# Accounting Work Skills

Tutorial

AAT Diploma Pathway Unit 31

Michael Fardon

Roger Petheram

osborne
BOOKS

Published by Osborne Books Limited
Unit 1B Everoak Estate
Bromyard Road
Worcester WR2 5HP
Tel 01905 748071
Email books@osbornebooks.co.uk
Website www.osbornebooks.co.uk

Design by Richard Holt
Cover image from Getty Images

Printed by CPI Antony Rowe Limited, Chippenham

British Library Cataloguing in Publication Data
A catalogue record for this book is available from the British Library

ISBN 978 1905777 020

# Contents

Introduction

## Present financial data for internal and external use

## Operate a computerised accounting system

## Perform effectively in the workplace

# Acknowledgements

The authors wish to thank the following for their help with the production of the text and illustrations in this book: Rob Fardon, Mike Gilbert, Claire McCarthy, Jon Moore, Steve Tubb and Wendy Yates.

The publisher would also like to thank Debbie Board for helping to produce and test the Sage computer accounting exercises.

The publisher is indebted to the Association of Accounting Technicians for its generous help and advice to our authors and editors during the preparation of this text, and for permission to reproduce extracts from the Specifications for the Diploma Pathway. Thanks also go to the Association of Accounting Technicians, *Accounting Technician* and the Health and Safety Executive for permission to reproduce web pages.

# Authors

**Michael Fardon** has extensive teaching experience of a wide range of banking, business and accountancy courses at Worcester College of Technology. He now specialises in writing business and financial texts and is General Editor at Osborne Books. He is also an educational consultant and has worked extensively in the areas of vocational business curriculum development.

**Roger Petheram** has lectured at Worcester College of Technology on a wide range of accounting, business and management courses for a number of years. He previously worked as a senior accountant for the Health Service. He is currently senior editor for accounting texts at Osborne Books, with particular responsibility for the AAT Series.

# Introduction

*Accounting Work Skills Tutorial* has been written to cover the requirements of Unit 31 of the AAT Diploma Pathway. The book is divided into three sections, which reflect the three Elements of Unit 31:

Section 1    Present financial data for internal and external use (Element 31.1)

Section 2    Operate a computerised accounting system (Element 31.2)

Section 3    Perform effectively in the workplace (Element 31.3)

The book contains a substantial amount of new material which has been written specifically to cover the demands of the Unit 31 Simulation.

**Section 1** probably presents more challenges to students than any other area, so it need not necessarily be tackled first, but it is a critical topic – particularly the consolidation and presentation of accounting data. This section also contains a brief and optional introduction to financial statements. This is not part of the Unit specification, but the writers – in consultation with tutors delivering the Unit – firmly believe that any study of performance indicators would benefit greatly from a basic knowledge of financial statements.

**Section 2** provides a new suite of Sage Line 50 (version 11) accounting exercises based closely on the requirements of the second part of the Simulation. The exercises are far simpler than Osborne Books' previous computerised accounting material and do not require any pre-loaded data.

**Section 3** provides the background knowledge and understanding needed for the 'take-away' third section of the Simulation. It will be of particular value to students who may not have immediate access to the workplace.

*Accounting Work Skills Workbook* is the companion volume to this tutorial text. It provides useful practice material in the form of additional questions for each chapter (including further computerised accounting exercises) and two practice simulations to prepare students thoroughly for their Unit assessment. The answers to the Workbook are contained in the *Accounting Work Skills Tutor Pack,* available on request, and to students with tutor permission, from Osborne Books (01905 748071).

If you have any feedback on the content of this book, or suggestions about the delivery of the Unit, please feel free to contact our editorial team on 01905 748071.

Michael Fardon and Roger Petheram

Summer 2006

# 1 Management accounting – costs and coding

Managers of a business or organisation will need information from the accounting system to help them in decision-making, planning and control. In this chapter we look at:

- the information they need from the accounts system

- the differences between financial accounting and management accounting

- the structure of organisations

- costs (materials, labour and expenses) and income

- cost centres, profit centres and investment centres

- the use of coding for costs and income

## PERFORMANCE CRITERION COVERED

**unit 31: ACCOUNTING WORK SKILLS**

**element 13.1**

**present financial data for internal and external use**

A    recognise cost centres and elements of costs and extract and code income and expenditure from orders and invoices

## WHO IS A MANAGER?

The word 'manager' includes anybody within the business or organisation who is involved in decision-making, planning and control. The description extends to the 'line manager' (a term which has largely replaced 'supervisor').

Look at the statements below and decide which of these people are managers:

- the managing director of a bank takes the decision to develop e-banking

- the government's health secretary plans to cut hospital waiting lists

- the finance director is controlling the company's spending to ensure that the bank overdraft limit is not exceeded

- the office manager decides to buy a new Xentra photocopier for use in the office

- the accounts supervisor plans to run the computer payroll program next Tuesday

- the accounts assistant controls the petty cash float

The answer is that all of the above are managers because the statements involve **decision-making** (managing director of the bank, office manager), planning (health secretary, accounts supervisor), and **control** (finance director, accounts assistant). We can see, therefore, that the concept of management is broadly-based. In fact, we can say that everybody is responsible for something: making decisions, planning what to do and controlling the progress of work.

Clearly there are different levels of management and it is important to recognise that any information for the use of a manager must be tailored to meet the user's needs. For example, the accounts supervisor will wish to know about a bad debt of £50, but this will be of little or no concern to the managing director (who *would* want to know about a bad debt of £50 million!).

Read through the examples shown below and then relate them to the management of the business where you work, or to an organisation that you know about:

**Decision-making**

- higher level: 'I have taken the decision to close our factory in Wales'
- intermediate level: 'I have decided to buy a new photocopier for the office'
- lower level: 'I will pay this petty cash claim'

**Planning**
- higher level: 'We need to start planning the firm's expansion programme'
- intermediate level: 'I am planning to increase overtime working in the production department next month'
- lower level: 'I plan to extract a trial balance first thing tomorrow'

**Control**
- higher level: 'Last month's group sales were up by ten per cent'
- intermediate level: 'Costs for organic baked beans were reduced by five per cent last month'
- lower level: 'I have balanced the petty cash book'

The conclusion to be drawn is that we are all managers, but at different levels. For example, within an accounts office, the accounts assistant will be responsible for a different level of management to the line manager who will, in turn, be responsible for a different level of management to the departmental manager.

## ACCOUNTING INFORMATION FOR MANAGERS

The accounting records provide the management of a business or organisation with information to:

- assist with decision-making, for example by giving income from sales, and expenditure costs, of different products or services
- assist with planning, for example by giving details of income and expenditure that can then be estimated for the future
- assist with control, for example by comparing estimates of what was expected to happen with details of what has actually happened

All of these aspects use known information from the accounting records, but some also include estimates of what is likely to happen in the future; these estimates are usually based on what has happened in the past.

The accounting records that you will have studied in Unit 30 'Introductory Accounting' are based on actual transactions that have taken place – this type of accounting is referred to as **financial accounting**. **Management accounting**, on the other hand, involves taking the actual transactions, looking at them in different ways, and estimating them for the future in order to provide information for management.

To use a simple example to illustrate the differences: how much you or a friend *actually* earned last year is financial accounting information; how much you or your friend *expect* to earn next year is management accounting information.

In the sections which follow we will look in more detail at the differences between these two types of accounting.

## WHAT IS FINANCIAL ACCOUNTING?

**Financial accounting** is concerned with recording financial transactions that have happened already, and with providing information from the accounting records, for example, in order to prepare VAT returns, and trial balance (the starting point for the preparation of the profit and loss account and balance sheet – see Chapter 2).

The main features of financial accounting are:
- it records transactions that have happened already
- it looks backwards to show what has happened in the past
- it is arithmetically accurate – there are no estimated amounts
- it often fulfils a legal requirement to keep accounts (in order to prepare VAT returns, and tax returns for HM Revenue & Customs showing income and expenditure)
- it maintains confidentiality of information (eg payroll details, VAT returns)

## WHAT IS MANAGEMENT ACCOUNTING?

**Management accounting** is concerned with looking at actual transactions in different ways from financial accounting. In particular, the costs of each product or service are considered both in the past and the likely costs in the future. In this way, management accounting is able to provide information to help the business or organisation plan for the future.

The main features of management accounting are:
- it uses accounting information to summarise transactions that have happened already and to make estimates for the future
- it looks in detail at the costs – materials, labour and expenses (explained later in this chapter) – and the sales income of products and services
- it looks forward to forecast what is likely to happen in the future
- it may use estimates where these are the most useful or suitable form of information
- it provides management with reports that are needed to run the business or organisation

- it provides management information as frequently as circumstances demand – speed is often vital as information may go out-of-date very quickly
- it maintains confidentiality of information (eg payroll details)

## FUNCTIONS AND STRUCTURES OF AN ORGANISATION

So far in this chapter we have stressed the need for management information within a business or an organisation. It is important to be able to appreciate that businesses and other organisations vary widely in size and structure. A one-person business will operate very differently from Tesco or your local authority.

What is common to all businesses and organisations is that, like the human body, they all carry out the same functions on a day-to-day basis. An efficient information flow between the functions within businesses and organisations is therefore very important. The diagram below illustrates the functions that are common to most organisations.

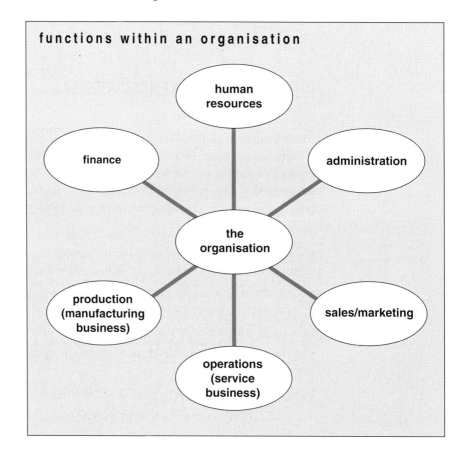

The functions in the diagram have very different responsibilities:

- **finance** – provides financial accounting and management accounting services
- **human resources** – provides the staff to run the business, hires new staff, lays-off surplus staff, negotiates pay and overtime rates and conditions of service, trains and develops staff
- **administration** – ensures the overall smooth running of the organisation by providing office support
- **sales/marketing** – organises the promotion and sales or provision of the products or services of the business or other organisation
- **production** – the organisation and operation of the production process in a manufacturing business, including buying materials, incurring labour costs and other expenses and ensuring that production quality and targets are met
- **operations** – the organisation and operation of the provision of services to customers

As businesses grow larger so the functions within the organisation grow more complex. For example, a large manufacturing business may be subdivided into divisions for each product it makes, or even parts of the manufacturing process; a service business may subdivide into different geographical areas.

The way in which the business/organisation is organised will have implications for the operation of financial accounting and management accounting systems:

- for recording and analysing sales and other income
- for analysing and forecasting costs related to the different functions

## COSTS AND INCOME

### costs

Each of the functions of the organisation incurs **costs** – eg administration costs, production costs – and some of the functions will generate income, eg from sales of products or services.

The accounting system should be able to supply management information about costs and income for each function of the organisation, and answer questions such as:

- what were the sales for products A and B last month?
- what was the payroll cost of the administration department last year?

- what was our income from operations in the last quarter?
- how much was our expenditure on marketing last year?

In order to provide such information we need to consider the main costs and income and then see how it is analysed to the different functions of the business or organisation.

### classification of costs

All businesses and organisations, whether they manufacture products or provide services incur **costs**, which can be broken down into three elements:

- materials
- labour
- expenses

**Materials costs** include the cost of:

- **raw materials** and components bought for use by a manufacturing business
- **products** bought for resale by a shop or a wholesaler

Materials range from sheet metal and plastics used in a car factory, computer chips and other components bought in by a computer manufacturer to tins of baked beans and DVD players bought in by a supermarket for resale.

**Labour costs** refers to the payroll costs of all employees of a business or other organisation. These costs include the money paid to manufacturing workers, people employed in service industries and the public sector (college lecturers, for example). The expense to the business or organisation in each case is know as **gross pay**. This can be subdivided in many cases into:

- **basic pay:** the amount of pay  the employee is contracted to receive before any additions or deductions are made – this could be, for example, a wage of £300 per week or a salary of £15,000 a year
- **overtime:** an agreed hourly rate of pay applied for extra hours worked
- **bonus:** an extra amount paid to reward productivity or loyalty, eg a sales rep who meets or exceeds sales targets, a production team that exceeds production targets, an employee with an outstanding attendance record

**Expenses** refers to all other running costs of the business or organisation that cannot be included under the headings of materials and labour. Examples include:

- **running costs:** rent, heating, telephone, advertising, insurance
- **services** such as cleaning and security
- **consumables:** such as stationery and printer toner

### income

The main source of income for the private sector is from the sale of products or services. There may also be other, smaller, amounts of income, eg interest received on bank balances, rental income if a part of the premises is let to a tenant, government grants and allowances for setting up a new business or buying new technology.

For the public sector, the main sources of income for central and local government are from taxes and rates. Government owned or controlled organisations either receive grants and allowances or, in the case of trading businesses in the public sector, such as the Post Office, receive income from the products and services that they supply.

## COST CENTRES

In order to provide management with information from the accounting system, the costs – materials, labour and expenses – need to be analysed between the different functions, or sections, within the business or organisation. This is achieved by the use of cost centres.

**Cost centres are sections of a business to which costs can be charged.**

A cost centre can be any function or section of the organisation. In a manufacturing business it can be an entire factory, a department of a factory, or a particular stage in the production process. In a service industry it can be a shop, or group of shops in an area, a teaching department or a resources centre within a college, a ward or operating theatre in a hospital.

Any section of a business can be a cost centre – each of the functions within the organisation that we considered earlier in this chapter would be appropriate cost centres. A manager or supervisor will be responsible for each cost centre and it is this person who will be asking for information from the accounts system.

### analysis of costs to different cost centres

When the cost centres of an organisation have been established it is necessary to ensure that the accounts system is able to give information to the manager of each cost centre. In order to do this, separate accounts are established for each cost centre to cover the main cost headings. For example, labour costs can be split between 'wages and salaries: production', 'wages and salaries: administration', 'wages and salaries: human resources', and so on. By analysing costs in this way the accounts system is able to provide the cost centre manager with information about how much has been spent by, or charged to, the centre over the last month, quarter, half-year, or year. This information will help the manager to:

- plan for the future, eg by using actual costs, will be able to forecast next year's costs
- make decisions, eg by comparing the costs of different products or services, helping to decide whether to increase or decrease output
- control costs, eg by comparing actual costs with budgeted costs will be able to take steps, where necessary, to reduce costs

In this way the accounts system is able to tell the manager what has happened – at least in terms of financial information.

## where does the information come from?

The sources of information to enable the analysis of costs include:

- purchase orders and purchase invoices, for materials and expenses costs
- payroll schedules, for labour costs
- invoices and cash receipts, for expenses costs

The amounts of each cost are then analysed to the cost centre which has incurred the cost: the diagram below shows how this process works. In practice an organisation may have a written 'policy manual' which will give details of which costs are to be charged to which cost centre. The categories of cost will be **coded** on the relevant source document – eg an invoice.

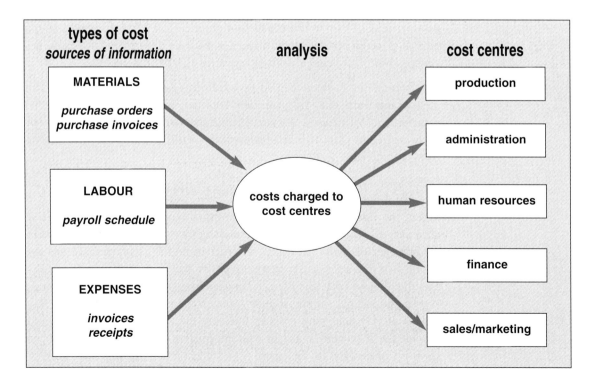

## PROFIT CENTRES

In some organisations the cost centre approach of analysing costs is taken to a further level by also analysing **sales income** to centres. Because sales income less costs equals profit, such centres are called **profit centres**. The source of information on sales often comes from sales orders and sales invoices.

**Profit centres are sections of a business to which costs can be charged, income can be identified, and profit can be calculated.**

From this definition we can see that profit centres account for both costs and income. It follows, therefore, that profit centres will be based on sections of the business that make products or services (incur costs) and sell them to customers (receive income from sales). For example, Waterwells Books is a 'high street' bookshop which also runs a website bookshop. It has its website bookshop as a profit centre, as shown below.

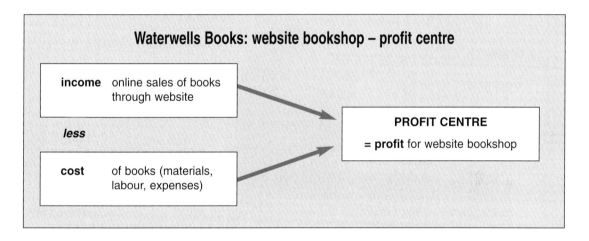

Note that many cost centres provide support services within a business or organisation and so cannot become profit centres because they do not have any significant income. For example, the administration department of a business is a cost centre to which costs can be charged, but it does not receive any income. As we have seen profit centres incur costs and also generate income.

Managers of profit centres will be requiring information from the accounting system about the costs incurred and the income generated by their centre. By deducting costs from income they can quantify the profit made and can make comparisons with previous periods (eg last month, last quarter, last year) and also with other profit centres (eg 'our profit was higher than yours last month').

## INVESTMENT CENTRES

A further development of profit centres is to consider profit in relation to the amount of money invested in the centre. For **investment centres** the profit of the centre is compared with the amount of money the business has put in to earn that profit.

**Investment centres are sections of a business where profit can be compared with the amount of money invested in the centre.**

Profit is usually compared with money invested by means of a percentage as shown in the diagram which follows for the Waterwells Books website bookshop.

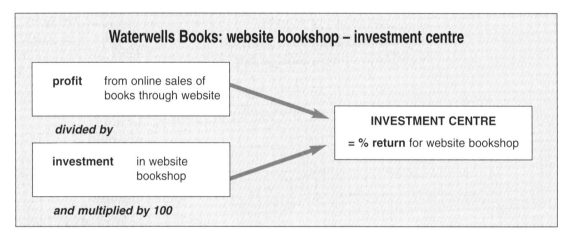

Managers of investment centres will wish to make comparisons of the return on investment for the current period with that of previous periods, and also with the other investment centres of the business, eg 'have we done better than last year?', 'how do we compare with the other investment centres?'

## ANALYSIS OF COSTS AND INCOME – CODING

### what is coding?

Coding is the means by which costs, income and expenditure are analysed to centres (cost centres, profit centres or investment centres). A number is written on each source document received (eg sales invoice, purchase invoice, receipt, etc) to analyse it to a particular centre, and to indicate the type of cost, income or expenditure, represented by the document. The following code is a typical example which might be used by Waterwells Books and written on an invoice received for advertising costs:

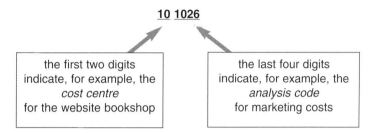

The code 101026 (above) indicates to the book-keeper who is recording items in the accounts that the amount of the prime document is to be debited to 'marketing costs – website bookshop' account. Note that, from the six-digit code used here:

– the first two digits indicate the cost centre

– the last four digits indicate the analysis code

The six-digit code used here is only one example of coding – a business can use whatever coding system suits it best – any combination of letters or numbers. For example, Waterwells Books could use letters for the cost centres and numbers for the analysis, so WB 1026 could be used for the website bookshop (WB) cost centre, with the analysis to marketing costs (1026). Whatever system of coding is in use, it must be recorded in the organisation's **policy manual**. This book (or file) states how all operations within the organisation are to be carried out, so that they can be followed, on a consistent basis, by anybody at any time.

A practical point for the establishment of code numbers is that you would not initially use consecutive numbers but would leave plenty of 'gaps' for future development of the system. For example, a business with three cost centres would not code these as 11, 12 and 13; instead it would be more sensible to use 10, 20 and 30 – leaving plenty of space for any new cost centres.

The analysis codes will group together the three main costs of materials, labour and expenses, and the income items, as shown in the example shown on the next page.

This example uses cost centre numbers in increments of tens (ie 10, 20, 30 etc) and a four-digit analysis. With this system the code numbers should not be too difficult to use on a day-to-day basis and will provide the right level of detail. Note that the policy manual will give the full list of codes and this should be referred to as and when necessary.

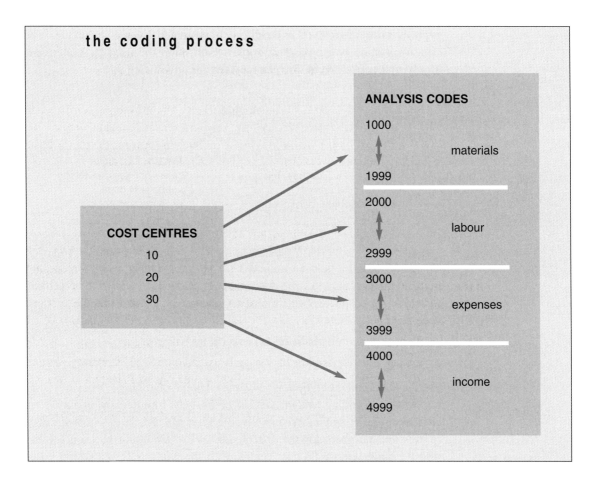

Within the accounts department of a business or organisation, it is necessary to code source documents, both received (purchase invoices, receipts) and issued (copies of sales invoices). The person carrying out such coding – the coding clerk – must work to high standards of accuracy – wrong coding of a document will lead to it being posted to the wrong account in the accounts system, which will lead to incorrect information being supplied to the managers, which could in turn lead to wrong decision-making.

The way in which documents are coded varies from one organisation to another. For some, the code number is written on the document and marked clearly; others use a rubber stamp to provide a layout on which can be indicated the code number and the initials of the person entering the code.

For a coding system to work well:

- codes should provide the correct level of detail, ie cost/profit centre code and analysis code

- coding of documents must be accurate

- code numbers must be complete, ie the full code to be indicated, and not just the cost/profit centre or the analysis code
- coding of documents must be carried out at regular intervals within the timescales required by the organisation

The objective of coding is to provide correct analysis so as to give information from the accounts system to managers. By analysing costs and income to cost (and other) centres we can answer questions such as 'how much was the basic pay for my cost centre last month?'; 'how much was the overtime?'.

## problems and errors with coding

No administration system within an organisation is completely free of problems and 'fool-proof'. With coding the main problem is in deciding the cost centre and the analysis code to be used – the source document may not be clear as to which centre has incurred the cost and what type of cost it is. The procedures manual may help but, if not, such items will have to be referred to the line manager (who may need to make further enquiries).

As with much of the work of the accounts department, a high level of confidentiality is needed in coding costs and income. Confidentiality ensures that the accounts department works independently of the other cost (and profit) centres – although some queries may have to be resolved by reference to the centres – and also ensures that management information is accurate.

### wrong codes

An error of coding occurs when a wrong code is applied to a prime document. This will lead to the item being posted to the incorrect account in the accounts system. As a result, the costs of one cost centre will be overstated and those of another will be understated; similarly income will be overstated in one profit centre but will be understated in another.

Wrong coding means that the accounts system is inaccurate for internal management use within the business or organisation. (External suppliers and buyers of goods and services are unaffected as they will still be paid the amounts due to them, or will receive sales invoices for the correct amounts.) Incorrect management information is being supplied, which could lead to wrong estimates for next year (being based on current-year figures), or to wrong decisions being made.

### excessive volumes

The coding clerk will also be on the look out for excessive volumes of costs or income. This occurs when the wrong quantity of costs or income is shown on the source document, and the volume is much greater than the amounts normally seen.

## other discrepancies in documentation

As well as wrong codes and excessive volumes, the coding clerk will be on the lookout for discrepancies in documentation. These can include invoices addressed to the wrong organisation or invoices for fictitious expenses.

- **wrong organisations**

    An error that, in theory, should not slip through the accounts system is where source documents for costs relate to a different business or organisation. The coding clerk should check carefully that the documents do relate to the organisation, and are not for another business or organisation with a similar name.

- **fictitious expenses**

    The coding clerk must also watch for an unscrupulous business that sends out invoices for fictitious expenses – for example, to cover the cost of an unwanted entry in a trade directory (which may never be published). Because amounts are small and do not raise suspicions, such invoices are often paid by larger businesses and organisations.

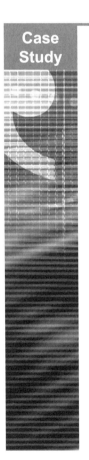

**Case Study**

# WYVERN ROYAL HOSPITAL TRUST – CODING THE COSTS

## situation

Wyvern Royal Hospital Trust is a National Health Service hospital. You are an assistant in the accounts department and today you are working on the subsidiary (purchases) ledger. For accounting purposes the hospital is divided into a number of cost centres or income centres. The following are the codes for some of the departments which are cost centres:

| | |
|---|---|
| x-ray department | cost centre code 10 |
| casualty | cost centre code 20 |
| pharmacy | cost centre code 30 |
| physiotherapy | cost centre code 40 |

The following posting sheet for purchase invoices has been handed to you by the accounts supervisor, Pippa Farrell, who asks you to complete the coding column for the costs (ie the right-hand column):

**WYVERN ROYAL HOSPITAL TRUST**

**Posting sheet: purchase invoices**

| Supplior | Department | Description | Amount | Coding |
|---|---|---|---|---|
| | | | £ | |
| Zodak Films | x-ray | x-ray film | 4,250.57 | |
| Wye Plaster Co | casualty | fine-grade plaster | 754.93 | |
| Beech Drugs plc | pharmacy | drugs | 2,941.26 | |
| Tyax Sports Ltd | physiotherapy | rowing machines | 3,248.36 | |
| Electro Ltd | x-ray | repairs to scanner | 1,495.22 | |
| WR Industries plc | casualty | disposable gloves | 472.33 | |
| Country Pie Co | kitchen | pies (various) | 528.36 | |
| Wyvern Cleaning Co | casualty | cleaning services | 2,871.89 | |

Check list total  |16,562.92|

Prepared by  *Ginger Waterman*  Date  *17 June 2006*

Checked by  *Lucinda Luz*  Date  *19 June 2006*

Coded by  _____  Date  _____

Posted by  _____  Date  _____

The accounts supervisor has given you the coding list which includes the following:

| cost | code no |
|---|---|
| cleaning materials | 3200 |
| contract cleaning | 3225 |
| dressings and plaster | 1100 |
| electricity and gas | 1350 |
| exercise equipment | 1900 |
| laundry contract | 3250 |
| mechanical and electrical repairs | 3250 |
| medicines and drugs | 1500 |
| uniforms and disposables | 1600 |
| x-ray film | 1125 |

You are to complete the coding section of the posting sheet as far as you are able. Any items you are not able to code are to be queried by e-mail to the accounts supervisor asking for the appropriate code(s).

## solution

Using the cost centre codes and the cost codes, the posting sheet is coded as follows:

## WYVERN ROYAL HOSPITAL TRUST

**Posting sheet: purchase invoices**

| Supplier | Department | Description | Amount | Coding |
|----------|-----------|-------------|-------:|--------|
| | | | £ | |
| Zodak Films | x-ray | x-ray film | 4,250.57 | 101125 |
| Wye Plaster Co | casualty | fine-grade plaster | 754.93 | 201100 |
| Beech Drugs plc | pharmacy | drugs | 2,941.26 | 301500 |
| Tyax Sports Ltd | physiotherapy | rowing machines | 3,248.36 | 401900 |
| Electro Ltd | x-ray | repairs to scanner | 1,495.22 | 103250 |
| WR Industries plc | casualty | disposable gloves | 472.33 | 201600 |
| Country Pie Co | kitchen | pies (various) | 528.36 | |
| Wyvern Cleaning Co | casualty | cleaning services | 2,871.89 | 203225 |

Check list total   16,562.92

Prepared by   *Ginger Waterman*   Date   *17 June 2006*

Checked by   *Lucinda Luz*   Date   *19 June 2006*

Coded by   _____   Date   _____

Posted by   _____   Date   _____

As you are unable to complete the coding it is important to be able to describe the problem and refer it to the appropriate person. Accordingly, you send the following e-mail to the accounts supervisor, Pippa Farrell:

---

Pippa.Farrell@wrht.swest.nhs.uk   20/6/06   10:32.16

To:  Pippa.Farrell

From: A.Student

I have been coding the purchases invoices but I don't have a cost centre code and cost code for one of the items. The cost centre is the kitchen and the cost code is for pies (presumably the code will be for food). Can you please advise me?

---

The accounts supervisor replies by e-mail as follows:

---

A.Student@wrht.swest.nhs.uk   20/6/06   11:44.51

To:  A.Student

From: Pippa.Farrell

Further to your e-mail this morning, the cost centre code for the kitchen is 60; the cost code for food is 3825.

---

You are now able to complete the posting sheet with the code 603825. You sign as the person coding it, date it, and pass it on for posting to the subsidiary (purchases) ledger and the purchases ledger control account by the data input clerk.

**Chapter Summary**

- Managers are people in a business or organisation who are involved in decision-making, planning and control.

- Managers make use of
  - financial accounting to provide reports on past transactions
  - management accounting to provide reports which summarise transactions that have happened in the recent past and to make estimates for the future

- The main functions within an organisation include:
  - finance
  - human resources
  - administration
  - sales/marketing
  - production (in a manufacturing business)
  - operations (provision of services to customers)

- The three elements of cost comprise
  - *materials costs*:
    raw materials and components, products bought in for resale
  - *labour*:
    the payroll costs of employees – basic pay, overtime and bonuses
  - *expenses*:
    all other running costs, services and consumable items

- Costs are analysed between the different functions or sections of a business or organisation by the use of cost centres.

- Profit centres include an analysis of costs and income to show the profit (income less costs) in defined sections of the business or organisation.

- Investment centres relate profit to the amount of money invested in the centre (section of the business or organisation), and express it as a percentage return on investment.

- Coding is the means by which costs and income are analysed to cost/profit/investment centres.

- Errors in coding and discrepancies in documentation include
  - wrong codes
  - excessive volumes
  - wrong organisations
  - fictitious expenses

| Key Terms | financial accounting | is concerned with recording financial transactions that have happened already, and with providing information from the accounting records |
|---|---|---|
| | management accounting | uses accounting information to summarise transactions that have happened in the recent past and to make estimates for the future |
| | costs | comprise materials, labour and expenses |
| | income | the sale of products or services |
| | cost centre | section of a business to which costs can be charged |
| | profit centre | a section of a business to which costs can be charged, income can be identified, and profit can be calculated |
| | investment centre | a section of a business where profit can be compared with the amount of money invested in the centre, and can be expressed as a percentage return on investment |
| | coding | a code number written on a source document to identify it with a particular cost/profit/investment centre and to indicate the type of cost or income |

# Student Activities

**1.1** What are the three main functions of a manager?

**1.2** What are the two types of information that the accounting system is able to provide for managers?

**1.3** What are the main differences between financial accounting and management accounting?

**1.4** Study the following accounting activities and decide which of them are financial accounting and which are management accounting:

    (a)    recording purchases invoices in the subsidiary (purchases) ledger

    (b)    listing sales invoices in the sales day book

    (c)    using last year's sales figure to estimate next year's sales

    (d)    reporting last year's cost of materials

(e)     analysing costs between different cost centres

(f)     calculating the return on investment of an investment centre

**1.5**   (a)   Explain the difference between
- cost centre
- profit centre
- investment centre

(b)   Suggest likely cost centres for
- a school or a college
- a manufacturing business which makes two product lines

(c)   Give examples of cost centres in your workplace, or an organisation with which you are familiar.

**1.6**   You work as an accounts assistant at City News and Books, a company which owns a group of shops selling newspapers and magazines, books and stationery. The accounting system has been set up to show costs, income and money invested for each of these three sections of the business: newspapers and magazines, books, stationery.

The finance director has requested details for each section of costs and income for last year, and the amount of money invested in each section at the end of the year. (She says that all figures can be to the nearest £000.)

The accounts supervisor asks you to deal with this request and you go to the accounts and extract the following information for last year:

|  | Newspapers and magazines | Books | Stationery |
|---|---|---|---|
|  | £000s | £000s | £000s |
| Costs: materials | 155 | 246 | 122 |
| labour | 65 | 93 | 58 |
| expenses | 27 | 35 | 25 |
| Sales | 352 | 544 | 230 |
| Money invested | 420 | 850 | 250 |

The accounts supervisor asks you to present the information for the finance director in the form of a memorandum which shows the costs, profit, and return on investment for each section of the business.

**1.7** You are an accounts assistant at Eagle Books, a large publisher. The business is split into four divisions: educational textbooks, novels, children's books and sports books. The accounts system is arranged so that each division is a profit centre. There is also a separate cost centre for administration.

An extract from the company's policy manual is as follows:

| cost or profit centre number | cost or profit centre name |
|---|---|
| 20 | educational textbooks |
| 30 | novels |
| 40 | children's books |
| 50 | sports books |
| 60 | administration |

| analysis code | cost or income |
|---|---|
| 1050 | paper |
| 2100 | basic pay |
| 2150 | overtime |
| 2200 | bonus payments |
| 2300 | holiday pay |
| 2400 | sick pay |
| 3050 | authors' royalties |
| 3100 | rates |
| 3150 | heating and lighting |
| 3200 | telephone |
| 3500 | building maintenance |
| 3525 | computers and equipment maintenance |
| 3550 | vehicle running costs |
| 3700 | advertising |
| 4050 | sales to bookshops |
| 4250 | sales to wholesalers |

The following source documents have been received today (amounts are net of VAT, where applicable):

(a) copy of a sales invoice showing the sale of £14,750 of educational textbooks to Orton Book Wholesalers Limited

(b) printer's bill of £22,740 for paper for printing sports books

(c) payroll summary showing overtime of £840 last month in the children's book section

(d) payment of £1,540 for advertising sports books in the magazine 'Sport Today'

(e) telephone bill of £1,200 to be split equally between all cost and profit centres

(f)     royalties of £88,245 paid to children's book authors

(g)     copy of sales invoice showing the sale of £1,890 of novels to the Airport Bookshop

You are to code the above transactions using the policy manual extract given.

Your supervisor asks you to provide a summary of the day's costs and income, analysed between materials, labour, expenses, and income. You know that the coding system is split into the following categories:

| code numbers | category |
| --- | --- |
| 1000 – 1999 | materials |
| 2000 – 2999 | labour |
| 3000 – 3999 | expenses |
| 4000 – 4999 | income |

Reply to your supervisor by means of a memorandum or an email.

*This chapter explains how financial accounting reports – known as the 'financial statements' – can be extracted from the records to provide information about how the organisation is performing. This process involves a number of stages:*

- *extracting a trial balance – a list of account balances – from the accounting records*

- *constructing a profit and loss account, which indicates profitability*

- *constructing a balance sheet, which indicates the financial strength of the organisation*

- *passing this information both to the management of the business and also to outsiders such as banks who will want to know how the business is performing*

## OPTIONAL CHAPTER

## IMPORTANT NOTE TO CERTIFICATE LEVEL STUDENTS – PLEASE READ!

### why learn about financial statements?

*The financial statements covered in this chapter – the profit and loss account and the balance sheet – do not, strictly speaking, form part of AAT Certificate studies, and you will not be assessed on them at this level of the Diploma Pathway. They will, however, feature prominently in the exams at Advanced Certificate and Diploma levels.*

*The reason why they are introduced in this chapter is because it is important to appreciate that the data contained in the financial statements form the basis of a number of the financial 'performance indicators' which are assessed at Certificate level and covered in the next chapter – for example 'net profit percentage' and 'return on capital employed'. Unless you know what 'net profit' and 'capital employed' are and how they are calculated, you may not understand what they signify in your assessment tasks.*

### how to approach this chapter

- *read it through carefully*
- *make notes on the definitions of net profit, gross profit and capital*
- *consolidate what you have learned by carrying out some of the activities*

*Remember – you do not have to read this chapter and you will certainly not be assessed on its contents in Unit 31, but studying it will make more sense of the next chapter and will greatly help your accounting studies. If in doubt, ask your tutor's advice.*

# FROM TRIAL BALANCE TO FINANCIAL STATEMENTS

You will know from your studies of Unit 30 'Introductory Accounting' that the **trial balance** is prepared from a list of the account balances in the ledger. Set out below is the year-end trial balance of Carlo Danieli who runs a business selling Italian food.

| Trial balance of Carlo Danieli as at 31 December 2006 | | |
|---|---|---|
| | Debit | Credit |
| Name of account | £ | £ |
| Stock (at 1 January 2006) | 12,500 | |
| Purchases | 105,000 | |
| Sales | | 155,000 |
| Administration | 6,200 | |
| Wages | 20,500 | |
| Rent paid | 3,750 | |
| Telephone | 500 | |
| Interest paid | 4,500 | |
| Travel expenses | 550 | |
| Premises | 100,000 | |
| Machinery | 20,000 | |
| Debtors | 15,500 | |
| Bank | 450 | |
| Cash | 50 | |
| Capital | | 75,000 |
| Drawings | 7,000 | |
| Loan from bank | | 50,000 |
| Creditors | | 16,500 |
| | 296,500 | 296,500 |

You will know from your studies in Unit 30 that the trial balance is part of the checking process which proves the arithmetical accuracy of the accounting data. You will also appreciate from your later studies that it forms the basis for the preparation of financial statements:

- the **profit and loss account** – which shows the amount of profit (or loss) made by an organisation such as a business

- the **balance sheet** – which gives an idea of the financial strength of an organisation, showing what the organisation owns and what it owes, and how it is financed

## PROFIT AND LOSS ACCOUNT

### a definition

**A profit and loss account is a financial statement which summarises the revenue and expenses of a business for an accounting period and shows the overall profit or loss.**

The profit and loss account – also known as the profit statement – uses information from the accounting records as shown by the trial balance:

- the sales (or turnover) of the business
- the purchases made by the business
- the overheads of running the business, such as administration, wages, rent paid, telephone, interest paid, travel expenses

The amount of sales is the revenue of the business, while the amounts of purchases and overheads are the expenses of the business. Study the layout of the example of a profit and loss account on the next page.

### the accounting period

The profit and loss account covers a set period of time – an accounting period – frequently a year of business activity. Often the financial year-end is the same as the calendar year-end, ie 31 December.

Businesses may also produce financial statements such as the profit and loss account at regular intervals during the year as an aid to financial management. If a computer accounting program is used, it is a simple matter of printing it out from the financial reports menu (or icon).

The important point to remember is that the accounting period must be stated in the heading of the profit and loss account.

### calculations in the profit and loss account

As mentioned above, the profit and loss account consists of a basic calculation:

REVENUE less EXPENSES  =  PROFIT (or LOSS)

If revenue is greater than expenses, then the business has made a profit; if expenses are greater than revenue, then a loss has been made.

The profit and loss account is presented in a vertical format, ie it runs down the page. Two columns are used for money amounts: the right-hand column contains sub-totals and totals, while the left-hand column is used for listing individual amounts (eg overheads) which are then totalled and carried to the right-hand column.

There are a number of terms in the profit and loss account which you will encounter in your studies:

- **Sales** is the revenue of the business for the accounting period.

- **Cost of Sales** is what it says it is: the cost of what the organisation has sold (eg stock sold by a shop, cars made by BMW)

- **Gross profit** is the profit made after Cost of Sales has been deducted from Sales

- **Net profit** is the profit made after all the other running expenses (overheads) have been deducted – it is this 'bottom line' line figure which is the most significant indicator of performance, as we will see in the next chapter.

The profit and loss account of Carlo Danieli is shown below.

**Profit and loss account
of Carlo Danieli for the year ended 31 December 2006**

|  | £ | £ |
|---|---|---|
| Sales | | 155,000 |
| Cost of Sales | | 107,000 |
| Gross profit | | 48,000 |
| Less overheads: | | |
| Administration | 6,200 | |
| Wages | 20,500 | |
| Rent paid | 3,750 | |
| Telephone | 500 | |
| Interest paid | 4,500 | |
| Travel expenses | 550 | |
| | | 36,000 |
| Net profit | | 12,000 |

## BALANCE SHEET

**A balance sheet is a financial statement which shows the assets, liabilities and capital of a business at a particular date.**

Balance sheets are different from profit and loss accounts which show profits for a time period such as a year. Balance sheets show the state of the business at one moment in time – things could be somewhat different tomorrow. A balance sheet is often described as a 'snapshot' of a business at one moment in time.

The money amounts of these assets, liabilities, and capital are taken from the accounting records of the business.

The balance sheet lists:

### assets

Assets are 'items' owned by the business, such as premises, vehicles, stock for resale, debtors (amounts owed by customers), cash, money in the bank.

### liabilities

Liabilities are amounts owed by the business, such as creditors (amounts owed by the business to suppliers), any bank overdraft and loans.

### capital

The capital is the amount of the owner's finance put into the business and profits built up over the years.

### layout of the balance sheet

The balance sheet shows the value of the assets used by the business to make profits and how they have been financed. This concept may be expressed as follows:

ASSETS minus LIABILITIES  = CAPITAL

The balance sheet shows the asset strength of the business, in contrast to the profit and loss account, which shows the profits from the trading activities.

A more detailed example of a balance sheet, using the figures from Carlo Danieli's trial balance (see page 25) is shown on the next page. Note that it is presented in a vertical format, and assets and liabilities are listed under the headings of fixed assets, current assets, current liabilities, long-term liabilities, and capital: these terms are explained after the balance sheet.

| Balance sheet of Carlo Danieli as at 31 December 2006 | £ | £ |
|---|---|---|
| **Fixed assets** | | |
| Premises | | 100,000 |
| Machinery | | 20,000 |
| | | 120,000 |
| **Current assets** | | |
| Stock | 10,500 | |
| Debtors | 15,500 | |
| Bank | 450 | |
| Cash | 50 | |
| | 26,500 | |
| **Less Current liabilities** | | |
| Creditors | 16,500 | |
| **Working capital** | | 10,000 |
| | | 130,000 |
| **Less Long-term liabilities** | | |
| Loan from bank | | 50,000 |
| **NET ASSETS** | | 80,000 |
| **FINANCED BY** | | |
| **Capital** | | |
| Opening capital | | 75,000 |
| Add net profit (from profit & loss account) | | 12,000 |
| | | 87,000 |
| Less drawings | | 7,000 |
| | | 80,000 |

We will now explain each of the main headings, starting from the top of the balance sheet.

## fixed assets

**Fixed assets** are the long-term items owned by a business which are not bought with the intention of selling them off in the near future, eg premises, machinery, vehicles, office equipment, furniture, etc. When a business buys new fixed assets, this expenditure is called capital expenditure (in contrast to revenue expenditure which is the cost of the overheads shown in the profit and loss account).

## current assets

**Current assets** are short-term assets which change regularly, eg stocks of food in a shop, debtors (amounts owed to the business by customers), bank balances and cash. These items will alter as the business trades, eg stocks will be sold, or more will be bought; debtors will make payment to the business, or sales on credit will be made; the cash and bank balances will alter with the flow of money paid into the bank account, or as withdrawals are made.

Fixed and current assets are listed from the top, starting with the most permanent, ie premises, and working through to the most liquid, ie nearest to cash: either cash itself, or the balance at the bank.

## current liabilities

These are liabilities (items owed) which are due for repayment within twelve months of the date of the balance sheet, eg creditors (amounts owed by the business to suppliers), and any bank overdraft.

## working capital

This is the excess of current assets over current liabilities, ie current assets minus current liabilities = working capital. Without adequate working capital, a business will find it difficult to continue to operate as it may find it cannot pay its bills when they are due to be paid.

## long-term liabilities

These liabilities represent loans to the business where repayment is due in more than one year from the date of the balance sheet; they are often described as 'bank loan', 'long-term loan', or 'mortgage'.

## net assets

This is the total value of assets used by the business, ie fixed and current assets minus current and long-term liabilities. The net assets are financed by the owner(s) of the business, in the form of **capital**. The total of the net assets therefore equals the total of the 'financed by' section – and so the balance sheet 'balances'. This total is sometimes referred to as **capital employed**.

## capital

**Capital** is the stake of the owner(s) of the business, and is a liability of a business, ie it is what the business owes the owner. It is made up of money invested and profits made over time. In practice, it is unlikely to be repaid as it is the permanent capital of the business. In the case shown here, the capital is Carlo's stake in the business (it is all his). In the case of a limited company, the capital would be made up of investors' shares and accumulated profit.

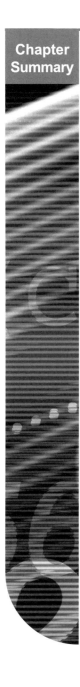

**Chapter Summary**

- The profit and loss account and the balance sheet are the principal financial statements of a business and are produced as part of the financial accounting process.

- The trial balance with its debit and credit columns contains figures which are used in the construction of the financial statements of a business.

- The profit and loss account shows the profit or loss made by a business over an accounting period (normally a year).

- The gross profit in the profit and loss account of a business which sells a manufactured product shows the trading profit achieved. This is the sales figure minus the cost of sales total (the cost of the goods which have actually been sold in the accounting period).

- The net profit shows the profit after overheads have been deducted. In the case of a trading company it is calculated as gross profit less overheads.

- The balance sheet shows the assets (items owned), liabilities (items owed) and capital of a business at a particular date in time. The formula is:

  *Assets minus Liabilities equals Capital.*

- The assets in a balance sheet are either short-term current assets such as stock, debtors, cash and money in the bank, or long-term fixed assets such as machinery.

- The liabilities in a balance sheet are either current liabilities (due within a year) or long-term liabilities such as bank loans.

- Capital is the investment of the owner in the business and can include profits which have built up over time.

| **Key Terms** | | |
|---|---|---|
| | **profit & loss account** | a financial statement which measures the profit made by a business over an accounting period |
| | **cost of sales** | the cost to a trading business of the value of the stock actually sold during the accounting period |
| | **gross profit** | trading profit: sales minus cost of sales |
| | **overheads** | the running costs of the business |
| | **net profit** | owner's profit: gross profit less overheads |
| | **balance sheet** | a financial statement which shows at any one time how a business is financed, its working capital position and the owner's capital |
| | **current assets** | items owned by a business for the short term |
| | **fixed assets** | items owned by a business over the long term |
| | **current liabilities** | items owed by a business and due for repayment within twelve months |
| | **long-term liabilities** | items owed by a business and not due for repayment within twelve months |
| | **working capital** | short-term funds used to finance the day-to-day operations of the business |
| | **net assets** | total assets less total liabilities – what the business is worth – equal to capital |
| | **capital** | the investment by the owner in a business and accumulated profits |

# Student Activities

**2.1** What are the two main financial statements produced from the trial balance of an organisation?

**2.2** What is the difference between a profit and loss account and a balance sheet? Include a definition of both financial statements in your answer.

**2.3** (a) How is net profit calculated?

(b) Who would be interested in the net profit of a large company like Tesco, and why?

**2.4** (a) How is the capital of a business calculated from its assets and liabilities?

(b) What is normally included in the capital of a business?

**2.5** You are given figures which have been calculated from the year-end trial balance of Guy Rossiter who runs a local pizza delivery business:

|                    | £       |
|--------------------|---------|
| Sales              | 400,000 |
| Cost of Sales      | 125,000 |
| Overheads/expenses | 175,000 |
| Fixed assets       | 120,000 |
| Current assets     | 85,000  |
| Current liabilities| 55,000  |

Use these figures to calculate Guy's

(a) gross profit for the year

(b) net profit for the year

(c) net assets

(d) capital

Explain what each of these four figures means.

In this chapter we take a detailed look at the financial information recorded within organisations and used by management. We look at the way the information is reported in the form of:

- performance indicators relating to productivity, cost per unit, the utilisation of resources and profitability

- specific ratios and percentages: gross profit margin, net profit margin and the return on capital employed

In the next chapter we examine the way in which this type of information can be presented in the form of tables, charts and graphs.

## PERFORMANCE CRITERION COVERED

### unit 31: ACCOUNTING WORK SKILLS

### element 13.1

### present financial data for internal and external use

C    provide, in the given format, comparisons of data as requested, to include ratios and performance indicators

## PERFORMANCE INDICATORS

In simple terms a **performance indicator** is a method of expressing by way of a formula how well a business is performing in certain areas:

- **productivity** – how well it is using its available resources
- **cost per unit** – how much it costs to produce each item it makes
- **resource utilisation** – how well it is making use of its workforce and equipment
- **profitability** – how much return it is making on its sales and capital employed

Remember that more businesses are now in the service sector than in manufacturing: the terms 'product' or 'item sold' apply equally to holidays, audits carried out, sessions in the gym, as to manufactured goods such as cars and packets of crisps.

Before we explain these performance indicators in more detail, we will first explain **percentages**, as they are often used – and not always understood.

## USING PERCENTAGES

### a quantity as a percentage of another quantity

**A percentage is a proportion of a whole – where the whole equates to the number 100 – as a basis for comparison.**

If you eat half a pizza you have eaten 50% because the whole pizza is equated to 100 and the part you have eaten is 50 'parts' of that 100.

When dealing with numbers you will often need to make comparisons. A **fraction** is often the starting point. For example there may be two accounting classes studying at the same level. One class (Class A) has 20 students and the other (Class B) has 16 students. The classes could be analysed as follows:

|  | Class A | Class B |
|---|---|---|
| students | 20 | 16 |
| females | 12 | 8 |
| students who pass | 18 | 12 |

If you ask what proportion of students in each class are female, you could use a fraction. The numbers used in the fraction show that proportion:

$$\text{Class A: } \frac{12}{20} \qquad \text{Class B: } \frac{8}{16}$$

But this still does not give you a clear comparison of the proportion of females in each class. You can achieve this by turning each fraction into a percentage which will relate both classes to a base number 100:

$$\text{percentage} = \frac{\text{top number in the fraction x 100}}{\text{bottom number in the fraction}}$$

This works out as:

Class A:

$$\frac{12 \text{ x } 100}{20} = 60\%$$

Class B:

$$\frac{8 \text{ x } 100}{16} = 50\%$$

The situation is now clear: Class A is 60% female, Class B is 50% female.

If you now turn again to the table on the previous page, you will be able to work out the percentage pass rate of each class:

Class A: $\dfrac{18 \text{ students pass}}{20 \text{ student total}}$  Class B: $\dfrac{12 \text{ students pass}}{16 \text{ student total}}$

You can then convert this to a percentage:

Class A:

$$\frac{18 \text{ x } 100}{20} = 90\%$$

Class B:

$$\frac{12 \text{ x } 100}{16} = 75\%$$

The next question, of course, is whether there is any connection between the number of females in the class and the pass rate!

We will now look at some more formulas using percentages.

### finding a percentage of an amount

Suppose that you earn £19,500 a year and are given a 5% pay rise. What extra money will you be awarded (ignoring what the tax 'man' will take)?

The formula for working out a percentage of an amount is:

$$\frac{\text{amount x percentage}}{100}$$

The calculation is: $\dfrac{£19,500 \text{ x } 5}{100} = £975 \text{ (before tax!)}$

This formula is useful for calculating VAT or interest. You can, of course, use your percentage button on your calculator to perform this calculation.

### increasing an amount by a given percentage

Suppose that your sales figures for this year are £925,000. Your finance director wants to see an 8% increase in sales next year. What will your sales have to be next year to meet this target?

The formula for this calculation is:

$$\frac{\text{amount} \times (100 + \text{percentage increase})}{100}$$

The calculation is: $\frac{£925,000 \times (100 + 8)}{100} = £999,000$ sales

An easy way of doing this is £925,000 × 1.08 = £999,000 sales

## decreasing an amount by a given percentage

The formula here is similar to the one above. Suppose the finance director also wants to cut the annual wages bill of £450,000 by 5%. The formula is:

$$\frac{\text{amount} \times (100 - \text{percentage decrease})}{100}$$

The calculation is: $\frac{£450,000 \times (100 - 5)}{100} = £427,500$ wages bill

An easy way of doing this is £450,000 × 0.95 = £427,500.

We will now look in detail at performance indicators, a number of which are expressed as percentages.

# PRODUCTIVITY

If you say that you have had a 'productive' day you mean that you have achieved a great deal despite all the circumstances. For a business or organisation which manufactures a product or provides a service 'productivity' measures

**the level of output (goods manufactured or services provided) in relation to the cost of producing the product or service**

## labour productivity

*Labour productivity* is normally measured by dividing the output (the number of items produced or services provided) over a given period (eg week, year) by the number of employees. Take, for example, a travel agency business which employs 4 staff and aims to arrange 500 holidays in a week.

The productivity (the output per* week) is calculated as follows:

$$\text{output per* employee} = \frac{\text{output (500 holidays)}}{\text{number of employees (4)}} = \frac{500}{4} = 125$$

*Note here the use of the word 'per' which compares the output to something else such a time value – in the same way that one refers to 'kilometres per hour' for speed or 'units per week' for car production.

It is common practice to compare **actual** output against the benchmark of **expected** output. For example, the travel agency may have set 125 holidays per week as the expected level of productivity per employee, but over a four week period with 4 staff it achieves the results shown below. The right-hand column shows productivity per employee.

| period | holidays booked | productivity |
|--------|-----------------|--------------|
| Week 1 | 520 | 130 |
| Week 2 | 600 | 150 |
| Week 3 | 440 | 110 |
| Week 4 | 580 | 145 |

A further method of measuring labour productivity, which is useful when there is a variety of products and a fluctuating number of employees is to compare output in money terms (eg the sales figure) and the number of hours worked over a given period:

$$\text{labour productivity (sales per hour)} = \frac{\text{output (£) over a given period}}{\text{hours worked over a given period}}$$

## efficiency

The efficiency of an organisation – expressed as a percentage – is calculated by comparing actual output (in units) with expected (standard) output:

$$\text{efficiency \%} = \frac{\text{actual output (units) } \times \ 100}{\text{expected/standard output (units)}}$$

In the case of the travel agency on the previous page, the efficiency percentage in week 1 in which 520 holidays have been booked (against the expected 500) is:

$$\text{efficiency \%} = \frac{520 \text{ (actual output) } \times \ 100}{500 \text{ (expected output)}} = 104\%$$

It is then a simple calculator operation (dividing actual output by expected output) to see that the efficiency in the other weeks was: 120% in week 2, 88% in week 3 and 116% in week 4.

## other productivity measures

Organisations often find it useful to compare output over a given period with factors other than labour.  Examples in the manufacturing sector include:

machine productivity  =  $\dfrac{\text{sales (£) over a given period}}{\text{machine hours for the period}}$

capital productivity  =  $\dfrac{\text{sales (£) over a given period}}{\text{capital employed (see page 43)}}$

Examples in the services industries include:

in a supermarket (sales per employee):  $\dfrac{\text{sales (£) over a given period}}{\text{employees}}$

at a college (contact hours per lecturer):  $\dfrac{\text{total student contact hours}}{\text{lecturers employed}}$

## cost per unit

Another performance indicator is the cost per unit.

**cost per unit is the cost of producing each unit**

This is calculated using the formula

cost per unit  =  $\dfrac{\text{cost of production over a given period}}{\text{number of units produced over a given period}}$

This performance indicator provides useful information because costs can be compared over different time periods. It must be remembered that the 'unit' ('cost unit') referred to can be produced by a service industry as well as in a manufacturing process. Costs can be worked out for:

| 'producer' | unit |
| --- | --- |
| BMW | car produced |
| Kelloggs | packet of cereal produced |
| police force | offence dealt with |
| fire service | incident dealt with |

Further detail can be extracted by relating the number of units produced to different cost classifications of cost, eg advertising cost per unit, labour cost per unit, distribution cost per unit. These all assist management in monitoring performance and identifying problem areas.

## resource utilisation

The major resources of any organisation – whether in the manufacturing or in the services sector – are **labour** and **equipment**. The ideally efficient organisation will ensure that its employees and its equipment are working 'flat out' all the time. Resource utilisation in this case will obviously be 100% and there is no **idle time** or **slack time**:

- **idle time** – hours in the working day spent by employees *not* working, not through any fault of their own, but because of factors such as computer/machine breakdown, power cuts, or simply because the work in hand is finished and no other task has been allocated

- **slack time** – hours in the working day during which machinery and equipment is not in productive use, eg a printing press switched off because there are no books or catalogues to print

Resource utilisation – for labour and for equipment – can be measured as a percentage. Clearly the higher the percentage, the better:

$$\text{resource utilisation \%} = \frac{\text{actual hours worked} \times 100}{\text{hours available for working}}$$

Monitoring of resource utilisation will highlight any problem areas and enable management to take decisions, eg to reduce the contracted hours of the workforce, to lay off staff, to sell or replace machinery. Of course the management also has a major responsibility in operations management to plan for efficient working of staff and machine utilisation.

## profitability

One of the principal objectives of any business is to make a profit which will benefit the owners, employees and customers. This objective also extends to other organisations such as charities and public sector services, but the motives are different – a charity helps a good cause and a public service aims to be efficient, given the resources that are available.

There are a number of ways of measuring profit performance, normally expressed as percentages, but traditionally and perhaps misleadingly called **ratios**. We will deal with some of these in the next section. Before examining the ways in which profit is measured it is important to appreciate the way in which profit is calculated. As you will know from the last chapter, a business will normally  draw up a **profit and loss account** from the accounting records. Now refresh your memory by studying the notes and the profit and loss account format illustrated on the next page.

| PROFIT AND LOSS ACCOUNT | | |
|---|---|---|
| | £ | £ |
| **Sales** | | 600,000 |
| *less*    **Cost of sales** | | 360,000 |
| *equals*    **Gross profit** | | 240,000 |
| | | |
| *less*    **Overheads**: | | |
| Administration/labour | 85,000 | |
| Selling and distribution | 50,000 | |
| Finance costs | 15,000 | |
| | | 150,000 |
| | | |
| *equals*    **Net profit** | | 90,000 |

**sales**
this figure represents the sales for the period (often a year); it may be sales of a product or it may be sales of a service (eg fees for a management consultant)

**cost of sales**
this figure is what it has cost the business to acquire what has actually been sold during the period, eg raw materials for a manufacturer or stock bought from wholesalers in the case of a shop (cost of sales is also often known as 'cost of goods sold')

**gross profit**
**sales minus cost of sales** – this gives an indicator of the 'mark-up' of a business, eg a shop buying jeans in at £15 a pair and selling them at £35 – the gross profit on the jeans will be £20, ie £35 minus £15

**overheads**
these are expenses which have to be paid, such as insurance, advertising, rates, power bills; they are not normally directly related to the level of sales; they are deducted from gross profit

**net profit**
**gross profit minus overheads** – this is essentially sales minus all costs, and represents the final profit figure the business has achieved for the period

## RATIO ANALYSIS

We will now explain the performance indicators relating to profitability:

- gross profit margin
- net profit margin
- return on capital employed

As noted earlier, these indicators are often known as accounting **ratios**: although they express a relationship between two figures, they are often quoted as percentages.

### gross profit margin

$$\text{gross profit margin \%} = \frac{\text{gross profit} \times 100}{\text{sales}}$$

This percentage shows the proportion of gross profit (sales less cost of sales) to the sales figure for the period. In the example profit and loss account shown on the previous page the calculation is:

$$\text{gross profit margin \%} = \frac{£240,000 \times 100}{£600,000} = 40\%$$

In other words, for every £100 of sales, gross profit is £40. An organisation should expect to see this percentage stay fairly constant from year-to-year, and to be similar to the gross profit margin of other organisations in the same line of business. Gross profit margins in different types of business will vary widely: a jeweller will have a high margin and a food supermarket a low margin, reflecting the length of time it takes to sell the stock.

### net profit margin

In the same way, **net profit margin** relates net profit to sales.

$$\text{net profit margin \%} = \frac{\text{net profit} \times 100}{\text{sales}}$$

This percentage relates net profit (gross profit less overheads) to the sales figure for the period. In the example profit and loss account shown on the previous page the calculation is:

$$\text{net profit margin \%} = \frac{£90,000 \times 100}{£600,000} = 15\%$$

The business is making £15 overall profit on every £100 of sales. Ideally an organisation would hope to see this percentage increase from year-to-year, as this profit figure represents funds which can be used in expanding the business. If the percentage falls over time the management will be concerned: sales may be falling or expenses may be increasing (or both).

## return on capital employed (ROCE)

return on capital employed %     =     $\dfrac{\text{net profit} \times 100}{\text{capital}}$

As we saw in the last chapter, **capital** is the investment in the business made by the owner(s) plus profits. Capital is not found in the profit and loss account but at the bottom of the balance sheet – the statement of what the business owns and owes. The return on capital employed is exactly what it says it is – it is the percentage return made on the owner's investment.

This ratio involves a closer look at the balance sheet of a business. An example of a sole trader balance sheet is shown on the next page. As we saw in the last chapter, it is essentially an equation based on a 'snapshot' of a business at a particular moment in time:

> **assets** (items owned by the business) – shown in the top half
>
> *minus*
>
> **liabilities** (items owed by the business) – shown half-way down
>
> *equals*
>
> **capital** (capital and profit) – shown at the bottom

**Net assets** are total assets less total liabilities. They are equal to the owner's stake or investment in the business.

## definitions of return on capital employed (ROCE)

Note that the sole trader business shown on the next page is the simplest form of business; a limited company, on the other hand, may have a complex capital structure made up of different types of shares and other forms of funding; the profit and loss account, too, will be more complex. These, however, are subject areas covered in AAT units studied later along the Diploma pathway, and you do not need to pay attention to them at this stage.

In this text we will adopt the simple formula:

return on capital employed %     =     $\dfrac{\text{net profit} \times 100}{\text{capital}}$

## SOLE TRADER BALANCE SHEET

**Fixed assets**

| | | |
|---|---|---|
| Premises | | 250,000 |
| Machinery | | 18,000 |
| Vehicle | | 15,000 |
| | | 283,000 |

**Current assets**

| | | |
|---|---|---|
| Stock | 24,000 | |
| Debtors | 15,000 | |
| Bank | 13,500 | |
| | 52,500 | |

*Less* **Current liabilities**

| | | |
|---|---|---|
| Creditors | 25,500 | |
| **Working capital** | | 27,000 |
| | | 310,000 |

*Less* **Long-term liabilities**

| | | |
|---|---|---|
| Bank loan | | 10,000 |
| **NET ASSETS** | | 300,000 |

**FINANCED BY**

| | | |
|---|---|---|
| Capital | | 240,000 |
| *Add* Profit | | 90,000 |
| *Less* drawings | | 30,000 |
| | | 300,000 |

assets

less

liabilities

equals

capital

*balance sheet format*

If we then apply this to the balance sheet shown on the previous page:

return on capital employed %     =     $\dfrac{£90,000 \times 100}{£300,000}$     = 30%

This sole trader is clearly running a very profitable enterprise: he or she is achieving a 30% return on the money tied up in the business – better than any bank account.

Note, however, that profit does not equal cash which can be drawn out of the business. The profit earned will have been ploughed back into the business and will be represented by the assets on the balance sheet, eg the bank balance, stocks, machinery and so on.

### more formulas!

It must be stressed that the **return on capital employed (ROCE)** formula already quoted above is not the only way of calculating return on capital employed. There are alternative formulas for this performance indicator. For example, in some circumstances, the term 'capital employed' can include long-term liabilities such as fixed bank loans. The £10,000 bank loan in the balance sheet on the previous page could in certain circumstances be added to the capital figure of £300,000, which would then produce a return on capital employed of 29%.

The term 'capital employed' clearly mean different things to different types of business.

But you do not have to worry about having to learn different formulas for return on capital employed – they will always be provided for you in AAT assessments.

## PERFORMANCE INDICATORS AND PERFORMANCE REPORTING

The performance indicators and ratios explained so far are commonly used in periodic performance reports prepared by businesses. They enable the owner(s) of the business and other interested parties such as lenders and investors to monitor the financial 'health' of the business. Performance indicators also help the owner(s) of the business to assess **quality** as it relates to the business: not only production, but aspects such as customer service and supplier deliveries. Constant improvement can be implemented as feedback is received.

In the Case Study which follows we analyse the performance of Citro Plc, a soft drinks manufacturer, and provide comments which can be used in the reporting process (see Chapter 5).

# CITRO PLC: PERFORMANCE INDICATORS

## situation

Citro Plc is a company which manufactures soft drinks. It operates three separate production divisions in the UK: Citro North, Citro South and Citro West. Performance figures for the last three months have just been made available. What do they say about the performance of the company's three divisions and about the company as a whole?

| | CITRO NORTH | CITRO SOUTH | CITRO WEST | TOTAL |
| --- | --- | --- | --- | --- |
| | £000s | £000s | £000s | £000s |
| **profit and loss data** | | | | |
| Sales | 400 | 600 | 500 | 1,500 |
| Cost of sales | 250 | 375 | 375 | 1,000 |
| Gross profit | 150 | 225 | 125 | 500 |
| Overheads | 85 | 150 | 100 | 335 |
| Net profit | 65 | 75 | 25 | 165 |
| **balance sheet data** | | | | |
| Capital employed | 1,300 | 1,250 | 1,250 | 3,800 |
| **other data** | | | | |
| Employees | 120 | 130 | 135 | 385 |
| Total labour hours available | 55,200 | 63,000 | 75,000 | 193,200 |
| Total hours worked | 54,720 | 62,400 | 69,660 | 186,780 |
| Units produced and sold | 320,000 | 400,000 | 325,000 | 1,045,000 |
| Target unit production | 300,000 | 360,000 | 375,000 | 1,035,000 |

You have been asked to calculate performance indicators and ratios for the three month period (as far as the data allows) and to comment on your findings. The areas you are looking at are:

- **productivity** – how well Citro is using its available resources
- **cost per unit** – how much it costs to produce each item sold
- **resource utilisation** – how well Citro is making use of resources, eg its workforce
- **profitability** – what return Citro is making on its sales and its capital employed

You first draw up the table of results shown on the next page, and then you add your comments under the four headings listed above.

|  | CITRO NORTH | CITRO SOUTH | CITRO WEST | TOTAL |
|---|---|---|---|---|
| **PRODUCTIVITY** | | | | |
| **labour productivity** | | | | |
| units/employees | 2667 | 3077 | 2407 | 2714 |
| sales (£)/hours | £7.31 | £9.62 | £7.18 | £8.03 |
| **capital productivity** | | | | |
| sales (£)/ capital employed | £0.31 | £0.48 | £0.40 | £0.39 |
| **efficiency %** actual output/target output | 107% | 111% | 87% | 101% |
| **COST PER UNIT** production cost*/units sold *cost, in this case = Cost of Sales | £0.78 | £0.94 | £1.15 | £0.96 |
| **RESOURCE UTILISATION** labour utilisation% actual hours/available hours | 99% | 99% | 93% | 97% |
| **PROFITABILITY** | | | | |
| **Gross profit margin %** gross profit/sales | 37.5% | 37.5% | 25% | 33.3% |
| **Net profit margin %** Net profit/sales | 16.3% | 12.5% | 5.0% | 11.0% |
| **Return on capital employed %** net profit/capital employed | 5.0% | 6.0% | 2.0% | 4.3% |

**important note to students**

You will not be required in your assessment to comment on the data you have produced or to recommend action. This is the responsibility of management. The comments set out on the next page are included so that you can appreciate the significance of the figures you have produced.

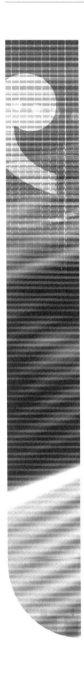

### comments on productivity

There are two measures of *labour productivity*. They link

- the number of employees to units produced
- hours worked to the sales income from the units sold

The *labour productivity* of the three divisions follows the same pattern over the three month period: Citro North and Citro South have higher labour productivity (2,667 and 3,077 units per employee, whereas Citro West is the least productive (2,407 units per employee).

Citro West is also the least *efficient:* 87% against 107% (Citro North) and 111% (Citro South). The *capital productivity* of the three divisions is reasonably consistent.

### comments on cost per unit

These figures are not strictly comparable because each division manufactures a different range of products, each of which will have different levels of cost. The figures that will need to be compared are the three-monthly results for *each division* over a period of time to pick up any trend.

### comments on resource utilisation

Citro North and Citro South are performing very well with 99% of available hours worked. Again Citro West is the weakest division with labour utilisation of only 93%.

### comments on profitability

Gross profit margin is consistent at 37.5% at Citro North and Citro South; Citro West is less profitable at 25%. This pattern is repeated for net profit margin and return on capital employed.

### overall conclusion

All companies are profitable and achieving a reasonable level of productivity. Citro West is the weakest performer. Management may need to investigate this division, and look particularly at:

- working practices – to improve labour utilisation and efficiency
- containing costs – to improve profitability

Management will also need to look at the figures for the other financial periods so that trends over time can be established and analysed.

### a note on formal reports . . .

As this Case Study shows, once the figures have been extracted, some skill is needed in reporting the information and in presenting it in a meaningful way. But the stage we have reached here is only a 'halfway house' in this respect – in Chapter 5 we continue the Case Study, having looked at the format of the report and the ways in which information can be presented in the form of graphs and charts.

**Case Study**

# CITRO PLC: PERFORMANCE REPORTING USING A COMPUTER SPREADSHEET

## situation

You have been asked to set up a spreadsheet to produce the figures in the Citro Performance Report.

You first set up the spreadsheet headings and then enter the formulas. These are shown on the screen below.

☐ Citro

| | A | B | C | D | E |
|---|---|---|---|---|---|
| 1 | | North | South | West | Total |
| 2 | | £'000s | £'000s | £'000s | £'000s |
| 3 | Profit and Loss Account Data | | | | |
| 4 | Sales | | | | =SUM(B4:D4) |
| 5 | Cost of sales | | | | =SUM(B5:D5) |
| 6 | Gross profit | =B4-B5 | =C4-C5 | =D4-D5 | =E4-E5 |
| 7 | Overheads | | | | =SUM(B7:D7) |
| 8 | Net Profit | =B6-B7 | =C6-C7 | =D6-D7 | =E6-E7 |
| 9 | | | | | |
| 10 | Balance Sheet Data | | | | |
| 11 | Capital employed | | | | =SUM(B11:D11) |
| 12 | | | | | |
| 13 | Other Data | | | | |
| 14 | Employees | | | | =SUM(B14:D14) |
| 15 | Total Hours Available | | | | =SUM(B15:D15) |
| 16 | Total Hours Worked | | | | =SUM(B16:D16) |
| 17 | Units Produced and Sold | | | | =SUM(B17:D17) |
| 18 | Target Production | | | | =SUM(B18:D18) |
| 19 | | | | | |
| 20 | PERFORMANCE INDICATORS AND RATIOS | | | | |
| 21 | *Productivity* | | | | |
| 22 | Labour Productivity | | | | |
| 23 | Output per worker | =B17/B14 | =C17/C14 | =D17/D14 | =E17/E14 |
| 24 | Sales revenue per hour worked | =B4*1000/B16 | =C4*1000/C16 | =D4*1000/D16 | =E4*1000/E16 |
| 25 | Capital Productivity | | | | |
| 26 | Sales revenue per £ capital employed | =B4/B11 | =C4/C11 | =D4/D11 | =E4/E11 |
| 27 | Efficiency% | | | | |
| 28 | Actual output/target output | =B17/B18 | =C17/C18 | =D17/D18 | =E17/E18 |
| 29 | COST PER UNIT | | | | |
| 30 | cost of sales / units sold | =B5*1000/B17 | =C5*1000/C17 | =D5*1000/D17 | =E5*1000/E17 |
| 31 | RESOURCE UTILISATION | | | | |
| 32 | labour utilisation% | | | | |
| 33 | actual hours /available hours | =B16/B15 | =C16/C15 | =D16/D15 | =E16/E15 |
| 34 | PROFITABILITY | | | | |
| 35 | Gross profit margin% | | | | |
| 36 | Gross profit/sales | =B6/B4 | =C6/C4 | =D6/D4 | =E6/E4 |
| 37 | Net profit % | | | | |
| 38 | Net profit/sales | =B8/B4 | =C8/C4 | =D8/D4 | =E8/E4 |
| 39 | Return on Capital Employed% | | | | |
| 40 | Net profit/capital employed | =B8/B11 | =C8/C11 | =D8/D11 | =E8/E11 |
| 41 | | | | | |
| 42 | | | | | |

Your next task is to enter the financial data in the appropriate cells. This then automatically calculates the performance indicators, as shown in the screen below.

| | A | B | C | D | E |
|---|---|---|---|---|---|
| 1 | | North | South | West | Total |
| 2 | | £'000s | £'000s | £'000s | £'000s |
| 3 | Profit and Loss Account Data | | | | |
| 4 | Sales | 400 | 600 | 500 | 1500 |
| 5 | Cost of sales | 250 | 375 | 375 | 1000 |
| 6 | Gross profit | 150 | 225 | 125 | 500 |
| 7 | Overheads | 85 | 150 | 100 | 335 |
| 8 | Net Profit | 65 | 75 | 25 | 165 |
| 9 | | | | | |
| 10 | Balance Sheet Data | | | | |
| 11 | Capital employed | 1300 | 1250 | 1250 | 3800 |
| 12 | | | | | |
| 13 | Other Data | | | | |
| 14 | Employees | 120 | 130 | 135 | 385 |
| 15 | Total Hours Available | 55200 | 63000 | 75000 | 193200 |
| 16 | Total Hours Worked | 54720 | 62400 | 69660 | 186780 |
| 17 | Units Produced and Sold | 320000 | 400000 | 325000 | 1045000 |
| 18 | Target Production | 300000 | 360000 | 375000 | 1035000 |
| 19 | | | | | |
| 20 | PERFORMANCE INDICATORS AND RATIOS | | | | |
| 21 | PRODUCTIVITY | | | | |
| 22 | Labour Productivity | | | | |
| 23 | Output per worker | 2667 | 3077 | 2407 | 2714 |
| 24 | Sales revenue per hour worked | £7.30 | £9.62 | £7.18 | £8.03 |
| 25 | Capital Productivity | | | | |
| 26 | Sales revenue per £ capital employed | £0.31 | £0.48 | £0.40 | £0.39 |
| 27 | Efficiency % | | | | |
| 28 | Actual output/target output | 107% | 111% | 87% | 101% |
| 29 | COST PER UNIT | | | | |
| 30 | cost of sales / units sold | £0.78 | £0.94 | £1.15 | £0.96 |
| 31 | RESOURCE UTILISATION | | | | |
| 32 | labour utilisation % | | | | |
| 33 | actual hours /available hours | 99% | 99% | 93% | 97% |
| 34 | PROFITABILITY | | | | |
| 35 | Gross profit margin % | | | | |
| 36 | Gross profit/sales | 37.5% | 37.5% | 25.0% | 33.3% |
| 37 | Net profit % | | | | |
| 38 | Net profit/sales | 16.3% | 12.5% | 5.0% | 11.0% |
| 39 | Return on Capital Employed % | | | | |
| 40 | Net profit/capital employed | 5.0% | 6.0% | 2.0% | 4.3% |
| 41 | | | | | |

When you have studied the figures and made notes about what you are going to say in your report, you will then extract spreadsheet charts which you can paste into your word-processed report.

You are particularly worried about the performance of Citro West and decide to extract comparative bar charts for the three Citro divisions, which show

- efficiency percentages

- the Return on Capital Employed percentages

These charts are shown in the continuation of this Case Study on page 86.

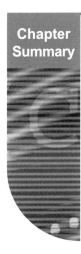

**Chapter Summary**

- Performance within a business is measured by means of formulas, percentages and ratios – known as performance indicators. These cover:
  - productivity – how well the business is using its available resources
  - cost per unit – how much it costs the business to produce each item it makes
  - resource utilisation – how well the business is making use of its workforce and equipment
  - profitability – how great a return the business is making on its sales

  These performance indicators are covered in the Key Terms section below.

- An important managerial skill, once the performance indicators have been extracted, is to comment and report on them.

- Spreadsheets are often used by organisations to calculate performance indicators.

**Key Terms**

| | |
|---|---|
| **percentage** | A percentage is a proportion of a whole where the whole equates to the number 100 for comparison |
| **productivity** | the level of output (goods manufactured or services provided) in relation to the cost of producing the product or service |
| **labour productivity** | $\dfrac{\text{output (units)}}{\text{number of employees}}$   *or . . .*<br><br>$\dfrac{\text{output (sales £)}}{\text{hours worked}}$ |
| **capital productivity** | $\dfrac{\text{output (sales £)}}{\text{capital employed}}$ |
| **efficiency %** | $\dfrac{\text{output (units) x 100}}{\text{expected (standard) units}}$ |
| **cost per unit** | $\dfrac{\text{cost of production over a given period}}{\text{number of units produced over a given period}}$ |
| **resource utilisation %** | $\dfrac{\text{actual hours worked x 100}}{\text{hours available for working}}$<br>note: this can apply to both labour hours and machine hours |
| **gross profit margin %** | $\dfrac{\text{gross profit x 100}}{\text{sales}}$ |
| **net profit margin %** | $\dfrac{\text{net profit x 100}}{\text{sales}}$ |
| **return on capital employed %** | $\dfrac{\text{net profit x 100}}{\text{capital employed}}$ |

# Student Activities

**3.1**   Helicon Limited is a holiday company, specialising in holidays on the Adriatic coast. It operates two independent offices, one in Cardiff, the other in Newcastle.  A breakdown of the costs of the two offices is as follows:

|  | Cardiff | Newcastle |
| --- | --- | --- |
|  | £000 | £000 |
| Holiday (cost of sales) | 428 | 310 |
| Marketing | 96 | 40 |
| Staffing | 120 | 76 |
| Financial Costs | 24 | 14 |
| General Office costs | 48 | 26 |
| Total costs | 716 | 466 |

*The following questions ask you to work out percentages. Round your answers to the nearest whole unit percentage.*

(a)   What percentage of the combined cost of the two offices is represented by the costs incurred by the Cardiff office?

(b)   What percentage of the total staff costs is borne by the Newcastle office?

(c)   What percentage of the Cardiff office's total costs is represented by its staff costs?

(d)   The sales manager in Newcastle is predicting a 12% rise in holiday sales next year. What would the Newcastle holiday cost of sales be if they rose by 10%?

(e)   The Cardiff accounts manager wants to see a 15% reduction in staffing costs next year. What would this cost be?

(f)   Helicon Limited has to pay for most of its holiday costs in Euros. At the beginning of the year 1 Euro cost GB£0.65. During the year the pound fell in value by 10% against the Euro.

How much would 1 Euro cost in GB£ at the end of the year?

How do you think this would affect Helicon Limited's profits, bearing in mind that holiday prices are fixed at the beginning of the year?

**3.2**  Severn Car Insurance Brokers employ five sales staff. They record between them the following number of new policies arranged each month of the year:

| | | | |
|---|---|---|---|
| January | 600 | July | 890 |
| February | 545 | August | 675 |
| March | 655 | September | 465 |
| April | 680 | October | 750 |
| May | 550 | November | 670 |
| June | 615 | December | 560 |

The expected average monthly number of policies is 625

**You are to calculate**:

(a)  the monthly labour productivity (output per employee)

(b)  the monthly efficiency percentage (to the nearest %)

(c)  the average monthly labour productivity (a) and average efficiency (b) over the year

Set out your results in a table and comment on the figures. If you are not sure about how to calculate averages, please see page 65.

**3.3**  Sentinel Security installs domestic alarm systems. During the year it records the following figures for systems installed and total costs incurred:

| month | units | costs | month | units | costs |
|---|---|---|---|---|---|
| January | 20 | £4,000 | July | 20 | £4,000 |
| February | 25 | £4,800 | August | 21 | £4,200 |
| March | 22 | £4,400 | September | 26 | £4,900 |
| April | 30 | £5,500 | October | 28 | £5,000 |
| May | 32 | £5,600 | November | 30 | £5,600 |
| June | 28 | £5,200 | December | 26 | £5,000 |

**You are to calculate**

(a)  the monthly cost per unit (to the nearest £)

(b)  the average annual cost per unit

Set out your results in a table comparing units sold, costs and unit costs. Comment on the figures. If you are not sure about how to calculate averages, please see page 65.

**3.4** Cool Designs provides a computer graphic design service. The business employs eight staff who all work a seven hour day, five days a week. During the course of a week their timesheets record the total daily hours worked: Monday 56, Tuesday 50, Wednesday 28, Thursday 56, Friday 48.

**You are to calculate**:

(a) the labour utilisation percentage for each day (to the nearest %)

(b) the labour utilisation percentage for the week

State why you think idle time may have occurred and how it might reflect on working practices.

**3.5** Trend Toys plc is a UK manufacturer planning to capture the Christmas market with its new 'RoboZapper' toy which has been heavily advertised in the pre-Christmas period. In the month of November the marketing campaign proves very successful, demand takes off and orders flood in. In order to cope with this increased demand, extra staff are taken on and overtime is worked in the factory and in the despatch department. Extra raw materials have to be purchased from new suppliers, and the price negotiated for these materials is higher than Trend Toys normally pays.

The following figures are reported for the four weeks of November.

| Production figures for the Trend RoboZapper: | | | | |
|---|---|---|---|---|
| | *Week 1* | *Week 2* | *Week 3* | *Week 4* |
| Sales (£) | 240,000 | 300,000 | 330,000 | 360,000 |
| Units produced and sold | 16,000 | 20,000 | 22,000 | 24,000 |
| Expected output (units) | 15,500 | 19,000 | 20,000 | 21,000 |
| Cost of production (£) | 120,000 | 150,000 | 190,000 | 210,000 |
| Hours worked | 4,000 | 4,700 | 4,850 | 5,150 |
| Capital employed (£) | 1,500,000 | 1,500,000 | 1,500,000 | 1,500,000 |

**You are to** calculate for each week:

(a) labour productivity (sales [£] per hour worked) – to the nearest £

(b) capital productivity (sales per £1 of capital employed) – to the nearest p

(c) efficiency percentage – to the nearest %

(d) cost per unit

Set out your results in the form of a table.

Optional task: comment on the trends shown.

**3.6** The accounts office of Witley Agricultural Machines Limited has brought together the sales and costs figures for the four quarters of the financial year (which ends on 31 December):

|  | Jan-March | April-June | July-Sept | Oct-Dec |
|---|---|---|---|---|
| Sales | 280,000 | 350,000 | 375,000 | 210,000 |
| Cost of sales | 168,000 | 217,000 | 221,250 | 128,100 |
| Overheads | 70,000 | 77,000 | 80,000 | 65,000 |

**You are to** calculate for each quarter *and* for the whole financial year:

(a)     the gross profit and the gross profit percentage (to the nearest %)

(b)     the net profit and the net profit percentage (to the nearest %)

and for the financial *year* only:

(c)     return on capital employed of £1.25 million

Set out your results in the form of a table.

Optional task: comment on your results.

You could use a spreadsheet to set out and calculate the data. A suggested format is shown below.

|  | Jan-March | April-June | July-Sept | Oct-Dec | Total |
|---|---|---|---|---|---|
| Sales (£) |  |  |  |  |  |
| Cost of sales (£) |  |  |  |  |  |
| Gross profit  (£) |  |  |  |  |  |
| Gross profit % |  |  |  |  |  |
| Overheads (£) |  |  |  |  |  |
| Net profit (£) |  |  |  |  |  |
| Net profit % |  |  |  |  |  |
| ROCE % |  |  |  |  |  |

# 4 Charts, averages and indices

## this chapter covers . . .

In this chapter we examine the techniques used in presenting performance indicators in the form of tables, charts and graphs. Specifically we explain:

- the construction of tables and the use of 'time series' data
- the visual presentation of this data in the form of:
  - line graphs
  - bar charts
  - pie charts
- the way in which averages work and the ways in which they can be used to forecast future data trends
- the techniques of changing numbers when comparing figures over a period of time in order to allow for changing price levels – either by using percentages or by using index numbers

## PERFORMANCE CRITERIA COVERED

### unit 31: ACCOUNTING WORK SKILLS

### element 13.1

### present financial data for internal and external use

C    provide, in the given format, comparisons of data as requested, to include ratios and performance indicators

D    adjust data to allow for changing price levels

# TIME SERIES ANALYSIS

### a definition

Time series analysis is a phrase which means

**'comparing figures recorded over a period of time.'**

In an accounting context time series analysis can include annual, quarterly, monthly or weekly comparison of figures for:

* sales

* cost of sales

* overhead costs

* gross and net profit

In short, 'time series analysis' is a technical term for the commonly-used technique of comparing results from different accounting periods.

### constructing a time series table

In many of the Assessments and Student Activities that you will be doing, the data is already set out in a table. If you are processing the figures at work you may have to construct a table; alternatively the table may be in 'pro-forma' form (ready made) or it may be output from a computer information system, or be completed as a computer spreadsheet. Look at the example shown below, and read the notes that follow.

| Sphere Paints PLC  Summary Profit Statement | | | | |
|---|---|---|---|---|
| | Year 1 £000s | Year 2 £000s | Year 3 £000s | Year 4 £000s |
| Sales | 500 | 970 | 1,430 | 1,912 |
| Cost of sales | 250 | 505 | 750 | 985 |
| Gross profit | 250 | 465 | 680 | 927 |
| Overheads | 185 | 370 | 548 | 780 |
| Net profit | 65 | 95 | 132 | 147 |

* the title clearly sets out the subject matter of the data

* each time period is allocated a vertical column

* each time period is clearly headed up (it could be a year, a month or a week)

- the units are stated below the time period – here £000s are chosen to prevent the table being cluttered up with unnecessary zeros
- the variables (ie sales, costs, profits) are set out in the left-hand column
- lines are added to clarify the table – it is not necessary in this case to draw a line under each variable as the columns can easily be read across; if, however, there was a large number of columns, lines would be helpful

### presenting a time series – graphs and charts

Figures set out in a table can be interpreted: upward and downward trends can be detected by reading across the rows of figures, in other words by **interpreting the time series**. A much clearer idea of trends can be obtained by presenting the time series in the form of a graph or chart which will provide a very visual concept of each trend. This process can be carried out manually or by using a computer spreadsheet or charting package. The graphs and charts which follow on the next few pages were produced by a simple spreadsheet program into which the figures above had been input.

## LINE GRAPH

The simplest form of visual representation of a time series is the **line graph**.

A line graph – which can be in a straight line or a curve – shows the relationship between two variables. One variable will always depend on the other. They are known as:

- the **independent variable** – the measurement that is at a fixed interval
- the **dependent variable** – the figure that will depend on the independent variable

A common independent variable is time, and a common dependent variable is money but as you will see from the table shown below, it is not the only fixed measurement.

| independent variable | dependent variable |
|---|---|
| time (years) | sales (£) |
| units produced | costs of production (£) |
| income level (£) | number of holidays per year |
| working out in gym (hours) | calories burned up |

Now study the diagram shown on the next page and read the notes which follow.

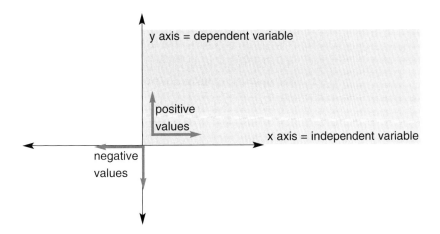

- the **independent variable** (eg years) is set out on the **horizontal** 'x' axis
- the **dependent variable** (eg sales) is set out on the **vertical** 'y' axis
- the line graph can show negative figures as well as positive figures (eg a company showing a loss over a period of years), but the most common format shows the area shaded in grey – ie both variables being positive; it is this format which is illustrated below

Now study the graph shown below and note the points made in grey text.

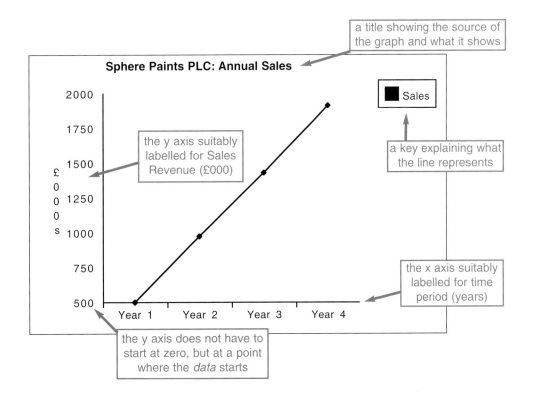

### showing trends on line graphs

The graph shown below has added the gross profit and net profit figures for Sphere Paints PLC from the table on page 61. It shows simply and clearly the upward trends in a way that the table of raw data is unable to do.

The graph is also useful in that it shows the **comparative** trends – ie sales are increasing proportionally more than gross profit, and gross profit is increasing proportionally more than net profit – as you would expect. The visual effect is quite dramatic in its impact.

On the technical side, note:

• the scaling has changed on the 'y' axis – it now goes down to zero

• each of the  lines is identified by a label (or a key could be used)

• the title has changed

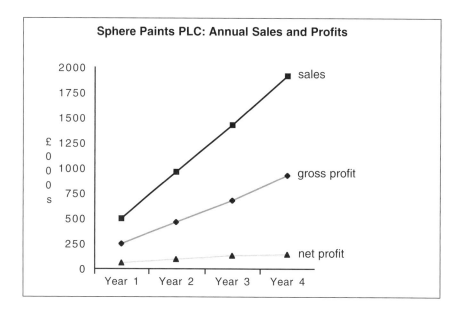

### extrapolation of trend lines

Sometimes a trend line on a line graph can be extended beyond the plotted points to **forecast** a future trend.  If a sales line, for example, shows that sales have increased by approximately 10% a year for the last five years, it is possible to plot a point for next years's sales 10% above this years figure. This is known as **extrapolation**. It is really no more than an educated guess and should be treated with caution.

In the next section we will look at the way in which these same trends can be illustrated by means of a **bar chart**.

## BAR CHARTS

A bar chart is a chart which sets out a series of bars, the height of which indicates the extent of the dependent variable. It is normal to set out a bar chart along the horizontal 'x' axis (so that they look like high-rise buildings) but the practice can be varied so that they stretch left to right from the 'y' axis.

Bar charts can be simple, compound or component, depending on what data comparisons need to be made.

### simple bar chart

The simple bar chart is the most common type. It works on the same basis as a line graph and illustrates a trend. Set out below is a simple bar chart which uses the sales figures for Sphere Paints PLC from the table on page 57. Compare it with the line graph on page 59.

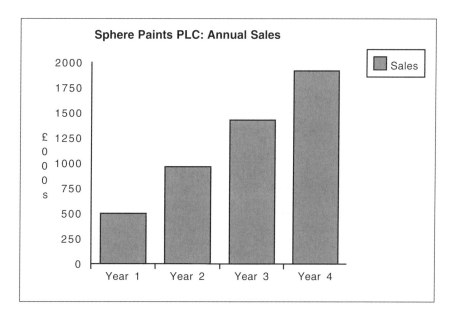

Note that:

- the labelling conventions are the same as for a line graph – here the bars are given a shading identity
- the 'y' axis goes down to zero – the whole length of the bar is needed (this is different from the line graph scaling)
- the bars are separated – this is common, but not essential – they can be drawn so that their sides touch

## compound bar chart

Just as it is possible to draw a line graph with more than one line, it is also possible to construct a bar chart with more than one set of data for each independent variable – eg sales and profits for each year. This is known as a **compound bar chart**. An example, constructed from the table of data on page 57 is shown below.

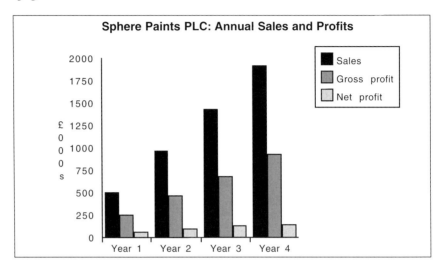

## component bar chart

A component bar chart is a bar chart which divides each bar into segments, showing how the total for each bar is made up. For example, if the annual sales totals for Sphere Paints PLC were made up of totals for three sales divisions A, B and C, each bar could be shown as having three segments.

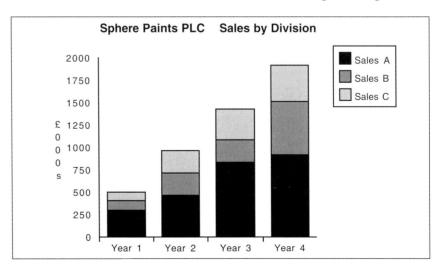

## percentage component bar chart

Another way of presenting the sales data is to express the divisional sales figures as **percentages** of the annual sales total in a percentage component bar chart. Each bar is then the same height, ie 100%, and the subdivisions show the trends of divisional sales over the four years. In this case you can see that the performance of Division A as a percentage of total sales fluctuates substantially each year, a trend that is not shown on the ordinary component chart (previous page) which indicates a steady increase. This is the type of trend that the management might be advised to investigate.

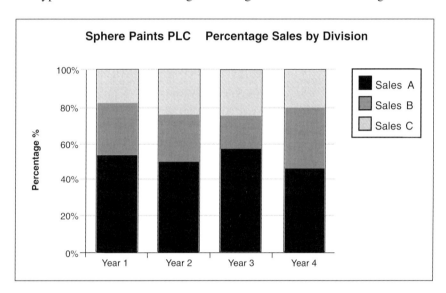

These divisional trends could also be presented in the form of a line graph:

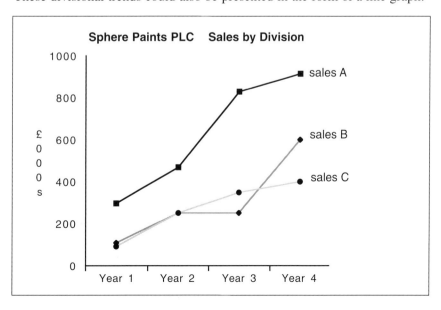

## PIE CHARTS

A **pie chart** is a circle divided into sectors to represent in the correct proportions the parts of a whole. It is called a pie chart because, like a meat or fruit pie, it can be cut into 'slices'.

Line graphs and bar charts are suitable for the presentation of **time series** data – data which varies from time period to time period. Pie charts, on the other hand, are useful in showing the breakdown of a whole into its constituent parts at a particular moment in time.

Pie charts can be constructed by hand, or by using a computer spreadsheet or charting package. If you are constructing a pie chart by hand you will need a calculator, accurate drawing equipment and a protractor.

If you take Sphere Paints PLC's sales figures for Year 1 you will equate the total sales of £500,000 with the whole pie circle. This will be divided into segments, each of which will proportionally represent a divisional sales figure. As the angle at the centre of a circle is 360° it is necessary to work out the angle for each segment individually. The formula is as follows:

$$\frac{\text{Divisional sales figure} \times 360°}{\text{Total sales figure}} = \text{the angle at the centre for the segment (°)}$$

Applying the formula to the Year 1 divisional sales figures for Sphere Paints PLC, the calculation is:

| Sales Division | Calculation | | Angle of segment (°) |
|---|---|---|---|
| Division A | $\dfrac{£300,000 \times 360°}{£500,000}$ | = | 216 |
| Division B | $\dfrac{£110,000 \times 360°}{£500,000}$ | = | 79.2 |
| Division C | $\dfrac{£90,000 \times 360°}{£500,000}$ | = | 64.8 |

If you then carry out the same procedure for Year 2, you can construct pie charts as set out on the next page. Note the labelling and shading, and the fact that the degrees are not indicated (they are of no interest to the reader). The percentages are of more significance. They can be worked out by dividing the number of degrees for each sector by 360 and multiplying by 100.

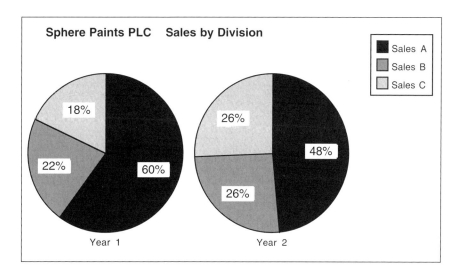

Sphere Paints PLC    Sales by Division

Sales A
Sales B
Sales C

18%
22%
60%
Year 1

26%
48%
26%
Year 2

## USING AVERAGES

A statistical technique which is useful when reporting on a series of performance figures is the use of **averages**. There are three commonly-used types of average: the mean, the median and the mode.

### which average?

Suppose the finance manager of a kitchen installation business wanted to know for budgeting purposes the average job completion time in days, from initial enquiry through to final installation. He has just received the figures for the jobs completed last month. The figures are (in days):

20, 25, 35, 35, 35, 36, 37, 55, 60, 65, 65

What is the average job completion time? We will look in turn at the mean, median and mode averages.

### the mean

The arithmetic mean is probably the most commonly used and statistically reliable form of average.

**The arithmetic mean is the sum of all the figures divided by the number of figures.**

The sum of  20, 25, 35, 35, 35, 36, 37, 55, 60, 65, 65  =  468

The arithmetic mean   $=$   $\dfrac{468}{11}$   $=$   42.6 days

This tells the manager that, on average, a job takes approximately 43 days to complete. This will help him in the planning and budgeting process. Note:

- the result is not a whole number of days – rounding up to 43 is necessary
- the result takes into account all values – if there had been an exceptional job taking 165 days instead of 65, the result will have been a mean average of $568 \div 11 = 51.6$ days, a possibly distorted result

## the median

**The median is the value of the middle figure in a series of figures.**

Note that if there is no middle figure, as with an even number of values, the median is the arithmetic mean of the two figures nearest to the middle.

Here the median is 20, 25, 35, 35, 35, **36**, 37, 55, 60, 65, 65   =   36 days.

This will not be as helpful to the manager as the mean in this context; it is useful because it is not distorted by extreme values (eg 165 days) – the mean, however, is more reliable because an equal weighting is given to each value.

## the mode

**The mode is the value that occurs most often in a series.**

In this case the most common period is 35 days (3 jobs), followed closely by 65 days (2 jobs). Note that these two time periods are very widely dispersed. This would suggest that this type of average is not as helpful in the planning process. The mode is more useful in areas such as market research in answering questions such as

'How much do people on average spend on a fast food meal?'

'What is the most commonly occurring size of T shirt?'

## USING AVERAGES IN FORECASTING

Forecasts in the reporting process are based on information about the way in which trends have established themselves in the past and are showing themselves in the present. It is then assumed that these trends will continue into the future. If one takes a profits trend, for example, established in the past, it is possible to predict a trend for the future by using a number of techniques, including the **moving average**.

**The use of moving averages is the technique of repeatedly calculating a series of different arithmetic mean values for a dependent variable along a time series to produce a trend graph.**

A moving average will move forward in time (the independent variable), step by step along the trend line, calculating a new average from the given data at each step, removing in the averaging process data which is literally "out of line" with the trend.  Some data will be above the line, some below it;  in the averaging process these fluctuations will offset each other to produce a smoother line.  The following example, assuming we are in the future – in 2015 – shows the profit figures of a company,  Arco Plc, over 15 years.

| Year | annual profit | 5 Year Moving Average |
|------|---------------|-----------------------|
|      | £M | £M |
| 2001 | 10 | |
| 2002 | 4 | |
| 2003 | 8 | 64 ÷ 5 =12.8 |
| 2004 | 18 | 17.6 |
| 2005 | 24 | 20.8 |
| 2006 | 34 | 21.6 |
| 2007 | 20 | 23.2 |
| 2008 | 12 | 26.4 |
| 2009 | 26 | 26.8 |
| 2010 | 40 | 26.4 |
| 2011 | 36 | 30.4 |
| 2012 | 18 | 34.0 |
| 2013 | 32 | 34.0 |
| 2014 | 44 | |
| 2015 | 40 | |

This table has been produced as follows:

- the profit figures were plotted on a line graph (see next page)
- a five-yearly fluctuating cycle was noted
- the profit figures for the first five years were added and divided by five to find the first of the moving averages:

  $(10 + 4 + 8 + 18 + 24 = 64;\ 64 ÷ 5 = 12.8)$

- the next arithmetic mean is calculated over the five years 2002 to 2006, ie the average moves forward a year:

  $(4 + 8 + 18 + 24 + 34 = 88;\ 88 ÷ 5 = 17.6)$

- the process is repeated for the following years until the data is exhausted
- the moving average line is plotted on the same axes as the annual profit

This line graph shows that the moving average smooths out the fluctuations, plotting a profit trend line which could be extended to provide an estimate of profit in, say, 2017, as on the graph on the next page.

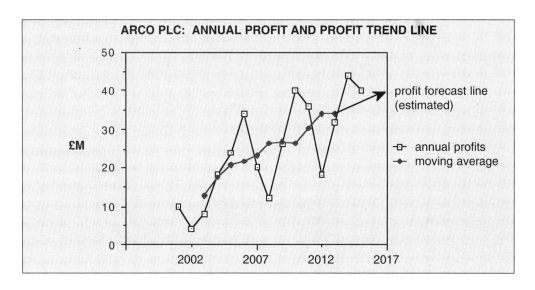

### forecasting using the incremental method

The profit forecast line to 2017 on the graph shown above is merely a guess based on the trend shown by the moving average. It is possible, however, to plot this forecast line on the graph by working out the average increase ('increment') in the moving averages (the trend). In the case shown here this will be the **average annual increase in profits**. This average increase can then be applied to subsequent years for forecasting purposes.

The arithmetic is as follows.

1   Calculate the moving averages (see previous page) and set the results out in a table (see next page)

2   Calculate the increments (increases) in the annual moving average, starting in 2004 by deducting £12.8M from £17.6M = £4.8M.

3   Repeat this process as far as you are able for each year. If the result is negative, show it in brackets. For example, the increment in 2010 is £26.4M minus £26.8M, which produces a minus figure, written as (£0.4M).

4   Add up all the increments, making sure to deduct any minus figures in the process. Here the total is £21.2M.

5   Divide the total of the increments by the number of increments to produce an average annual increment. The calculation is £21.2M ÷ 10 = £2.12M

Another way of calculating an average annual increment is by using a formula. This is normally quicker than working out each increment individually. The formula applied to this example is:

$$\frac{(\textit{Last moving average} - \textit{First moving average})}{(\textit{Number of moving averages} - 1)} = \frac{(£34.0M - £12.8M)}{10} = £2.12M$$

We can now use this average annual increment of £2.12M to produce a profit forecast beyond 2015, which is the last year for which we have data.

The arithmetic is as follows (see also the graph on the next page):

1    Decide how far in the future you want the forecast to extend. Here it is the year 2017.

2    Extend the moving average line on the graph (it goes up to 2013), increasing the profit by £2.12M a year. If you want the profit forecast to go up to 2017, this will involve plotting another *four* points, ie 2014, 2015, 2016, 2017, with the increment of £2.12M each time.

From this you can see that the *forecast* profit for 2017 will be:

£34M (the moving average for 2013)  +  £8.48M  (ie 4 x £2.12M)

=  £42.48M.

| calculation of increments in an annual moving average | | | |
|---|---|---|---|
| Year | annual profit | moving average | annual increment |
| | £M | £M | £M |
| 2001 | 10 | | |
| 2002 | 4 | | |
| 2003 | 8 | 12.8 | |
| 2004 | 18 | 17.6 | 4.8 |
| 2005 | 24 | 20.8 | 3.2 |
| 2006 | 34 | 21.6 | 0.8 |
| 2007 | 20 | 23.2 | 1.6 |
| 2008 | 12 | 26.4 | 3.2 |
| 2009 | 26 | 26.8 | 0.4 |
| 2010 | 40 | 26.4 | (0.4) |
| 2011 | 36 | 30.4 | 4.0 |
| 2012 | 18 | 34.0 | 3.6 |
| 2013 | 32 | 34.0 | 0.0 |
| 2014 | 44 | | |
| 2015 | 40 | | |

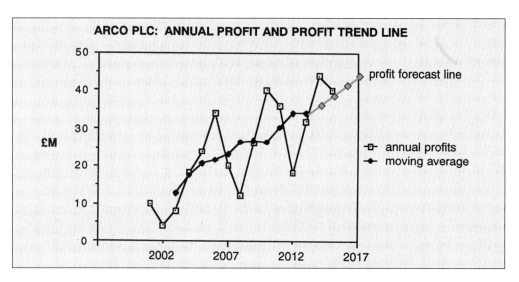

## ADJUSTING FOR PRICE RISES: PERCENTAGE METHOD

### the problem of inflation

If there is inflation in an economy it means that the value of money is falling because prices keep rising. The problem that inflation creates is that any year-to-year comparison of figures such as sales and costs is distorted because one cannot then compare 'like with like'.

### a solution – using percentages

Accountants will sometimes adjust comparative figures to allow for inflation. For example, if sales of a certain product line last year (Year 1) were £100,000 and selling prices since then have risen by 5%, the sales figure for this year (Year 2) is not a reliable comparison. If the Year 1 figure is to be meaningfully compared with the Year 2 figure, it will need to be adjusted. The formula used is simple:

$$\frac{\text{Year 1 figure x (100 + \% rise in cost or price)}}{100} = \text{updated Year 1 figure}$$

ie    $\dfrac{£100,000 \text{ x } (100 + 5)}{100} = £105,000$

To make things simpler, when using a calculator all you need to key in is:

£100,000 x **1.05**  =  £105,000

Here the percentage increase (5%) is added to 100 and the decimal point shifted two places to the left.

**Case
Study**

# THYME PRODUCTS LTD – ADJUSTING PRIOR YEAR'S FIGURES FOR INFLATION

## situation

The management of Thymo Limited, which makes herbal medicines, are concerned that the current year-end performance figures they have just received do not show the whole picture. They are aware that costs rose last year with inflation and that as a result the sales prices they charged also went up. Do these sales and cost figures show an increase or a fall? Adjustments will clearly need to be made to demonstrate this.

The figures they have received are as follows:

|  | Year 1 (actual) £ | Year 2 (actual) £ |
|---|---|---|
| Sales | 200,000 | 260,000 |
| Materials costs | 100,000 | 102,000 |
| Overheads costs | 75,000 | 90,000 |

It looks like all the figures have gone up from Year 1 to Year 2 , but management  also learn that sales prices increased by 5%, materials costs by 4% and overheads costs by 6%.

They ask you to adjust the Year 1 figures and then calculate a percentage increase or decrease  for sales, materials costs and overhead costs.

## solution

This calculations are as follows:

|  | Year 1 (*adjusted*) £ | Year 2 (actual) £ | Difference £ | % |
|---|---|---|---|---|
| Sales | **210,000**[1] | 260,000 | + 50,000 | + 23.8 |
| Materials costs | **104,000**[2] | 102,000 | – 2,000 | – 1.9 |
| Overheads costs | **79,500**[3] | 90,000 | + 10,500 | + 13.2 |

Calculations:

[1] $\dfrac{£200,000 \times (100 + 5)}{100} = £210,000.$  Difference = £260,000 – £210,000 = £50,000.

Percentage increase is £50,000/£210,000 x 100

= 23.8%

[2] $\dfrac{£100,000 \times (100 + 4)}{100} = £104,000.$  Difference = £102,000 – £104,000 =  – £2,000.

Percentage decrease is – £2,000/£104,000 x 100

= – 1.9%

[3] $\dfrac{£75,000 \times (100 + 6)}{100} = £79,500.$  Difference = £90,000 – £79,500 = £10,500.

Percentage increase is £10,500/£79,500 x 100

= 13.2%

## ALLOWING FOR CHANGES IN PRICES: INDEX NUMBERS

### performance figures as index numbers

A further method of presenting a numeric trend over a time period is converting the figures in question into a series of **index numbers**.

**An index is a sequence of values where one base value is equated to 100 and the other values are proportionally related to 100.**

The object of using an index system is to simplify comparison of complex values by replacing the complicated figures with simple ones, all related to a base of 100.

It is therefore possible to convert periodic performance figures such as sales and profits to index numbers in order to analyse trends much more easily. The procedure for doing this is explained at the bottom of the page.

### RPI: price levels as index numbers

Another form of index is the Retail Price Index (RPI) which regularly looks at the price of a defined 'shopping basket' of products in the UK economy and gives them an index number related to a base year. This index charts the rise in the level of prices. This is important to businesses because if prices are rising sharply, a true comparison of performance figures becomes difficult. There is no point in saying that sales in money terms have increased by 10% when the level of prices has risen by 15% – in this case the volume of sales may actually have gone down.

### calculating index numbers

The procedure for creating an index series is as follows:

■ Take a series of values, for example the total sales for Osborne PLC over four years:

|  |  |
|---|---|
| Year 1 | £500,000 |
| Year 2 | £520,000 |
| Year 3 | £525,000 |
| Year 4 | £535,000 |

■ Equate the first figure (the base year) with 100, ie say £500,000 = 100

■ Convert each of the subsequent years' figures to index numbers by applying the formula:

$$\frac{\text{other year's figure} \times 100}{\text{base year figure}} = \text{index number of other year}$$

The calculation for the index for the sales of Osborne PLC is therefore:

| | | | |
|---|---|---|---|
| Year 1 | £500,000 (base year figure) | = | 100 |
| Year 2 | $\frac{£520,000 \times 100}{£500,000}$ | = | 104 |
| Year 3 | $\frac{£525,000 \times 100}{£500,000}$ | = | 105 |
| Year 4 | $\frac{£535,000 \times 100}{£500,000}$ | = | 107 |

The indices (index numbers) for the four years are therefore: 100, 104, 105 and 107. There would seem to be a modest upward trend in sales. Or is there? Suppose that for the four years in question the prices of goods and services in the economy had been rising sharply – in other words in real terms the value of money had been declining. It follows that sales **in real terms** may also have been declining. Using index numbers it is possible to compare the sales trend with inflation. The table below shows the RPI (Retail Price Index) as quoted for the four years in question:

| | RPI index | Osborne sales index |
|---|---|---|
| Year 1 | 150 | 100 |
| Year 2 | 160 | 104 |
| Year 3 | 170 | 105 |
| Year 4 | 182 | 107 |

It is clear from this exercise that sales are increasing at a slower rate than the level of prices: the RPI index figures are increasing at a higher rate. In the next section we will see how these sales figures can be adjusted to **sales in real terms** by using the RPI index figures.

### converting figures to adjust for price changes

The following formula is used to present the sales trend in the light of the rise in the price level as shown by the RPI:

$$\frac{\text{Sales figure for year in question} \times \text{RPI index for Year 1}}{\text{RPI index for year in question}} = \text{Adjusted sales figure}$$

For Year 2, therefore, the calculation is:

$$\frac{£520,000 \times 150}{160} = \text{Adjusted sales figure of } £487,500$$

For Year 3 the calculation is:

$$\frac{£525,000 \times 150}{170} = \text{Adjusted sales figure of } £463,235$$

For Year 4, therefore, the calculation is:

$$\frac{£535,000 \times 150}{182} = \text{Adjusted sales figure of } £440,934$$

The sales figures can then be presented in a table as follows:

| Year | Actual sales figures £ | Sales figures adjusted by RPI index £ |
|---|---|---|
| Year 1 | 500,000 | 500,000 |
| Year 2 | 520,000 | 487,500 |
| Year 3 | 525,000 | 463,235 |
| Year 4 | 535,000 | 440,934 |

It is clear from these adjusted figures that sales **in real terms** are on a serious decline: although the actual figure for Year 4 is £535,00, when adjusted for the change in price levels as measured by the RPI, it is only £440,934.

## Chapter Summary

- Performance reports contain the presentation of figures – money amounts, units produced hours – over a period of time. This is known as time series analysis.

- Time series analysis normally starts with the presentation of the figures in a table; these are the raw data from which can be constructed a variety of graphs and charts, either on paper or on a computer.

- A line graph is a simple and effective way of showing trends over time. More than one line can be displayed on a line graph.

- A bar chart also illustrates trends and can be in simple form (one variable charted) or compound (a number of variables charted separately) or component (showing the make-up of a figure in a single bar).

- A pie chart – a circular 'pie' divided into slices – shows the proportional make-up of a single figure. A pie chart is not so helpful in showing trends as it is limited to a single time period.

- When analysing periodic performance figures it is important to be able to use averages. There are three types of average: the mean (arithmetic), the median (the middle figure in a series) and the mode (the most common figure).

■ The use of moving averages enables a trend to be established when the figures in the time series vary widely; this technique also enables a future trend to be forecast.

■ One effect of inflation is to change the value of money amounts in a time series, which makes comparison of year-to-year figures unreliable. This can be avoided by adjusting figures by applying a percentage method. This enables reliable comparisons to be made from one year to the next.

■ A series of index numbers enables a set of complex time series values (eg sales over five years) to be related to a base figure of 100. This makes comparison of the values much simpler.

■ The Retail Price Index (RPI) charts changes in price levels in the UK economy over time. It is useful – particularly when prices are rising rapidly – to adjust a set of time series figures (eg sales) to the RPI index. This will show the actual trend of the time series figures.

| **Key Terms** | | |
|---|---|---|
| **time series analysis** | | the comparison of a set of figures recorded over a period of time |
| **line graph** | | a visual representation of a time series |
| **independent variable** | | the measurement on a line graph which is set at fixed intervals – this is often time – on the horizontal axis |
| **dependent variable** | | the measurement on a line graph which depends on the independent variable, eg sales, profit, on the vertical axis |
| **simple bar chart** | | a chart which sets out a series of bars, the height of which indicates the extent of the independent variable |
| **compound bar chart** | | a bar chart which displays more than one set of data (and more than one bar) for each independent variable |
| **component bar chart** | | a bar chart which divides each bar into segments which shows how the total for each bar is made up |
| **percentage component bar chart** | | a component bar chart where all the bars are the same height and shows the segments as percentages of each bar |

**pie chart**                        a circle divided into sectors to represent in the correct proportion the parts of a whole – like a pie divided into 'slices'

**arithmetic mean**                  an average worked out as the sum of all the figures in a series divided by the number of figures

**median**                           an average which is the value of a middle figure in a series of figures

**mode**                             an average which is the value that occurs most often in a series

**moving average**                   the technique of repeatedly calculating a series of different arithmetic mean values for a dependent variable along a time series to produce a trend graph

**incremental forecasting**          producing a trend line by working out the average increase in trend figures and using the average increase as a basis for forecasting

**inflation**                        the fall of the value of money in an economy as a result of a rise in the general level of prices

**index**                            a sequence of values where one base value is equated to 100 and the other values are proportionally related to 100

**Retail Price Index (RPI)**         an index which represents the price of a 'shopping basket' of products in the UK economy over time – it measures the price level and is an indicator of inflation

# Student Activities

**4.1**  A colleague hands you the following table which is to be used in a performance report. What is wrong with it? Redraft it as you think it should appear and construct a line graph to illustrate sales and profitability. Note: the figures for sales, cost of sales and overheads are known to be correct.

| Gemini PLC | | | | |
|---|---|---|---|---|
| | **Year 1** | **Year 2** | **Year 3** | **Year 3** |
| Sales | 1,000 | 1,250 | 1,300 | 1,450 |
| Cost of sales | 500 | 650 | 650 | 700 |
| Gross profit | 500 | 600 | 640 | 750 |
| Overheads | 350 | 350 | 380 | 400 |
| Net profit | 250 | 300 | 260 | 350 |

**4.2**  The table below shows the divisional sales figures for Newbury Products PLC.

| Newbury Products PLC   Sales by Division | | | | |
|---|---|---|---|---|
| | **Year 1** £000s | **Year 2** £000s | **Year 3** £000s | **Year 4** £000s |
| Sales Division A | 400 | 500 | 550 | 600 |
| Sales Division B | 100 | 250 | 350 | 400 |
| Sales Division C | 350 | 300 | 250 | 300 |
| Total Sales | 850 | 1,050 | 1,150 | 1,300 |

**You are to:**

(a)  Construct a compound bar chart showing the sales for all three divisions over the four years. Make brief comments on the trends shown.  Is this the best form of chart to use to show these trends?

(b)  Construct a component bar chart using the same data. Comment on the differences between the charts in (a) and (b) and state in what circumstances you would use them.

(c)  Construct pie charts for Year 1 and Year 4 and comment on what they do and do not show.

**4.3**   Calculate the average (mean, median and mode) hourly rate of shop floor workers pay from the following figures:

£5.50, £5.75, £5.80, £5.85, £5.90, £8.00, £10.00, £10.00, £35.00.

Which average figure are you likely to use if you are compiling a report on wage costs, and why?

**4.4**   The following figures represent the number of unit sales (measured in millions) of a highly successful new computer game 'Final Frontier' over the last 12 weeks, following a worldwide advertising campaign promoting the product.

3, 5, 10, 5, 7, 12, 7, 9, 17, 8,10,18

(a)   Set up a table to work out a moving average on these figures, using a three point moving average as a basis for your calculation. Calculate to the nearest decimal place.

(b)   Calculate the average increment of the moving averages (to the nearest decimal place).

(c)   Plot the original figures and the moving average figures on a line graph. Include a forecast for the next three weeks using the average increment you have calculated. (Note: you need to allow for 15 weeks on your graph).

**4.5**   The following figures represent the quarterly unit sales of a range of swimwear by BigSplash PLC over the last 4 years.

|      | Quarter 1 | Quarter 2 | Quarter 3 | Quarter 4 |
|------|-----------|-----------|-----------|-----------|
| 2001 | 2,000     | 4,500     | 6,000     | 2,000     |
| 2002 | 3,000     | 5,000     | 7,500     | 3,000     |
| 2003 | 4,000     | 6,500     | 8,500     | 4,000     |
| 2004 | 5,000     | 8,000     | 10,000    | 5,000     |

(a)   Set up a table to work out a moving average on these figures, using a four point moving average as a basis for your calculation.

(b)   Calculate the average quarterly increment in the trend (to the nearest unit).

**4.6**   The year-end accounts for Crimson Computers Limited are being prepared. Figures relating to revenue and expenses have been drawn up in a table which compares current year results with the figures from the previous year. Inflation has been affecting costs and sales prices during the year and so the table also shows the relevant increase in costs and the rise in sales prices charged.

|                    | Last year (£) | Current year (£) | inflationary rise (%) |
|--------------------|---------------|------------------|-----------------------|
| Sales              | 420,000       | 430,000          | 5% price increase     |
| Cost of goods sold | 185,000       | 200,000          | 4% rise in costs      |
| Wages and salaries | 85,000        | 95,000           | 5% rise in costs      |
| Other overheads    | 56,000        | 65,000           | 4% rise in costs      |

**You are to:**

(a)    Adjust last year's figures for the appropriate percentage rise.

(b)    Calculate the difference between the figures for the two years, noting whether the difference total is positive or negative.

(c)    Calculate the percentage rise or decrease.

Set out your results in an appropriate table. In the case of each Item (sales and costs), explain what has happened during the year in terms of the figures calculated and the trends shown.

**4.7**    The following table shows the sales and net profit figures for Pilot Design Consultancy for the last five years, together with the Retail Price Index for those years.

| Pilot Design Consultancy: sales and profitability | | | |
|---|---|---|---|
| | Sales (£) | Net profit (£) | RPI |
| Year 1 | 350,000 | 45,000 | 155 |
| Year 2 | 355,000 | 46,000 | 163 |
| Year 3 | 365,000 | 48,000 | 169 |
| Year 4 | 380,000 | 48,500 | 176 |
| Year 5 | 390,000 | 49,000 | 189 |

**You are to:**

(a)    Convert the sales and net profit figures into index numbers, using year one as the base. Comment on the trends shown.

(b)    Adjust (to the nearest £) the sales and net profit figures for the changing price levels shown by the RPI indices. Comment on the trends shown.

# 5 Report writing

In this chapter we examine written reports:

- the context in which reports are written
- the report format
- interpreting data for use in reports
- techniques used in report writing
- the importance of keeping to deadlines

## PERFORMANCE CRITERION COVERED

### unit 31:  ACCOUNTING WORK SKILLS

### element 13.1

### present financial data for internal and external use

C   provide, in the given format, comparisons of data as requested, to include ratios and performance indicators

# REPORT WRITING

## the report in context

Reports are written in a wide variety of contexts; they may be very long or they may be very short. Examples of long reports include the report to shareholders produced by companies. The principles are essentially the same: performance is reported, commented on and recommendations normally made. The important point about a report is that it should set out information clearly and concisely and come to a firm conclusion. It should also be submitted within the given timescale.

In your accounting studies you may be asked to produce a variety of report forms, for example

- a short memorandum passing on information

- a 'proforma' report where defined information has to be filled in boxes on a form – this format can also be computer-based, eg on a spreadsheet

- a more extended document – maybe one or two pages – setting out financial data and analysis, normally for the benefit of management, and suggesting a specific course of action or investigation – this type of report is often known as the 'short formal report'

As you may have to write a formal report as part of your Diploma studies, it is explained and illustrated in the pages that follow.

## report format

Reports normally fall into a series of sections. These sections can be given a formal heading, eg 'introduction', or they can be left as a series of self-contained paragraphs. For the purposes of your studies, it is suggested that you use the headings – they help to concentrate the mind and they do make the document look clearer and more structured. The sections commonly found in a report are shown below. These can, of course, be varied to suit the situation. There is no 'right' or 'wrong' format.

## decimal numbering systems

Reports which have a complex structure of headings and subheadings often use a decimal numbering system for the various sections. These tend to be longer reports and you may not need to use this system for Unit 31.

Each section is given a number (eg 1.0) and any subsection within that section is given a number after a decimal point (ie 1.1, 1.2, 1.3), and subdivisions of that are given a further decimal point and a number (eg 1.1.1, 1.1.2). Each section and subsection (and sub-subsection) is progressively indented from the left margin, as seen in the example on the next page.

| |
|---|
| **2.0 Procedure** |
| 2.1 Source material |
| 2.1.1 Sales budget |
| 2.1.2 Production budget |

## CONTENTS OF A REPORT

When reading this section, refer to the report format shown opposite.

### title and preliminaries

A report is always given a title. It is also common practice for a report, like a memorandum, to be addressed from one person to another. Job titles are normally added to these names. The report should also be dated.

### introduction

This section, sometimes called 'Terms of Reference' will set out the circumstances and scope of the report:

• the person who requested it

• the ground it has to cover

• the date by which it has to be submitted

• whether it has to make any recommendations

For example: 'This report, requested by the Finance Director, will analyse the revenues and costs for the three divisions of Sphere Paints for the last three financial years and will make recommendations for improving future performance. The report is due for completion by March 30.'

### procedure

This section will set out the methods used, eg 'Data produced by the Accounts Department was used for this report. A table of financial data is included in the body of this report.'

### findings

This will set out the main findings and trends, highlighting figures and commenting on performance indicators; these can be set out in the form of tables, graphs and charts (see the next chapter).

This section can also be used to point out any limitations of the data, eg 'this was an exceptional year because the accounting policies changed' or 'the factory was burnt down' or 'the business was taken over' . . . and so on.

---

report to ..............................(name + job title)     report date .............................................

report from .........................(name + job title)

**REPORT TITLE  (in capitals)**..................................................................................................

**introduction/terms of reference**
Circumstances and scope of the report – what it covers, why it is being written, for whom, and when.

**procedure**
Where the data comes from and how it is used.

**findings**
The data is set out and analysed. Any limitations of the findings will be highlighted.

**conclusions**
A summary of the findings – with comments.

**recommendations**
Recommendations made on the basis of the conclusions reached.

**appendices**
Extra data included here if there is not room for it in the findings.

---

*short formal report format*

## conclusions

This section summarises and makes comments on the findings so that recommendations may follow if required.

## recommendations

If required by the report, recommendations should be made based on the conclusions reached.

## appendices

If some of the data is too bulky to go in the main 'findings' section, it can be included in an appendix – eg three years' profit and loss statements and balance sheets, stock reports or budget reports. An appendix can also be used for graphs and charts imported from a spreadsheet.  If there is more than one appendix, the appendices are normally numbered.

## HINTS ON REPORT WRITING

Writing a successful report is an exercise in communication. You have to get a message across clearly, accurately and on time.

Before starting the actual report, make sure that:

- you have all the facts and figures needed – you may need to construct or complete a table or spreadsheet which sets out performance indicators
- you have checked all the calculations
- you have planned out the report – you may need to 'rough out' a series of points on a separate piece of paper, a process which will help you come to a reasoned conclusion
- you know what format of report is to be used

When putting pen to paper (or fingers to keyboard), bear in mind the following points:

| | |
|---|---|
| **be clear** | Avoid using complex words and phrases when simple ones will do – for example: |
| | *'Sales have improved at Citro North'* |
| | is far preferable to: |
| | *'The recorded level of turnover has seen a significant uplift at the Citro North operating division.'* |
| **be brief** | Remember that the person reading the report will not have hours to spare. Keep the text brief – for example: |
| | *'The stock level will need examining'* |
| | is preferable to: |
| | *'It is my view that the levels of stock maintained should become the subject of a thorough investigation.'* |
| **be objective** | Avoid using 'I' and 'We' which are subjective, but instead be objective – for example: |
| | *'Citro West's low liquidity is likely to be the result of a high stock level'* is far preferable to |
| | *'In my view, Citro West's poor liquidity may be a result of their having too much stock.'* |
| | Giving opinions is a form of subjectivity and should be avoided. Statements beginning 'In my view. . . ' or 'I think that . . .' should be avoided as they suggest that what follows is based on guesswork rather than on fact. |

| | |
|---|---|
| **avoid slang** | Using slang is lazy and should be avoided at all costs. |

For example:

*'It is recommended that management should take measures to improve profitability'*

is far better than

*'I think that these results are rubbish – they could be improved a lot.'*

Do not write 'don't' – which is the spoken version – but 'do not' and similarly 'could not' rather than 'couldn't'.

| | |
|---|---|
| **be accurate** | Always check that figures quoted in the text tally with the data provided. If you are calculating ratios and percentages, always carry out the calculation twice and make sure you are using the right figures. If you are using a spreadsheet check that the input is correct – and get someone else to check it for you – remember that 'garbage in . . . garbage out'. |

## PRODUCING THE REPORT

If you refer to the Citro Plc Case Study in the Chapter 3 (see page 46) you will see that all the performance indicators have been set out in a table that is reproduced on the next page, and 'comments' have been added. These comments are a form of report to management: they highlight the main trends and pinpoint weaknesses. They conclude with recommendations relating to the weakest performing division of the business. These comments could be rewritten in the form of a structured short report, as shown on the pages which follow the table of results.

### using a word-processing program

The report will normally be word-processed, as the format 'template' will then be on file in the organisation. The following checklist sets out word-processing techniques with which you should be familiar and be prepared to use in a report where appropriate:

*   setting out headings – emboldening and enlarging
*   setting out data in tables and formatting tables
*   indenting text and numbering paragraphs, if this is required
*   importing ('pasting') graphics into the text, eg graphs and charts

# CITRO PLC: PERIODIC PERFORMANCE REPORT

## situation

The table below shows the performance of Citro PLC's three sales divisions for the three months ended 31 March. You have been asked to prepare a performance report for the Finance Director, Brian Cousins.

|  | CITRO NORTH | CITRO SOUTH | CITRO WEST | TOTAL |
|---|---|---|---|---|
| **PRODUCTIVITY** | | | | |
| **labour productivity**<br>units/employees | 2667 | 3077 | 2407 | 2714 |
| sales (£)/hours | £7.31 | £9.62 | £7.18 | £8.03 |
| **capital productivity**<br>sales (£)/<br>capital employed | £0.31 | £0.48 | £0.40 | £0.39 |
| **efficiency %**<br>actual output/target output | 107% | 111% | 87% | 101% |
| **COST PER UNIT**<br>production cost*/units sold<br>•cost, in this case = Cost of Sales | £0.78 | £0.94 | £1.15 | £0.96 |
| **RESOURCE UTILISATION**<br>labour utilisation%<br>actual hours/available hours | 99% | 99% | 93% | 97% |
| **PROFITABILITY** | | | | |
| **Gross profit margin %**<br>gross profit/sales | 37.5% | 37.5% | 25.0% | 33.3% |
| **Net profit margin %**<br>Net profit/sales | 16.3% | 12.5% | 5.0% | 11.0% |
| **Return on capital employed %**<br>net profit/capital employed | 5.0% | 6.0% | 2.0% | 4.3% |

You word process the report set out on the next few pages. The supporting numerical data (see previous page) will have been processed on a spreadsheet, and appropriate charts extracted and imported into the appendix to the report.

The text of the report will be checked for accuracy within your Department and then sent to the Finance Director. The report may then be referred to the Board of Directors and decisions made at that level if it is thought appropriate.

---

**from**   Stew Dent, Accounts Assistant

**to**     Brian Cousins, Finance Director          **date**  10 April 2006

## CITRO PLC QUARTERLY PERFORMANCE REPORT

**(for the three months ended 31 March 2006)**

### INTRODUCTION

This report, produced by the Finance Department as part of its normal reporting procedure will set out the performance indicators for the three operating divisions of Citro PLC: Citro North, Citro South and Citro West for the three months ended 31 March 2006. It will compare the performance and make recommendations based on its findings by 18 April 2006.

### PROCEDURE

The data for this report has been compiled as part of the monthly management reporting process by the Finance, Production and Sales Departments. A table of financial data and appropriate charts are included in the body of this report.

### FINDINGS

**productivity**

The *labour productivity* of the three divisions follows the same pattern over the three month period: Citro North and Citro South have higher labour productivity (2,667 and 3,077 units per employee), whereas Citro West is the least productive (2,407 units per employee).

Citro West is also the least *efficient:* 87% against 107% (Citro North) and 111% (Citro South).

The *capital productivity* of the three divisions is reasonably consistent, averaging 39p of sales per £1 of capital employed.

## cost per unit

The figures for cost per unit are not strictly comparable because the three divisions manufacture a different range of products, each of which will has a different level of cost.

## labour utilisation

Citro South and Citro North are performing very well with 99% of available hours worked. Again Citro West is the weakest division with labour utilisation of only 93%

## profitability

*Gross profit margin* is consistent at 37.5% at Citro North and Citro South; Citro West is less profitable at 25%. This pattern is repeated for net profit margin and return on capital employed: the margins for Citro North and Citro South are satisfactory, whereas the results for Citro West are less so.

It should be pointed out that the table does not show figures for the other financial quarters; this additional data will enable trends to be established and analysed.

## CONCLUSIONS

All divisions are profitable and achieving a reasonable level of productivity. Citro West is the weakest performer in terms of efficiency, labour utilisation and profitability. Profitability in particular is weak, pointing to a higher level of costs in this division.

## RECOMMENDATIONS

Management may need to investigate areas in Citro West such as:

* working practices – to improve labour utilisation and efficiency
* containing costs – to improve profitability

The results of these investigations will enable management to take measures to improve performance in these areas.

### important note to students

You may not be required in your assessment to comment on the data you have produced or to recommend action, as is in this report. You should read your assessment instructions carefully to see what exactly you are required to do with the data you have produced. Study the practice assessments in the Osborne Books' *Accounting Work Skills Workbook*.

## APPENDIX

The bar charts shown below demonstrate the weakness of the Citro West division in terms of its efficiency and its return on capital employed.

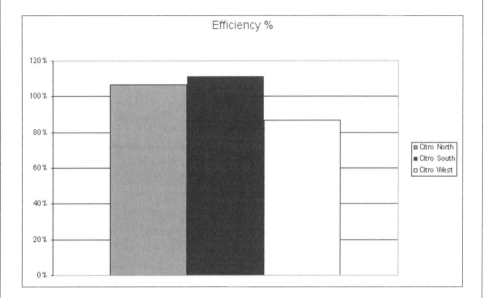

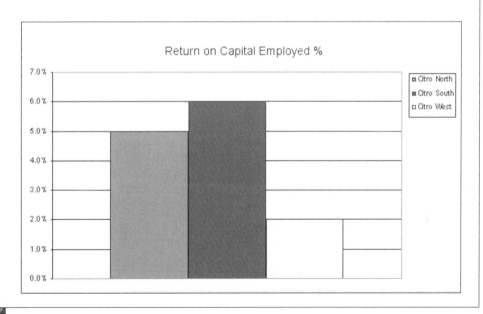

**Chapter Summary**

- Reports are written in a wide variety of contexts and can vary in length.

- Periodic performance reports produced to present accounting data normally take the form of a short formal report.

- The sections of the report normally include:
    - report title and preliminaries (date, sender, recipient)
    - the Introduction (or 'Terms of Reference') – what it is about
    - Procedure – the sources used
    - Findings – presentation and analysis of data
    - Conclusions
    - Recommendations
    - Appendices – data which is too bulky for the 'Findings' section

- Guidelines for report writing state that a report should:
    - be clear
    - be brief
    - be objective rather than subjective
    - avoid slang
    - be accurate

- Reports should be completed within the given deadlines.

**Key Terms**

| | |
|---|---|
| **short formal report** | a brief formally structured report (see 'sections' above), often used within an organisation for management purposes |
| **terms of reference** | the section of the report which sets out the scope and content, date of submission and intended recipient |
| **procedure** | the section of the report which sets out the sources used and the methods used to extract the data |
| **findings** | the section of the report which sets out the data, analyses it and comments on it; it also highlights any limitations of the data |
| **conclusions** | the section of the report which comes to a firm conclusion about the findings |
| **recommendations** | the section of the report which makes recommendations – if required – on the basis of the conclusions reached |
| **appendices** | the section of the report which contains data used in the 'Findings', but which is too extensive to be quoted in full in the 'Findings' – eg financial statement |

# Student Activities

5.1 Refer to Student Activity 3.5 on page 54. If you have not already done this Activity you should do it now – the text is set out below in the grey box. When you have completed your table and drafted your comments

**you are to . . .**

Produce a short formal report based on your comments. Use today's date, your name (job title – Assistant, Accounts Department) and address the report to the Finance Director (invent a name). The report should be headed up with the section headings (Introduction, Procedure etc) and include a Recommendations section. The table of performance indicators should be included as an Appendix. Use a word-processing program for the report text and the table.

Trend Toys plc is a UK manufacturer planning to capture the Christmas market with its new 'RoboZapper' toy which has been heavily advertised in the pre-Christmas period.

In the month of November the marketing campaign proves very successful, demand takes off and orders flood in. In order to cope with this increased demand, extra staff are taken on and overtime is worked in the factory and in the despatch department.

The following figures are reported for the four weeks of November.

| Production figures for the Trend RoboZapper: | | | | |
|---|---|---|---|---|
| | Week 1 | Week 2 | Week 3 | Week 4 |
| Sales (£) | 240,000 | 300,000 | 330,000 | 360,000 |
| Units produced and sold | 16,000 | 20,000 | 22,000 | 24,000 |
| Expected output (units) | 15,500 | 19,000 | 20,000 | 21,000 |
| Cost of production (£) | 120,000 | 150,000 | 190,000 | 210,000 |
| Hours worked | 4,000 | 4,700 | 4,850 | 5,150 |
| Capital employed (£) | 1,500,000 | 1,500,000 | 1,500,000 | 1,500,000 |

**You are to** calculate for each week:

(a)    labour productivity  (based on output related to hours worked)

(b)    capital productivity (sales per £1 of capital employed)

(c)    efficiency  percentage

(d)    cost per unit

Set out your results in the form of a table and comment on the trends shown.

**5.2** Oasis Computers sells hardware and software from a chain of shops. It has representation in three towns: Kidderport, Stourminster and Persham.

Each shop is self-accounting. The figures for the first six months of the year have just been brought together:

|  | Kidderport | Stourminster | Persham | Total |
|---|---|---|---|---|
|  | £ | £ | £ | £ |
| **financial information** |  |  |  |  |
| Sales | 120,000 | 95,000 | 110,000 | 325,000 |
| Cost of sales | 65,000 | 55,000 | 72,000 | 192,000 |
| Gross profit | 55,000 | 40,000 | 38,000 | 133,000 |
| Overheads | 40,000 | 29,000 | 36,000 | 105,000 |
| Net profit | 15,000 | 11,000 | 2,000 | 28,000 |
| Capital employed | 150,000 | 120,000 | 135,000 | 405,000 |
| **non-financial information** |  |  |  |  |
| Employees | 5 | 4 | 6 | 15 |
| Hours worked | 4,375 | 3,600 | 5,100 | 13,075 |
| Floor space of shop | 500m² | 450m² | 625m² | 1,575m² |
| Units sold | 2,400 | 1,900 | 2,200 | 6,500 |

**You are to**

Calculate appropriate ratios and percentages for all three shops and the business as a whole, covering the areas listed below. You should set out your results in the form of a table.

Use a spreadsheet if you can to process and present the data.

(a) labour productivity – relating units to employees, and sales to hours worked

(b) capital productivity – sales per £1 of capital employed (to the nearest p)

(c) cost per unit – units sold related to cost of sales plus overheads

(d)  resource utilisation – sales per square metre of floor space

(e)  gross profit percentage (to the nearest %)

(f)  net profit percentage (to the nearest %)

(g)  return on capital employed (to the nearest %)


Then, having discussed your findings within your student group (if this is possible), word process a short formal report to Bill Bates, General Manager of Oasis Computers. Use your own name (job title – Assistant, Accounts Department).

The report should be headed up with the section headings (Introduction, Procedure etc) and include a Recommendations section. The table of performance indicators and ratios should be included as an Appendix, preferably imported from the spreadsheet.

# Consolidating and reporting information

In the last few chapters we have explained and illustrated:

- the ways in which performance indicators can be applied to data which has been extracted from an organisation

- the statistical techniques that can be applied to this data, producing graphs and charts to illustrate situations and trends.

- the use of spreadsheets to help in these processes

Your studies also require that you are able to consolidate this data, which may come from different operating divisions of a business. You will also need to make adjustments to the data. You may then be required to bring data together to produce a single profit and loss account, for example, and then to analyse the figures, extract performance indicators and produce graphs and charts to incorporate in a short report.

## PERFORMANCE CRITERION COVERED

### unit 31: ACCOUNTING WORK SKILLS

### element 13.1

### present financial data for internal and external use

B    Consolidate and reconcile data from different parts of an organisation into a given format, adjusting for internal transfers as necessary.

## CONSOLIDATING INFORMATION

Reporting on the performance of a business which is based in one location, or which has a simple product range, is a straightforward affair. Financial and production data can be brought together to produce performance indicators such as labour productivity and net profit margin for the benefit of management. Many computer accounting programs can do this automatically and spreadsheets can be set up to process the data so that sales, profits and stock levels can be monitored, and action taken if the need arises.

### the need for consolidation of data

The situation becomes more complex when data has to be consolidated from different parts of an organisation, for example:

- the **different branches of a service business** such as a retailer which operates through a chain of shops in different towns
- the **different divisions of a manufacturer of goods** – for example a company making digital radios which is divided into:
  - a manufacturing division (building the electronics)
  - an assembly division (putting the electronics into the cases)
  - a sales and administration division (marketing, selling and distributing the radios)

In both these examples, financial and production data has to be consolidated so that financial statements for the business as a whole can be constructed and performance indicators extracted.

In this chapter we will deal with each of these two examples in turn.

## CONSOLIDATION OF 'BRANCH' DATA

Some organisations consist of a number of separate 'branches' – for example travel agents, shops, hotels – all of which keep separate accounting records of sales and expenses, and in some cases stock. In these cases the accounting data will need to be consolidated to produce a single financial statement or report which will provide 'the whole picture'. This is normally a case of simple arithmetic, and can easily be set up on a spreadsheet.

Take, for example, a business which runs a chain of shops in three separate locations and has the main office at one of the locations. The profitability for a period such as a month can easily be calculated by consolidating the figures for all three branches, as seen in the Case Study that follows.

# ABC RETAIL: CONSOLIDATING INFORMATION

## situation

ABC Retail Limited operates three shops – Branch A, Branch B, and Branch C. The table below shows the revenue and costs which provide the data for the Profit & Loss Account for the company for the month of March.

**ABC RETAIL LIMITED**

| | Branch A £ | Branch B £ | Branch C £ |
|---|---|---|---|
| Sales | 50,000 | 65,000 | 75,000 |
| Opening Stock | 20,000 | 22,000 | 25,000 |
| Purchases | 25,000 | 30,000 | 36,000 |
| Closing stock | 18,000 | 21,000 | 24,000 |
| Cost of goods sold | 27,000 | 31,000 | 37,000 |
| Wages | 12,000 | 18,000 | 20,000 |
| Other overheads | 8,000 | 8,000 | 8,000 |

You have been asked to enter the figures in a table (shown below) to consolidate the results of the three branches in a total column and to calculate:

- gross profit percentage
- net profit percentage

**ABC RETAIL LIMITED**

**Profit and Loss Account for March**

| | Branch A £ | Branch B £ | Branch C £ | Total £ |
|---|---|---|---|---|
| Sales | 50,000 | 65,000 | 75,000 | 190,000 |
| Opening Stock | 20,000 | 22,000 | 25,000 | 67,000 |
| Purchases | 25,000 | 30,000 | 36,000 | 91,000 |
| Closing stock | 18,000 | 21,000 | 24,000 | 63,000 |
| Cost of goods sold | 27,000 | 31,000 | 37,000 | 95,000 |
| **Gross Profit** | **23,000** | **34,000** | **38,000** | **95,000** |
| Wages | 12,000 | 18,000 | 20,000 | 50,000 |
| Other overheads | 8,000 | 8,000 | 8,000 | 24,000 |
| Total overheads | 20,000 | 26,000 | 28,000 | 74,000 |
| **Net Profit** | **3,000** | **8,000** | **10,000** | **21,000** |

Your next step is to set up a spreadsheet to calculate the gross and net profit percentages and to extract a chart showing the net profit performance of the three branches of ABC Retail Limited (see next page).

## spreadsheet calculating gross and net profit margins

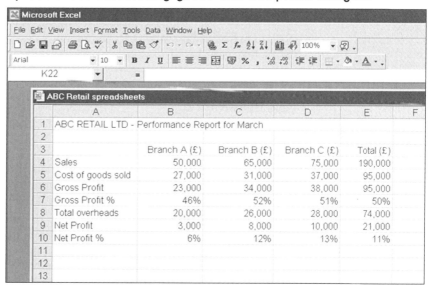

| | A | B | C | D | E | F |
|---|---|---|---|---|---|---|
| 1 | ABC RETAIL LTD - Performance Report for March | | | | | |
| 2 | | | | | | |
| 3 | | Branch A (£) | Branch B (£) | Branch C (£) | Total (£) | |
| 4 | Sales | 50,000 | 65,000 | 75,000 | 190,000 | |
| 5 | Cost of goods sold | 27,000 | 31,000 | 37,000 | 95,000 | |
| 6 | Gross Profit | 23,000 | 34,000 | 38,000 | 95,000 | |
| 7 | Gross Profit % | 46% | 52% | 51% | 50% | |
| 8 | Total overheads | 20,000 | 26,000 | 28,000 | 74,000 | |
| 9 | Net Profit | 3,000 | 8,000 | 10,000 | 21,000 | |
| 10 | Net Profit % | 6% | 12% | 13% | 11% | |
| 11 | | | | | | |
| 12 | | | | | | |
| 13 | | | | | | |

## pie chart showing comparative net profit for the three shops

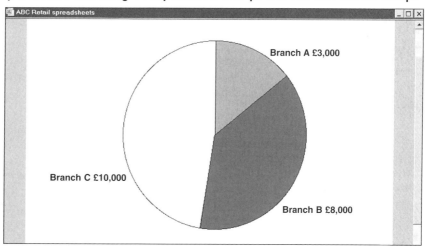

Branch A £3,000

Branch C £10,000

Branch B £8,000

# DEALING WITH STOCK TRANSFERS

## transfers of stock with added margin

It is not uncommon for different divisions of a business to transfer stock between themselves as the need arises. Individual companies in large manufacturing groups may even 'sell' stock or manufactured items to each other and add on a profit margin. For example, a company manufacturing car engines may transfer them to another company in the group which produces the finished vehicles, charging the engine at cost plus an agreed margin.

## transfers of stock at cost

In some businesses which involve divisions or 'branches', the transfer of the stock may be carried out *at cost*. No margin will be added on. Examples of this include transfers of stock between shops and transfers between divisions of a company, eg transfers of finished products between a manufacturing division and a sales division. **Your studies of Unit 31 will always deal with these transfers at cost.**

## recording transfers of stock

These transfers need to be recorded by the individual branches or divisions, together with the sales, purchases, expenses and stock figures as appropriate. But the important point is that **transfers should not be included in the sales or purchases of the group.** If the transfers are recorded as part of sales (transfers out) or purchases (transfers in) for branches or divisions, **they should be deducted or excluded when compiling the group figures.**

It is likely that the transfers will be recorded separately (not as part of sales and purchases), as in the table below. In this particular case a 'transfer out' is shown as a minus and a 'transfer in' as a plus. You will see that the net effect of the transfers between the branches on the total group is zero.

| ABC RETAIL LIMITED | | | | |
|---|---|---|---|---|
| | Branch A £ | Branch B £ | Branch C £ | Total £ |
| Sales | 50,000 | 65,000 | 75,000 | 190,000 |
| Opening Stock | 20,000 | 22,000 | 25,000 | 67,000 |
| Purchases | 25,000 | 30,000 | 36,000 | 91,000 |
| Closing stock | 18,000 | 21,000 | 24,000 | 63,000 |
| Stock transfers | – 2,000 | + 800 | + 1,200 | zero |

## the problem of stock in transit

But what would happen, if at the end of the month, £200 of stock from Branch A had been sent off to Branch B, but had not yet arrived, or had not yet been recorded by Branch B? You would be able to detect this because the total figure for transfers out would not equal the total for transfers in. In the case of the table shown above the transfer total column would not be zero, but would be shown as – £200. The situation here is:

- Branch A has recorded the stock as having been despatched and so will have reduced its closing stock figure by £200

- Branch B will not have made any adjustments to its figures at all
- There will be £200 of stock missing from the total group closing stock

**The rule is therefore that the value of stock in transit should be:**

- **added back to the closing stock of the branch which sent it**
- **deducted from the total of the stock transferred by that branch**

In other words, stock in transit should be treated as if it is still at the branch which sent it. In this case the closing stock of Branch A will be £18,000 + £200 = £18,200 and the transfer figures will become:

– £1,800 (Branch A)   + £600 (Branch B)   + £1,200 (Branch C)  =  zero

**Case Study**

# COOLTIME: CONSOLIDATING BRANCH INFORMATION

## situation

CoolTime is a chain of three fashion shops, owned by Julie Mye. The main shop and the office is in Staines, and the other two shops are in Bracknell and in Slough. You work as an accounts assistant in Staines and report directly to Julie Mye. Part of your job requires you to compile information every Monday on the financial performance of the three shops for the previous trading week. The data from Bracknell and Slough is sent to you by email. The data for last week is as follows:

| Julie Mye, trading as CoolTime Transactions for the week ended 3 April | | | |
|---|---|---|---|
| | *Staines* | *Bracknell* | *Slough* |
| | £ | £ | £ |
| Sales | 20,200 | 10,590 | 11,850 |
| Purchases | 9,800 | 3,100 | 4,220 |
| Wages | 3,200 | 2,200 | 2,300 |
| Other overheads | 2,750 | 2,800 | 2,600 |
| Opening stock | 18,000 | 10,500 | 14,250 |
| Closing stock | 16,900 | 9,800 | 12,900 |
| Stock transfers to Bracknell and Slough | 1,200 | | |
| Transfers from Staines | | 450 | 550 |

**Notes**

- On 3 April £200 of stock was transferred to Bracknell from Staines. This was not recorded in the books of Bracknell until 5 April.

- No adjustments for the stock transfers that were recorded (see table above) need to be made to the sales or purchases figures of the three branches.

### required

1   Check the data received from the three shops and adjust the appropriate figures for any stock in transit.

2   Using the data produced in (1), draw up a profit and loss account for the week ended 3 April.

3   Draw up a performance report on a spreadsheet which calculates the following performance indicators (use percentages correct to two decimal places):
(a)   gross profit margin
(b)   net profit margin

4   Compile a short word-processed report addressed to Julie Mye, commenting on the performance of the three shops and incorporating the data and chart produced in tasks 1 to 4.

### solution

### 1 adjusting the data for stock transfers

Before the profit and loss account can be drawn up, adjustment must be made for the £200 of stock in transit from Staines to Bracknell which is causing a discrepancy. Transfers 'out' total £1,200 and transfers 'in' total £1,000 (£550 plus £450), a difference of £200.

The solution is to treat the stock as if it has not left Staines:

- add £200 back to the Staines closing stock figure:
  £16,900 + £200 = £17,100

- deduct £200 from the Staines transfer figure:
  £1,200 − £200 = £1,000

The group total closing stock figure will now be correct and the net total effect of the transfers will be zero:

   − £1,000 (Staines) + £450 (Bracknell) + £550 (Slough) = zero

**note**

No stock transfer adjustments need to be made to the sales and purchases figures in this Case Study, as they have already been carried out.

### 2  drawing up the profit and loss account

The profit and loss account can now be drawn up.

Note that the closing stock figure of the Staines branch has been adjusted upwards by £200 to £17,100 for the stock in transit, which is now treated as being back at Staines again. Otherwise all the other figures are unaltered. The formulas used are:

**Cost of goods sold** = Opening stock + Purchases − Closing stock

**Gross profit** = Sales − Cost of goods sold

**Net profit** = Gross profit − Total overheads

| | Staines £ | Bracknell £ | Slough £ | Total £ |
|---|---|---|---|---|
| | | | | |

**Julie Mye, trading as CoolTime**

**Profit and Loss Account Account for the week ended 3 April**

| | Staines £ | Bracknell £ | Slough £ | Total £ |
|---|---|---|---|---|
| **Sales** | 20,200 | 10,590 | 11,850 | 42,640 |
| Opening Stock | 18,000 | 10,500 | 14,250 | 42,750 |
| Purchases | 9,800 | 3,100 | 4,220 | 17,120 |
| Closing stock | 17,100 | 9,800 | 12,900 | 39,800 |
| **Cost of goods sold** | 10,700 | 3,800 | 5,570 | 20,070 |
| **Gross Profit** | 9,500 | 6,790 | 6,280 | 22,570 |
| Wages | 3,200 | 2,200 | 2,300 | 7,700 |
| Other overheads | 2,750 | 2,800 | 2,600 | 8,150 |
| Total overheads | 5,950 | 5,000 | 4,900 | 15,850 |
| **Net Profit** | 3,550 | 1,790 | 1,380 | 6,720 |

## 3  drawing up the performance report

Julie will want to see the performance indicators which can be extracted from these figures. She will be particularly interested in:

- sales revenue from each of the branches
- gross profitability (a minimum of 50% is targeted by the management)
- net profitability (a minimum of 15% is targeted by the management)

The spreadsheet is shown below. Charts could also be extracted to illustrate this data.

| | A | B | C | D | E | F | G | H |
|---|---|---|---|---|---|---|---|---|
| 1 | Cooltime - Performance Report: week ending 3 April | | | | | | | |
| 2 | | | | | | | | |
| 3 | | Staines (£) | Bracknell (£) | Slough (£) | Total (£) | | | |
| 4 | Sales | 20,200 | 10,590 | 11,850 | 42,640 | | | |
| 5 | Cost of goods sold | 10,700 | 3,800 | 5,570 | 20,070 | | | |
| 6 | Gross Profit | 9,500 | 6,790 | 6,280 | 22,570 | | | |
| 7 | Gross Profit % | 47.03% | 64.12% | 53.00% | 52.93% | | | |
| 8 | Total overheads | 5,950 | 5,000 | 4,900 | 15,850 | | | |
| 9 | Net Profit | 3,550 | 1,790 | 1,380 | 6,720 | | | |
| 10 | Net Profit % | 17.57% | 16.90% | 11.65% | 15.76% | | | |
| 11 | | | | | | | | |
| 12 | | | | | | | | |

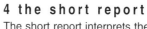

## 4 the short report

The short report interprets the data and performance indicators calculated in tasks 1 to 4. These, together with any charts produced, will be included as appendices to the short report, the purpose of which is to highlight points that should be made to the owner.

Report to Julie Mye                                          date .................
Report from A Student

**COOLTIME PERFORMANCE REPORT FOR WEEK ENDED 3 APRIL**

**Introduction**
This report has been produced as part of the regular weekly performance reporting of the three shops in the CoolTime chain.

**Procedure**
The data for this report has been received from each of the three branches: Staines, Bracknell and Slough. The data has been processed at the Staines office.

**Findings**
The gross profit percentages are as follows:

| | |
|---|---|
| Staines | 47.03% |
| Bracknell | 64.12% |
| Slough | 53.00% |

The Bracknell and Slough results are comfortably above the 50% minimum figure targeted by management. The Staines result of 47.03% may reflect a number of sales promotions (sales price reductions) offered by that store last week in order to stimulate sales, and so does not give cause for concern.

The net profit percentages are as follows:

| | |
|---|---|
| Staines | 17.57% |
| Bracknell | 16.90% |
| Slough | 11.65% |

The only figure that gives cause for concern here is the Slough figure of 11.65% which falls well short of the 15% minimum targeted by management.

**Conclusions**
The profitability of the CoolTime group of stores continues to be very satisfactory, with the exception of the net profitability of the Slough branch.

**Recommendations**
The Slough branch should be asked to provide a breakdown of its overheads for the last month so that they can be analysed and discussed with the shop manager, with a view to improving bottom line net profit.

**Appendices**
Data tables and charts.

> **Note to students**
> As an alternative to the short report format shown here, you may also use a more informal approach and state your findings using bullet points or emboldened headings. Ask your tutor for guidance, or, in the case of an assessment, read the instructions very carefully.

## CONSOLIDATING DATA FROM DIFFERENT DIVISIONS

Another scenario in which reported data can be consolidated might involve a business where there are separate divisions which pass stock and goods to each other as part of the manufacturing and sales process. At the beginning of the chapter we gave the example of a company that manufactures radios which pass through:

- a **manufacturing division**, which puts together the electronic components

- an **assembly division** which assembles the radios and puts them in boxes with appropriate packing materials and printed instructions and warranty

- a **sales and administration division** which markets, sells and distributes the radios

All three divisions:

- incur **costs** (labour, materials and overheads)

- receive **revenue** – ie the value of the radios that they pass on to another division, or, in the case of sales and administration, the sales revenue from their customers

It is therefore possible to construct for each division a **statement of costs and revenue**. These can then be **consolidated** into an overall statement of costs and revenue which forms the basis of the **profit and loss account** of the business. Study the diagram below.

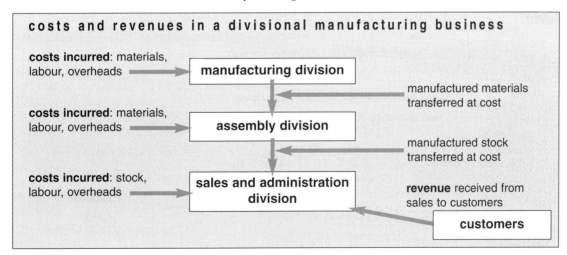

Note that any internal transfers of stock (at varying stages of assembly) between divisions will be **recorded** at **cost price**, but of course no actual money will change hands. The sales division will add a profit margin when selling to its external customers, and this is when the money revenue is received. The Case Study which follows shows how this data is consolidated.

# SOLARIO MANUFACTURING: CONSOLIDATING DATA

## situation

Solario Manufacturing Limited is a high-tech company set up by its owner Soni Djim to manufacture solar powered portable radios which are starting to prove very popular with the environmentally-conscious public.

The business is organised in three divisions:

- the Manufacturing Division buys in the components and makes the electronic content
- the Assembly Division assemble the radios, using the electronic content and materials for the casing and packaging
- the Sales and Administration Division takes the finished stock of radios and sells them to the customers; it also manages the administration of the company

At the end of the accounting year (30 June 2006) you have been asked to consolidate the summary cost statements for the Manufacturing and Assembly Divisions with the summary cost and revenue statement for the Sales and Administration Division to produce a total statement of costs and revenues. You have asked to note that:

- all transfers between divisions are accounted for at cost
- the effects of any transfers between divisions must be removed when preparing the consolidated statement

## solution

The first statement is the Cost Statement of the Manufacturing Division. Note that:

- the costs involved are raw materials, labour costs and factory overheads
- the bottom line shows the actual cost of the manufactured electronic content of the radios passed to the Assembly Division

**Cost Statement: Manufacturing Division**
**Year ended 30 June 2006**

| | | £ |
|---|---|---|
| | Opening stock of raw materials | 65,000 |
| add | Purchases of raw materials | 460,000 |
| | | 525,000 |
| less | Closing stock of raw materials | 72,000 |
| | Total usage of raw materials | 453,000 |
| add | Factory labour costs | 350,000 |
| add | Factory overheads | 250,000 |
| | **Transfer cost to Assembly Division** | **1,053,000** |

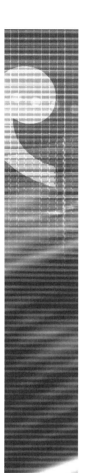

The next stage is the Cost Statement of the Assembly Division. This Division finishes the manufacturing process and passes the completed radios to the Sales and Administration Division. The radios are transferred at cost price (see the bottom line), ie the total cost of manufacture, including factory labour and overheads.

**Cost Statement: Assembly Division**
**Year ended 30 June 2006**

| | | £ |
|---|---|---:|
| | Opening stock of raw materials | 52,000 |
| add | Purchases of raw materials from external suppliers | 250,000 |
| **add** | **Transfer cost from Manufacturing Division** | **1,053,000** |
| | | 1,355,000 |
| less | Closing stock of raw materials | 85,000 |
| | Total usage of raw materials | 1,270,000 |
| add | Factory labour costs | 325,000 |
| add | Factory overheads | 355,000 |
| | **Transfer cost to Sales and Administration Division** | **1,950,000** |

The final stage of the process (shown below) is to draw up the Cost and Revenue Statement of the Sales and Administration Division. This statement starts with the revenue received from sales of the radios and then deducts the manufacturing cost of the radios sold and the wages and administration costs of the Division. The resultant bottom line shows the net profit of the company (ie total revenue less total costs).

**Cost and Revenue Statement: Sales and Administration Division**
**Year ended 30 June 2006**

| | | £ | £ |
|---|---|---:|---:|
| | Sales | | 4,000,000 |
| | Cost of goods sold: | | |
| | Opening cost of finished goods | 150,000 | |
| **add** | **Transfer cost from Assembly Division** | **1,950,000** | |
| | | 2,100,000 | |
| less | Closing stock of finished goods | 140,000 | |
| | Total cost of goods sold | 1,960,000 | |
| add | Sales and administration salaries | 600,000 | |
| add | Other sales and administration costs | 700,000 | |
| | Total costs | | 3,260,000 |
| | **Net profit** | | **740,000** |

The next step in the process is to consolidate the figures from the three statements on the last two pages into a Consolidated Statement of Revenues and Costs, which essentially shows the 'whole picture' of Costs and Revenues for the company over the period of a year and calculates the net profit.

Solario Limited has a spreadsheet which it uses for this purpose. When completing this spreadsheet you must make sure that you remove the effects of any transfers between divisions, in this case the £1,053,000 transfer from Manufacturing to Assembly.

The completed spreadsheet is shown below. Study it carefully, comparing it with the three statements on the previous two pages, so that you know where the figures come from and how the transfers are eliminated.

Note that in cell D11 (highlighted below for illustration purposes) the figure £217,000 has been arrived at by making the following adjustment:

| | |
|---|---|
| Assembly Division Cost Statement Total usage of raw materials | £1,270,000 |
| *less* transfer cost of transfer from Manufacturing Division | £1,053,000 |
| *equals* net total usage of raw materials by Assembly Division | £217,000 |

Note also that the total consolidated cost of goods sold (£1,960,000) is equal to the transfer cost to Sales & Administration plus the difference between its opening and closing stock, ie £1,950,000 + £10,000 = £1,960,000.

| | A | B | C | D | E | F |
|---|---|---|---|---|---|---|
| 1 | Solario Ltd: Consolidated Statement of Revenues and Costs | | | | | |
| 2 | Year ended 30 June 2006 | | | | | |
| 3 | | | | | | |
| 4 | | | Manufacturing | Assembly | Sales and admin | Consolidated |
| 5 | | | £ | £ | £ | £ |
| 6 | | | | | | |
| 7 | | Sales | | | 4,000,000 | 4,000,000 |
| 8 | | | | | | |
| 9 | | Cost of goods sold | | | | |
| 10 | | Opening stock of finished goods | | | 150,000 | 150,000 |
| 11 | plus | Total usage of raw materials | 453,000 | 217,000 | | 670,000 |
| 12 | plus | Total factory labour | 350,000 | 325,000 | | 675,000 |
| 13 | plus | Total factory overheads | 250,000 | 355,000 | | 605,000 |
| 14 | | | 1,053,000 | 897,000 | 150,000 | 2,100,000 |
| 15 | less | Closing stock of finished goods | | | 140,000 | 140,000 |
| 16 | | Total cost of goods sold | 1,053,000 | 897,000 | 10,000 | 1,960,000 |
| 17 | | | | | | |
| 18 | | Gross profit | | | | 2,040,000 |
| 19 | | | | | | |
| 20 | less | Sales and administration salaries | | | | 600,000 |
| 21 | less | Other sales and administration costs | | | | 700,000 |
| 22 | | | | | | 1,300,000 |
| 23 | | Net profit | | | | 740,000 |

## USING THE CONSOLIDATED DATA

The Case Study set out above shows how accounting data can be consolidated. It is important to appreciate that this data will now be used to calculate performance criteria for management (as described in Chapter 3) and also may need to be adjusted to allow for price changes and inflation (as described in Chapter 4). We will now continue the Solario Limited Case Study to show how this is done.

**Case Study**

# SOLARIO MANUFACTURING: PERFORMANCE REPORTING

## task 1 – calculating the performance indicators

You have been asked by the management of Solario Limited to calculate some performance indicators. They have sent you an email:

Please calculate for the financial year ending 30 June 2006:

1  gross profit margin ( to nearest %)

2  net profit margin (to nearest %)

3  return on capital employed (to nearest %)

4  manufacturing cost (£) of each radio produced

5  sales revenue (£) per employee

Note the following data:

- Capital employed for year ended 30 June 2006          £12 million
- Number of radios produced in year ended 30 June 2006          156,800
- Staff employed in the year ended 30 June 2006          296

Your workings for these performance indicators are as follows:

| **gross profit margin %** | = | $\dfrac{\text{gross profit} \times 100}{\text{sales}}$ |
|---|---|---|
| | = | $\dfrac{2{,}040{,}000 \times 100}{4{,}000{,}000}$ |
| | = | 51% |

| **net profit margin %** | = | $\dfrac{\text{net profit} \times 100}{\text{sales}}$ |
|---|---|---|
| | = | $\dfrac{740{,}000 \times 100}{4{,}000{,}000}$ |
| | = | 19% |

| **return on capital employed %** | = | $\dfrac{\text{net profit} \times 100}{\text{capital employed}}$ |
|---|---|---|
| | = | $\dfrac{740{,}000 \times 100}{12{,}000{,}000}$ |
| | = | 6% |

| **manufacturing cost per radio** | = | $\dfrac{£1{,}950{,}000}{156{,}800 \text{ radios}}$ |
|---|---|---|
| | = | £12.44 |

| **sales revenue per employee** | = | $\dfrac{£4{,}000{,}000}{296 \text{ employees}}$ |
|---|---|---|
| | = | £13,513.51 |

### solution 1

You present the data you have calculated in the form of an email or a memo as follows:

| Performance indicators for the year ended 30 June 2006 | | |
| --- | --- | --- |
| Gross profit margin % | = | 51% |
| Net profit margin % | = | 19% |
| Return on capital employed % | = | 6% |
| Manufacturing cost per radio | = | £12.44 |
| Sales revenue per employee | = | £13,513.51 |

### task 2 – adjusting the figures for price rises

You have been asked to provide further management information in the form of a comparison of the company's costs and revenues for the last two financial years: 2005 and 2006. Because of changing price levels, you will have to adjust (increase) the figures for 2005 by certain percentages so that a true comparison can be made with the figures for 2006. The changes over the year are:

• selling prices have risen by 5%

• raw materials costs have risen by 3%

• the cost of factory labour has risen by 4%

• factory overheads have risen by 5%

• sales and administration salaries have risen by 4%

• other sales and administration costs have risen by 5%

### solution 2

You process the data on the computer spreadsheet shown at the top of the next page.

The two columns on the right are the original unadjusted figures for 2005, the two columns on the left show the same set of results, but the cells which have a grey background have been adjusted by the percentages listed above so that they be compared more accurately with the 2006 figures.

For example the rise of 5% in sales prices has been adjusted as follows:

£3,500,000 x 1.05 (ie 100% + 5% rise) = £3,675,000.

Similarly the 3% rise in raw materials prices is adjusted as follows:

£650,000 x 1.03 (ie 100% + 3% rise) = £669,500.

and so on . . .

| | A | B | C | D | E | F |
|--|---|---|---|---|---|---|
| 1 | Solario Ltd: Consolidated Statement of Revenues and Costs | | | | | |
| 2 | Year ended 30 June 2005 | | | | | |
| 3 | | | | | | |
| 4 | | | Adjusted | | Unadjusted | |
| 5 | | | £ | £ | £ | £ |
| 6 | | | | | | |
| 7 | | Sales | | 3,675,000 | + 5% | 3,500,000 |
| 8 | | | | | | |
| 9 | | Cost of goods sold | | | | |
| 10 | | | | | | |
| 11 | | Opening stock of finished goods | 130,000 | | 130,000 | |
| 12 | add | Total usage of raw materials | 669,500 | | 650,000 + 3% | |
| 13 | add | Total factory labour | 655,200 | | 630,000 + 4% | |
| 14 | add | Total factory overheads | 630,000 | | 600,000 + 5% | |
| 15 | | | 2,084,700 | | 2,010,000 | |
| 16 | less | Closing stock of finished goods | 150,000 | | 150,000 | |
| 17 | | Total cost of goods sold | | 1,934,700 | | 1,860,000 |
| 18 | | | | | | |
| 19 | | Gross profit | | 1,740,300 | | 1,640,000 |
| 20 | | | | | | |
| 21 | less | Sales and administration salaries | 582,400 | | 560,000 + 4% | |
| 22 | | | | | | |
| 23 | less: | Other sales and administration costs | 714,000 | | 680,000 + 5% | |
| 24 | | | | 1,296,400 | | 1,240,000 |
| 25 | | Net profit before taxation | | 443,900 | | 400,000 |

## task 3 – comparing the two years

Your final task also involves a spreadsheet. You are required to compare selected figures from the 2006 consolidated statement of costs and revenues with the adjusted 2005 figures and calculate the difference (variance) between them, both as a money amount and also as a percentage.

The calculations you will have to perform in each case are:

2006 figure (£) – adjusted 2005 figure (£) = variance (£).

To work out the percentage variance use the formula:

$$\frac{\text{variance (£)} \times 100}{\text{earlier year figure (£)}} = \text{variance percentage}$$

## solution 3

| | A | B | C | D | E |
|--|---|---|---|---|---|
| 1 | Solario Ltd: Comparison of actual 2006 results with adjusted 2005 results | | | | |
| 2 | | | | | |
| 3 | | | | | |
| 4 | | Actual 2006 | Adjusted 2005 | Variance | Variance |
| 5 | | £ | £ | £ | % |
| 6 | | | | | |
| 7 | Sales | 4,000,000 | 3,675,000 | 325,000 | 8.8 |
| 8 | | | | | |
| 9 | Gross profit | 2,040,000 | 1,740,300 | 299,700 | 17.2 |
| 10 | | | | | |
| 11 | Sales and administration salaries | 600,000 | 582,400 | 17,600 | 3.0 |
| 12 | | | | | |
| 13 | Other sales and administration costs | 700,000 | 714,000 | -14,000 | -2.0 |
| 14 | | | | | |
| 15 | Net profit before taxation | 740,000 | 443,900 | 296,100 | 66.7 |
| 16 | | | | | |

## UNIT 31 ASSESSMENT

The Solario Case Study on the previous six pages has been included because it will give you a good idea of what to expect in your Unit 31 assessment. Remember that you are also likely to have to provide a written (or word processed) report on the figures produced in the assessment.

There are a number of practice assessments in the Osborne Books Accounting Work Skills Workbook, and you will see that they follow the pattern of this Case Study

Your assessment is also likely to require you to use the performance indicators to complete a report form issued by an external body, for example an application for finance from a bank. This is covered in the next chapter.

If you carry out the Student Activities at the end of this chapter, you should be well prepared for the Unit assessment.

**Chapter Summary**

- Businesses which operate separate branches or divisions will have to consolidate data from those separate divisions when compiling financial statements and performance reports.

- Businesses which operate separate branches or divisions and which deal with stock or finished products may get involved in transferring the stock or products between the branches or divisions.

- The net total of all transfers at cost should be zero as a transfer into one branch or division (a positive figure) is numerically equal to the same transfer from another branch or division (a negative figure).

- When compiling financial data for performance reports, businesses must take care to account for stock or products 'in transit' as these can cause discrepancies.

- Any stock in transit must be accounted for by the branch or division sending it. This may involve adding it back into the closing stock of that branch or division and deducting it from the total of transfers out of the branch or division.

- Consolidation of data can also take place with businesses which operate different divisions, typically in a manufacturing company where the data from manufacturing, assembly, sales and administration departments can be brought together to produce a consolidated statement of revenues and costs.

- Transfers of stock between these divisions will normally (as with branches) be made at cost price. These transfers must be taken out of the calculation when consolidation of data takes place.

- When comparing the financial results of two years it may be necessary to apply a percentage adjustment to one set of figures to compensate for increases in costs and sales prices. A more accurate comparison can then be made.

| Key Terms | | |
|---|---|---|
| | **consolidation** | the combination of financial and other data from separate operating branches or divisions of an organisation |
| | **stock transfers** | transfers of stock or other products between separate branches or divisions of a business |
| | **stock in transit** | stock or other products which have been transferred from one branch or division of a business to another |
| | **statement of costs and revenue** | a statement, similar to a profit and loss account, which calculates profit as the difference between revenue and costs |

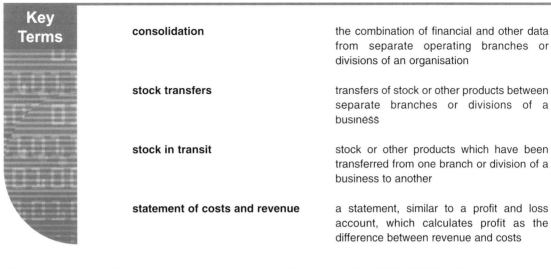

# Student Activities

**6.1** FitMan Wholesale Limited is a mens clothes supplier which has two branches.

On 28 March 2006 £1,000 of stock was transferred from the Hornchurch branch to the Basildon branch at cost. This was not recorded in the books of the Basildon branch until 3 April.

Complete the gross profit calculations for FitMan Wholesale Limited, having made appropriate adjustments for stock in transit. If you wish, set up the calculation on a spreadsheet.

Remember:

- Cost of goods sold = opening stock + purchases – closing stock

- Gross profit = Sales – Cost of goods sold

| FITMAN WHOLESALE LIMITED | | | |
|---|---|---|---|
| **Profit and Loss Account (extract) for week ended 31 March 2006** | | | |
| | **Hornchurch** | **Basildon** | **Total** |
| | £ | £ | £ |
| Sales | 71,000 | 55,000 | |
| Opening Stock | 32,000 | 24,000 | |
| Purchases | 35,000 | 25,000 | |
| Closing stock | 31,000 | 23,000 | |
| Cost of goods sold | | | |
| Gross Profit | | | |

**6.2**　Complete the gross profit calculations for the retail group shown below. If you wish, set up the calculation on a spreadsheet.

Make appropriate adjustments for stock in transit. No adjustments need to be made to the sales or purchases figures. Remember that cost of goods sold = opening stock + purchases − closing stock.

| XYZ RETAIL LIMITED | | | | |
| --- | --- | --- | --- | --- |
| Profit and Loss Account (extract) for week ended 31 March 2006 | | | | |
| | **Branch X** | **Branch Y** | **Branch Z** | **Total** |
| | £ | £ | £ | £ |
| Sales | 80,000 | 75,000 | 80,000 | |
| Opening Stock | 30,000 | 22,000 | 25,000 | |
| Purchases | 40,000 | 37,000 | 38,000 | |
| Closing stock | 28,000 | 21,000 | 24,000 | |
| Cost of goods sold | | | | |
| Gross Profit | | | | |
| Transfers from X | 2,000 | | | |
| Transfers to Y and Z | | 1,000 | 500 | |

Note: On 29 March  £500 of stock was transferred from Branch X to Branch Y. This was not recorded in the books of Branch Y until 3 April.

**6.3**　Your name is Owen Gerrard and you work as an accounts assistant for Anne Field Enterprises, a sole trader business which operates two sports shops in the North West, one in Liverpool and one in Southport.

You work in the Liverpool office and are currently collecting the quarterly financial figures for the two branches so that you can consolidate them into a single profit and loss account.

The figures provided by the two branches are shown below. They include net transfers of stock at cost price between the two shops. Your line manager has told you that these transfers, which are included among the sales and purchases, should not be included in the consolidated figures.

The records from the Liverpool shop show that £200 of stock was sent to the Southport branch on 30 June. This stock in transit was not recorded in the Southport records until 2 July.

**Anne Field Enterprises: Profit and Loss Account data for 3 months ended 30 June 2006**

| | Liverpool Branch | | Southport Branch | |
|---|---|---|---|---|
| | £ | £ | £ | £ |
| Sales | | 120,000 | | 100,500 |
| Transfers to Southport at cost | | 5,100 | | - |
| | | 125,100 | | |
| Opening stock | 56,000 | | 46,000 | |
| Purchases | 61,000 | | 53,000 | |
| Transfers from Liverpool at cost | - | | 4,900 | |
| | 117,000 | | 103,900 | |
| Less closing stock | 52,500 | | 48,500 | |
| Cost of goods sold | | 64,500 | | 55,400 |
| Gross Profit | | 60,600 | | 45,100 |
| Overheads | | 48,000 | | 39,400 |
| Net Profit | | 12,600 | | 5,700 |

You note from the records that the combined profit and loss account figures for the two shops for the same period in 2005 were as follows:

| | £ |
|---|---|
| Sales | 185,000 |
| Cost of goods sold | 112,000 |
| Gross profit | 73,000 |
| Overheads | 62,000 |
| Net profit | 11,000 |

**You are to:**

(a)    Consolidate the figures from the two shops into a profit and loss account for the business for the three months ended 30 June 2006, making the necessary adjustments to exclude transfers of stock, and stock in transit. No further adjustments need be made.

(b)    Draw up a table setting out comparative figures for the two years, including: sales, cost of goods sold, gross profit, gross profit percentage, overheads, net profit, net profit percentage (percentages should be calculated to two decimal places). Use a spreadsheet if possible.

(c)    Draw up (or extract from a spreadsheet) a compound bar chart showing for the two years
    •    sales revenue
    •    gross profit
    •    net profit

(d)    Write comments on the combined performance of the two shops over the two years. Use a wordprocessing package and set out your comments clearly using emboldened headings and bullet points.

**6.4** Chronos Manufacturing Limited makes digital clocks, employing 315 people in its factory in Newtown, Wales. The company is organised in three divisions:

> **Electronics Division** manufactures the clock mechanisms from imported components.

> **Casings Division** completes the manufacturing process by installing the mechanisms in a variety of clock casings, ranging from reproduction antique to ultra modern. When the products leave Casings Division they are ready for despatch to customers.

> **Administration Division** organises the marketing and sales of the clocks and also provides the other support functions of the company.

At the end of the financial year you are handed the summary cost statements for the Electronics and Casings Divisions and the cost and revenue statement of the Administration Division.

**You are** to consolidate the data from these three statements on the spreadsheet on the next page. You may set up the spreadsheet if you wish. You should note that all transfers between divisions are at cost and the effects of them should be removed when preparing the consolidated statement.

---

**Cost Statement: Electronics Division**

**Year ended 30 June 2006**

| | | £ |
|---|---|---:|
| | Opening stock of raw materials | 32,500 |
| add | Purchases of raw materials | 230,000 |
| | | 262,500 |
| less | Closing stock of raw materials | 36,000 |
| | Total usage of raw materials | 226,500 |
| | | |
| add | Factory labour costs | 176,400 |
| add | Factory overheads | 131,600 |
| | **Transfer cost to Casings Division** | **534,500** |

---

**Cost Statement: Casings Division**

**Year ended 30 June 2006**

| | | £ |
|---|---|---:|
| | Opening stock of raw materials | 25,500 |
| add | Purchases of raw materials from external suppliers | 126,700 |
| **add** | **Transfer cost from Electronics Division** | **534,500** |
| | | 686,700 |
| less | Closing stock of raw materials | 41,000 |
| | Total usage of raw materials | 645,700 |
| | | |
| add | Factory labour costs | 181,000 |
| add | Factory overheads | 174,300 |
| | **Transfer cost to Administration Division** | **1,001,000** |

**Cost and Revenue Statement: Administration Division**

**Year ended 30 June 2006**

|  |  | £ | £ |
|---|---|---:|---:|
| | Sales | | 1,876,000 |
| | Cost of goods sold: | | |
| | Opening cost of finished goods | 75,600 | |
| **add** | **Transfer cost from Casings Division** | **1,001,000** | |
| | | 1,076,600 | |
| less | Closing stock of finished goods | 71,900 | |
| | Total cost of goods sold | 1,004,700 | |
| add | Sales and administration salaries | 310,000 | |
| add | Other sales and administration costs | 356,000 | |
| | Total costs | | 1,670,700 |
| | **Net profit** | | **205,300** |

| | A | B | C | D | E | F |
|---|---|---|---|---|---|---|
| 1 | | Chronos Manufacturing Limited: Consolidated statement of cost and revenues | | | | |
| 2 | | Year ended 30 June 2006 | | | | |
| 3 | | | | | | |
| 4 | | | Electronics Division | Casings Division | Admin Division | Consolidated |
| 5 | | | £ | £ | £ | £ |
| 6 | | | | | | |
| 7 | | Sales | | | | |
| 8 | | | | | | |
| 9 | | Cost of goods sold | | | | |
| 10 | | Opening stock of finished goods | | | | |
| 11 | plus | Total usage of raw materials | | | | |
| 12 | plus | Total factory labour | | | | |
| 13 | plus | Total factory overheads | | | | |
| 14 | | | | | | |
| 15 | less | Closing stock of finished goods | | | | |
| 16 | | Total cost of goods sold | | | | |
| 17 | | | | | | |
| 18 | | Gross profit | | | | |
| 19 | | | | | | |
| 20 | less | Administration salaries | | | | |
| 21 | less | Administration costs | | | | |
| 22 | | | | | | |
| 23 | | Net profit | | | | |

**6.5** Helios Limited makes compact weather 'stations' which record and compile data such as daily sunshine hours, rainfall, wind speed and atmospheric pressure. The company employs 220 people in its factory in Milton Keynes. The company is organised in three divisions:

> **Manufacturing Division** manufactures the internal mechanisms for the weather stations.

> **Assembly Division** completes the manufacturing process by assembling the mechanisms

> **Administration Division** organises the marketing and sales of the weather stations and provides the other support functions of the company.

At the end of the financial year you are handed the summary cost statements for the Manufacturing and Assembly Divisions and the cost and revenue statement of the Administration Division.

**You are** to consolidate the data from these three statements on the spreadsheet on the next page. You may set up the spreadsheet if you wish. You should note that all transfers between divisions are at cost and the effects of them should be removed when preparing the consolidated statement.

---

**Cost Statement: Manufacturing Division**

**Year ended 30 June 2006**

|  |  | £ |
|---|---|---:|
|  | Opening stock of raw materials | 48,750 |
| add | Purchases of raw materials | 345,000 |
|  |  | 393,750 |
| less | Closing stock of raw materials | 54,000 |
|  | Total usage of raw materials | 339,750 |
|  |  |  |
| add | Factory labour costs | 264,600 |
| add | Factory overheads | 196,500 |
|  | **Transfer cost to Assembly Division** | **800,850** |

---

**Cost Statement: Assembly Division**

**Year ended 30 June 2006**

|  |  | £ |
|---|---|---:|
|  | Opening stock of raw materials | 38,250 |
| add | Purchases of raw materials from external suppliers | 190,050 |
| **add** | **Transfer cost from Manufacturing Division** | **800,850** |
|  |  | 1,029,150 |
| less | Closing stock of raw materials | 61,500 |
|  | Total usage of raw materials | 967,650 |
|  |  |  |
| add | Factory labour costs | 271,500 |
| add | Factory overheads | 261,450 |
|  | **Transfer cost to Administration Division** | **1,500,600** |

Cost and Revenue Statement: Administration Division

Year ended 30 June 2006

|  |  | £ | £ |
|---|---|---|---|
| | Sales | | 2,814,000 |
| | Cost of goods sold: | | |
| | Opening cost of finished goods | 96,000 | |
| add | **Transfer cost from Assembly Division** | **1,500,600** | |
| | | 1,596,600 | |
| less | Closing stock of finished goods | 93,100 | |
| | Total cost of goods sold | 1,503,500 | |
| add | Sales and administration salaries | 450,000 | |
| add | Other sales and administration costs | 525,000 | |
| | Total costs | | 2,478,500 |
| | **Net profit** | | **335,500** |

| | A | B | C | D | E | F |
|---|---|---|---|---|---|---|
| 1 | | Helios Limited: Consolidated statement of cost and revenues | | | | |
| 2 | | Year ended 30 June 2006 | | | | |
| 3 | | | | | | |
| 4 | | | Manufacturing | Assembly | Administration | Consolidated |
| 5 | | | £ | £ | £ | £ |
| 6 | | | | | | |
| 7 | | Sales | | | | |
| 8 | | | | | | |
| 9 | | Cost of goods sold | | | | |
| 10 | | Opening stock of finished goods | | | | |
| 11 | plus | Total usage of raw materials | | | | |
| 12 | plus | Total factory labour | | | | |
| 13 | plus | Total factory overheads | | | | |
| 14 | | | | | | |
| 15 | less | Closing stock of finished goods | | | | |
| 16 | | **Total cost of goods sold** | | | | |
| 17 | | | | | | |
| 18 | | **Gross profit** | | | | |
| 19 | | | | | | |
| 20 | less | Administration salaries | | | | |
| 21 | less | Administration costs | | | | |
| 22 | | | | | | |
| 23 | | **Net profit** | | | | |

**6.6**

> **Note**
>
> This activity continues the scenario introduced in Activity 6.5. You should check with your tutor that your calculations for Activity 6.5 are correct before proceeding with Activity 6.6.

**(a)**   You have been asked by the management of Helios Limited to calculate some performance indicators. They have asked you to work out for the financial year ending 30 June 2006:

1    gross profit margin ( to nearest %)

2    net profit margin (to nearest %)

3    return on capital employed (to nearest %)

4    manufacturing cost (£) of each weather station

5    sales revenue (£) per employee

They provide you with the following data:

| | |
|---|---|
| Capital employed for year ended 30 June 2006 | £5 million |
| Number of weather stations produced in year ended 30 June 2006 | 100,040 |
| Staff employed in the year ended 30 June 2006 | 200 |

They ask you to set the data out ready for presentation, either in a Powerpoint slide, or in a wordprocessed format, eg a table, with an appropriate heading.

**(b)**   You have been asked to provide further management information in the form of a comparison of the company's costs and revenues for the last two financial years: 2005 and 2006.

Because of changing price levels, you will have to adjust (increase) the figures for 2005 by certain percentages so that a true comparison can be made with the figures for 2006. The changes over the year are:

•    selling prices have risen by 4%

•    raw materials costs have risen by 2%

•    the cost of factory labour has risen by 3%

•    factory overheads have risen by 4%

•    sales and administration salaries have risen by 3%

•    other sales and administration costs have risen by 4%

The data should be entered in the 'adjusted' column of the spreadsheet at the top of the next page.

**(c)**   You have been asked to compare the adjusted 2005 figures with the 2006 results and enter them on the spreadsheet shown at the bottom of the next page. You need to work out the difference in the figures over the two years, both in money amounts and also in percentage terms.

You have also been asked to make brief comments on the the performance of the business over the two years. Set out your comments in a word processed file, using a table for the figures and headings and bullet points for your comments as appropriate.

|  | A | B | C | D | E | F |
|---|---|---|---|---|---|---|
| 1 | Helios Ltd: Consolidated Statement of Revenues and Costs | | | | | |
| 2 | Year ended 30 June 2005 | | | | | |
| 3 | | | | | | |
| 4 | | | Adjusted | | Unadjusted | |
| 5 | | | £ | £ | £ | £ |
| 6 | | | | | | |
| 7 | | Sales | | | | 2,550,000 |
| 8 | | | | | | |
| 9 | | Cost of goods sold | | | | |
| 10 | | | | | | |
| 11 | | Opening stock of finished goods | | | 95,000 | |
| 12 | add | Total usage of raw materials | | | 475,000 | |
| 13 | add | Total factory labour | | | 488,000 | |
| 14 | add | Total factory overheads | | | 425,000 | |
| 15 | | | | | 1,483,000 | |
| 16 | less | Closing stock of finished goods | | | 96,000 | |
| 17 | | Total cost of goods sold | | | | 1,387,000 |
| 18 | | | | | | |
| 19 | | Gross profit | | | | 1,163,000 |
| 20 | | | | | | |
| 21 | less | Administration salaries | | | 395,000 | |
| 22 | | | | | | |
| 23 | less: | Administration costs | | | 498,000 | |
| 24 | | | | | | 893,000 |
| 25 | | Net profit before taxation | | | | 270,000 |

|  | A | B | C | D | E |
|---|---|---|---|---|---|
| 1 | Helios Ltd: Comparison of actual 2006 results with adjusted 2005 results | | | | |
| 2 | | | | | |
| 3 | | | | | |
| 4 | | Actual 2006 | Adjusted 2005 | Variance | Variance |
| 5 | | £ | £ | £ | % |
| 6 | | | | | |
| 7 | Sales | | | | |
| 8 | | | | | |
| 9 | Gross profit | | | | |
| 10 | | | | | |
| 11 | Net profit | | | | |
| 12 | | | | | |
| 13 | Factory labour costs | | | | |
| 14 | | | | | |
| 15 | Administration salaries | | | | |
| 16 | | | | | |

## this chapter covers . . .

In this chapter we examine a range of reports that organisations may have to complete and send to external bodies. These are required from time-to-time by a variety of external agencies:

- organisations that award grants and provide finance, eg the Department of Trade and Industry and banks

- regulatory bodies such as HM Revenue & Customs

We also stress the need to make sure that reports being sent off are:

- authorised by the appropriate person

- checked carefully for accuracy

- sent off on time and as required by the outside body

It is essential that confidentiality is observed when dealing with external reporting:

- documents should be stored securely

- information should only be passed to other people authorised to receive it

## PERFORMANCE CRITERION COVERED

unit 31: ACCOUNTING WORK SKILLS

element 13.1

present financial data for internal and external use

F    Prepare external reports in the given format observing confidentiality requirements.

## WHO NEEDS REPORTS?

As well as the requirement for internal reporting seen so far in this book, organisations will need from time-to-time to complete returns to external bodies. In this chapter we will present a series of Case Studies covering all the main types of return, showing how information held by the organisation is entered onto the form.

Most returns are on 'pro-forma' forms – ie the information is entered in boxes or on defined lines on pre-printed pages. This makes the information easier to identify and to collect by the organisation completing the return, and easier to process by the body asking for it.

### grant awarding bodies

If an organisation needs to raise money there are banks and other financial companies which will provide loans and public sector (government owned or controlled) bodies which will provide grants, and, in some cases, loans. Details of these sources of finance are available through Chambers of Commerce and Business Link offices.  Any application for finance or a grant will invariably involve sending the organisation financial and non-financial details, as we will see in the Case Studies. Examples of finance and grant-awarding bodies include:

• banks

• local authorities

• the Department of Trade and Industry

• the European Commission

### trade associations

A trade association is basically a membership 'club' for businesses in a particular trade, eg ABTA (Association of British Travel Agents) and the Publishers Association. As well as safeguarding and promoting the interests of businesses in those sectors, trade associations collect data from their individual members for statistical purposes and in some cases to produce directories. This data, for a retailing organisation (for example), might include details such as the level of annual sales (within certain bands), terms of trade (discounts given) and the number of employees. The accounting function of a retailer – whether it be a small shop or a major retail chain – may well have to send in these details on a regular basis.

## regulatory bodies

Organisations are subject by law to a variety of external regulations and need periodically to provide returns to the bodies that administer those regulations. Examples include:

- **HM Revenue & Customs** which requires
    - details of payroll (employer's P35 annual return)
    - tax liabilities (self-assessment form for sole traders, accounts for larger businesses)
    - regular completion of a VAT 100 (VAT return) by VAT-registered businesses  (this process is covered in Chapter 9)

- **Companies House** which regulates the running of limited companies and requires an annual return from companies and the filing of accounts for larger companies

## authorisation of returns

All reports and returns sent to external agencies should go through a rigorous checking and authorisation procedure. There should be no short cuts in the process. Checks should ensure that all the information required is present and in the correct format. External reports and returns should also be sent off on time; most organisations will set up a diary system to ensure that this happens. Some returns will require an authorised signature; this should not be overlooked. This aspect of reports and returns cannot be stressed too highly: there are fines for late company returns and also for errors on VAT returns, even if the error was accidental. Late submission of VAT returns can sometimes trigger off a VAT inspection, which is not something to be welcomed!

## confidentiality of data

An important accounting skill for any employee is the use of judgement in keeping accounting data confidential. As noted above, employees should never disclose information about the organisation without authority. Financial data should be stored securely: paper files should be kept away from any public access areas, and computer files (eg computer accounting systems) should be password protected.

Fraud is currently all too common. Any requests for financial information should be referred to a higher authority, particularly requests over the internet for confirmation of banking details. This type of scam is designed to provide thieves with the data they need for siphoning off money from unsuspecting bank accounts. Confidentiality nowadays requires a special degree of alertness.

## CASE STUDIES

The remainder of this chapter is made up of two Case Studies which explain what reports and returns are likely to be encountered and how they will be completed.

They are:

- Trading figures for a bank – Ace Furniture Limited
- Application for an Export Award – Helios Vision

The VAT return will be covered in detail in Chapter 9 (see pages 148 to 149).

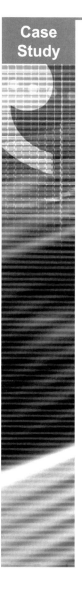

**Case Study**

# TRADING FIGURES FOR THE BANK: ACE FURNITURE

### situation

Ace Furniture is a small shop run by David Rill selling quality design furniture to a wide range of commercial and private customers. Much of the furniture is imported; many of the customers pay on credit.

Two years ago Ace Furniture took out a long-term loan of £75,000 from National Bank plc to help set up its present premises.

As part of the financing arrangements Ace Furniture agreed to provide management accounting figures for the bank on a quarterly basis so that the bank could monitor the progress of the business. If the business was running into difficulties, the bank could pick up the warning signs from these performance indicators.

The quarterly performance indicators required for the return comprise the following:

■ Sales

■ Gross profit

■ Overhead costs

■ Net profit

■ Return on Capital Employed

This data is extracted from the accounting records of the business. A summary of the accounting data, together with workings, is shown on the next page and the completed return to the bank on the page that follows.

# Ace Furniture

## Extract from quarterly Management Accounts

Accounting period:          3 months to 31 March 2007

Date prepared              1 April 2007

Prepared by:               Vin Eere

### Results

|  | £ |
|---|---|
| Sales | 240,000 |
| Cost of Sales | 168,000 |
| Gross profit | 72,000 |
| Overhead costs | 48,000 |
| Net profit | 24,000 |
| Total assets | 650,000 |
| Working Capital | 120,000 |
| Owner's Capital | 300,000 |

### Workings

Gross profit %  $= \dfrac{£72,000 \times 100}{£240,000} = 30\%$

Net profit %  $= \dfrac{£24,000 \times 100}{£240,000} = 10\%$

Return on capital employed  $= \dfrac{£24,000 \times 100}{£300,000} = 8\%$

# National Bank Plc

## Quarterly Management Accounts

| | |
|---|---|
| Name of customer: | D Rill trading as Ace Furniture |
| Quarter ended: | 31 March 2007 |

**Accounting Data Required:**

| | |
|---|---|
| Sales (£) | £240,000 |
| Gross profit (£) | £72,000 |
| Gross profit % | 30% |
| Overhead costs (£) | £48,000 |
| Net profit (£) | £24,000 |
| Net profit % | 10% |
| Return on capital employed %<br><br>Note: Formula required = $\dfrac{\text{net profit} \times 100}{\text{owner's capital}}$ | 8% |

Authorised signature of customer    S Crew

Date    1 April 2007

**Case Study**

# APPLICATION FOR AN EXPORT AWARD: HELIOS VISION

## situation

Helios Vision Plc is a fast-growing UK manufacturer of fashion sunglasses. This company has been particularly successful in exporting to the USA and Australia. One of its success stories is the distinctive 'Cool Shade' brand which was adopted by Brad Street, star of the American TV soap 'Sunrise Park'.

The Board of Directors has decided to apply for a Government-backed Export Award for smaller businesses – over £50,000 worth of cash and professional services are available. Applications for awards are competitive. Eligible businesses must be: independent UK-based businesses, manufacturers or providers of services, employers of no more than 250 people and not a previous award winner.

On the financial side, applicants must:

• show growth in export earnings over the last 3 years

• achieve at least £100,000 in export earnings over the most recent year

The application involves:

• an entry form signed by the Managing Director (see opposite)

• a Statement of Export Achievement on one side of A4 paper

John Brandon, the MD, has asked the Sales Department to provide the written statement. It is your job to complete the figures in Part 2b of the form shown opposite.

## solution

You research the accounting records and extract the following figures, which you set out in a table ready for checking and transferring to the form. You also contact the payroll supervisor for employee numbers over the last three years.

| HELIOS VISION PLC | | | |
|---|---|---|---|
| Year to: | 31.12.04 | 31.12.05 | 31.12.06 |
| | £ | £ | £ |
| UK Sales | 487,612 | 542,373 | 680,063 |
| Export Sales | 105,961 | 189,731 | 249,500 |
| Total Sales | 593,573 | 732,104 | 929,563 |
| Net profit (after tax) | 71,725 | 93,763 | 121,811 |

When the figures have been checked and authorised, the form should be completed and passed to the MD's office for signature by John Brandon and submission by 20 May – the stipulated deadline.

# ENTRY FORM
(Please type or print clearly using a ball point pen)

## PART 1 — Full name and address

| | |
|---|---|
| Chairman/Managing Director | JOHN BRANDON |
| Company Name | HELIOS VISION |
| Company Address | UNIT 17 HARTBURY ESTATE |
| | MEREFORD |
| County & Postcode | MRL 5HN Tel: 01902 743193 Fax: 01902 743748 |
| Parent Company (if any) | — |
| Subsidiaries (if any) | — |
| Total number of employees in Group (incl. Directors & employees of parent & subsidiary companies) | 120 |
| Type of Company: Manufacturing ✓ Service ◇ (Please tick) | |
| Description of products or services exported from the UK: | SUNGLASSES |

## PART 2 — Figures (Please tick one box to show which Award you are applying for)

**2a** **Entry for Regional Award** ✓
The Best Exporting Company of the Year will be selected from the Regional Winners. Figures must be provided for the latest three complete financial years,

**2b** **Entry for Best Newcomer Award** ◇
Figures must be provided for the first full year of exporting

| Full financial years ended MONTH | YEAR | Number of employees (Applicant firm only) | Export earnings | Whole annual turnover | Net profit after tax |
|---|---|---|---|---|---|
| DEC | 2004 | 98 | £105,961 | £593,573 | £71,725 |
| DEC | 2005 | 107 | £189,731 | £732,104 | £93,763 |
| DEC | 2006 | 120 | £249,500 | £929,563 | £121,811 |

## PART 3 — Statement of Export Achievement

A Statement of Export Achievement (not exceeding one side of A4 paper) must be submitted with this entry. Its scope is at the discretion of the entrant company but should include a short resume of the business, a description of its products/services and most importantly, details of how current export success has been achieved. Points of particular interest are sales and marketing methods, market research methods and export management.

Statement attached (Please tick) ✓

## PART 4 — Certification

➤ We submit this entry and attach a TYPED ONE-PAGE statement of export achievement. We undertake to submit immediately our latest audited Report and Accounts and an Auditor's Certificate supporting the figures in Part 2 above, in the event of our company being included on the preliminary shortlist.

➤ We hereby certify that all the particulars supplied by us in our entry are correct to the best of our knowledge and belief and comply with definitions set out and that no material information has been withheld.

➤ We accept the rules and conditions of entry A to D and agree to abide by the decisions of the Panel of Judges and the sponsors on all matters relating to these Awards.

Date 11 April 2007  Signature (of Chairman or Managing Director) _J. Brandon_

The Award Administrator will acknowledge receipt of your entry and will advise you whether or not you have been included on the preliminary shortlist in due course. You will be provided with a reference number which you should quote in any correspondence concerning this application.

**Chapter Summary**

■ Organisations may from time-to-time need to make returns to outside bodies.

■ The returns are normally on pre-printed forms, but occasionally an additional written text may be required.

■ The types of bodies requiring returns are
- grant awarding bodies and providers of finance, eg banks
- trade associations
- regulatory bodies such as HM Revenue & Customs

■ The returns should be completed in the format and manner in which they are requested by the outside agency.

■ It is essential that all completed returns are carefully checked, authorised and sent off within the stipulated deadline.

■ It is also essential that the confidentiality of the data being sent off is respected by the organisation.

**Key Terms**

**pro-forma** — a preprinted form with a defined format

**public sector bodies** — organisations which are government-owned or government controlled

**regulatory body** — public sector bodies which regulate the operation of organisations

**trade association** — a membership 'club' for a particular trade, responsible for safeguarding interests and, in some cases, regulation

**HM Revenue & Customs** — the government agency responsible for the direct taxation of individuals and organisations (the Inland Revenue) and the administration of import and export duties and Value Added Tax (HM Customs)

# Student Activities

**7.1**   Romona Smith is the owner/manager of a franchised gift shop in Stourford. The business is called 'Cute Ideas' and is supplied from the franchisor in Kettering.

The franchisor in Kettering requires a regular return of information from its franchisees (shops). Each shop is set an agreed quarterly sales target. Sales are divided into:

- Category A (books and cards)

- Category B (novelties)

Each quarter a form (see next page)  is sent to shop owners requesting

- sales figures

- variances from targets (amounts)

- variances from target in the form of percentage deviation from the targets

A box is also supplied for comments by the shop owner.

The franchisor takes as commission 10% of the sales figure each quarter as part of the franchise agreement, and a box is included on the form for calculation of this payment.

When the form is completed it is returned to the franchisor together with a commission cheque within fifteen days of the end of the quarter.

It is the first week in April. Romona has just reached the end of her January - March trading quarter and has to fill in the form from the accounting information she has printed out from her computer:

|  | Target (£) | Actual (£) |
|---|---|---|
| Sales A | 15,000 | 13,500 |
| Sales B | 21,000 | 18,000 |

Romona tells you that the last three months have not been good for a number of reasons – bad weather keeping customers away, a similar shop opening up two doors away, road works and customers being short of cash after Christmas.

**You are to:**

(a)   Enter the sales figures on the form

(b)   Calculate the variances (amounts and percentages – to the nearest £ and %)

(c)   Calculate the commission due

(d)   Provide comments in the space

(e)   Sign and date the form in Romona's name (assume the current year, first quarter)

| CUTE IDEAS Trading Report | Quarter ended ......../......./....... | | | |
|---|---|---|---|---|
| £ | | £ | £ variance | % variance |
| Sales A (actual) | Sales Target A | | | |
| Sales B (actual) | Sales Target B | | | |
| Total Sales (actual) | Total Sales Target | | | |
| 10% Commission on sales £ | (cheque enclosed) | | | |
| **Comments** | | | | |
| **signature** | **date** | | | |

**7.2** Electro Supplies is a computer supplies business run by Les Pratt. He has borrowed £50,000 from the bank to finance his business, and as part of the arrangement he has to supply financial details to the bank every three months.

Some figures for the last quarter have been extracted for Les as follows:

```
Sales            £340,000
Cost of Sales    £255,000
Overheads         £68,000
Owner's capital  £425,000
```

You are to calculate the following and then complete the form on the next page:

(a) gross profit and gross profit percentage

(b) net profit and net profit percentage

(c) return on capital employed, using the formula shown on the form

Show your workings on a separate piece of paper.

# Great Western Bank Plc

## Quarterly Management Accounts

**Customer:**        Flectro Supplies

**Quarter ended:**   31 March 2007

**Please complete details in the column on the right:**

| | |
|---|---|
| **Sales (£)** | |
| **Gross profit (£)** | |
| **Gross profit %** | |
| **Overhead costs (£)** | |
| **Net profit (£)** | |
| **Net profit %** | |
| **Return on capital employed %**<br><br>Note: Formula required  =  net profit x 100 / owner's capital | |

**Authorised signature of customer** ........................................

**Date** ........................................

# 8 Basic principles of VAT

## this chapter covers . . .

In this chapter we explain what Value Added Tax (VAT) is and how it works in practice. We cover the following areas:

- a definition of Value Added Tax
- the various rates of VAT
- registration for VAT
- VAT on sales (output tax) and VAT on purchases (input VAT)
- the timing of VAT – the 'tax point'
- VAT invoices – the different types and what they involve
- VAT on imports and exports

In the next chapter we will examine the accounting records that need to be kept for VAT and how they provide the information for the VAT return.

## PERFORMANCE CRITERION COVERED

unit 31: ACCOUNTING WORK SKILLS

element 13.1

present financial data for internal and external use

F    Prepare external reports in the given format observing confidentiality requirements.

## VAT AND REGULATION OF VAT

### a definition

**Value Added Tax (VAT) is a tax on the sale of goods and services**

VAT is not only charged in the UK: many countries charge VAT (or a similar sales tax), and at varying rates. VAT – essentially a tax on spending – is an important source of revenue for any government. In the UK, VAT is also a tax on *imports* into the country. VAT is charged at a standard percentage rate (currently 17.5% in the UK) on *business* transactions.

### VAT regulation and sources of information

The body which regulates and collects VAT in the UK is HM Revenue & Customs. This public sector agency combines the operations of the Inland Revenue and what was formerly HM Customs & Excise.

Customs Notice 700, the 'VAT Guide', issued by HM Revenue & Customs is a useful booklet which explains and interprets the VAT regulations. The 'VAT Guide' is available free of charge from local VAT offices and from the HM Revenue & Customs website – www.hmrc.gov.uk

### an overview of VAT

Most suppliers of goods and services charge VAT, unless, of course, there is no VAT payable, as in the case of the sale of food and young children's clothes. There is a registration threshold set by the government each year, normally in the March Budget. If this figure is exceeded (or is likely to be exceeded), a supplier must by law register with HM Revenue & Customs to become what is known as a taxable person.

The effect of this registration means that the supplier (taxable person)

- must charge VAT on chargeable supplies (ie goods and services)
  - this is known as **output tax**

- can reclaim VAT paid on most supplies received
  - this is known as **input tax**

As most businesses are run to make a profit – ie more money will be received from sales than is spent on supplies – most businesses will charge more VAT (output tax) than they pay (input tax). The difference between these two must be paid to HM Revenue & Customs.

If a business trades in goods or services on which no VAT is payable (eg books or sewerage services) the business will pay more VAT than it will charge, so it can reclaim the difference from HM Revenue & Customs.

The business owner will have to complete a VAT Return (Form VAT 100) or make an Electronic VAT Return (EVR) on a regular basis – normally quarterly – to account to HM Revenue & Customs for the amount of VAT due or refundable. This is covered in the next chapter.

Note that when a person has been registered for VAT, a registration certificate will be issued giving full details of registration, including the VAT number which is normally quoted on VAT invoices issued to states within the EU.

### VAT – a tax on the final consumer

VAT is a tax which is paid by the final consumer of the goods.

If we take, for, example, a member of the public buying a computer for £705, the amount paid includes VAT of £105 (ie 17.5% of £600). The buyer stands the cost of the VAT, but the VAT is actually paid to HM Revenue & Customs by all those involved in the manufacturing and selling process.

This procedure is illustrated by the flow chart shown on the opposite page. You will see that the right hand column shows the amount of VAT paid to HM Revenue & Customs at each stage in the process. The supplier of raw materials, the manufacturer and the shop all pay over to HM Revenue & Customs the difference between VAT on sales (outputs) and VAT on purchases (inputs), but this amount is collected from the next person in the process. It is the consumer who foots the VAT bill at the end of the day. The VAT is paid to the shop, but as you can see from the diagram, the tax has already been paid (or will soon be paid) to HM Revenue & Customs.

## RATES OF VAT

There are currently three rates of VAT in the UK:

- standard rate                                                       17.5%
- reduced rate (eg on energy-saving products)        5%
- zero rate                                                             0%

Zero-rated supplies are not the same as exempt supplies, although the result is the same – no VAT is charged. We will now look at these types of supply

### zero-rated supplies

Zero-rated supplies are goods and services taxed at 0%. This may sound odd, but all it means is that the supplies are taxable, but the government has decided that no tax should be charged, normally because the goods are an essential part of spending and to tax them would place a burden on the less well-off. Examples of zero-rated supplies include (see page 136):

## collection of Value Added Tax

| manufacture and sale of a computer | | VAT payments to HM Revenue & Customs |
|---|---|---|
| **supplier of materials** | • keeps £200<br>• pays £35 to HM Revenue & Customs | £35 |
| sells materials for £200 plus £35 VAT = £235 | | *plus* |
| **manufacturer** | • keeps £440<br>• pays £42 to HM Revenue & Customs (difference between £77 collected and £35 paid to supplier) | £42 |
| adds on margin and sells computer for £440 plus £77 VAT = £517 | | *plus* |
| **shop** | • keeps £600<br>• pays £28 to HM Revenue & Customs (difference between £105 collected and £77 paid to supplier) | £28 |
| adds on margin and sells computer for £600 plus £105 VAT = £705 | | *plus* |
| **final consumer** | • pays nothing <u>directly</u> to HM Revenue & Customs (the £105 has all been paid to the shop) | £0 |
| buys computer for £600 plus £105 VAT = £705 | | *equals*<br><br>£105 |

- food bought in shops, but not in restaurants
- young children's clothes and shoes
- transport – eg bus and train fares
- newspapers, magazines and books

Note also that goods and services exported from the UK are usually zero-rated. Exports and imports within the EU are known as **acquisitions**.

The important point here is that **businesses that sell zero-rated goods can reclaim the VAT charged** (the input tax) on supplies that they have bought. For example, there was no VAT charged on this book, but the publisher was able to reclaim the VAT paid on the cost of the book, for example the paper used. The situation with exempt supplies is quite different.

### exempt supplies

Whereas zero-rated supplies are chargeable – at 0% – exempt supplies are not chargeable at all. Also, **a supplier who supplies only VAT-exempt goods or services cannot reclaim any input VAT**. Examples of supplies that are exempt include:

- certain types of insurance
- postal services from the Post Office
- education and healthcare
- betting and gambling, burials and cremations

You should read the 'VAT Guide' which illustrates these points further. (This is available on www.hmrc.gov.uk as Notice 700).

### tax points

The **tax point** of a taxable supply is the date on which it is recorded as taking place for the purposes of the tax return.

For goods the basic tax point is normally when the goods are sent to the customer or taken away by the customer. For services the basic tax point is normally when the service is performed.

## VAT INVOICES

When a VAT-registered supplier sells standard-rated goods or services to another VAT-registered person, the supplier must give or send to the purchaser within 30 days of the supply a VAT invoice which contains information about the goods or services supplied. A copy  of the invoice should be kept on file (paper or electronic) by the supplier.

The requirements for the contents of a VAT invoice are laid down by HM Revenue & Customs in common with the regulations of all EU member states. The information on the invoice should include:

- an invoice number
- the name and address of the supplier
- the VAT number of the supplier – this is compulsory if the supply is made within the EU, but is commonly quoted anyway
- the date of the invoice
- the purchaser's name and address
- a description (the 'details') of the goods or services supplied, eg shirts or hours of an accountant's time
- the quantity of goods (eg 4 shirts) or the extent of the service (eg 4 hours of accountant's time)
- the unit price, eg the cost of each shirt or hour (or consultation)
- the total charge made, excluding VAT
- the total amount of VAT charged – this must be in sterling – but note that the VAT rate and VAT amounts for individual items do not have to be shown
- the total charge made, including VAT – this also has to be in sterling

Study the invoices shown on the next two pages and see how they differ.

### calculations on VAT invoices

VAT is calculated as a percentage of the cost of the goods. If invoiced goods cost £100, the VAT (at the standard rate of 17.5%) is calculated as:

$$\frac{£100 \times 17.5}{100} \quad = \quad £17.50$$

If the amount of VAT calculated comes out at more than 2 decimal places, you should round *down* to the nearest penny. On the invoice opposite:

$$\frac{£75 \times 17.5}{100} \quad = \quad £13.125 \text{ (rounded down to £13.12)}$$

Guidance relating to rounding may be found in the 'VAT Invoices' section of the 'VAT Guide'. For example, there are rules relating to complex rounding methods when calculating VAT on individual items or 'lines' on a VAT invoice.

The important factor is that any rounding is consistently applied. The method of rounding down shown here is recommended by HM Revenue & Customs. It is simple, and tried and tested.

# SALES INVOICE

## Trend Designs
Unit 40 Elgar Estate, Broadfield, BR7 4ER
Tel 01908 765365  Fax 01908 7659507  Email lisa@trend.u-net.com
VAT Reg GB 0745 4172 20

invoice to

```
Crispins Fashion Store
34 The Arcade
Broadfield
BR1 4GH
```

| | |
|---|---|
| invoice no | 787906 |
| account | 3993 |
| your reference | 1956 |
| date/tax point | 21 04 07 |

deliver to

`as above`

| details | quantity | unit price | amount (excl VAT) | VAT rate % | VAT amount £ |
|---|---|---|---|---|---|
| Schwarz 'T' shirts (black) | 20 | 5.50 | 110.00 | 17.5 | 19.25 |
| Snugtight leggings (black) | 15 | 12.50 | 187.50 | 17.5 | 32.81 |

**terms**
Net monthly
Carriage paid
E & OE

| | |
|---|---|
| **Total (excl VAT)** | 297.50 |
| **VAT** | 52.06 |
| **TOTAL** | 349.56 |

This invoice has been issued by a supplier of fashion clothes, Trend Designs, to Crispins Fashion Store on 21 April (the tax point).

All the requirements of a VAT invoice are met: both items sold are charged at the standard rate of tax and the unit price is shown. The VAT total of £52.06 will recorded as output (sales) tax for Trend Designs and as input (purchases) tax for Crispins Fashion Store.

Note that it is not compulsory to show the VAT rate and VAT amount for each item when the same rate applies to all items on the invoice. It is quite sufficient to show the VAT total (as here) on the invoice.

# ──── SALES INVOICE ────

## Paragon Printers
Partners: Edwin Parry, George Dragon
Unit 43 Elgar Estate, Broadfield, BR7 4ER
Tel 01908 765312  Fax 01908 7659551  Email Ed@paragon.u net.com  VAT Reg GB 0745 4672 71

invoice to

| | |
|---|---|
| Prime Publicity Ltd | |
| 4 Friar Street | |
| Broadfield | |
| BR1 3RG | |

| | |
|---|---|
| invoice no | 787923 |
| account | 3993 |
| your reference | 47609 |
| date/tax point | 07 05 07 |

deliver to

as above

| details | unit price | amount (excl VAT) | VAT rate % | VAT amount £ |
|---|---|---|---|---|
| Printing 2,000 A4 leaflets | 189.00 | 189.00 | zero | 00.00 |
| Supplying 2,000 C4 envelopes | 75.00 | 75.00 | 17.5 | 13.12 |

**terms**
Net monthly
Carriage paid
E & OE

| | |
|---|---|
| **Total (excl VAT)** | 264.00 |
| **VAT** | 13.12 |
| **TOTAL** | 277.12 |

This invoice has been issued by a commercial printer, Paragon Printers, to Prime Publicity Limited on 7 May (the tax point) for goods delivered.

Note that in this case there are two rates of VAT involved: printing is zero-rated and stationery is standard rated. Where there are mixed VAT rates, as here, the two rates and VAT amounts must be quoted.

The VAT total of £13.12 will be recorded as output tax for Paragon Printers and as input tax for Prime Publicity Ltd.

### zero-rated and exempt supplies

If you supply goods which are zero-rated or exempt, invoices issued must show this fact and also that no VAT amount is payable. An invoice for zero-rated or exempt supplies must be issued if there is a mixture of rates (as on the opposite page).

### less detailed invoices – amounts under £250

If the amount charged for the supply is £250 or less (including VAT) a less detailed invoice may be issued. This type of invoice must show:

*   the name and address of the supplier
*   the date of supply
*   a description of the goods or services
*   the total charge payable for each item, *including* VAT

If you are given, as in this case, a total amount which does not show the VAT amount, you may need to work out both the VAT content and also the amount before VAT is added (the 'VAT exclusive' amount).  The formula for working out the amount before VAT is added is

$$\text{total amount including VAT} \quad \times \quad \frac{100}{117.5} \quad = \quad \text{amount excluding VAT}$$

The VAT exclusive amount in a receipt for £117.50 is therefore

$$£117.50 \times \frac{100}{117.50} = £100$$

A quick way to calculate the VAT exclusive amount on a calculator is to divide the total amount by 1.175.

Another way to work out the VAT element in a VAT inclusive price is to use the **VAT fraction**, which for 17.5% is $7/47$. For an overall total (ie VAT-inclusive total) of £117.50 the calculation is:

$$\frac{£117.50 \times 7}{47} = £17.50 \text{ VAT included in the £117.50}$$

### working out the VAT to be charged

If you are given the goods amount before VAT and need to work out the VAT amount, you apply the formula:

$$\text{amount} \times \frac{17.5}{100} \text{ (ie the VAT rate)} = \text{VAT payable}$$

VAT chargeable on £100 is therefore $£100 \times \frac{17.5}{100} = £17.50$

**Chapter Summary**

- Value Added Tax (VAT) is a sales tax on most goods and services imposed by governments in a number of different countries to raise revenue.

- VAT is administered and collected in the UK by HM Revenue & Customs.

- VAT is paid by the final consumer but is collected and paid to HM Revenue & Customs by the businesses involved in the selling and manufacturing processes.

- VAT is charged at different rates: standard, reduced (domestic fuel) and zero. These (except for zero rate) may be changed from time-to-time.

- A person must register for VAT if annual sales liable to VAT exceed (or are likely to exceed) an annual threshold.

- A VAT-registered person must pay to HM Revenue & Customs the VAT charged on sales (output tax) less tax on purchases (input tax). If input tax exceeds output tax a refund is due. The payment or refund is calculated on the regular VAT return (VAT 100).

- The recording of the date of the sales and purchases is important in this calculation – the date of payment is the tax point.

- A VAT-registered supplier must in most circumstances issue a VAT invoice to the buyer. The VAT invoice must contain defined items of information relating to the transaction.

- VAT is also a tax on the import or acquisition of goods and services from overseas states.

- Exports to EU and non-EU countries are normally zero-rated.

**Key Terms**

| | |
|---|---|
| **Value Added Tax** | a tax on the sale of goods and services |
| **supplier** | a person who sells goods and services |
| **taxable person** | a supplier who has been registered for VAT; a person can be a sole trader, a partnership, a limited company, a group of companies, a club or association, a charity |
| **output tax** | VAT on sales of goods and services |
| **input tax** | VAT on purchases of goods and services |

| | |
|---|---|
| **VAT 100** | the HM Revenue & Customs VAT Return, which calculates VAT to be paid or refunded by off setting input tax and output tax |
| **standard rate** | the basic percentage rate at which VAT is calculated – currently 17.5% in the UK |
| **reduced rate** | a reduced rate allowed for domestic fuel – currently 5% in the UK |
| **zero-rated goods** | supplies which are liable to VAT, but at zero % |
| **exempt goods** | supplies which are not liable to VAT |
| **tax point** | the date on which the supply is recorded for the purposes of the VAT Return – normally the date of the invoice |
| **VAT invoice** | an invoice recording the taxable supply (the sale) containing specific required details; for lower value transactions (under £250) the invoice may be less detailed |
| **acquisitions** | imports within the Single Market |

# Student Activities

**8.1** What does VAT tax?

**8.2** What is the difference between input tax and output tax?

**8.3** In what circumstances may a supplier reclaim VAT from HM Revenue & Customs?

**8.4** Why does the final consumer pay all the VAT on chargeable goods and services, but pay nothing personally to HM Revenue & Customs?

**8.5** What are the three rates of VAT currently charged in the UK?

**8.6** Explain the difference between the terms 'zero-rated' and 'VAT-exempt'. Give three examples of each.

**8.7** The invoice below has been issued as a VAT invoice. What is wrong with it?

## SALES INVOICE

### Trend Designs
Unit 40 Elgar Estate, Broadfield, BR7 4ER
Tel 01908 765365  Fax 01908 7659507  Email lisa@trend.u-net.com VAT Reg 1745 4572 33

invoice to

```
Persephone Fashion
45 The Broads
Broadfield
BR1 8UH
```

| details | quantity | amount (excl VAT) | VAT rate % | VAT amount £ |
|---|---|---|---|---|
| Bianca 'T' shirts | 42 | 209.58 | 17.5 | 36.68 |

**terms**
Net monthly
Carriage paid
E & OE

| | |
|---|---|
| **Total (excl VAT)** | 209.58 |
| **VAT** | 36.68 |
| **TOTAL** | 273.26 |

**8.8** Your business receives five invoices from a VAT registered trader.  The amounts are:

£87.50, £41.12, £47.00, £55.75, £99.05

Your colleague notes that

- none of the invoices has the VAT amount listed separately – there is just a total on each which includes the amount for the goods and VAT combined  (ie the figures quoted above)

- the invoices have all the other details you would expect to see on a VAT invoice

**You are to:**

(a)    state whether the invoices are valid VAT invoices

(b)    calculate the VAT on each invoice so that you can enter up the purchases day book

# 9 VAT accounting and the VAT return

*In this chapter we explain:*

- *the records a VAT-registered business needs to keep to record VAT on sales and on purchases and expenses*

- *the treatment of VAT in manual accounts and computer accounts*

- *the way the figures are collected from the accounting records to supply information for the VAT Return*

- *the completion of the VAT Return Form VAT 100*

## PERFORMANCE CRITERIA COVERED

### unit 31: ACCOUNTING WORK SKILLS

### element 13.1

### present financial data for internal and external use

F    *Prepare external reports in the given format observing confidentiality requirements.*

G    *Identify VAT inputs and outputs and complete a VAT return.*

## RECORDING VAT

### VAT and VAT records

The accounting system of a VAT-registered business should record:

- input tax on purchases and expenses
- output tax on sales

It must be appreciated that accounting systems vary substantially from business to business, but the basic principles will remain the same: data has to be collected periodically (normally quarterly) so that input tax can be set off against output tax for the completion of the VAT Return.

### records for output tax (sales)

You will be familiar with the use of **day books** and the **cash book** and **petty cash book** from your Unit 30 studies. Day books are central to the recording of VAT in the accounting system. Records for **output tax** include:

**sales day book**

This lists all sales made on credit and has an analysis column for VAT which is totalled periodically.

**credit notes issued**

Any credit given (eg for returned goods, adjustments for overcharges) may involve VAT and deduction should be made from output tax. Sometimes a separate sales returns day book, with a VAT analysis column, will be kept by the business.

**cash book**

This includes a VAT analysis column and records details of other receipts not on credit which involve output tax, eg cash sales. Note that receipts for credit sales in the cash book should be ignored.

### records for input tax (purchases and expenses)

Records for input tax include:

**purchases day book**

This lists all purchases made on credit and has an analysis column for VAT which is totalled periodically.

**credit notes received**

Any credit received (eg for returned goods) may involve VAT and deduction should be made from input tax. Sometimes a separate purchases returns day book, with a VAT analysis column, will be kept by the business.

**cash book**

This lists all the expenses paid by the business; VAT for non-credit items should be taken from the cash book analysis column. VAT on payments for credit purchases should be ignored. A **petty cash book** with a VAT column may also be used to list small expenses and will need to be accounted for.

## VAT control account

The central record for any VAT-registered business book-keeping system is the VAT control account into which all input and output tax is entered. The balance of VAT control account represents the amount owing to (or due from) HM Revenue & Customs.

The diagram below is based on the layout recommended by HM Revenue & Customs in the 'VAT Guide'. It shows entries for a supplier who normally has a surplus of output tax over input tax, ie the supplier pays VAT every quarter to HM Revenue & Customs.

You should note that the control account shown is not a double-entry account in the strict sense, for example, items such as credit notes are deducted on each side rather than being entered on the opposite side. In practice the VAT control account will be maintained in whatever way the accounting system – manual or computerised – requires. The important point is that the entries used for the VAT Return are all accounted for in a consistent way.

You are unlikely to be asked to construct a VAT control account for your assessment, but it is useful to know about it and what it contains. You are more likely to be asked to complete a VAT return by extracting details from the daybooks (see pages 148 to 149).

## VAT control account – summary of entries

| VAT deductible (input tax) | VAT payable (output tax) |
|---|---|
| Purchases Day Book VAT monthly totals, *less* any credit notes received | Sales Day Book VAT monthly totals, *less* any credit notes issued |
| Cash Book – items not in Purchases Day Book | Cash Book – items not in Sales Day Book |
| Petty Cash Book – VAT on small expenses | |
| Acquisitions from EU states | Acquisitions from EU states |
| Corrections of errors from previous periods | Corrections of errors from previous periods |
| Bad debt relief claimed | |
| = TOTAL TAX DEDUCTIBLE | = TOTAL TAX PAYABLE |
| | *less* TOTAL TAX DEDUCTIBLE |
| | *equals* TAX PAYABLE ON VAT RETURN |

## computer accounts – VAT control account

The VAT control account shown on the previous page assumes that all the VAT data is transferred manually from the accounting records. If a business operates a computer accounting program, normally every transaction that involves VAT will automatically post the VAT element to VAT control account, eg sales, purchases, journal entries, payment or repayment of VAT.

The reports available will vary according to the sophistication of the program. Up-to-date programs will do all the work for the supplier, including the production of a screen and a printout at the end of the VAT period with figures needed for the VAT Return. The business which relies on this system must make sure that the VAT data is correct before VAT Return is processed. A computer VAT Return screen is shown below.

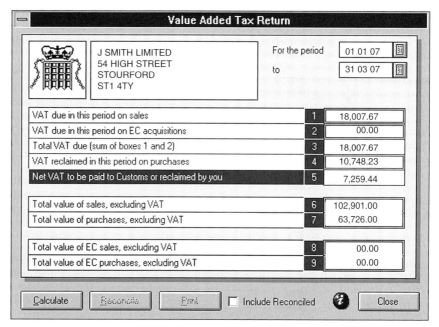

Less sophisticated programs may merely produce summaries of sales and purchases day books and cash books, and a transaction history of VAT Account over the VAT period. If this account history of VAT Account is used for extracting the data for the VAT Return, care must be taken to adjust for payment or repayment of VAT relating to the previous period during the VAT quarter, as this will automatically post to VAT account, but is clearly is not classed as a taxable output or input (you cannot tax tax!). If this is the case:

- payment of VAT to HM Revenue & Customs must be deducted from the input tax total

- repayment of VAT received from HM Revenue & Customs must be deducted from the output tax total

## THE VAT RETURN – FORM VAT 100

When the VAT figures have been transferred to the VAT control account and the amount of VAT due or reclaimable has been calculated, the VAT Return can then be completed. The form is completed as follows:

**1** The total VAT due on sales and other outputs. This total should be adjusted for the VAT on any credit notes issued in the period and any output VAT omitted (amounts under £2,000 ) on previous returns.

**2** VAT due on acquisitions from other EU states.

**3** The total of boxes 1 and 2.

**4** The total VAT reclaimed on purchases and other inputs (less VAT on any credit notes). This total includes tax on acquisition of goods from other EU states, amounts (under £2,000) not claimed on previous returns and any bad debt relief claimed (see next page for an explanation of this)

**5** Take the figures in boxes 3 and 4, deduct the smaller from the larger and enter the difference in box 5. If the figure in box 3 is more than the figure in box 4, this is the amount payable to HM Revenue & Customs. If the figure in box 3 is smaller than the figure in box 4, the amount in box 5 will be repaid to the supplier completing the form.

**6** The total of sales and outputs excluding any VAT. This will include exempt, standard and zero-rated supplies and supplies to EU member states. Remember to adjust the total for any credit notes.

**7** The total of purchases (inputs) excluding any VAT. This includes standard, zero and exempt supplies, imports and acquisitions from EU states. Remember to adjust the total for any credit notes.

**8** The total of supplies of goods and related services, excluding VAT, to EU states.

**9** The total of acquisition of goods and related services, excluding VAT, from EU states.

### notes on completion of VAT 100

- if a VAT payment is being enclosed, the relevant box should be ticked
- the form should be signed by an authorised person
- the form should be returned by the due date shown on the form in the envelope provided (normally one month after the end of the VAT period)
- do not leave any boxes blank – enter 'none' if there is no figure to insert

Note that VAT registered organisations now have the option of sending the VAT Return electronically by Electronic VAT Return (EVR).

**For the period**
01 01 07  to  31 03 07

SPECIMEN

625 454 7106 52 100 03 99  Q25147

JAMES FULLER
65 LABURNUM GARDENS
BEXHILL-ON-SEA
EAST SUSSEX
BN5 6TR

| Registration Number | Period |
|---|---|
| 454 7106 52 | 03 07 |

**You could be liable to a financial penalty if your completed return and all the VAT payable are not received by the due date.**

**Due date:** 30  04  07

For
Official
Use

Before you fill in this form please read the notes on the back and the VAT leaflet *"Filling in your VAT return"*. Fill in all boxes in ink, and write 'none' where necessary. Don't put a dash or leave any box blank. If there are no pence write "00" in the pence column. **Do not** enter more than one amount in any box.

| For official use | | | £ | p |
|---|---|---|---|---|
| | VAT due in this period on **sales** and other outputs | **1** | 31,353 | 61 |
| | VAT due in this period on **acquisitions** from other **EC Member States** | **2** | 183 | 05 |
| | Total VAT due **(the sum of boxes 1 and 2)** | **3** | 31,536 | 66 |
| | VAT reclaimed in this period on **purchases** and other inputs (including acquisitions from the EC) | **4** | 14,826 | 92 |
| | Net VAT to be paid to Customs or reclaimed by you **(Difference between boxes 3 and 4)** | **5** | 16,709 | 74 |
| | Total value of **sales** and all other outputs excluding any VAT. **Include your box 8 figure** | **6** | 179,163 | 00 |
| | Total value of **purchases** and all other inputs excluding any VAT. **Include your box 9 figure** | **7** | 84,725 | 00 |
| | Total value of all **supplies** of goods and related services, excluding any VAT, to other **EC Member States** | **8** | none | 00 |
| | Total value of all **acquisitions** of goods and related services, excluding any VAT, from other **EC Member States** | **9** | 1,046 | 00 |

**Retail schemes.** If you have used any of the schemes in the period covered by this return, enter the relevant letter(s) in this box.

If you are enclosing a payment please tick this box.

✓

DECLARATION: You, or someone on your behalf, must sign below.

I, .......... JAMES FULLER .......... declare that the
(Full name of signatory in BLOCK LETTERS)

information given above is true and complete.

Signature .......... S. Fuller .......... Date .. 11 April 2007 ..

**A false declaration can result in prosecution.**

0038584

**VAT 100** (Half)

PCU (June 1996)

L

*a completed VAT Return Form VAT 100*

## A NOTE ON BAD DEBT RELIEF

As you will know from your studies of Unit 30, a **bad debt** is an amount owing which a supplier writes off in the books because he/she is unlikely ever to be paid – the buyer may have 'gone bust' for example.

What happens if output VAT paid over to HM Revenue & Customs on the VAT Return is not received six or more months later by the supplier because the debt is written off as bad? In other words, the business will have paid the VAT amount to HM Revenue & Customs, but is unlikely ever to receive it from the customer.

HM Revenue & Customs allows a refund of amounts like this to all suppliers through the VAT Return – this is known as **bad debt relief**.

Bad debt relief is available:

- for debts which are more than six months overdue
- when the output VAT has already been paid to HM Revenue & Customs
- when the debt has been written off in the supplier's accounts

Bad debt relief is accounted for on the VAT Return by adding it to the Box 4 total (VAT reclaimed on purchases).

## DEALING WITH THE VAT OFFICE

The normal point of contact with HM Revenue & Customs is the local VAT office. The staff are willing to help suppliers with advice and as regulatory bodies they are also likely to want to make sure that a supplier keeps accurate VAT records.

From time-to-time a supplier may receive an inspection visit from VAT officers who will go through the records with the proverbial 'toothcomb' to ensure that all the necessary documentation and accounting records are in order, VAT Returns are being submitted on time and VAT is not being underpaid or overpaid.

Any VAT queries or problems should be referred to the local office through the appropriate channels. If your firm's accounts office is involved, this means an authorised official (supervisor or section head) should telephone or write to the VAT office. Typical a typical query might be:

*"Are these goods standard-rated or zero-rated"*

Now read through the Case Study that follows. It shows you how the VAT 100 (VAT return) form is completed from accounting held by a business. It is the type of procedure you would carry out in a Unit 31 assessment.

**Case Study**

# COMPLETING THE VAT RETURN: TOPO TOYS

### situation

You work in the Accounts Department of Topo Toys Limited, a manufacturer of small toy furry animals, which have proved very popular with children.

It is the first week of April and it is your job to complete the VAT Return to HM Revenue & Customs for the quarter ended 31 March 2007. You have to complete the VAT 100 form, ready for signature by Mikki Topo.

You have extracted the data from the company's day books and have set it out in the table shown below. You have also been presented with a note about a large bad debt recently written off by the company.

**Sales day book totals: quarter ended 31 March 2007**

|  | January | February | March | Total |
|---|---|---|---|---|
|  | £ | £ | £ | £ |
| UK sales: standard rated | 120,000 | 130,000 | 135,000 | 385,000 |
| EU sales: zero-rated | 50,100 | 49,800 | 42,900 | 142,800 |
| Total | 170,100 | 179,800 | 177,900 | 527,800 |
| VAT on UK sales | 21,000 | 22,750 | 23,625 | 67,375 |

**Purchases day book totals: quarter ended 31 March 2007**

|  | January | February | March | Total |
|---|---|---|---|---|
|  | £ | £ | £ | £ |
| Purchases/expenses | 95,000 | 99,000 | 102,000 | 296,000 |
| VAT on purchases/expenses | 16,625 | 17,325 | 17,850 | 51,800 |

PLUTO PALACE RETAIL - BAD DEBT

Please note that an invoice for £2,820 (including VAT) issued to Pluto Palace Retail Ltd on 1 April 2006 was written off as a bad debt on 30 January 2007.

Please adjust the VAT 100 to claim bad debt relief . In case you have not done this procedure before, you add the VAT onto the VAT on purchases and expenses for the quarter (Box 4) to claim it back.

Thanks. Minnie. 01/02/07.

## solution

The figures entered in the VAT 100 are as follows:                    £

Boxes 1 & 3   The VAT on UK Sales figure is take from the
              Sales Day Book total column                          67,375

Boxes 2 & 9   There are no acquisitions from other EU States            -

Box 4         The VAT reclaimed is made up of two figures:

              VAT on purchases and expenses:                      51,800
              Bad debt relief on invoice for £2,820 in
              which the VAT element is £420
              (calculation: £2,820  x  7/47):                        420
                                                                  _____
                                                                  £52,220

Box 5         This figure is Box 3 minus Box 4                     15,155

Box 6         Total Sales from Sales Day Book Total column        527,800

Box 7         Total purchases from Purchases Day Book             296,000

Box 8         Total EU Sales, zero-rated                          142,800

Note that the name of the person signing the form is entered and also that the
box on the left-hand side is ticked, indicating that a cheque will be enclosed.

Before you fill in this form please read the notes on the back and the VAT leaflet *"Filling in your VAT return"*. Fill in all boxes clearly in ink, and write 'none' where necessary. Don't put a dash or leave any box blank. If there are no pence write **"00"** in the pence column. **Do not** enter more than one amount in any box.

| For official use | | £ | p |
|---|---|---|---|
| | VAT due in this period on **sales** and other outputs **1** | 67,375 | 00 |
| | VAT due in this period on **acquisitions** from other **EC Member States** **2** | NONE | |
| | Total VAT due **(the sum of boxes 1 and 2)** **3** | 67,375 | 00 |
| | VAT reclaimed in this period on **purchases** and other inputs (including acquisitions from the EC) **4** | 52,220 | 00 |
| | Net VAT to be paid to Customs or reclaimed by you **(Difference between boxes 3 and 4)** **5** | 15,155 | 00 |
| | Total value of **sales** and all other outputs excluding any VAT. **Include your box 8 figure** **6** | 527,800 | 00 |
| | Total value of **purchases** and all other inputs excluding any VAT. **Include your box 9 figure** **7** | 296,000 | 00 |
| | Total value of all **supplies** of goods and related services, excluding any VAT, to other **EC Member States** **8** | 142,800 | 00 |
| | Total value of all **acquisitions** of goods and related services, excluding any VAT, from other **EC Member States** **9** | NONE | 00 |

If you are enclosing a payment please tick this box.

✔

DECLARATION: You, or someone on your behalf, must sign below.

I, MIKKI TOPO ................................................................ declare that the
(Full name of signatory in BLOCK LETTERS)

information given above is true and complete.

Signature ............................................... Date ...............
A false declaration can result in prosecution.

0041633

L

**VAT 100** (half)

**Chapter Summary**

■ VAT-registered businesses may use manual or computerised accounting systems. The normal sources of accounting data for the completion of the VAT Return are:
   - sales and purchases day books (for credit items)
   - cash book and petty cash book (for non-credit items)

■ The accounting data is normally compiled in a VAT control account which calculates the amount due to HM Revenue & Customs by setting off VAT on sales (output tax) and VAT on purchases and expenses (input tax).

■ An organisation may claim back the VAT paid to HM Revenue & Customs on a debt which has gone bad and has been written off in its books. This is done through the VAT return by adding the VAT amount to the total of input (purchases) VAT claimed.

■ Computer accounting systems will normally keep a running VAT account to which all transactions involving VAT are posted. Some programs will additionally produce a VAT return printout.

■ The VAT Return and payment (if required) should be completed and despatched within the timescale allowed (normally a month from the end of the VAT period); the VAT 100 should be signed by an authorised person.

**Key Terms**

| | |
|---|---|
| **VAT Control Account** | an essential account which collects all the accounting data needed for the VAT Return; it may be maintained manually or by a computer accounting system |
| **VAT Return** | Form VAT 100 is completed by VAT-registered suppliers at the end of each VAT period in order to calculate the amount of VAT due to HM Revenue & Customs or reclaimable from them; it also records statistical data about EU acquisitions |
| **bad debt relief** | a scheme available for any registered supplier whereby output VAT paid over to HM Revenue & Customs on a debt which has subsequently (over 6 months after the due date) gone bad is reclaimable through the VAT 100 |

# Student Activities

**9.1** You work for a firm of accountants and have been asked to complete the VAT 100 forms for four VAT-registered businesses. You collate the following details from their accounting records. The figures represent the day book totals for the last quarter.

|  | Business: Uno Ltd | Business: Duo Brothers | Business: Tray PLC | Business: Quattro PLC |
|---|---|---|---|---|
| **Sales day book** | £ | £ | £ | £ |
| UK sales: standard rated | 120,000 | 185,000 | 98,000 | 2,760,000 |
| EU sales: zero-rated | - | 22,511 | 5,100 | 590,800 |
| VAT on UK sales | 21,000 | 32,375 | 17,150 | 483,000 |
| **Purchases day book** | £ | £ | £ | £ |
| Purchases/expenses (UK) | 65,000 | 80,000 | 45,000 | 1,497,000 |
| VAT on purchases (UK) | 11,375 | 14,000 | 7,875 | 261,975 |

You are also told the following, and are asked to make the necessary adjustments.

(a) Duo Brothers have written off invoices totalling £9,400 (including VAT) as bad debts, and all the invoices qualify for bad debt relief.

(b) Quattro PLC find that in the previous VAT quarter their total of VAT on UK Sales was incorrect and that it should have been £455,000 and not £454,000 as recorded on the VAT 100 form.

**You are to** complete the summary report on the next page. The 'Box numbers' correspond with the box numbers on the appropriate VAT 100 Form. Ensure that the adjustments to the data fromDuo Brothers and Quattro PLC are included in this report.

|  | Business: Uno Ltd £ | Business: Duo Brothers £ | Business: Tray PLC £ | Business: Quattro PLC £ |
|---|---|---|---|---|
| **Box 1** VAT on sales and other outputs (UK) |  |  |  |  |
| **Box 2** VAT on acquisitions from EU (non UK) |  |  |  |  |
| **Box 3** Box 1 plus Box 2 |  |  |  |  |
| **Box 4** VAT reclaimed on purchases/expenses (UK & EU) |  |  |  |  |
| **Box 5** VAT to be paid or reclaimed (difference between Box 3 and Box 4) |  |  |  |  |
| **Box 6** Total value of sales (UK & EU) |  |  |  |  |
| **Box 7** Total of purchases/expenses (UK & EU) |  |  |  |  |
| **Box 8** Total value of sales (EU excluding UK) |  |  |  |  |
| **Box 9** Total value of purchases/expenses (EU excluding UK) |  |  |  |  |

**9.2** You work in the Accounts Department of Bennett Trading Limited.

It is the first week of April and you have been asked to complete the VAT Return to HM Revenue & Customs for the quarter ended 31 March 2007.

You have been presented with the extracts from the company's day books shown below.

**Sales day book totals**

**Quarter ended 31 March 2007**

|  | January | February | March | Total |
|---|---|---|---|---|
|  | £ | £ | £ | £ |
| UK sales: standard rated | 520,000 | 550,000 | 490,000 | 1,560,000 |
| EU sales: zero-rated | 43,100 | 44,800 | 36,900 | 124,800 |
| Total | 563,100 | 594,800 | 526,900 | 1,684,800 |
| VAT on UK sales | 91,000 | 96,250 | 85,750 | 273,000 |

**Purchases day book totals**

**Quarter ended 31 March 2007**

|  | January | February | March | Total |
|---|---|---|---|---|
|  | £ | £ | £ | £ |
| Purchases/expenses | 276,000 | 310,000 | 284,000 | 870,000 |
| VAT on purchases/expenses | 48,300 | 54,250 | 49,700 | 152,250 |

A note was attached to the extracts from the accounts:

A invoice for £1,410 (including VAT) issued to Duff Builders Ltd on 7 July 2006 was written off as a bad debt on 28 February 2007.

PLEASE ADJUST the VAT 100 to claim bad debt relief (ie add the VAT onto the VAT on purchases for the quarter to claim it back).

Thanks. Asaf. 01.03.07.

**You are to** complete the VAT 100 on the opposite page for the signature of Ralph Postgate. You should leave spaces for his signature and the date.

Before you fill in this form please read the notes on the back and the VAT leaflet *"Filling in your VAT return"*. Fill in all boxes clearly in ink, and write 'none' where necessary. Don't put a dash or leave any box blank. If there are no pence write **"00"** in the pence column. **Do not** enter more than one amount in any box.

|  | | £ | p |
|---|---|---|---|
| For official use | VAT due in this period on **sales** and other outputs  **1** | | |
| | VAT due in this period on **acquisitions** from other **EC Member States**  **2** | | |
| | Total VAT due **(the sum of boxes 1 and 2)**  **3** | | |
| | VAT reclaimed in this period on **purchases** and other inputs (including acquisitions from the EC)  **4** | | |
| | Net VAT to be paid to Customs or reclaimed by you **(Difference between boxes 3 and 4)**  **5** | | |
| | Total value of **sales** and all other outputs excluding any VAT. **Include your box 8 figure**  **6** | | 00 |
| | Total value of **purchases** and all other inputs excluding any VAT. **Include your box 9 figure**  **7** | | 00 |
| | Total value of all **supplies** of goods and related services, excluding any VAT, to other **EC Member States**  **8** | | 00 |
| | Total value of all **acquisitions** of goods and related services, excluding any VAT, from other **EC Member States**  **9** | | 00 |

If you are enclosing a payment please tick this box.

DECLARATION: You, or someone on your behalf, must sign below.

I, ........................................................................ declare that the
(Full name of signatory in BLOCK LETTERS)

information given above is true and complete.

Signature ................................................ Date ................................
**A false declaration can result in prosecution.**

L

0041633

**VAT 100** (half)   SPECIMEN

# 10 Computer systems and accounting software

This chapter introduces the basics of computer systems – the hardware and the software used. It deals with the skills needed for the everyday use of computers and computer programs. These include:

- the procedures for starting up and closing down a computer system

- the use of passwords

- how to use the software: accessing, inputting and printing data

- saving data and maintaining systems for backing up

- knowing what to do when something goes wrong

## PERFORMANCE CRITERIA COVERED

### unit 31: ACCOUNTING WORK SKILLS

### element 31.2

### Operate a computerised accounting system

A    Power up the computer and use passwords to access the system, software and data files.

B    Save, back up and print data files.

F    Exit from software and safely close down the computer.

# INTRODUCTION TO COMPUTER ACCOUNTING PACKAGES

## a growth area

Although a few organisations, particularly small businesses, still use paper-based accounting systems, many are now operating computerised accounting systems. Businesses can buy 'off-the shelf' accounting programs from suppliers such as Sage, and customise them to their particular needs.

## links with traditional book-keeping

You will know that your study of book-keeping and accounts concentrates largely on paper-based systems. The reason for this is that when you use a paper-based system you have to do all the work manually, so you can understand the theory that underlies the system: you prepare the documents, make entries in the accounts, balance the cash book, and so on. You know where all the figures are entered, and why they are entered. If you know how a paper-based system works, you will be in a much better position to be able to understand the operation of a computer-based system.

## comparison with other types of computer program

Computer accounting packages – such as the Sage Line 50 series of products – make use of many of the functions of the other types of computer program already described in this chapter. Most computer accounting packages contain:

- word processing functions – eg the facility to write memos and notes
- a series of databases – eg details of customers, stock items held
- calculation facilities – eg invoices where the operator inputs figures and the program automatically generates VAT amounts and totals
- charting and graphing facilities – eg charting of activity on a customer account

## facilities

A typical computer accounting program will offer a number of facilities:

- on-screen input and printout of sales invoices and credit notes
- automatic updating of customer accounts with sales transactions
- recording of suppliers' invoices
- automatic updating of supplier accounts with details of purchases
- recording of money paid into the bank
- recording of payments to suppliers and for expenses

## management reports

A computer accounting program can provide instant reports for management, for example:

- an aged debtors' summary – showing who owes you what and for what periods of time
- activity reports on customer and supplier accounts
- activity reports on expenses accounts

## advantages of a computer accounting program

Computer accounting programs, like the other computer programs outlined in this chapter, are popular because they offer a number of distinct advantages over paper-based systems:

- they tend to be more accurate because they rely on single-entry input (one amount per transaction) rather than double-entry book-keeping
- they can provide the accounting function of the organisation with a clear and up-to-date picture of what is happening
- they can print VAT Returns and other useful reports for management
- they save time, and therefore money

The diagram below shows a menu bar setting out the structure of a Sage computer accounting program.

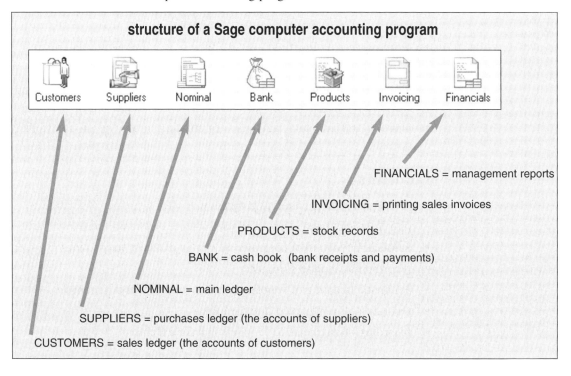

**structure of a Sage computer accounting program**

Customers    Suppliers    Nominal    Bank    Products    Invoicing    Financials

FINANCIALS = management reports

INVOICING = printing sales invoices

PRODUCTS = stock records

BANK = cash book (bank receipts and payments)

NOMINAL = main ledger

SUPPLIERS = purchases ledger (the accounts of suppliers)

CUSTOMERS = sales ledger (the accounts of customers)

## STARTING UP A COMPUTER SYSTEM

There are a number of visual safety checks that you must perform when starting up a computer system.

### hardware components

Are all the hardware components there? Check to see if the main processing unit and peripherals such as screens, printers, back-up drives and scanners are in place and have not been moved by a cleaner or removed for maintenance, or worse still, by a thief!

If there is a problem, you should refer it to someone in a position of responsibility who will be able to deal with it. Clearly if equipment is missing, it will need to be dealt with urgently.

*have you checked the power supply?*

### power plugs

Is everything plugged in correctly? Check the following:

- are the mains plugs in place and is the electrical supply up and running?

- check any power supply surge protectors are correctly in place (these protect against surges in current which might damage sensitive electronic devices such as computers)

- are the mains plugs plugged in properly?

If there is any problem here you should either fix it yourself if you are able, or refer it to someone in a position of responsibility who will be able to deal with it.

### peripheral plugs and cables

In a standalone system (one computer on its own) the main processing unit should be connected to a variety of devices such as mouse, keyboard, monitor and peripheral units such as printer, scanner and back-up device such as a zip drive.

A quick visual check will tell you whether these devices are all securely plugged in.

You should also check that the internet connection is plugged in.

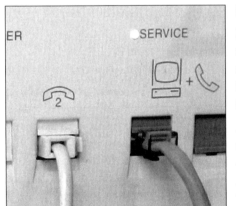

*are you connected?*

If you are working on a network system you will need to check your work station connections. Peripheral devices such as printers may be situated elsewhere in the office and will not be connected directly to your machine. In this case you will be able to check on screen once the computer is up and running.

Lastly, and very importantly, check that cables are not positioned dangerously, where people could trip over them and possibly injure themselves. This is part of your personal responsibility under the Health and Safety regulations (see Chapter 19). You may be able to deal with dangerous cabling yourself, or, if you are not able to put it right, you should refer the problem to someone in a position of responsibility who will be able to deal with it.

### powering up

When all these checks have been carried out, you should switch on the computer(s) in the usual way and hopefully experience a trouble-free session operating the computer system.

## USING PASSWORDS

Before getting going on the computer you are likely to have to use **passwords** to enable you to gain access to:

- the computer itself, for example if you are using a workstation on a network – this is a **system password**

- particular computer programs, some of which may enable you to access sensitive or confidential information – eg the accounting software – this is a **software password**

We will deal with the security aspect of passwords in the next chapter. We will concentrate here on the practical aspects of passwords as part of the starting up procedure.

### system passwords – logging on

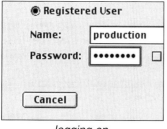

*logging on*

If you are working on a network you have to 'log on' as a user before you can use a computer workstation. You may have to give a user name and also a unique password. The user name will normally show on the screen as you input it, but the password will show as a series of dots or asterisks. The example on the left shows someone logging onto a computer in the production department. Logging on is a simple process, and you may well be familiar with it because it is normally used when you log onto the internet.

## software passwords – accessing a program

Passwords are also needed to protect sensitive and confidential data held on the computer system. This is particularly important in the areas of staff records and also in the case of financial data processed by computer accounting programs.

One solution to the problem of unauthorised employees gaining access to sensitive financial data is the use of **passwords** to gain access to the computer program. Many larger businesses will employ a number of people who need to operate the computer accounting system; they will be issued with an appropriate password. Businesses can also set up **access rights** which restrict certain employees to certain activities and prevent them from accessing more sensitive areas such as the making of payments from the bank account.

When an employee comes to operate, for example, a Sage computer accounting package, he or she will be asked to 'log on'. In the example from Sage Line 50 shown below a person called Tom enters his log on name and a password (CRUISE).

The next screen from Sage Line 50 (see below) shows that Tom and Britney are the two people authorised to access the program. Tom has full access, which means that he can access all the functions of the program. Britney, however, has partial access. She is only allowed to deal with Customers, Suppliers and the Nominal (Main) Ledger. She cannot access the Bank records.

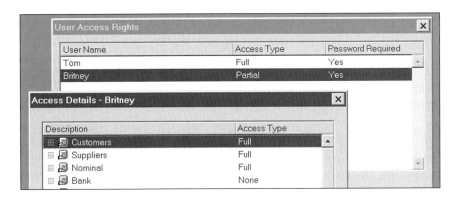

## USING SOFTWARE

Using software involves a number of processes:

### opening up the program

You should know how to open up the program in the first place, using a password where appropriate (see previous page).

### accessing files that you need

The files that you use may be in a familiar folder, or you may have to use a search routine to locate a file, a text document or chart that has been created, or a download from the internet. You need to be tidy in the way that you organise and name files, otherwise you may 'lose' or accidentally overwrite files, in which case you have to go to your back-up (assuming you have one!)

### saving documents

It is critically important to save the data that you input on a frequent and systematic basis (some programs do this automatically). As mentioned above, you should use a logical file naming system when you are saving for the first time and make sure that you know into which folder you have saved a file. There is more on 'saving' on page 166 when we deal with shutting down the computer system.

### printing documents

If you use a standalone computer system, the printer will be connected directly to the computer and, as long as it is connected properly, you will be able to print out documents from the 'Print' command. If you use a network you will have to select the printer on-screen and then give the 'Print' command. You may then find that your document will join a print queue and you will then have to locate it when it is printed.

If you are using a computer accounting program you will be able to print out documents such as daybooks, account activity, aged debtor analyses, trial balances, invoices, credit notes and statements.

## BACKING-UP FILES

You will also need to **back-up** the data generated by the computer. There is no set rule about when you should do this, but it should be at least at the end of every day and preferably when you have completed a run of inputting.

If you are working on a network, you can normally save to your files to your work station's hard disk and also to the server. If you have a standalone computer system, the back-up files should be saved to some form of storage device. This may take the form of a disk drive in the workstation itself or it may be an external drive.

Data can be backed up onto a variety of media:

- floppy disks (cheap, traditional but limited in storage capacity)
- Zip disks (higher capacity, higher price)
- tape drive
- writable or rewriteable CDs (cheap and disposable)

Another back-up option is to send files by email and keep them secure at a remote location, although this option would be limited by file size.

## naming the back-up files

It is important when creating a back-up file that you allocate a sensible filename to it, so that the file can be easily identified. Normally the computer will assign a default name and automatically add a suffix identifying the program that created it, eg SAGEBACK.001 in a Sage program. Of course, the name can be overwritten and replaced with a more meaningful name such as the date.

## back-up policy

It is important that an organisation works out a systematic policy for backup of its data. This should involve:

- backup held on more than one set of disks or other back-up media
- the backup data held off the premises
- periodic backup (eg backups at the end of each month) stored securely

A traditional solution is for the business to keep a set of back-up data (on disk or other media) for each working day, identified with the name of the day. At the end of each working day the data is backed up on the appropriate disks/media, which are kept securely on site, preferably under lock and key.

As a further security measure, a second back-up could be kept as an off-site reserve. This would be backed up at the end of each day and taken off-site by an employee.

With this system in place the business has double security for its valuable data.

It should also be mentioned that any discs used should be replaced periodically (every three months, for example) as they wear out in time and the data can become corrupted.

## CLOSE DOWN

Closing down the computer system correctly is important because a variety of problems can arise if the correct procedures are not followed.

When you wish to shut down you should:

- exit each program by using the 'close' command – this will warn you if you have any unsaved files still open and will enable you to save your work; it will also make sure that the program starts up properly next time the computer is used

- use the correct command from the operating system to close the computer down

If you are using a work station on a network and need to keep the computer turned on – perhaps for someone else to use – you should log off, making sure that all your files are closed, saved and backed up.

## GETTING HELP

*don't try and fix it yourself unless you know what you are doing!*

A computer system that goes wrong can be very frustrating, not only for the organisation, but also for the customers that deal with it. Try booking a holiday at a travel agent when the 'system is down'.

If there is a problem, it should be fixed as soon as possible. If the problem happens to you, and you cannot deal with it yourself, you should know where you can get help.

The type of problems that you are likely to encounter include:

- **hardware** faults – eg a printer that jams, toner that runs out

- **software** faults – program files that corrupt so that the program will not start

- **corrupt data** or **deleted** or **overwritten** data files which stop your normal work flow

### hardware failure

There will be times when you have equipment failures. If this happens, the problem should be referred to the person in the organisation who deals with the equipment. It is not advisable to 'have a go' yourself, unless it is a simple matter such as replacing a printer ribbon or cartridge. Many businesses will have back-up computers which can run the software and which can be loaded with your last back-up data disk. There may also be 'on-site' support provided under contract by the supplier of the hardware.

### software failure

Software problems can be more complex. If it is a case of not knowing how to carry out a particular operation, refer the matter to someone who does. Help is always at hand through HELP menus, on-line support or telephone technical support to which the business is likely to have subscribed. The rule is again, do not 'have a go' yourself unless you know what you are doing. If a program crashes, it may be necessary to restart the computer. If the program refuses to work after repeated attempts, it may have become corrupted, in which case it may need to be re-installed by a technician.

### corrupted, deleted or overwritten data files

Problems can also be caused if a data file you are using

- becomes **corrupt**, ie it becomes unusable and will not open or print, or both

- gets **deleted** by accident when you are tidying up your computer desktop and sending what you think are redundant files into the trash can

- is accidentally **overwritten** by an older version of a file, and in the process wipes out the work you may have done on the file

In these cases you have to rely on your back-up files and hope that they are up-to-date. If you are unable to access them yourself (if, for example, you work on a network) you may need help.

The Case Study that follows illustrates the various problems that can be encountered when running a computer system, and explains the way an employee can overcome those problems.

---

**Case Study**

## SORTING PROBLEMS

Noor is an accounts assistant at Spira PLC, an insurance company, based in Staines. She works alongside her line manager, Jim Slater.

It is the end of the month and she has been given two tasks to carry out:

1   Printing out all the customer statements ready for mailing.

2   Compiling sales reports for management. These involve inputting sales data into a spreadsheet, extracting charts and pasting them into a word-processing file.

Noor has not been having a very good day at all, and has encountered a number of problems.

## problem 1 – paper out

Noor works on a standalone machine which is used for computer accounting – data input, invoicing and production of reports such as trial balances and aged debtors analyses. The computer has a laser printer linked directly to it for the printing of these documents.

Today Noor has 150 statements of account to print out, fold, place in window envelopes and send out to customers. The statements are generated from a routine in the computer accounting program used by Spira PLC.

When the printer has been running for a while, Noor's computer gives a warning message saying that the printer tray is empty. The 'paper out' light is flashing on the printer.

## problem 2 – paper jam

Later in the print run, the printer jams and stops printing. Noor's computer flashes up a warning message and the paper jam light starts flashing on the printer.

## problem 3 – a missing file

Noor has been asked to update a sales figures spreadsheet with the figures for the month. She looks in the 'Sales Figures' folder on her hard disk and cannot find the file. She does a 'Search' routine, but the answer comes back 'File not Found'.

## problem 4 – software problems

Noor has extracted a chart from a spreadsheet file and needs to export it into a word-processing file as part of a sales report to management. Unfortunately the word-processing file refuses to open when she clicks on it. She then tries to open it through the word-processing file menu, but the program refuses to open. She tries restarting the computer, but still the word-processing program will not start.

The solutions to Noor's problems are as follows:

## solution 1 – paper out

Filling up the paper tray on a printer is normally a task most employees would be expected to carry out, as it does not involve any great technical skill. Noor would no doubt be able to replenish the paper supply to enable the printer to complete the statements.

## solution 2 – paper jam

Again, most modern printers can easily be opened up so that paper jams can be cleared. If, however, the paper has torn at all, the job may prove more difficult. If this is the case, Noor should report the matter to her line manager so that a technician can be called in to unjam the printer.

### solution 3 – a missing file

It would appear that the required file has somehow been accidentally deleted from the computer.

Noor needs to obtain a back-up copy of the file. This should be available in the office. If Noor is not sure where it is located, she should ask her line manager. When the file is found it should be restored onto the computer so that Noor can resume her work.

### solution 4 – software problems

The problem of the faulty software is more serious. it appears that the program files have been corrupted and as a result they do not work.

Noor should report the matter to her line manager who can then arrange for a technician to re-install the program files onto the computer and overwrite the corrupt software. The program files will normally be held in CD form in the office.

**Chapter Summary**

- Computer accounting programs combine the functions of a number of different programs – they act as a database and spreadsheet and can generate text and data for use in other programs.

- Visual checks should be made when starting up a computer system. These include checks of hardware and peripherals, power plugs, plugs for peripherals and all cabling.

- Passwords are used for gaining access to data held on a computer system. Passwords are used both for logging on and also for gaining access to different software packages. They can also be used for restricting access to certain types of data.

- Good computer housekeeping involves a strict routine for saving and naming files. It is important to have a consistent back-up policy and ensure that an off-site back up is always maintained.

   - A routine for shutting down a computer system should also be established. A system that is not shut down correctly can cause problems when the system is next powered up.

   - If problems arise with a computer system, immediate assistance should be sought if the fault cannot be remedied by the employee.

**Key Terms**

| | |
|---|---|
| **hardware** | the computer equipment on which the computer programs run |
| **software** | the computer programs which enable the computer to work and carry out its functions |
| **main processing unit** | the main computer unit which runs the software |
| **peripheral** | an item of hardware – such as an external disk drive or scanner – which is connected to the main processing unit |
| **standalone system** | a computer system which is not linked to other computers |
| **network system** | a computer system which links a number of computers and shared peripherals – also known as an intranet |
| **internet** | a telephone link to an internet service provider giving access to the worldwide web (www) |
| **password** | a series of letters and/or numbers which are required by the system to enable a computer user to gain access to the system, to software, or certain types of data |

# Student Activities

**10.1** You work in the parts department of a local independent garage which runs a standalone computer system to run its accounts and keep records of its stock. The computer is a traditional 'tower' set up with monitor, mouse, keyboard, printer and external zip drive to back-up files at the end of each day.

It is part of your job to operate the computer system, mainly to print invoices for jobs carried out and to check part availability.

Write a numbered checklist of the visual checks to the system you would carry out when you come in the morning, and before you turn the computer on.

**10.2** (a)    Describe the difference between a system password and a software password.

(b)    Explain why the two types of passwords are necessary.

**10.3** Give an example of a back-up policy adopted by an organisation. Your source could be an organisation with which you are familiar, information from a friend, or the text in this chapter.

**10.4** Computer printers are invaluable when they work well, but can disrupt the work flow when they stop working for one reason or another.

Investigate and list the reasons why a printer might stop working, and in each case state whether the computer operator would be expected to fix the problem, or whether assistance would need to be obtained from elsewhere.

# 11 Data security

This chapter explains how data held on computer file is kept secure. Security helps to prevent:

- loss of the data through accidental means, eg disk corruption, viruses
- loss of the data to an unauthorised person, eg someone hacking into the system

Security is maintained through:

- careful use of passwords
- making sure computer hardware and data is located in a safe place
- identifying and dealing with risks to hardware and data

The chapter also deals with the legal regulations relating to the use of computers and the handling of computer data.

## PERFORMANCE CRITERIA COVERED

### unit 31:  ACCOUNTING WORK SKILLS

### element 31.2

### Operate a computerised accounting system

E    Maintain security and confidentiality of data, passwords, disks etc, so that potential risks are minimised.

G    Identify the possible impact of relevant legislation and regulations.

## INTRODUCTION TO DATA SECURITY

A business that uses computers will have invested thousands of pounds in buying equipment and in training staff to operate it. A business that neglects to look after the equipment and the data that it holds is potentially throwing this money down the drain.

What are the dangers?

### dangers to the data

The data held on the computer is irreplaceable once lost and so must be kept securely both on the computer system and also in the form of back ups.

Back-up systems were discussed in the last chapter (pages 166-167). An essential element of data security is the maintenance of a foolproof back-up system and the secure location of back-up disks, both on-site and off-site.

The data must be kept securely to prevent interference from outside and inside the business:

- people such as competitors or criminals outside the business may try to gain access to the data either directly (through 'hacking' if the computer is linked to the internet) or through an employee who can be persuaded to obtain the information

- employees of the business may try to access the data in order to work a fraud – through the payroll, for example, or by making bogus payments to external bank accounts which they control

In this chapter we look at the various precautions that can be taken to minimise these risks.


## PASSWORD PROTECTION

We have seen in the last chapter (pages 164-165) that passwords are needed to access:

- the computer system itself (system passwords)
- the software run on the computer system (software passwords)

Security of passwords can be enhanced by individuals choosing 'unbreakable' passwords (see next page).

The organisation can also increase security by ensuring that passwords are changed regularly and when they have been compromised (ie guessed by someone else).

## basic rules of choosing an individual password

1   Do not use the word 'password' (it does happen).

2   Combine letters and numbers if possible.

3   Do not use your own name or date of birth.

4   Make it so that you can remember the password easily and avoid forgettable combinations such as z9ad2w8y7d –- try the name and birthday of your first girlfriend/boyfriend, Lisa0511, for example, but avoid using similar details relating to your present partner (because people will guess them).

5   Never write the password down where people can see it, and never put it on a post-it note stuck on the computer monitor (it does happen).

When you have chosen a password, make sure that nobody stands watching you when you are logging on; the password appears as dots on the screen, but people can work out what you are typing on the keyboard.

If you suspect that someone has worked out your password, change it. If you do not know how to, seek assistance.

## organisational procedures for password security

An organisation should ensure that passwords are changed regularly, every couple of months, for example. This will ensure that if an unauthorised person has obtained a password, it can only be used for a limited period.

An organisation should ensure that if there is any suspicion that a password has been 'leaked', there should be a wholesale change of passwords.

## IDENTIFYING SECURITY RISKS

Data on computer file needs to be protected against:

*   **corruption** – ie when the file goes 'wrong' and does not work properly – either because of a virus or because of poor storage facilities

*   **loss** – when the file is deleted, accidentally or intentionally – by an employee or by a virus introduced from outside

*   **illegal copying** – by an employee copying a program or by someone 'hacking in' from outside through the internet connection

Clearly the threats to data therefore come both internally, from employees, and externally, from hackers or viruses.

## protecting data from internal risks

Much of the data held on computer file is sensitive and confidential in nature, for example:

- payroll details of employees
- financial details relating to customers

It is an unfortunate possibility that employees may be persuaded or paid by outsiders to obtain this information. As a result all employees should take reasonable precautions to prevent data that they are working from being used in this way. For example:

- if you leave your computer, do not leave sensitive data on screen, or the program running
- use a screensaver
- use passwords wherever possible
- if you print out a document with confidential information on it, do not leave it on the printer (or the photocopier!)

Another internal risk is **illegal copying** of computer data – often program files – by employees who 'borrow' disks to take home or 'lend' to friends. The answer here is to keep these types of files under strict control. A business using software will in any event have been granted a **licence** to use it, and any unauthorised copying will be a breach of that licence.

Careful and safe **storage** of computer data on various forms of media is also important. Heat and radiation can damage files held on disk, and the surface of CDs and DVDs can easily be scratched, causing corruption and data loss.

## protecting data from external risks

External risks to data include:

- thieves who steal data by stealing the computers on which it is held – computer laptops are particularly vulnerable
- external hackers who access files within an organisation by 'hacking in' from the internet and accessing files held – often on a network
- viruses sent into the computer system, either on a disk or through the internet

Protection against thieves can be achieved by rigorous security at the premises. CCTV is now commonly used to guard against crime. Laptops away from the premises should be kept under lock and key wherever possible, and preferably not left in cars. Hackers can be kept at bay by a 'firewall' on the internet portal of a computer network. A 'firewall' is software which keeps out all external interference and unwanted emails.

Computer viruses are dealt with in the next section.

## VIRUS PROTECTION

Computers are vulnerable to viruses. A **virus** is a destructive program which can be introduced into the computer either from a disk or from another computer. If the computer or server which runs the software is linked directly or indirectly to the internet, there is a danger that an incoming email with an attachment may introduce a virus.

Some viruses are relatively harmless and may merely display messages on the screen, others can be very damaging and destroy operating systems and data, putting the computer system completely out of action.

Most computers are now sold already installed with virus protection software which will:

• check for viruses

• destroy known viruses

• check for damage to files on the hard disk

• repair damage to files on the hard disk where possible

This software should be run and updated regularly so that it can deal with the latest viruses.

The screen below shows a virus protection program scanning the hard disk of a computer. As you can see, it has not yet found any infected files.

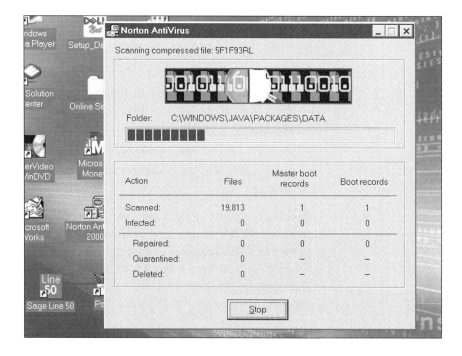

## precautions against viruses

There are a number of simple precautions which you can take against viruses:

- be wary of opening any unidentified email attachments which arrive
- use protective software to inspect any disk received from an outside source before opening up any file saved onto it
- make sure that your protective software is up to date – very often they will update automatically over the internet

If your protective software announces that you have a virus, you should report it at once and stop using your computer.

# LEGAL REGULATIONS

Any organisation using computer systems must comply with a number of legal requirements.

## data protection legislation

Businesses inevitably keep records of their customers and suppliers on file – either manually – a card index system, for example – or, more likely, on computer file. This is 'personal data'.

The **Data Protection Act (1998)** establishes rules for the processing of personal data. The Act follows the guidelines of an EC Directive and brings the UK in line with European legal principles. The Act applies to a filing system of records held on **computer**, eg a computer database of customer names, addresses, telephone numbers, sales details, or a **manual** set of accessible records.

People have the legal right to know what personal details about them are held by an organisation. They can apply in writing for a copy of the personal data held on file by the organisation; they may have to pay a fee.

The Data Protection Act reinforces the need for confidentiality in business dealings. A business should not without permission reveal:

- information about one customer to another customer
- information about its employees

## Copyright, Designs and Patents Act,1988

This Act states that it is illegal to copy computer software without the permission of the copyright owner (the writer of the software). This permission is normally granted by **licence**. Software piracy is policed by an independent organisation, FAST (Federation Against Software Theft). A person found copying software is liable to a fine and/or imprisonment!

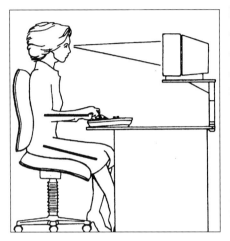

## Display Screen Equipment Regulations 1992

These Regulations set down rules for the use of computer workstations and VDU screens. A 'workstation' includes the computer equipment, furniture, space, light and atmosphere in which an employee works. Measures include:

- employees must have regular breaks
- employees must be offered eye tests
- equipment and furniture must conform to strict standards of safety and comfort

If these regulations are not complied with, the employee runs a number of risks, including: a bad back or a bad neck, eye strain, repetitive strain injury and stress.

These regulations apply to the organisation which employs computer operators. It must be remembered, too, that the employee has a responsibility to make sure that regular breaks are taken and that the correct posture is used when working at the computer.

### health and safety regulations

The law which governs the overall health and safety issue (including computer systems) is the **Health and Safety at Work Act 1974**. This sets out specific responsibilities and requirements for the employer and employee and is covered in detail in the next chapter.

### storing of documents

Business records are normally stored for at least six years (and a minimum of three years for payroll data). The Data Protection Act reinforces the requirement that personal data is kept securely and that it should be accurate. There are a number of legal reasons why financial data (which will include personal data) should be kept for this period of time:

- accounting records should be kept so that they can be inspected by the Inland Revenue if required (if there is a tax inspection)
- accounting records should be kept so that they can be inspected by HM Customs & Excise if required (if there is a VAT inspection)
- accounting records should be kept for at least six years in case they are needed as evidence in any legal action

**Chapter Summary**

■ Passwords restrict access to computer data and are an important aspect of data security. They should be kept secret by the employees that use them.

■ The organisation should arrange to change passwords on a regular basis, and should ensure that they are changed after any breach of password security.

■ Computer hardware and data (and back-ups) should be stored securely on the premises and in suitable environmental conditions. Any off-site back-ups should also be stored safely.

■ Organisations should be aware of the internal risks to data caused by corruption of files, loss and deletion of files and illegal copying.

■ Organisations should also be aware of the external risks to data caused by theft, hackers and computer viruses, and take precautions accordingly.

■ Confidentiality of data is very important, and data should not be made available without authorisation to outsiders. This is covered under the Data Protection Act.

■ Other legislation which affects computer operation includes VDU regulations, rules for the retention of data. and copyright (illegal copying).

**Key Terms**

| | |
|---|---|
| **password** | a collection of letters and/or numbers which give access to a computer system or specific software |
| **corruption** | loss of computer data possibly caused by poor storage conditions or a computer virus |
| **illegal copying** | unauthorised copying of computer files for personal use – a breach of copyright law |
| **hacker** | an individual who breaks into the computer system of an organisation from outside, through an internet connection, to steal or corrupt data |
| **virus** | a destructive or disruptive program introduced into a computer system from a disk or concealed in an email attachment |
| **firewall** | software which helps protect computer systems connected to the internet |
| **confidentiality of data** | keeping computer data secure and preventing unauthorised release to outsiders – covered under the Data Protection Act |

# Student Activities

**11.1** You work in an office which has a networked computer system.

Make up two passwords for your personal use, using a combination of letters and numbers from sources personal to you, eg names, ages, car registrations. The passwords should each have six characters.

Explain in each case why the password can be remembered by you and what the sources of the letters and numbers are. Also state why nobody else could guess them.

Note: do not quote passwords you use at work!

**11.2** Write a checklist of procedures or 'rules' that the staff of an organisation could adopt in order to protect the security of its computer passwords.

**11.3** Assume again that you work in an office which has a networked computer system.

You report directly to a line manager.

Describe what action you would take in the following circumstances:

(a) You notice on more than one occasion that a colleague is standing watching you as you input your system password.

(b) You receive an email with an attachment from someone you do not know. The email says 'Open me and be surprised!'

(c) You are having a heatwave and notice that a colleague has put some disks on the windowsill in full sunlight. They are marked 'on site back-up'

**11.4** There are many ways in which office work is regulated by law.

Identify which laws are relevant in the following cases.

Describe what action you would take if you were a line manager in the office concerned.

(a) An employee says to you as you leave work one day, 'Oh, by the way, I am just borrowing this spreadsheet program disk. Remind me to put it back in the morning. It should be OK, a lot of people have borrowed it!'

(b) A well-known customer telephones and asks one of the accounts assistants: 'Can you look on screen and let me know if your customer Jaques & Co is paying up on time? We are having trouble getting money out of them at the moment. I hope they are not going bust!' It is well known in the department that Jaques & Co are very bad at paying their invoices.

(c) An employee who is very busy inputting data, complains 'My back hurts something terrible when I get home, and my eyes feel really tired all the time. I think I need a change of job.

# 12 Computerised accounts – getting started

## this chapter covers . . .

This chapter explains how the account and ledger structure of the Sage Line 50 software used here relates to the accounts and ledger system you have studied in Unit 30. You will see that there are great similarities, although some of the terminology used is slightly different.

The chapter describes how a business – Rowan Limited – runs its accounting records on computer.

This chapter also covers the accounts in the Nominal Ledger (another term for the Main Ledger).

## PERFORMANCE CRITERIA COVERED

### unit 31: ACCOUNTING WORK SKILLS

### element 31.2

### Operate a computerised accounting system

C    Enter accounting transactions into computerised records.

D    Operate a computerised accounting system including output.

## INTRODUCTION TO COMPUTERISED ACCOUNTING

The three chapters that follow this introductory chapter take you through the computerised accounting requirements of Unit 31. It is recommended that you complete your study of Unit 30 before tackling these three chapters and their exercises.

The chapters contain text and Case Studies which explain how computerised accounting – using Sage software – works in practice. Most chapters conclude with an inputting exercise which enables you to enter accounting data into your computer and print out reports.

The chapters are written around a single business – Rowan Limited – which designs and markets fleece jackets and tops.

You will have to enter details of customers and suppliers invoices, credit notes and payments, as required by your course, and print out various daybooks, documents and reports as part of your Unit 31 assessment.

## WHY SAGE AND WHICH SAGE?

Osborne Books (the publisher of this book) has chosen Sage software for this text for two very good reasons:

1 Sage software is widely used in business and is recognised as a user-friendly and reliable product.

2 Osborne Books has used Sage itself for over ten years and is well used to the way it works.

The Sage software used for illustrating this book is Sage Line 50 Accountant Plus (Version 11) for Windows.

### screen illustrations

It should be appreciated that some training centres and businesses may be using older (or newer) versions, and so some of the screens may look slightly different. This does not matter. Using Sage is like driving different models of car – the controls may be located in slightly different places and the dashboard may not look exactly the same, but the controls are still there and they still do the same thing.

So, if the screens shown here look unfamiliar, examine them carefully and you will see that they contain the same (or very similar) Sage icons and functions as the version you are using.

## MANUAL AND COMPUTERISED RECORDS – AN OVERVIEW

The images shown on the far right of the diagram below are the icons on the Sage desktop which represent the different operating areas of the program. As you can see they very much relate to the ledger structure of the manual book-keeping system . . .

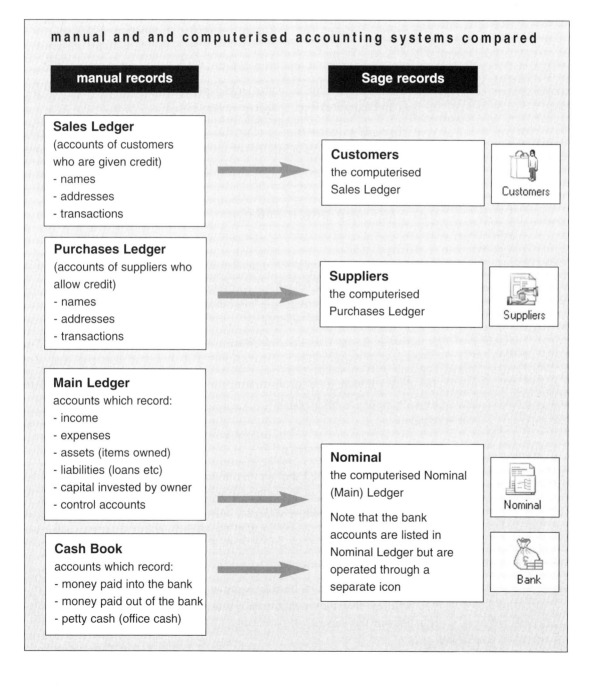

### differences between manual and computer records

The main difference to note between the manual and computerised accounting records is that the Main Ledger is called the **Nominal Ledger,** a term which is in common use in accounting. In these remaining chapters on computerised accounting we will therefore refer to 'nominal accounts' and 'nominal ledger' as well as to the 'main' ledger.

First, however, we will introduce Rowan Limited, the subject of our Case Study. We will then explain the way in which the Sage Nominal Ledger works.

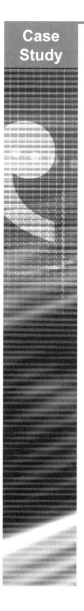

**Case Study**

# ROWAN LIMITED: COMPANY DETAILS

### the business

Rowan is a limited company run by Jo Dickinson. Rowan Limited manufactures fleece tops for the outdoor leisure and fashion market, operating from an industrial estate in Maidstone.

### setting up the accounting system

Jo uses Sage Line 50 software to run her accounts. Jo also runs her payroll on the computer, but this is run on a separate Sage program.

Jo has chosen Sage Line 50 because it will enable her to:

- record the invoices issued to her customers to whom she sells on credit
- pay her suppliers on the due date
- keep a record of her bank receipts and payments
- record her income and expenses, business assets and loans in a main (nominal) ledger

In short she will have a computerised accounting package which will enable her to record all her financial transactions, print out reports and manage her business finances, saving her time (and money) in running her accounting system.

When she first set up her Sage accounting system, Jo will have entered her company details on the computer in a facility known as Company Preferences in the SETTINGS menu. The entry screen is shown on the next page. The details include:

- address: Unit 34 Wordsworth Estate, Tennyson Road, Maidstone, Kent, ME4 5EW
- contact details: telephone, fax, email, website
- VAT registration number

The financial year start date of April 2007 is set up in 'Financial Year' in the SETTINGS menu.

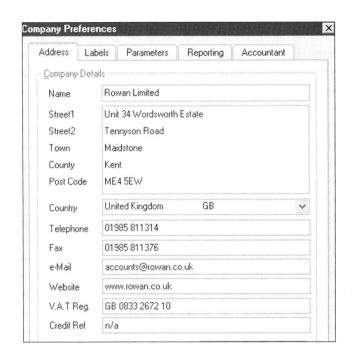

## SETTING UP THE NOMINAL (MAIN) LEDGER ACCOUNTS

The **nominal (main) ledger** accounts in any accounting system are the accounts which are not Subsidiary Ledger accounts, ie Customer accounts (Sales ledger) or Supplier accounts (Purchases ledger). Nominal accounts record income and expenses, assets, liabilities and capital.

In Sage the **bank account**s of the business (including Petty Cash account) are also **listed** in NOMINAL, but they are **operated** from a separate BANK icon, just as in a manual accounting system the bank transactions are recorded in a separate Cash Book.

When Jo Dickinson in the Rowan Limited Case Study set up her company she chose a set of nominal accounts automatically provided by the Sage program. She found that individual account names could be changed to suit the business at any time, for example types of products sold.

If you click on the NOMINAL icon in the Sage opening screen (Version 11 is used in this book) you will have a choice of 'layouts'. The Analyser layout groups the accounts into broad categories called the Chart of Accounts.The List layout (shown opposite) lists each individual nominal account.

To see these, you will need to click on the drop-down arrow in the Layout box. The List screen is illustrated on the next page. You can scroll down this screen on the computer to see the complete list of nominal accounts

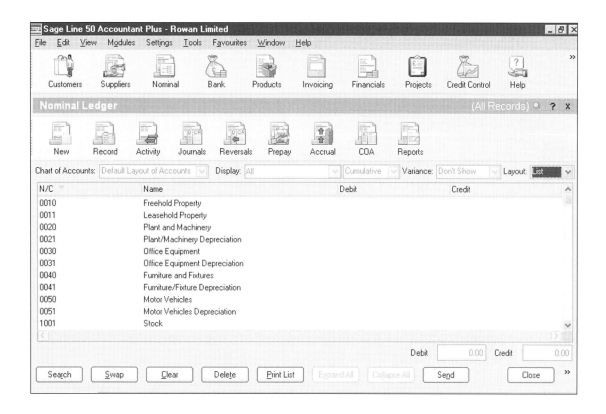

■ A computerised accounting system has a similar structure to a manual accounting system. It is just the terminology which is different:

   – 'Customers' is the Sales Ledger

   – 'Suppliers' is the Purchases ledger

   – 'Nominal' is the Main Ledger which additionally contains the bank accounts

■ A range of nominal ledger accounts is already set up in Sage. Individual account names can be personalised to the business.

**Note**

There are no Student Activities in this introductory chapter.
The first set of inputting exercises, including the setting up of
Rowan Limited on a Sage system, is in the next chapter.

# 13 Computerised accounting – credit sales

this chapter covers . . .

A business that sells on credit will invoice the goods or services supplied and then receive payment at a later date.

It is essential that details of the invoice are entered in the computerised accounting records so that the sale can be recorded and the amount owed by the customer logged into the accounting system.

A credit note is dealt with by a computerised accounting program in much the same way as an invoice (in terms of the input screens used.)

This chapter continues the Rowan Limited Case Study. It shows how to set up new customer records and how details of invoices and credit notes are entered into the computerised accounting records.

The next chapter looks at how the invoices and credit notes issued by suppliers are dealt with by a computerised accounting program.

## PERFORMANCE CRITERIA COVERED

### unit 31: ACCOUNTING WORK SKILLS

### element 31.2

### Operate a computerised accounting system

C    Enter accounting transactions into computerised records.

D    Operate a computerised accounting system including output.

## SETTING UP NEW CUSTOMER RECORDS IN THE SALES LEDGER

The first step is to input all the details of the customers to whom the business sells on credit. The type of details required include:

- customer code (this can be letters, numbers or a mixture of both)
- customer name and address
- credit limit
- trading terms

Study the input on the first Sage 'Customer Record' screen below.

## INVOICES, CREDIT NOTES AND SAGE

### the book-keeping background

The totals of invoices and credit notes have to be entered into the accounting records of a business. They record the sales and refunds made to customers who have bought on credit – the **debtors** of the business (known in Sage as Customers).

The amounts from these documents combine to provide the total of the **Sales Ledger**, which is the section of the accounting records which contains all the debtor (Customer) balances. The total of the debtor accounts is recorded in the **Sales Ledger Control Account** (known in Sage as Debtors Control Account). This tells the business how much in total is owing from customers who have bought on credit. The Sales Ledger Control Account is maintained in the Main Ledger, known in Sage as the 'Nominal Ledger'.

## methods of recording invoices and credit notes

When a business uses a computer accounting program such as Sage, it will have to make sure that the details of each invoice and credit note issued are entered into the computer accounting records. Businesses using Sage accounting programs have two alternatives: batch entry and computer printed invoices.

## batch entry

The business produces the invoices independently of the computer program (eg it types or writes them out) and then enters the invoice details into the computer accounting program on a **batch invoice** screen. A 'batch' is simply a group of items (eg a 'batch' of cakes in the oven). The term is used in this context to describe a group of invoices which are all input at one time. This may not be on the day that each invoice is produced – it may be the end of the week, or even the month.

It is normal practice to add up the totals of all the actual invoices that are being input – the 'batch total' – and check this total against the invoice total calculated by the computer from the actual input. This will pick up any errors. A batch invoice entry screen with four invoices input is shown below.

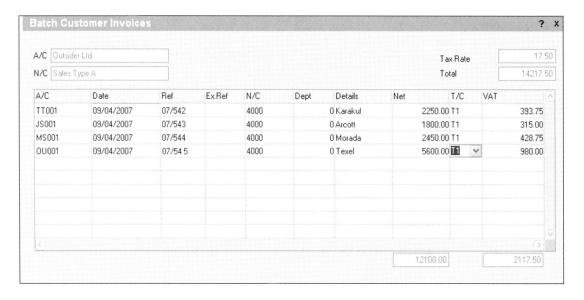

## notes on the data entry columns:

- 'A/C' column contains the customer account reference
- 'Date' is the date on which each invoice was issued
- 'Ref' column is the invoice number (note that they are consecutive)
- 'Ex.Ref' is optional – it could be used for the purchase order number

■ 'N/C' column is the nominal account code which specifies which type of sale is involved

■ 'Dept' is optional and is not used here

■ 'Details' describes the goods that have been sold

■ 'Net' is the amount of the invoice before VAT is added on

■ 'T/C' is the tax code which sets up the VAT rate that applies – here T1 refers to Standard Rate VAT, and is a default rate set up in Sage.

■ 'VAT' is calculated automatically

When the operator has completed the input and checked the batch totals with the computer totals, the batched invoices can be saved.

### computer printed invoices

Most versions of Sage include an invoicing function which requires the business to input the details of each invoice on screen. The computer system will then print out the invoices on the office printer – exactly as input. The invoices can either be for goods, or for a service provided. If the invoice is for goods, 'product' records with product codes will normally have to be set up in Sage, and the product code used each time stock is invoiced.

Service invoices do not require a product code, because no goods are involved in the transaction. An invoice input screen is shown below.

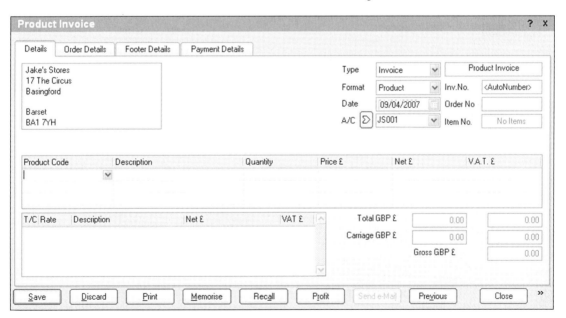

### important note: treatment of invoicing in this book

In this book we will concentrate on the batch entry method of recording invoices and credit notes. It is far simpler to operate and is common to all versions of Sage.

# ROWAN LIMITED:
# PROCESSING SALES INVOICES AND CREDIT NOTES

### entering customer details

The date is 9 April 2007.

Jo has some sales customer accounts to open.

She starts by entering the details she has on file. She does this in Sage by clicking on RECORD in CUSTOMERS. The first customer to input is Trinny's Togs. The information she wants to input is as follows:

| | |
|---|---|
| Account name | Trinny's Togs |
| Account reference | TT001 |
| Address | 24 Shaw Street |
| | Mereford |
| | MR4 6KJ |
| Contact name | Trish Marx |
| Telephone 01905 736271, Fax 01905 736388 | |
| Credit limit £10,000 | Payment terms 30 days |

Jo inputs the data on the 'Details' screen . . .

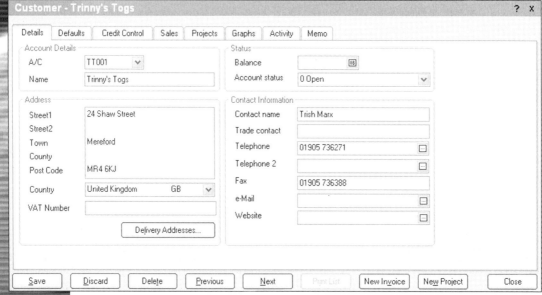

Having saved this data, Jo will go to the CREDIT CONTROL screen and input the credit limit, the 'payment due' of 30 (days), and tick the box marked 'Terms Agreed' and then Save again.

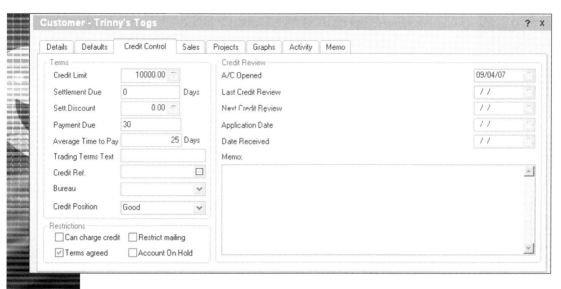

Jo will now repeat this process with the other customer records, checking carefully as she goes and saving each record as it is created.

Jo now needs to input her sales invoices and a credit note she has issued to one of her customers. The first invoice is shown below. Study it in conjunction with the notes on the next page.

# INVOICE

### ROWAN LIMITED

Unit 34 Wordsworth Estate,
Tennyson Road, Maidstone, Kent, ME4 5EW
Tel 01985 811314  Fax 01985 811376  Email sales@rowan.co.uk
VAT Reg GB 0833 2672 10

| invoice to | | | | invoice no | 07/542 |
|---|---|---|---|---|---|
| Trinny's Togs | | | | account | TT001 |
| 24 Shaw Street | | | | your reference | 47609 |
| Mereford | | | | date/tax point | 09 04 07 |
| MR4 6KJ | | | | | |

| description | quantity | price | unit | total |
|---|---|---|---|---|
| Karakul fleeces | 90 | 25.00 | each | 2,250.00 |

| terms | customer a/c reference | main ledger a/c number | goods total | 2,250.00 |
|---|---|---|---|---|
| Net monthly | | | | |
| Carriage paid | TT01 | 4000 | VAT | 393.75 |
| E & OE | | | TOTAL | 2,643.75 |

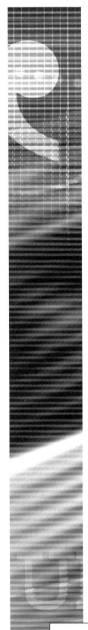

## coding the invoices

Jo will start with the invoice documents by identifying for each one:

- the relevant customer account reference
- the appropriate sales account number ('N/C')

She will enter these coding details in the boxes rubber-stamped on each invoice. The first invoice is shown on the previous page.

The customer account reference here is TT001 ('TT' stands for Trinny's Togs).

The main ledger account number is 4000, which is the usual 'nominal' account number used by Sage for Sales to customers.

## inputting the invoices

When Jo has coded all the invoices she will open the CUSTOMERS screen in Sage and click on the INVOICE icon. This will open the screen shown on the next page.

She must now:

- enter each invoice on a new line in Sage
- take the data from the invoice and input as follows, from the left:
  - customer account reference (the customer reference from the coding box)
  - date (9 April 2007)
  - invoice no. ('Ref'),
  - nominal code ('N/C'), here 4000 from the coding box on the invoice
  - product details
  - the amount before VAT ('net')
  - the T1 tax code for standard rate VAT (T/C)

Note: Jo must check each time that the VAT amount calculated on the screen is the same as the amount on the invoice. If there is a variation, the amount shown on screen should be changed to tally with the VAT on the document.

## checking the input

Before she input all the invoices Jo drew up on paper a 'batch' listing of the invoices. She should now check her original batch totals (the listing is shown below) against the computer totals (Net, VAT and Total). Once she is happy that her input is correct she should then Save.

| **BATCH LISTING – SALES INVOICES ISSUED** | | | | | |
|---|---|---|---|---|---|
| **invoice** | **name** | **date** | **details** | **net amount** | **VAT** |
| 07/542 | Trinny's Togs | 9/04/07 | Karakul | 2250.00 | 393.75 |
| 07/543 | Jake's Stores | 9/04/07 | Arcott | 1800.00 | 315.00 |
| 07/544 | Moorland Supplies | 9/04/07 | Morada | 2450.00 | 428.75 |
| 07/545 | Outsider Ltd | 9/04/07 | Texel | 5600.00 | 980.00 |
| Subtotals | | | | 12100.00 | 2117.50 |
| Batch total | | | | | 14217.50 |

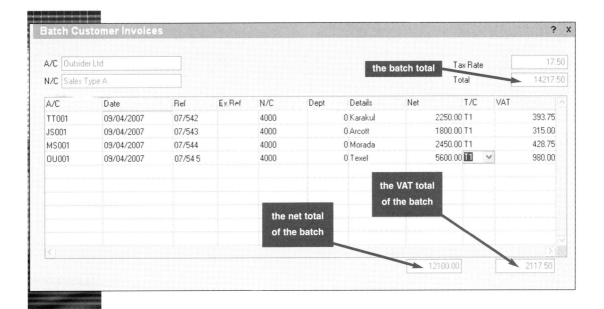

## checking the invoices are on the system

As a further check Jo could print out a Day Book Report. This can be obtained through the REPORTS icon on the CUSTOMER menu bar. The title of the report is 'Day Books: Customer Invoices (Detailed)' and the transaction date range to be entered in the Criteria box is 01/04/07 to 09/04/07. The report is shown below.

Hint: if you cannot see the REPORTS icon on the menu bar you may have to click on an icon on the right which shows a couple of arrows – this will take you to the REPORTS function.

### Rowan Limited
### Day Books: Customer Invoices (Detailed)

| Date From: | 01/04/2007 | | | | | | Customer From: | |
|---|---|---|---|---|---|---|---|---|
| Date To: | 09/04/2007 | | | | | | Customer To: | ZZZZZZZ |
| Transaction From: | 1 | | | | | | N/C From: | |
| Transaction To: | 99999999 | | | | | | N/C To: | 99999999 |
| Dept From: | 0 | | | | | | | |
| Dept To: | 999 | | | | | | | |

| TranNo. | Type | Date | A/C Ref | N/C | Inv Ref | Dept | Details | Net Amount | Tax Amount | T/C | Gross Amount |
|---|---|---|---|---|---|---|---|---|---|---|---|
| 1 | SI | 09/04/2007 | TT001 | 4000 | 07/542 | 0 | Karakul | 2,250.00 | 393.75 | T1 | 2,643.75 |
| 2 | SI | 09/04/2007 | JS001 | 4000 | 07/543 | 0 | Arcott | 1,800.00 | 315.00 | T1 | 2,115.00 |
| 3 | SI | 09/04/2007 | MS001 | 4000 | 07/544 | 0 | Morada | 2,450.00 | 428.75 | T1 | 2,878.75 |
| 4 | SI | 09/04/2007 | OU001 | 4000 | 07/545 | 0 | Texel | 5,600.00 | 980.00 | T1 | 6,580.00 |
| | | | | | | | Totals: | 12,100.00 | 2,117.50 | | 14,217.50 |

## batch credit note entry

Jo also has a credit note to input on 9 April. It is for Jake's Stores, a customer that has returned a faulty fleece. The credit note is shown below. Jo has already coded the document. The customer account reference is 'JS001' and the Sage main ledger account is again 4000.

Note: in the examples in this text, computerised accounting does not use a separate 'returns' account; instead it automatically debits returns to sales account.

---

# CREDIT NOTE

### ROWAN LIMITED
Unit 34 Wordsworth Estate,
Tennyson Road, Maidstone, Kent, ME4 5EW
Tel 01985 811314  Fax 01985 811376  Email sales@rowan.co.uk
VAT Reg GB 0833 2672 10

| to | | | |
|----|----|----|----|
| Jake's Stores<br>17 The Circus<br>Basingford<br>BA1 7YH | credit note no | | CN046 |
| | account | | JS001 |
| | your reference | | 71604 |
| | date/tax point | | 9 04 07 |

| description | quantity | price | unit | total |
|-------------|----------|-------|------|-------|
| Morada fleece | 1 | 35.00 | each | 35.00 |

| reason for credit: | customer a/c reference | main ledger a/c number | goods total | 35.00 |
|---|---|---|---|---|
| faulty goods | JS001 | 4000 | VAT | 6.13 |
| | | | TOTAL | 41.13 |

---

Jo will input the details from the credit note in much the same way as she processed the invoices. She will start by opening up the CUSTOMERS screen in Sage and clicking on the CREDIT icon.

This will show the screen shown at the top of the next page. She will then identify the account references for the customer and the Sales account numbers and input the credit note details as shown on the screen. When the input is complete she should check her batch totals against the computer totals (Net, VAT and Total). Once she is happy that her input is correct she should SAVE. Note that the input will be in red type.

## checking the credit note is on the system

As a further check Jo could print out a Day Book Report for credit notes. This can be obtained through the REPORTS icon on the CUSTOMER toolbar. The title of the report is 'Day Books: Customer Credits (Detailed)' and the transaction date range to be entered in the Criteria box is 01/04/07 to 09/04/07. The report is shown on the next page.

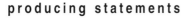

## producing statements

The Sage computerised accounting system is set up to print out statements of account for customers. This will normally be done at the end of the month, but 'one-off' statements can be issued on any date.

For example, if Jake's Stores asked for a statement of account as at 9 April. Jo would highlight Jake's Stores' account in the CUSTOMERS screen and select the STATEMENT icon. She might choose one of the A4 statement options and input a date range ending 09/04/2007 to show all transactions to that date. She would then print out the statement. Sage provides a variety of options for statement formats.

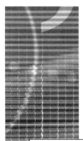

## aged debtors analysis

Sage can also print out a list showing how much each customer owes. This is known as an 'Aged Debtors Analysis' and can be printed as a summary (just the totals owed by each customer) or a detailed list (all invoices and credit notes). It can be accessed via REPORTS in CUSTOMERS.

Note that the appropriate customer(s) will need to be selected first, either on the screen list or by entering an account range.

### Rowan Limited
### Aged Debtors Analysis (Summary)

| Report Date: | 09/04/2007 | | | | | Customer From: | | |
| Include future transactions: | No | | | | | Customer To: | ZZZZZ | |
| Exclude later payments: | No | | | | | | | |

** NOTE: All report values are shown in Base Currency, unless otherwise indicated **

| A/C | Name | | Credit Limit | Turnover | Balance | Future | Current | Period 1 | Period 2 | Period 3 |
|-----|------|---|---|---|---|---|---|---|---|---|
| JS001 | Jake's Stores | £ | 10,000.00 | 1,765.00 | 2,073.87 | 0.00 | 2,073.87 | 0.00 | 0.00 | 0.00 |
| MS001 | Moorland Supplies | £ | 10,000.00 | 2,450.00 | 2,878.75 | 0.00 | 2,878.75 | 0.00 | 0.00 | 0.00 |
| OU001 | Outsider Ltd | £ | 10,000.00 | 5,600.00 | 6,580.00 | 0.00 | 6,580.00 | 0.00 | 0.00 | 0.00 |
| TT001 | Trixxy's Togs | £ | 10,000.00 | 2,250.00 | 2,643.75 | 0.00 | 2,643.75 | 0.00 | 0.00 | 0.00 |
| | Totals: | | | 12,065.00 | 14,176.37 | 0.00 | 14,176.37 | 0.00 | 0.00 | 0.00 |

## checking the input – the trial balance and the audit trail

Jo can now check the balances on her nominal (main) ledger accounts by producing a trial balance. This is produced through FINANCIALS by clicking on the TRIAL icon. Individual transactions to date can also be checked on the Audit Trail (Summary), printed in FINANCIALS by clicking Audit and choosing Summary. These two screen are shown below and on the next page.

Note that Sales Control Account on the Trial Balance is the net total of the VAT charged to customers.

### Rowan Limited
### Period Trial Balance

**To Period:** Month 1, April 2007

| N/C | Name | Debit | Credit |
|-----|------|-------|--------|
| 1100 | Debtors Control Account | 14,176.37 | |
| 2200 | Sales Tax Control Account | | 2,111.37 |
| 4000 | Sales Type A | | 12,065.00 |
| | Totals: | 14,176.37 | 14,176.37 |

## Rowan Limited
## Audit Trail (Summary)

| | | | | | | | | | | | | | |
|---|---|---|---|---|---|---|---|---|---|---|---|---|---|
| Date From: | | | 01/04/2007 | | | | | | | | Customer From: | | |
| Date To: | | | 09/04/2007 | | | | | | | | Customer To: | | |
| | | | | | | | | | | | | | |
| Transaction From: | | | 1 | | | | | | | | Supplier From: | | |
| Transaction To: | | | 99999999 | | | | | | | | Supplier To: | | |
| | | | | | | | | | | | | | |
| Dept From: | | | 0 | | | | | | | | N/C From: | | |
| Dept To: | | | 999 | | | | | | | | N/C To: | | |
| | | | | | | | | | | | | | |
| Exclude Deleted Tran: | | | No | | | | | | | | | | |

| No | Type | Date | A/C | N/C | Dept | Ref | Details | Net | Tax | T/C | Pd | Paid | V |
|---|---|---|---|---|---|---|---|---|---|---|---|---|---|
| 1 | SI | 09.04.2007 | TT001 | 4000 | 0 | 07/542 | Karakul | 2,250.00 | 393.75 | T1 | N | 0.00 | N |
| 2 | SI | 09.04.2007 | JS001 | 4000 | 0 | 07/543 | Arcott | 1,800.00 | 315.00 | T1 | N | 0.00 | N |
| 3 | SI | 09.04.2007 | MS001 | 4000 | 0 | 07/544 | Morada | 2,450.00 | 428.75 | T1 | N | 0.00 | N |
| 4 | SI | 09.04.2007 | OU001 | 4000 | 0 | 07/545 | Texel | 5,600.00 | 980.00 | T1 | N | 0.00 | N |
| 5 | SC | 09.04.2007 | JS001 | 4000 | 0 | CN046 | Morada returned | 35.00 | 6.13 | T1 | N | 0.00 | N |

**Note**

The printouts illustrated here show only the transactions carried out in the Case Study, for reasons of clarity of presentation. In reality there will be further transactions shown on the audit trail and a long list of nominal (main ledger) accounts on the trial balance.

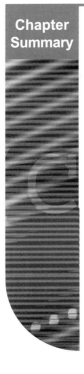

## Chapter Summary

■ The accounting records for selling on credit comprise the accounts of customers (debtors) in the Sales Ledger.

■ Setting up customer records in Sage involves the input of details such as names, addresses and account codes.

■ Details of invoices and credit notes issued are entered into the accounting records of a business. When a computer program is used the details will be input on screen.

■ Computerised accounting programs will either print out the invoices and credit notes after input, or will need to have the details of existing invoices and credit notes input, commonly in batches.

■ Computerised accounting programs will also print out statements of account on demand.

■ Further reports include the Aged Debtors Analysis, the Trial Balance and the Audit Trail.

| Key Terms | | |
|---|---|---|
| | **invoice** | the financial document issued by the seller which sets out the details of the goods sold or services provided, the amount owing and the date by which the amount is due |
| | **credit note** | the financial document – issued by the seller when goods are returned – which reduces the amount owing by the customer |
| | **batch** | a group of documents, eg invoices or credit notes |
| | **batch entry** | the input of a number of documents in a group |
| | **statement** | a financial document which is sent to the customer of a business, listing transactions on the account and advising the total amount owed |
| | **aged debtors analysis** | a list showing how much is owed by each customer |
| | **trial balance** | a list of the accounts of a business divided into two columns: |
| | | *debits* – assets and expenses |
| | | *credits* – income and liabilities |
| | | the two columns should have the same total, reflecting the workings of the double-entry book-keeping system |
| | **audit trail** | a list of transactions entered in the computer, in order of input |

# Student Activities

**Setting up the company**

Before carrying out the inputting exercises in this and the next two chapters you will need to set up Rowan Limited in your Sage system. This should be carried out from 'Company Preferences' and 'Financial Year' in the SETTINGS menu and should include the details set out in the Case Study in the last chapter (see the text and screen illustration on pages 185-186).

**13.1** The sales invoices shown below are the coded invoices input in the Rowan Limited Case Study in this chapter. Using these invoices you are to:

(a) Open accounts in the Sage sales ledger for each customer using the appropriate alphanumeric account reference (eg TT001 for Trinny's Togs). Each account is to have a credit limit of £10,000 and 30 days' terms agreed. Make up other details as appropriate. For the purposes of this exercise do not enter VAT registration numbers.

(b) Making sure that you have set the program date to 9 April 2007 (SETTINGS menu), enter the invoice details from the documents into the computer, as shown in the Case Study.

Check your totals against the batch listing on page 194 before saving and print out a Day Books: Customer Invoices (Detailed) Report to confirm the data that you have saved (see report printout on page 195).

---

| INVOICE | | | | | ROWAN LIMITED |
|---|---|---|---|---|---|

**ROWAN LIMITED**
Unit 34 Wordsworth Estate,
Tennyson Road, Maidstone, Kent, ME4 5EW
Tel 01985 811314  Fax 01985 811376  Email sales@rowan.co.uk
VAT Reg GB 0833 2672 10

invoice to

Trinny's Togs
24 Shaw Street
Mereford
MR4 6KJ

| | |
|---|---|
| invoice no | 07/542 |
| account | TT001 |
| your reference | 47609 |
| date/tax point | 09 04 07 |

| description | quantity | price | unit | total |
|---|---|---|---|---|
| Karakul fleeces | 90 | 25.00 | each | 2,250.00 |

**terms**

Net monthly

Carriage paid

E & OE

| customer a/c reference | main ledger a/c number |
|---|---|
| TT001 | 4000 |

| | |
|---|---|
| **goods total** | 2,250.00 |
| **VAT** | 393.75 |
| **TOTAL** | 2,643.75 |

# INVOICE

**ROWAN LIMITED**
Unit 34 Wordsworth Estate,
Tennyson Road, Maidstone, Kent, ME4 5EW
Tel 01985 811314  Fax 01985 811376  Email sales@rowan.co.uk
VAT Reg GB 0833 2672 10

invoice to

**Jake's Stores**
**17 The Circus**
**Basingford**
**BA1 7YH**

| invoice no | 07/543 |
| account | JS001 |
| your reference | 71631 |
| date/tax point | 09 04 07 |

| description | quantity | price | unit | total |
|---|---|---|---|---|
| **Arcott fleeces** | 60 | 30.00 | each | 1,800.00 |

**terms**

Net monthly

Carriage paid

E & OE

| customer a/c reference | main ledger a/c number |
|---|---|
| JS001 | 4000 |

| | |
|---|---|
| **goods total** | 1,800.00 |
| **VAT** | 315.00 |
| **TOTAL** | 2,115.00 |

# INVOICE

**ROWAN LIMITED**
Unit 34 Wordsworth Estate,
Tennyson Road, Maidstone, Kent, ME4 5EW
Tel 01985 811314  Fax 01985 811376  Email sales@rowan.co.uk
VAT Reg GB 0833 2672 10

invoice to

**Moorland Supplies**
**78 Green Hill Parade**
**Sheepworth**
**SH5 7GG**

| invoice no | 07/544 |
| account | MS001 |
| your reference | 9284 |
| date/tax point | 09 04 07 |

| description | quantity | price | unit | total |
|---|---|---|---|---|
| **Morada Fleeces** | 70 | 35.00 | each | 2,450.00 |

**terms**

Net monthly

Carriage paid

E & OE

| customer a/c reference | main ledger a/c number |
|---|---|
| MS001 | 4000 |

| | |
|---|---|
| **goods total** | 2,450.00 |
| **VAT** | 428.75 |
| **TOTAL** | 2,878.75 |

# INVOICE

**ROWAN LIMITED**
Unit 34 Wordsworth Estate,
Tennyson Road, Maidstone, Kent, ME4 5EW
Tel 01985 811314  Fax 01985 811376  Email sales@rowan.co.uk
VAT Reg GB 0833 2672 10

invoice to

Outsider Limited
Unit 45 Lakeside Estate
Illswater
IL5 8DS

| | |
|---|---|
| invoice no | 07/545 |
| account | OU001 |
| your reference | P7241 |
| date/tax point | 09 04 07 |

| description | quantity | price | unit | total |
|---|---|---|---|---|
| Texel fleeces | 140 | 40.00 | each | 5,600.00 |

**terms**
Net monthly
Carriage paid
E & OE

| customer a/c reference | main ledger a/c number |
|---|---|
| OU001 | 4000 |

| | |
|---|---|
| **goods total** | 5,600.00 |
| **VAT** | 980.00 |
| **TOTAL** | 6,580.00 |

**13.2** The credit note shown below is the coded credit note input in the Rowan Limited Case Study in this chapter. You are to input it into Sage on the computer as shown in the Case Study.

Check the totals before saving, and print out a Day Books: Customer Credits (Detailed) Report to confirm the data that you have saved (see printout on page 197).

| CREDIT NOTE | | | ROWAN LIMITED |
|---|---|---|---|
| | | | Unit 34 Wordsworth Estate, |
| | | | Tennyson Road, Maidstone, Kent, ME4 5EW |
| | | | Tel 01985 811314  Fax 01985 811376  Email sales@rowan.co.uk |
| | | | VAT Reg GB 0833 2672 10 |

| to | | credit note no | CN046 |
|---|---|---|---|
| Jake's Stores | | account | JS001 |
| 17 The Circus | | your reference | 47609 |
| Basingford | | date/tax point | 9 04 07 |
| BA1 7YH | | | |

| description | quantity | price | unit | total |
|---|---|---|---|---|
| Morada fleece | 1 | 35.00 | each | 35.00 |

| reason for credit: | customer a/c reference | main ledger a/c number | goods total | 35.00 |
|---|---|---|---|---|
| faulty goods | JS001 | 4000 | VAT | 6.13 |
| | | | TOTAL | 41.13 |

**13.3** You have been asked to prepare an Aged Debtors Analysis.

Run an Aged Debtor Analysis (Summary) Report (as at 9 April 2007) from REPORTS in CUSTOMERS. Print it out (see illustration on page 198).

**13.4** Your customer Jake's Stores asks you for a statement of account as at 9 April 2007.

Print out a statement (account JS001) from CUSTOMERS. (Note: there is a wide variety of statement layouts available; you should choose one which you think is appropriate).

**13.5** Print out a Trial Balance and Audit Trail (Summary) as at 9 April 2007 to show the balances of the Nominal (Main) Ledger and transactions to date.

The figures should agree with the Trial Balance shown on the next page. If they do, your input is correct. If there are any discrepancies you will need to identify and sort them out before tackling the inputting exercises in the next chapter.

The audit trail is also shown on the next page in case you need to track down any errors.

**Rowan Limited**
**Period Trial Balance**

**To Period:**    Month 1, April 2007

| N/C | Name | Debit | Credit |
|---|---|---|---|
| 1100 | Debtors Control Account | 14,176.37 | |
| 2200 | Sales Tax Control Account | | 2,111.37 |
| 4000 | Sales Type A | | 12,065.00 |
| | Totals: | 14,176.37 | 14,176.37 |

**Rowan Limited**
**Audit Trail (Summary)**

| Date From: | 01/04/2007 | | Customer From: | |
| Date To: | 09/04/2007 | | Customer To: | |
| Transaction From: | 1 | | Supplier From: | |
| Transaction To: | 99999999 | | Supplier To: | |
| Dept From: | 0 | | N/C From: | |
| Dept To: | 999 | | N/C To: | |
| Exclude Deleted Tran: | No | | | |

| No | Type | Date | A/C | N/C | Dept | Ref | Details | Net | Tax | T/C | Pd | Paid | V |
|---|---|---|---|---|---|---|---|---|---|---|---|---|---|
| 1 | SI | 09.04.2007 | TT001 | 4000 | 0 | 07/542 | Karakul | 2,250.00 | 393.75 | T1 | N | 0.00 | N |
| 2 | SI | 09.04.2007 | JS001 | 4000 | 0 | 07/543 | Arcott | 1,800.00 | 315.00 | T1 | N | 0.00 | N |
| 3 | SI | 09.04.2007 | MS001 | 4000 | 0 | 07/544 | Morada | 2,450.00 | 428.75 | T1 | N | 0.00 | N |
| 4 | SI | 09.04.2007 | OU001 | 4000 | 0 | 07/545 | Texel | 5,600.00 | 980.00 | T1 | N | 0.00 | N |
| 5 | SC | 09.04.2007 | JS001 | 4000 | 0 | CN046 | Morada returned | 35.00 | 6.13 | T1 | N | 0.00 | N |

**Reminder! Have you made a backup?**

# 14 Computerised accounting – credit purchases

This chapter should be read in conjunction with the last chapter 'Computerised accounting – credit sales' as it represents 'the other side of the coin' – invoices and credit notes as they are dealt with by the purchaser.

A business purchaser that buys on credit will receive an invoice for the goods or services supplied and will then have to pay at a later date.

Details of invoices and any credit notes received are entered by the purchaser into the account of the supplier in the computerised accounting records. In this way the total amount owing by the purchaser to the supplier is logged into the accounting system.

This chapter continues the Rowan Case Study. It shows how to set up new supplier records and how details of invoices and credit notes received are entered into supplier accounts in the computerised accounting records.

## PERFORMANCE CRITERIA COVERED

### unit 31: ACCOUNTING WORK SKILLS
### element 31.2

**Operate a computerised accounting system**

C    Enter accounting transactions into computerised records.

D    Operate a computerised accounting system including output.

## SETTING UP NEW SUPPLIER RECORDS

In the last chapter we saw how Rowan Limited set up customer records in the computerised Sales Ledger and then entered invoices and a credit note. In this chapter we illustrate the way in which supplier accounts are set up on the computer and supplier invoices and credit notes entered into the computer records. The processes are very similar, as you will see.

A typical supplier record screen is shown below:

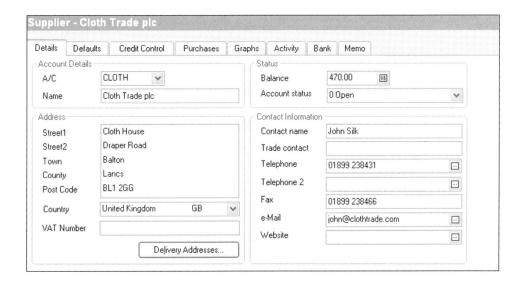

## THE BOOK-KEEPING BACKGROUND

Details of invoices and credit notes received have to be entered into the accounting records of a business that buys on credit. These documents record the sales and refunds made by suppliers who have sold on credit – the **creditors** of the business, known in Sage as 'Suppliers'.

The amounts from these documents combine to provide the total of the **Purchases Ledger**, which is the section of the accounting records which contains all the supplier accounts and their balances. The total of the **Purchases Ledger** is recorded in the **Purchases Ledger Control Account** (known in Sage as Creditors Control Account). This tells the business how much in total it owes to suppliers.

The documents received from the suppliers – invoices and credit notes – are recorded in the computer accounting system on the **batch** basis illustrated in the Case Study in the last chapter.

## PURCHASES AND EXPENSES AND CAPITAL ITEMS

One point that is very important to bear in mind is the difference between **purchases** and **expenses** and **capital items**, as it affects the nominal account codes used when inputting invoices and credit notes on the computer.

**Purchases** are items a business buys which it expects to turn into a product or sell as part of its day-to-day business. For example:

- a business that makes cheese will buy milk to make the cheese
- a supermarket will buy food and clothes to sell to the public

All these items are bought because they will be sold or turned into a product that will be sold. In Sage these purchases will be recorded in a **purchases account**, normally 5000, or a number in that category.

**Expenses,** on the other hand, are items which the business pays for which form part of the business running expenses (overheads), eg rent and electricity. Each expense has a separate nominal account number allocated in the Sage accounting system, by default in the range 6000 to 8299.

**Capital items** are 'one off' items that the business buys and intends to keep for a number of years, for example office equipment and furniture. These also have separate nominal account numbers in the Sage system, by default in the range 0010 to 0059.

The important point here is that all of these items may be bought on credit and each will have to be entered into the computerised accounting records, **but with the correct nominal account number.**

### Case Study

# ROWAN LIMITED: PROCESSING PURCHASE INVOICES AND CREDIT NOTES

### entering supplier details

Jo wishes to enter the details of a number of suppliers. She sets up her Supplier accounts by clicking on RECORD in SUPPLIERS. The date is still 9 April.

The first supplier to input is Johnson Threads. The information she wants to input is shown at the top of the next page. Below this data are the two input screens Jo will have to complete.

The first screen is for the contact details of Johnson Threads.

The second screen is for the credit limit and payment terms agreed by the supplier. The 'terms agreed' box will need be ticked on this second screen.

Account name          Johnson Threads

Account reference     JOHNS

Address               Avent House
                      Otto Way
                      New Milton
                      Norfolk
                      SR1 6TF

Contact name          Usha Patel

Telephone 01722 295875, Fax 01722 295611, Email sales@johnsonthreads.co.uk

Credit limit granted £10,000, payment terms 30 days of invoice date

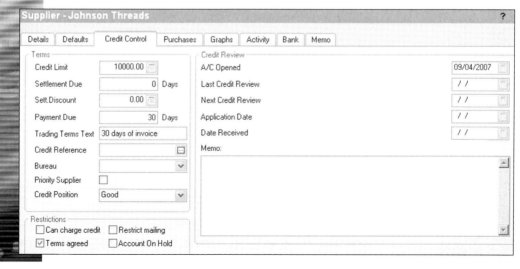

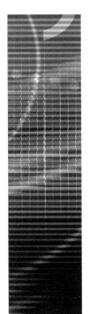

Jo will now repeat this inputting process with the other supplier records, checking carefully as she goes and saving each record as it is created.

Jo has a number of supplier invoices and a supplier credit note to input into the computerised accounting system.

### coding the invoices

Jo will start with the invoices by identifying for each one:

- the relevant supplier account reference
- the appropriate purchase account number ('N/C')

She will enter these in the boxes stamped on each invoice. The first invoice is shown below.

The supplier account reference here is JOHNS.

The main ledger account number (as here) is normally 5000, which is the usual 'nominal' account number used by Sage for purchases of materials from suppliers. The only exception to this is if the purchase is for a capital or expense item, such as a computer or an advertising cost, in which case the appropriate main ledger code ('nominal' code in Sage) should be used.

---

# INVOICE

## JOHNSON THREADS

Avent House, Otto Way
New Milton, SR1 6TF
Tel 01722 295875  Fax 01722 295611  Email sales@johnsonthreads.co.uk
VAT Reg GB 01982 6865 06

| invoice to | | |
|---|---|---|
| Rowan Limited<br>Unit 34 Wordsworth Estate<br>Tennyson Road<br>Maidstone<br>ME4 5EW | | |

| | |
|---|---|
| invoice no | 741736 |
| account | 94122 |
| your reference | 675 |
| date/tax point | 02 04 07 |

| description | quantity | price | unit | total |
|---|---|---|---|---|
| Assorted coloured thread | 200 | 3.00 | 5000m rolls | 600.00 |

**terms**

30 days

Carriage paid

E & OE

| customer a/c reference | main ledger a/c number |
|---|---|
| JOHNS | 5000 |

| | |
|---|---|
| **goods total** | 600.00 |
| **VAT** | 105.00 |
| **TOTAL** | 705.00 |

---

### inputting the invoices

When Jo has coded all the invoices she will open the SUPPLIERS screen in Sage and click on the INVOICE icon. This will open the screen shown on the next page.

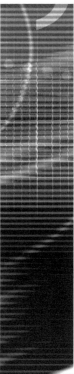

She must now:

- enter each invoice on a new line in Sage
- take the data from the invoice and input as follows, from the left:
  - customer account reference (the customer reference from the coding box)
  - date
  - invoice no. ('Ref'),
  - nominal code ('N/C'), here 5000 from the coding box on the invoice
  - product details
  - the amount before VAT ('net')
  - the T1 tax code for standard rate VAT (T/C)

Note that the Ex Ref, Project Ref & Cost Code columns are not used.

As with the input of sales invoices in the last chapter, Jo must check each time that the VAT amount calculated on the screen is the same as the amount on each invoice. Note that sometimes the VAT on the document will vary by a penny from the VAT on the screen. This is because Sage 'rounds' VAT up or down to the nearest penny, whereas the VAT authorities require that VAT is rounded down to the nearest penny. These one penny differences should be altered on the input screen to tally with the document VAT amount (but never the other way round!).

The batch suppliers' invoice screen will appear like this:

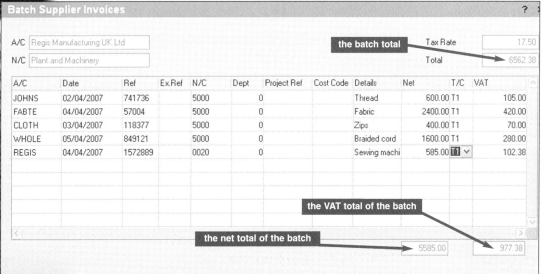

## checking the input

Before she input all the invoices Jo drew up on paper a 'batch' listing of the invoices. She should now check her original batch totals (the listing is shown at the top of the next page) against the computer totals (Net, VAT and Total). When she is happy with her input she should then SAVE.

**PURCHASE INVOICES RECEIVED – BATCH LISTING**

| invoice | name | date | details | net amount | VAT |
|---------|------|------|---------|-----------:|----:|
| 741736 | Johnson Threads | 2/04/07 | Thread | 600.00 | 105.00 |
| 57004 | Fabtech Ltd | 4/04/07 | Fabric | 2400.00 | 420.00 |
| 118377 | Cloth Trade plc | 3/04/07 | Zips | 400.00 | 70.00 |
| 849121 | Wholesale Textiles Ltd | 5/04/07 | Braided cord | 1600.00 | 280.00 |
| 1572889 | Regis Manufacturing UK Ltd | 4/04/07 | MG005 Sewing machine* | 585.00 | 102.38 |
| Subtotals | | | | 5585.00 | 977.38 |
| Batch total | | | | | 6562.38 |

\* Note: this machine is for use within the business and should be coded as a capital term. The appropriate main ledger ('nominal') default code in Sage is 0020 'Plant & Machinery'.

## checking the invoices are on the system

As a further check Jo prints out a Day Book Report. This can be obtained through the REPORTS icon on the SUPPLIER menu bar. The title of the report is 'Day Books: Supplier Invoices (Detailed)' and the transaction date range to be entered in the Criteria box is 01/04/07 to 09/04/07. The report appears as follows:

### Rowan Limited
### Day Books: Supplier Invoices (Detailed)

| Date From: | 01/04/2007 | | | | | | Supplier From: | | |
| Date To: | 09/04/2007 | | | | | | Supplier To: | | ZZZZZZ |

| Transaction From: | 1 | | | | | | N/C From: | | |
| Transaction To: | 99999999 | | | | | | N/C To: | | 99999999 |

| Dept From: | 0 |
| Dept To: | 999 |

| TranNo. | Type | Date | A/C Ref | N/C | Inv Ref | Dept | Details | Net Amount | Tax Amount | T/C | Gross Amount | V |
|---------|------|------|---------|-----|---------|------|---------|-----------:|-----------:|-----|-------------:|---|
| 6 | PI | 02/04/2007 | JOHNS | 5000 | 741736 | 0 | Thread | 600.00 | 105.00 | T1 | 705.00 | N |
| 7 | PI | 04/04/2007 | FABTE | 5000 | 57004 | 0 | Fabric | 2,400.00 | 420.00 | T1 | 2,820.00 | N |
| 8 | PI | 03/04/2007 | CLOTH | 5000 | 118377 | 0 | Zips | 400.00 | 70.00 | T1 | 470.00 | N |
| 9 | PI | 05/04/2007 | WHOLE | 5000 | 849121 | 0 | Braided cord | 1,600.00 | 280.00 | T1 | 1,880.00 | N |
| 10 | PI | 04/04/2007 | REGIS | 0020 | 1572889 | 0 | Sewing machine | 585.00 | 102.38 | T1 | 687.38 | N |
| | | | | | | | Totals | 5,585.00 | 977.38 | | 6,562.38 | |

## batch credit note entry

Jo also has a credit note to input on 9 April. It is from Fabtech Limited, and relates to some damaged fabric received. The credit note is shown at the top of the next page. Jo has already coded the document. The customer account reference is 'FABTE' and the Sage main ledger account is 5000 'Materials Purchases'.

Note that Sage computerised accounting does not use a separate 'returns' account; instead it requires you to debit purchases returns to Materials Purchases account 5000.

# CREDIT NOTE

**FABTECH LIMITED**
Unit 7 Roughway Estate,
Martley Road, Cookford, CO1 9GH
Tel 01843 265432  Fax 01843 265439  Email accounts@fabtech.co.uk
VAT Reg GB 0877 9333  06

to

Rowan Limited
Unit 34 Wordsworth Estate
Tennyson Road
Maidstone
ME4 5EW

| | |
|---|---|
| credit note no | 900736 |
| account | 92423 |
| your reference | 47601 |
| date/tax point | 3  04  07 |

| description | quantity | price | unit | total |
|---|---|---|---|---|
| Morello cotton FW11 | 50 | 3.00 | metre | 150.00 |

**reason for credit:**

damaged fabric

| customer a/c reference | main ledger a/c number |
|---|---|
| FABTE | 5000 |

| | |
|---|---|
| **goods total** | 150.00 |
| **VAT** | 26.25 |
| **TOTAL** | 176.25 |

Jo will input the details from the credit note in much the same way as she processed the invoices. She will start by opening up the SUPPLIERS screen in Sage and clicking on the CREDIT icon.

This will show the screen shown below.  When the input is complete she should check her batch totals against the computer totals (Net, VAT and Total). Once she is happy that her input is correct she should SAVE. Jo's batch sheet is shown on the next page.

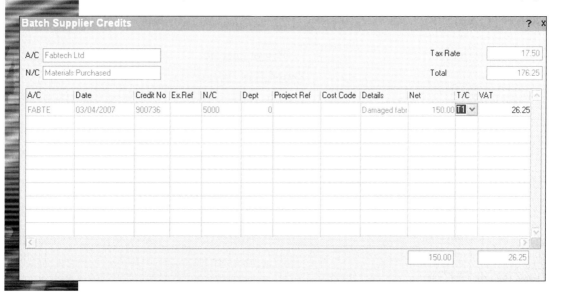

**Batch Supplier Credits**                                    ? X

| A/C | Fabtech Ltd | | | | Tax Rate | 17.50 |
| N/C | Materials Purchased | | | | Total | 176.25 |

| A/C | Date | Credit No | Ex.Ref | N/C | Dept | Project Ref | Cost Code | Details | Net | T/C | VAT |
|---|---|---|---|---|---|---|---|---|---|---|---|
| FABTE | 03/04/2007 | 900736 | | 5000 | 0 | | | Damaged fabr | 150.00 | T1 ∨ | 26.25 |

| | | |
|---|---|---|
| | 150.00 | 26.25 |

**CREDIT NOTES RECEIVED – BATCH LISTING**

| credit note | name | date | details | net amount | VAT |
|---|---|---|---|---|---|
| 900736 | Fabtech Ltd | 3/04/07 | Damaged fabric | 150.00 | 26.25 |
| Subtotals | | | | 150.00 | 26.25 |
| Batch total | | | | | 176.25 |

## checking the credit note is on the system

As a further check Jo could print out a Day Book Report for Supplier Credit notes. This can be obtained through the REPORTS icon on the SUPPLIERS toolbar. The title of the report is 'Day Books: Supplier Credits (Detailed)'. The report appears as follows:

### Rowan Limited
### Day Books: Supplier Credits (Detailed)

| Date From: | 01/04/2007 | | | | | | Supplier From: | | |
| Date To: | 09/04/2007 | | | | | | Supplier To: | ZZZZZZZ |
| Transaction From: | 1 | | | | | | N/C From: | |
| Transaction To: | 99999999 | | | | | | N/C To: | 99999999 |
| Dept From: | 0 | | | | | | | |
| Dept To: | 999 | | | | | | | |

| Tran No. | Type | Date | A/C Ref | N/C | Inv Ref | Dept | Details | Net Amount | Tax Amount | T/C | Gross Amount | V |
|---|---|---|---|---|---|---|---|---|---|---|---|---|
| 11 | PC | 03/04/2007 | FABTE | 5000 | 900736 | 0 | Damaged fabric | 150.00 | 26.25 | T1 | 176.25 | N |
| | | | | | | | Totals | 150.00 | 26.25 | | 176.25 | |

Jo can again check the balances on her nominal (main) ledger accounts by producing the trial balance shown below (it is produced by clicking on the TRIAL icon in FINANCIALS). It shows the control (total) accounts as follows:

Debtors control account £14,176.37 (the net total of the customer transactions)

Creditors control account £6,386.13 (the net total of the supplier transactions)

### Rowan Limited
### Period Trial Balance

**To Period :** Month 1, April 2007

| N/C | Name | Debit | Credit |
|---|---|---|---|
| 0020 | Plant and Machinery | 585.00 | |
| 1100 | Debtors Control Account | 14,176.37 | |
| 2100 | Creditors Control Account | | 6,386.13 |
| 2200 | Sales Tax Control Account | | 2,111.37 |
| 2201 | Purchase Tax Control Account | 951.13 | |
| 4000 | Sales Type A | | 12,065.00 |
| 5000 | Materials Purchased | 4,850.00 | |
| | Totals: | 20,562.50 | 20,562.50 |

Jo can also check how much she owes individual suppliers by printing an Aged Creditor Analysis (Summary) from REPORTS in SUPPLIERS.

## Rowan Limited

### Aged Creditors Analysis (Summary)

| | | | | | | | | | | |
|---|---|---|---|---|---|---|---|---|---|---|
| Report Date: | 09/04/2007 | | | | | Supplier From: | | | | |
| Include future transactions: | No | | | | | Supplier To: | ZZZZZZZ | | | |
| Exclude Later Payments: | No | | | | | | | | | |

** NOTE: All report values are shown in Base Currency, unless otherwise indicated **

| A/C | Name | Credit Limit | Turnover | Balance | Future | Current | Period 1 | Period 2 | Period 3 | Older |
|---|---|---|---|---|---|---|---|---|---|---|
| CLOTH | Cloth Trade plc | £ 10,000.00 | 400.00 | 470.00 | 0.00 | 470.00 | 0.00 | 0.00 | 0.00 | 0.00 |
| FABTE | Fabtech Ltd | £ 10,000.00 | 2,250.00 | 2,643.75 | 0.00 | 2,643.75 | 0.00 | 0.00 | 0.00 | 0.00 |
| JOHNS | Johnson Threads | £ 10,000.00 | 600.00 | 705.00 | 0.00 | 705.00 | 0.00 | 0.00 | 0.00 | 0.00 |
| REGIS | Regis Manufacturing UK Ltd | £ 10,000.00 | 585.00 | 687.38 | 0.00 | 687.38 | 0.00 | 0.00 | 0.00 | 0.00 |
| WHOLE | Wholesale Textiles Ltd | £ 10,000.00 | 1,600.00 | 1,880.00 | 0.00 | 1,880.00 | 0.00 | 0.00 | 0.00 | 0.00 |
| | Totals: | | 5,435.00 | 6,386.13 | 0.00 | 6,386.13 | 0.00 | 0.00 | 0.00 | 0.00 |

## checking nominal postings

Jo can check what has been posted to the Materials Purchased account (N/C 5000) by printing a Nominal Activity Report. She does this by going to NOMINAL (Layout: List), highlighting account 5000 and clicking REPORTS. The transaction date range is 1 April 2007 to 9 April 2007.

## Rowan Limited

### Nominal Activity

| | | | | | | |
|---|---|---|---|---|---|---|
| Date From: | 01/04/2007 | | | | N/C From: | |
| Date To: | 09/04/2007 | | | | N/C To: | 99999999 |
| Transaction From: | 1 | | | | | |
| Transaction To: | 99999999 | | | | | |

| N/C: | 5000 | | Name: | Materials Purchased | | | | Account Balance: | | 4,850.00 DR | | |

| No | Type | Date | Account | Ref | Details | Dept | T/C | Value | Debit | Credit | V | B |
|---|---|---|---|---|---|---|---|---|---|---|---|---|
| 6 | PI | 02/04/2007 | JOHNS | 741736 | Thread | 0 | T1 | 600.00 | 600.00 | | N | - |
| 7 | PI | 04/04/2007 | FABTE | 57004 | Fabric | 0 | T1 | 2,400.00 | 2,400.00 | | N | - |
| 8 | PI | 03/04/2007 | CLOTH | 118377 | Zips | 0 | T1 | 400.00 | 400.00 | | N | - |
| 9 | PI | 05/04/2007 | WHOLE | 849121 | Braided cord | 0 | T1 | 1,600.00 | 1,600.00 | | N | - |
| 11 | PC | 03/04/2007 | FABTE | 900736 | Damaged fabric | 0 | T1 | 150.00 | | 150.00 | N | - |
| | | | | | | | Totals: | | 5,000.00 | 150.00 | | |
| | | | | | | | History Balance: | | 4,850.00 | | | |

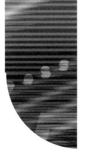

## what next?

Jo has now entered into her computer:

- customer and supplier details
- customer invoices and a credit note (in the last chapter)
- supplier invoices and a credit note (in this chapter)

The next chapter shows how she enters details of payments made to suppliers and payments received from customers.

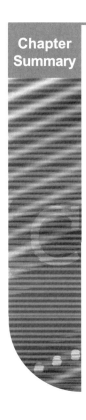

**Chapter Summary**

■ The accounting records for buying on credit comprise the accounts of suppliers (creditors) in the Purchases Ledger.

■ When a business buys on credit it will receive invoices and sometimes credit notes from its suppliers.

■ The details of invoices and credit notes received must be entered into the accounting records of a business. If a computer program is used the details are input on screen and reports may be printed out.

■ Setting up supplier records in Sage involves the input of details such as names, addresses and account codes.

■ In the case of supplier invoices and credit notes it is important that the correct Nominal account number is used to describe whether the transaction relates to purchases, expenses or capital items.

■ It is essential to check the details of invoices and credit notes before input and the details of input by printing out, for example, a day book report.

■ When a group of invoices or credit notes is input, it is common practice to list them and total them on a batch listing. This provides a useful check for the accuracy of the input.

**Key Terms**

| | |
|---|---|
| **credit purchase** | a purchase made where payment is due at a later date |
| **creditors** | suppliers to whom the business owes money |
| **purchases ledger** | the part of the accounting system where the suppliers' accounts are kept |
| **purchases** | items bought which will be turned into a product or be sold as part of day-to-day-trading |
| **expenses** | payments made which relate to the running of the business – also known as overheads |
| **capital items** | items bought which the business intends to keep |
| **batch** | a group of documents, eg invoices or credit notes |

# Student Activities

**14.1**   The purchase invoices shown below are the coded invoices input in the Rowan Limited Case Study in this chapter. You are to:

   (a)   Open accounts in the Sage purchases ledger for each supplier using the appropriate account reference (eg JOHNS for Johnson Threads).

   Make up contact names and other details which may not be on the invoices.

   For the purposes of this exercise do not enter VAT registration numbers.

   Each account is to to be marked with a credit limit of £10,000 and 30 days' terms agreed.

   (b)   Making sure that you have set the program date to 9 April 2007 (SETTINGS menu), enter the invoice details from the documents into the computer, as shown in the Case Study.

   Check your totals against the batch sheet before saving and print out a Day Books: Supplier Invoices (Detailed) Report to confirm the data that you have saved (see report printout on page 212).

---

# INVOICE         JOHNSON THREADS

Avent House, Otto Way
New Milton, SR1 6TF
Tel 01722 295875  Fax 01722 295611  Email sales@johnsonthreads.co.uk
VAT Reg GB 01982 6865 06

| invoice to | | | |
|---|---|---|---|
| Rowan Limited<br>Unit 34 Wordsworth Estate<br>Tennyson Road<br>Maidstone<br>ME4 5EW | invoice no | | 741736 |
| | account | | 94122 |
| | your reference | | 675 |
| | date/tax point | | 02 04 07 |

| description | quantity | price | unit | total |
|---|---|---|---|---|
| Assorted coloured thread | 200 | 3.00 | 5000m rolls | 600.00 |

| terms<br>30 days<br>Carriage paid<br>E & OE | customer a/c reference | main ledger a/c number | | |
|---|---|---|---|---|
| | JOHNS | 5000 | goods total | 600.00 |
| | | | VAT | 105.00 |
| | | | TOTAL | 705.00 |

# INVOICE

**FABTECH LIMITED**

Unit 7 Roughway Estate,
Martley Road, Cookford, CO1 9GH
Tel 01843 265432  Fax 01843 265439  Email accounts@fabtech.co.uk
VAT Reg GB 0877 9333  06

| invoice to | | | |
|---|---|---|---|
| Rowan Limited<br>Unit 34 Wordsworth Estate<br>Tennyson Road<br>Maidstone<br>ME4 5EW | invoice no | 57004 | |
| | account | 92423 | |
| | your reference | 672 | |
| | date/tax point | 04 04 07 | |

| description | quantity | price | unit | total |
|---|---|---|---|---|
| Fleece fabric, marine blue | 800 | 3.00 | metres | 2,400.00 |

| terms | customer a/c reference | main ledger a/c number | | |
|---|---|---|---|---|
| 30 days<br>Carriage paid<br>E & OE | FABTE | 5000 | goods total | 2,400.00 |
| | | | VAT | 420.00 |
| | | | TOTAL | 2,820.00 |

# INVOICE

## CLOTH TRADE PLC

Cloth House, Draper Road
Balton, BL1 2GG
Tel 01899 238431  Fax 01899 238466  Email sales@clothtrade.com
VAT Reg GB 08822 6865 03

| invoice to | | | |
|---|---|---|---|
| Rowan Limited<br>Unit 34 Wordsworth Estate<br>Tennyson Road<br>Maidstone<br>ME4 5EW | invoice no | 118377 | |
| | account | 4324 | |
| | your reference | 667 | |
| | date/tax point | 03 04 07 | |

| description | quantity | price | unit | total |
|---|---|---|---|---|
| Zips Z12, 200mm | 1000 | 0.40 | each | 400.00 |

| terms | customer a/c reference | main ledger a/c number | | |
|---|---|---|---|---|
| 30 days<br>Carriage paid<br>E & OE | CLOTH | 5000 | goods total | 400.00 |
| | | | VAT | 70.00 |
| | | | TOTAL | 470.00 |

# Wholesale Textiles Limited

**INVOICE**

Unit 34, Brunswick Estate
Brownville, BR1 9VC
Tel 01644 592382  Fax 01644 592313  Email sales@wholesaletextiles.co.uk
VAT Reg GB 9876 6112 08

invoice to

Rowan Limited
Unit 34 Wordsworth Estate
Tennyson Road
Maidstone
ME4 5EW

| | |
|---|---|
| invoice no | 849121 |
| account | R8913 |
| your reference | 673 |
| date/tax point | 05 04 07 |

| description | quantity | price | unit | total |
|---|---|---|---|---|
| Braided cord, Red | 40 | 40.00 | 500m rolls | 1,600.00 |

**terms**

30 days

Carriage paid

E & OE

| customer a/c reference | main ledger a/c number |
|---|---|
| WHOLE | 5000 |

| | |
|---|---|
| **goods total** | 1,600.00 |
| **VAT** | 280.00 |
| **TOTAL** | 1,880.00 |

---

**INVOICE**

# REGIS MANUFACTURING (UK) LTD

Regis House, Basil Park
Tewkesbury, GL8 8HG
Tel 01424 234575  Fax 01424 234534 Email accounts@regismanufacturing.co.uk
VAT Reg GB 98671 7624 09

invoice to

Rowan Limited
Unit 34 Wordsworth Estate
Tennyson Road
Maidstone
ME4 5EW

| | |
|---|---|
| invoice no | 1572889 |
| account | RL3221 |
| your reference | 671 |
| date/tax point | 04 04 07 |

| description | quantity | price | unit | total |
|---|---|---|---|---|
| MG005 sewing machine | 1 | 585.00 | each | 585.00 |

**terms**

30 days

Carriage paid

E & OE

| customer a/c reference | main ledger a/c number |
|---|---|
| REGIS | 0020 |

| | |
|---|---|
| **goods total** | 585.00 |
| **VAT** | 102.38 |
| **TOTAL** | 687.38 |

**14.2** The credit note shown below is the coded credit note input in the Rowan Limited Case Study in this chapter. You are to input it into Sage on the computer as shown in the Case Study.

Check the totals before saving, and print out a Day Books: Supplier Credits (Detailed) Report to confirm the data that you have saved (see report printout on page 214).

| CREDIT NOTE | | | FABTECH LIMITED |
|---|---|---|---|

Unit 7 Roughway Estate,
Martley Road, Cookford, CO1 9GH
Tel 01843 265432  Fax 01843 265439  Email accounts@fabtech.co.uk
VAT Reg GB 0877 9333  06

to

Rowan Limited
Unit 34 Wordsworth Estate
Tennyson Road
Maidstone
ME4 5EW

| | |
|---|---|
| credit note no | 900736 |
| account | 92423 |
| your reference | 47601 |
| date/tax point | 3 04 07 |

| description | quantity | price | unit | total |
|---|---|---|---|---|
| Morello cotton FW11 | 50 | 3.00 | metre | 150.00 |

**reason for credit:**
damaged fabric

| customer a/c reference | main ledger a/c number |
|---|---|
| FABTE | 5000 |

| | |
|---|---|
| goods total | 150.00 |
| VAT | 26.25 |
| TOTAL | 176.25 |

**14.3** When you have completed activities 14.1 and 14.2, print out a trial balance dated 9 April 2007.

Check your trial balance against the figures shown at the top of the next page. If you have any differences, print out and check the audit trail to identify any errors.

**14.4** Run and print out an Aged Creditors Analysis (Summary) from REPORTS in SUPPLIERS to show the position of the Purchases Ledger as at 9 April 2007 (see screen on the middle of the next page).

**14.5** Print a Nominal Activity Report for account 5000 Materials Purchased. You do this by going to NOMINAL (View Layout), highlighting account 5000 and clicking REPORTS. Use the date range 1 April to 9 April 2007.

Check the report against the printout at the bottom of the next page for accuracy.

Someone asks you why the invoice from Regis Manufacturing is missing from this report. What would your answer be?

## Rowan Limited
### Period Trial Balance

**To Period:**    Month 1, April 2007

| N/C | Name | Debit | Credit |
|---|---|---|---|
| 0020 | Plant and Machinery | 585.00 | |
| 1100 | Debtors Control Account | 14,176.37 | |
| 2100 | Creditors Control Account | | 6,386.13 |
| 2200 | Sales Tax Control Account | | 2,111.37 |
| 2201 | Purchase Tax Control Account | 951.13 | |
| 4000 | Sales Type A | | 12,065.00 |
| 5000 | Materials Purchased | 4,850.00 | |
| | Totals: | 20,562.50 | 20,562.50 |

---

## Rowan Limited
### Aged Creditors Analysis (Summary)

| | | |
|---|---|---|
| Report Date: | 09/04/2007 | |
| Include future transactions: | No | Supplier From: |
| Exclude Later Payments: | No | Supplier To:   ZZZZZZZZ |

** NOTE: All report values are shown in Base Currency, unless otherwise indicated **

| A/C | Name | Credit Limit | Turnover | Balance | Future | Current | Period 1 | Period 2 | Period 3 | Older |
|---|---|---|---|---|---|---|---|---|---|---|
| CLOTH | Cloth Trade plc | £ 10,000.00 | 400.00 | 470.00 | 0.00 | 470.00 | 0.00 | 0.00 | 0.00 | 0.00 |
| FABTE | Fabtech Ltd | £ 10,000.00 | 2,250.00 | 2,643.75 | 0.00 | 2,643.75 | 0.00 | 0.00 | 0.00 | 0.00 |
| JOHNS | Johnson Threads | £ 10,000.00 | 600.00 | 705.00 | 0.00 | 705.00 | 0.00 | 0.00 | 0.00 | 0.00 |
| REGIS | Regis Manufacturing UK Ltd | £ 10,000.00 | 585.00 | 687.38 | 0.00 | 687.38 | 0.00 | 0.00 | 0.00 | 0.00 |
| WHOLE | Wholesale Textiles Ltd | £ 10,000.00 | 1,600.00 | 1,880.00 | 0.00 | 1,880.00 | 0.00 | 0.00 | 0.00 | 0.00 |
| | Totals: | | 5,435.00 | 6,386.13 | 0.00 | 6,386.13 | 0.00 | 0.00 | 0.00 | 0.00 |

---

## Rowan Limited
### Nominal Activity

| | | | | |
|---|---|---|---|---|
| Date From: | 01/04/2007 | | N/C From: | |
| Date To: | 09/04/2007 | | N/C To: | 99999999 |
| Transaction From: | 1 | | | |
| Transaction To: | 99999999 | | | |

| N/C: | 5000 | Name: | Materials Purchased | | Account Balance: | 4,850.00 DR |
|---|---|---|---|---|---|---|

| No | Type | Date | Account | Ref | Details | Dept | T/C | Value | Debit | Credit | V | B |
|---|---|---|---|---|---|---|---|---|---|---|---|---|
| 6 | PI | 02/04/2007 | JOHNS | 741736 | Thread | 0 | T1 | 600.00 | 600.00 | | N | - |
| 7 | PI | 04/04/2007 | FABTE | 57004 | Fabric | 0 | T1 | 2,400.00 | 2,400.00 | | N | - |
| 8 | PI | 03/04/2007 | CLOTH | 118377 | Zips | 0 | T1 | 400.00 | 400.00 | | N | - |
| 9 | PI | 05/04/2007 | WHOLE | 849121 | Braided cord | 0 | T1 | 1,600.00 | 1,600.00 | | N | - |
| 11 | PC | 03/04/2007 | FABTE | 900736 | Damaged fabric | 0 | T1 | 150.00 | | 150.00 | N | - |
| | | | | | | | Totals: | | 5,000.00 | 150.00 | | |
| | | | | | | | History Balance: | | 4,850.00 | | | |

**Reminder! Have you made a backup?**

# Computerised accounting – payments

So far in this book we have dealt with accounts for customers and suppliers and entered details of financial documents. But we have not covered the way in which the computerised accounting system records the payment of money by customers to the business or by the business to suppliers.

The bank account is central to any accounting system as the payment of money is vital to all business transactions.

The bank account is used not only for payments by customers and to suppliers (credit transactions), but also for transactions for which settlement is made straightaway (cash transactions).

The Case Study in this chapter – a continuation of Rowan Limited – explains how payments made and received are recorded in the computerised accounting system.

The chapter concludes by illustrating other aspects of computerised accounting payments:

- dealing with cash payments
- the setting up of a petty cash account on the computer
- journal entries
- bad debt write off
- bank reconciliation statements

## PERFORMANCE CRITERIA COVERED

### unit 31: ACCOUNTING WORK SKILLS

### element 31.2

### Operate a computerised accounting system

C   Enter accounting transactions into computerised records.

D   Operate a computerised accounting system including output.

## THE BANK ACCOUNTS IN COMPUTER ACCOUNTING

The bank accounts and all the functions associated with them are found in Sage by clicking on the BANK icon in the main menu bar. The BANK screen then appears as shown below.

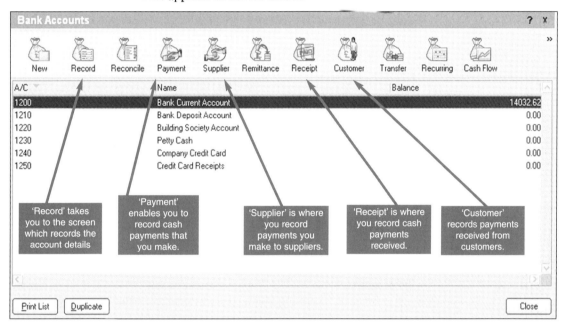

### types of bank account

The accounts listed above come from the default list provided by Sage for the Nominal (Main) Ledger. The business does not have to adopt all the bank accounts listed here, but may use some of them if it needs them:

■ **bank current account** records all payments in and out of the bank 'cheque' account used for everyday purposes – it is the most commonly used account

■ **bank deposit account** and **building society account** can be used if the business maintains interest-paying accounts for savings and for money that is not needed in the short term

■ **petty cash account** can be used if the business maintains a petty cash system in the office for small purchases such as stationery and stamps

■ **company credit card account** can be used if the business uses credit cards for its employees to pay for expenses

■ **credit card receipts account** can be used if the business receives a significant number of credit card payments from its customers

### cash or credit payments?

A number of icons on the menu bar record payments which are either:

■ **cash payments** – ie made straightaway without the need for invoices or credit notes

■ **credit payments** – ie made in settlement of invoices

The problem is, which is which? The rule is:

    =  **cash payments** (not involving credit customers or suppliers)

    =  **credit payments** (payments from customers and to suppliers in settlement of accounts)

### bank accounts in Sage

It must be stressed that if a Sage computerised account number is listed on the BANK screen it does not *have* to be used. It is there so that it can be used if the business needs it. The Bank Current Account for example, is always going to be used, assuming businesses always have bank current accounts!

## RECORDING PAYMENTS FROM CUSTOMERS

### how do payments arrive?

When a payment arrives from a customer who has bought on credit it will normally arrive at the business in one of two ways:

■ A cheque and **remittance advice**. A remittance advice is a document stating what the payment relates to – eg which invoices and credit notes.

■ A remittance advice stating that the money has been sent direct to the business bank account in the form of a **BACS payment** (a BACS [Bankers Automated Clearing Services] payment is a payment sent direct between the banks' computers and does not involve a cheque).

Examples of cheque and BACS remittance advices are shown on the next page. These relate to payments made to Rowan Limited – which features in the Case Studies in these computerised accounting chapters.

```
┌─────────────────────────────────────────────────────────────────────────────┐
│  TO                  REMITTANCE ADVICE   FROM                                 │
│ ┌──────────────────────────────────┐   ┌──────────────────────────────────┐  │
│ │ Rowan Limited                    │   │ Compsync                         │  │
│ │ Unit 34 Wordsworth Estate        │   │ 4 Friar Street                   │  │
│ │ Tennyson Road                    │   │ Broadfield                       │  │
│ │ Maidstone, ME4 5EW               │   │ BR1 3RF                          │  │
│ └──────────────────────────────────┘   │ Tel 01908 761234 Fax 01908 761987│ │
│                                         │ VAT REG GB 0745 8383 56          │  │
│  Account 3993          6 November 2007  └──────────────────────────────────┘  │
└─────────────────────────────────────────────────────────────────────────────┘
```

| date | your reference | our reference | payment amount |
|------|----------------|---------------|----------------|
| 01 10 07 | INVOICE 07/923 | 47609 | 277.30 |
| 10 10 07 | CREDIT NOTE CN59 | 47609 | (27.73) |
| | | **CHEQUE TOTAL** | 249.57 |

## BACS REMITTANCE ADVICE

FROM: Excelsior Fashions
17 Gatley Way
Bristol BS1 9GH

TO
Rowan Limited, Unit 34 Wordsworth Estate
Tennyson Road, Maidstone, ME4 5EW                  06 12 07

| Your ref | Our ref | | Amount |
|----------|---------|------|--------|
| 07/998 | 3323 | BACS TRANSFER | 465.00 |
| | | TOTAL | 465.00 |

THIS HAS BEEN PAID BY BACS CREDIT TRANSFER DIRECTLY INTO YOUR BANK ACCOUNT AT ALBION
BANK NO 11719881 SORT CODE 90 47 17 FOR VALUE 11 12 07

## customer payments and the accounting system

An incoming payment from a customer settling one or more invoices (less any credit notes) needs to be recorded in the accounting system:

- the balance of bank account will increase (a debit in double-entry)
- the balance of the customer's account (and the Sales Ledger Control Account ['Debtors Control Account' in Sage]) will decrease because the customer will owe less (a credit in double-entry accounting)

In computerised accounting the payment is input once and the entries will be automatically made from the same screen. Any settlement discount involved will also be entered on the screen and the account entries made automatically.

## the practicalities

The business will normally input a number of payments at one time on a regular basis, eg every week, using a batch of remittance advices as the source documentation, together with a totalled batch listing. The remittance advices will have all the details required (date, amount, invoices paid) and in the case of a BACS payment it is the only document relating to the payment the business will have.

The appropriate bank account should first be selected on the BANK screen and then the CUSTOMER icon selected to access the Customer Receipt input screen:

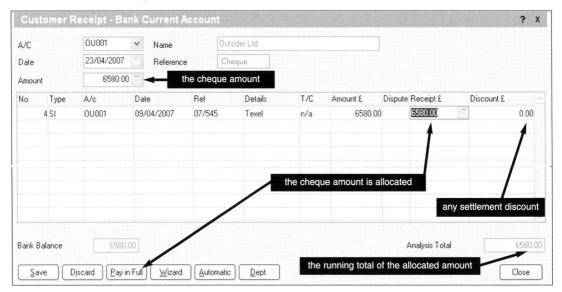

## processing the payments received

The procedure for recording the customer payment on this screen is to:

- input the customer account reference – this will bring up on screen the account name and all the outstanding amounts due on invoices

- input a reference if required – for example you might key in 'cheque' or 'BACS' or the numerical reference relating to the payment

- input the amount of the payment in the Amount box

- click on the 'Receipt' box of the invoice that is being paid

- click on the 'Pay in Full' button at the bottom

- if cash or settlement discount has been deducted from the payment, enter the net amount received in the Receipt box and the discount taken in the Discount box

- if there is more than one invoice being paid click on each of the items being paid; the Analysis Total box at the bottom will show a running total of the money allocated

- if there is a long list of invoices and a payment to cover them, click on 'Automatic' at the bottom and the computer will allocate the payment down the invoice list until the money amount of the payment runs out

- if a credit note is included in the net payment, click in the Receipt box on the credit note line first (recognised by SC in the *Type* column) and click on 'Pay in Full'; this picks up the value of the credit note and puts a minus figure in the analysis total; now you can pay any remaining invoices as shown above

- check that what you have done is correct and SAVE; details to check are:
  - customer, amount, invoices being paid and amount received
  - the amounts in the Amount box and the Analysis Total box should be the same (but see next point)

- if the amount received is greater than the amount allocated to outstanding invoices the extra payment will show as a 'Payment on Account' after you have saved

- if the amount received is less than the amount of the invoice(s) it is settling, the part-payment received should be allocated to the appropriate invoice(s) and the unpaid amount will show as outstanding on the Customer's account

- you should print out a Day Books: Customer Receipts (Summary) for these transactions from REPORTS in BANK to check that the total of the cheques (or BACS payments) received on your batch listing equals the total input into the computer

## RECORDING PAYMENTS TO SUPPLIERS

### what documents are involved?

A business pays its suppliers on the invoice due dates or after it receives a **statement** setting out the amounts due from invoices and any deductions made following the issue of credit notes.

Payment is often made by cheque, although some payments may be made by BACS transfer between the banks' computers. Payment is normally made in full, but occasionally a part-payment may be made. A typical payment cheque, together with a completed counterfoil (cheque stub) is shown on the next page. This relates to the Case Study in this chapter (see page 232).

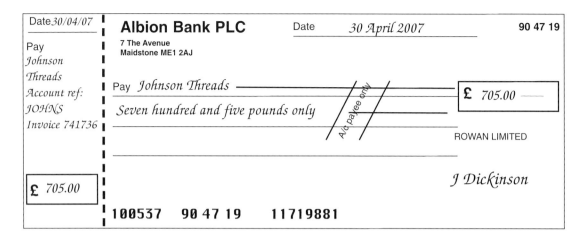

The business will send a **remittance advice** (see page 225) to the supplier with the cheque, or, if a BACS payment is being made, on its own. The remittance advice will normally provide the details for the input of the payment details on the computer.

Some programs can print remittance advices on the computer when the payment is sent off. If the business decides to do this, the payment details are likely to be taken from the completed cheque and counterfoil. Some computerised accounting programs which deal with long 'cheque runs' will also print the cheques themselves on special preprinted cheque stationery.

## supplier payments and the accounting system

Payment to a supplier settling one or more invoices (less any credit notes) needs to be recorded in the accounting system:

- the balance of bank account will decrease (a credit in double-entry)
- the balance of the supplier's account (and the Purchases Ledger Control Account ['Creditors Control Account' in Sage]) will decrease because the supplier will be owed less (a debit in double-entry accounting)

In computerised accounting the payment is input once and the entries will be automatically made from the same screen and the double-entry accounts posted automatically.

## processing the payments

As with customer receipts, the business will normally input a number of payments at one time on a regular basis, for example just after the cheques have been written out or the BACS payment instructions prepared.

The payments are input in Sage from the SUPPLIER icon on the BANK screen – after the appropriate bank account has been selected.

The procedure for recording the supplier payment is to:

- input the supplier reference in the box next to the word 'Payee' on the 'cheque' – this will bring up on screen the account name and all the outstanding amounts due on invoices

- input the cheque number on the cheque and alter the date if the cheque date is different

- input the amount of the payment in the amount box on the cheque; if it is a part payment the same procedure will be followed

- click on the Payment box of the invoice that is being paid  and click on the 'Pay in full' icon at the bottom; if there is more than one invoice being paid click on the items being paid as appropriate; any part payment will be allocated to the appropriate invoice(s) in the same way

- check that what you have done is correct (ie supplier, amount, invoices being paid), and SAVE

- print out a Day Books: Customer Payments (Summary) from REPORTS in BANK to check that the total of the cheques (or BACS payments) issued equals the total input on the computer

The treatment of settlement discount and credit notes is the same for supplier payments as for customer receipts (see page 226).

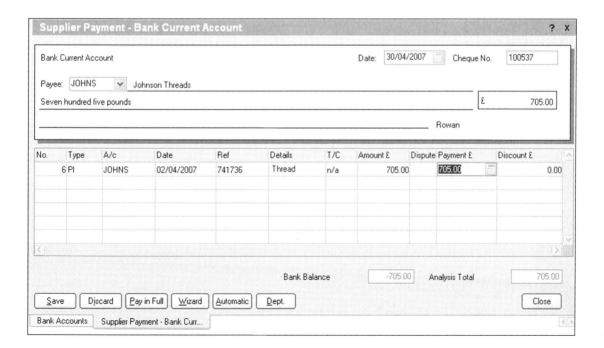

We will now look at the way in which Jo Dickinson's business, Rowan Limited, inputs its payments from customers and payments to suppliers on the computer.

# ROWAN LIMITED: PROCESSING PAYMENTS FROM CUSTOMERS AND TO SUPPLIERS

It is April 23 2007. Jo has received a BACS remittance advice from Jake's Stores and three cheques (with remittance advices) from her customers in settlement of invoices.

Jo also has two supplier invoices to pay. She deals with the payments received first.

### receipts from customers

The payments received are listed below.

| **cheques** | | |
|---|---|---|
| Outsider Ltd | £6580.00 | (pays invoice 07/545) |
| Moorland Supplies | £2878.75 | (pays invoice  07/544) |
| Trinny's Togs | £2500.00 | (part-pays invoice 07/542) |
| **BACS advice** | | |
| Jake's Stores | £2073.87 | (pays invoice 07/543 less c/note CN046) |
| Batch total | £14,032.62 | |

These four payments are entered into the computerised accounting system under CUSTOMER in the BANK section. The first payment is shown on the screen below.

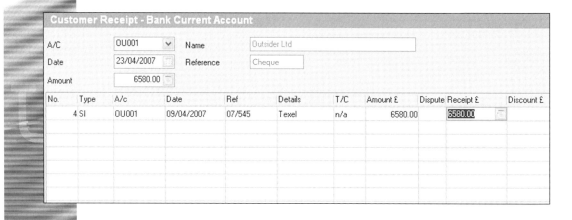

Jo then prints out a report 'Day Books: Customer Receipts (Summary)' from Reports in BANK, which shows the transactions she has processed.  This is illustrated below. She checks the total on the report against the batch total of the remittance advices (including the BACS advice) she has received.

### Rowan Limited
#### Day Books: Customer Receipts (Summary)

| | | | | | | | | | | | | |
|---|---|---|---|---|---|---|---|---|---|---|---|---|
| Date From: | | 01/04/2007 | | | | | | | Bank From: | | | |
| Date To: | | 30/04/2007 | | | | | | | Bank To: | | | 9999999 |
| Transaction From: | | 1 | | | | | | | Customer From: | | | |
| Transaction To: | | 99999999 | | | | | | | Customer To: | | | ZZZZZZ |

Bank  1200    Currency   Pound Sterling

| No | Type | Date | Account | Ref | Details | Net £ | Tax £ | Gross £ B |
|---|---|---|---|---|---|---|---|---|
| 12 | SR | 23/04/2007 | OU001 | Cheque | Sales Receipt | 6,580.00 | 0.00 | 6,580.00 N |
| 13 | SR | 23/04/2007 | MS001 | Cheque | Sales Receipt | 2,878.75 | 0.00 | 2,878.75 N |
| 14 | SR | 23/04/2007 | TT001 | Cheque | Sales Receipt | 2,500.00 | 0.00 | 2,500.00 N |
| 15 | SR | 23/04/2007 | JS001 | BACS | Sales Receipt | 2,073.87 | 0.00 | 2,073.87 N |
| | | | | | Totals £ | 14,032.62 | 0.00 | 14,032.62 |

Jo has noticed that her customer Trinny's Togs did not pay the full amount owed.

As a reminder to follow this up she highlights Trinny's Togs' account in CUSTOMERS and prints out a Customer Activity (Detailed) Report for this customer.

### Rowan Limited
#### Customer Activity (Detailed)

| | | | | | | |
|---|---|---|---|---|---|---|
| Date From: | 01/04/2007 | | | Customer From: | | |
| Date To: | 30/04/2007 | | | Customer To: | | ZZZZZZ |
| Transaction From: | 1 | | | N/C From: | | |
| Transaction To: | 99999999 | | | N/C To: | | 9999999 |
| Inc b/fwd transaction: | No | | | Dept From: | | 0 |
| Exc later payment: | No | | | Dept To: | | 999 |

** NOTE: All report values are shown in Base Currency, unless otherwise indicated **

A/C:  TT001   Name:  Trinny's Togs        Contact:              Tel:

| No | Type | Date | Ref | N/C | Details | Dept | T/C | Value | O/S | Debit | Credit |
|---|---|---|---|---|---|---|---|---|---|---|---|
| 1 | SI | 09/04/2007 | 07/542 | 4000 | Karakul | 0 | T1 | 2,643.75 p | 143.75 | 2,643.75 | |
| 14 | SR | 23/04/2007 | Cheque | 1200 | Sales Receipt | 0 | T9 | 2,500.00 | | | 2,500.00 |
| | | | | | Totals: | | | 143.75 | 143.75 | 2,643.75 | 2,500.00 |

Amount Outstanding        143.75

## payments to suppliers

It is now 30 April 2007. Jo has to make the following payments to her suppliers.

The two cheques are entered into the computerised accounting system under SUPPLIER in the BANK section. The first is shown in the example below.

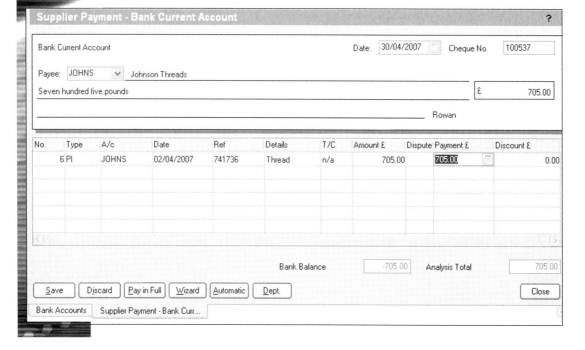

Jo then prints out a report Day Books: Supplier Payments (Summary) which shows the transactions she has processed. She checks the total on the report against the total of the cheques she has issued.

## Rowan Limited
### Day Books: Supplier Payments (Summary)

| Date From: | 01/04/2007 | | | Bank From: | |
|---|---|---|---|---|---|
| Date To: | 30/04/2007 | | | Bank To: | 999999 |
| Transaction From: | 1 | | | Supplier From: | |
| Transaction To: | 99999999 | | | Supplier To: | ZZZZZZ |

Bank 1200                    Currency  Pound Sterling

| No | Type | Date | Supplier | Ref | Details | Net £ | Tax £ | Gross £ | B |
|---|---|---|---|---|---|---|---|---|---|
| 16 | PP | 30/04/2007 | JOHNS | 100537 | Purchase Payment | 705.00 | 0.00 | 705.00 | N |
| 17 | PP | 30/04/2007 | REGIS | 100538 | Purchase Payment | 687.38 | 0.00 | 687.38 | N |
| | | | | | Totals £ | 1,392.38 | 0.00 | 1,392.38 | |

## CASH SALES

**Cash sales** made by a business are usually sales made 'over the counter'.

Cash sales can be made by cash, cheque or debit or credit card – they are not just notes and coins. The important point here is that the business should pay the money into the Bank Current Account as soon as possible – it will be safer in the bank and can be used to meet payments the business may have to make.

The input screen for cash sales is reached from the RECEIPT icon on the BANK menu bar. It looks like this:

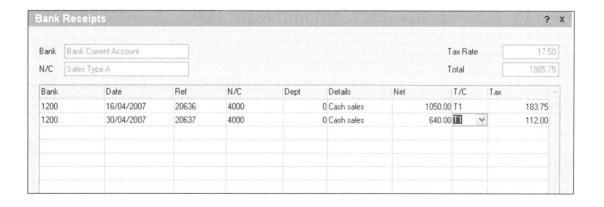

| Bank Receipts | | | | | | | | | | ? X |
|---|---|---|---|---|---|---|---|---|---|---|
| Bank | Bank Current Account | | | | | Tax Rate | | | | 17.50 |
| N/C | Sales Type A | | | | | Total | | | | 1985.75 |
| Bank | Date | Ref | N/C | Dept | Details | Net | T/C | Tax | | |
| 1200 | 16/04/2007 | 20636 | 4000 | 0 | Cash sales | 1050.00 | T1 | 183.75 | | |
| 1200 | 30/04/2007 | 20637 | 4000 | 0 | Cash sales | 640.00 | T1 | 112.00 | | |

### inputting bank receipts

Cash sales paid straight into the bank may be input from the bank paying-in slips recorded in the handwritten business cash book or from a sales listing sheet. These receipts are known in Sage as Bank Receipts and are input as follows:

- input the computer bank account number

- enter the date (usually the date the money is paid into the bank)

- enter a reference (this can be the reference number of the paying-in slip)

- input the appropriate nominal code (N/C) for the type of sales involved

- enter a description of the payment (eg 'cash sales') under 'Details'

- enter the net amount of the sales (ie the sales amount excluding VAT) and then click on T1 if the goods are standard rated for VAT – the computer will then automatically calculate the VAT amount for you and show it in the right-hand column

- check that the VAT amount shown agrees with your figure and change it on screen if it does not – there may be a rounding difference

- check the input details and totals and then SAVE

## CASH PAYMENTS

Most credit payments made by businesses, as we saw in the last chapter, are to suppliers for goods and services provided and paid for on invoice. But businesses also have to make payments on a day-to-day and cash basis (immediate payment) for a wide variety of running costs such as wages and telephone bills.

These payments are input from the screen reached by clicking on the PAYMENT icon on BANK.

Study the example shown on the next page. Here a variety of payments have been made by cheque and BACS from the Bank Current Account.

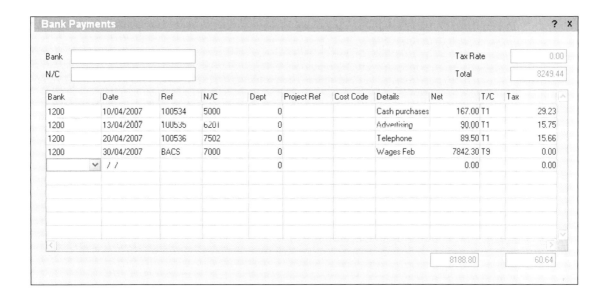

## inputting cash payments

Cash payments can be input from the handwritten business cash book (if one is used), or from the cheques issued and bills being paid (which should show any VAT element). The procedure for inputting is:

- input the computer bank account number

- enter the date (the date the payment is made)

- enter a reference (normally the cheque number or 'BACS' if the payment is a BACS payment)

- input the appropriate nominal code (N/C) for the type of expense involved

- enter a brief description of the nature of the payment (eg Telephone) under 'Details'

- enter the net amount of the payment (ie the amount excluding VAT) and then click on T1 if the product is standard rated for VAT – the computer will then automatically calculate the VAT amount for you and show it in the right-hand column

- check that the VAT amount shown agrees with your figure and change it on screen if it does not – there may be a rounding difference

## a note on VAT

The VAT rates used here are:

T1      purchases, advertising and telephone are all standard rated

T9      wages do not involve VAT

The code for a zero-rated item would have been T0. The code for a VAT exempt item would have been T2.

If you do not know what the VAT element of a payment figure is, enter the total figure in the 'Net' column and click on 'Calc.Net' at the bottom of the screen. The computer will then automatically calculate the VAT and adjust the Net figure accordingly.

## checking the input data

You will see that the screen on the previous page shows the Net, Tax and Total. These will automatically update as you enter the transactions. It is important to check your input against the source data for your input.

If you are entering the data as a batch of entries you should add up the three totals (Net, VAT and Total) manually and check them against the screen figures when you have finished your data entry, but before you Save.

As a final check you should print out a Day Book report (see example below) from Reports in BANK and check the entries against your handwritten records (your cash book, for example).

**Rowan Limited**

**Day Books: Bank Payments (Detailed)**

| Date From: | 01/04/2007 | | | | | | | | | Bank From: | | |
| Date To: | 30/04/2007 | | | | | | | | | Bank To: | 99999999 | |
| Transaction From: | 1 | | | | | | | | | N/C From: | | |
| Transaction To: | 99999999 | | | | | | | | | N/C To: | 99999999 | |
| Dept From: | 0 | | | | | | | | | | | |
| Dept To: | 999 | | | | | | | | | | | |

Bank: 1200    Currency: Pound Sterling

| No | Type | N/C | Date | Ref | Details | Dept | Net £ | Tax £ | T/C | Gross £ | V | B |
|----|------|-----|------|-----|---------|------|-----|-----|-----|-------|---|---|
| 20 | BP | 5000 | 10/04/2007 | 100534 | Cash purchases | 0 | 167.00 | 29.23 | T1 | 196.23 | N | N |
| 21 | BP | 6201 | 13/04/2007 | 100535 | Advertising | 0 | 90.00 | 15.75 | T1 | 105.75 | N | N |
| 22 | BP | 7502 | 20/04/2007 | 100536 | Telephone | 0 | 89.50 | 15.66 | T1 | 105.16 | N | N |
| 23 | BP | 7000 | 30/04/2007 | BACS | Wages | 0 | 7,842.30 | 0.00 | T9 | 7,842.30 | - | N |
| | | | | | | Totals £ | 8,188.80 | 60.64 | | 8,249.44 | | |

**Case Study**

# ROWAN LIMITED:
# CASH RECEIPTS AND PAYMENTS

It is April 30 2007 and Jo now has to input the various cash receipts and payments received and made during the month.

### cash receipts

Rowan Limited paid takings of cash sales into the bank current account twice during the month. The amounts recorded in the cash book are shown below. The reference quoted is the paying-in slip reference.

| Date | Details | Net amount (£) | VAT (£) | ref. |
|---|---|---|---|---|
| 16 April 2007 | Cash sales | 1,050.00 | 183.75 | 20636 |
| 30 April 2007 | Cash sales | 640.00 | 112.00 | 20638 |
| | | 1,690.00 | 295.75 | |

These sales receipts are entered into the computerised accounting system on the RECEIPTS screen reached from the BANK menu bar. Note that the Bank Current Account and the appropriate nominal sales code (N/C) are used each time.

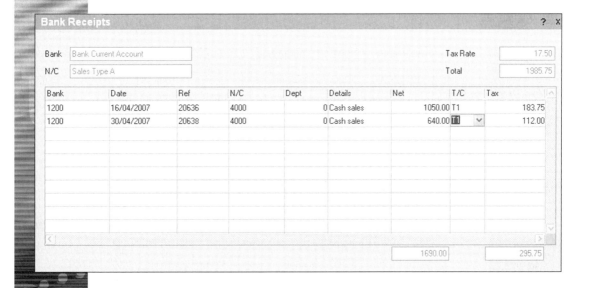

Jo then checks her listing totals against the on-screen totals for accuracy and clicks SAVE. She then prints out a report Day Books: Bank Receipts (Detailed) as a paper-based record of the transactions she has processed. This is shown below. She again checks the totals on the report against the totals on her original listing.

## Rowan Limited
### Day Books: Bank Receipts (Detailed)

| Date From: | 01/04/2007 | | | | | | | | Bank From: | |
|---|---|---|---|---|---|---|---|---|---|---|
| DateTo: | 30/04/2007 | | | | | | | | Bank To: | 99999999 |
| Transaction From: | 1 | | | | | | | | N/C From: | |
| Transaction To: | 99999999 | | | | | | | | N/C To: | 99999999 |
| Dept From: | 0 | | | | | | | | | |
| Dept To: | 999 | | | | | | | | | |

Bank:  1200        Currency:  Pound Sterling

| No | Type | N/C | Date | Ref | Details | Dept | Net £ | Tax £ T/C | Gross £ V B |
|---|---|---|---|---|---|---|---|---|---|
| 18 | BR | 4000 | 16/04/2007 | 20636 | Cash sales | 0 | 1,050.00 | 183.75 T1 | 1,233.75 N N |
| 19 | BR | 4000 | 30/04/2007 | 20638 | Cash sales | 0 | 640.00 | 112.00 T1 | 752.00 N N |
| | | | | | | Totals £ | 1,690.00 | 295.75 | 1,985.75 |

## cash payments

Jo sees from the company cash book that Rowan Limited has made a number of cash payments – by cheque – during the month for normal day-to-day running (revenue) expenses paid on a cash (immediate) basis. She makes a list as shown below, including among the details the Sage nominal account coding.

| Date | Code | Details | Net amount (£) | VAT (£) | chq no |
|---|---|---|---|---|---|
| 10/4/2007 | 5000 | Cash purchases | 167.00 | 29.23 | 100534 |
| 13/4/2007 | 6201 | Advertising | 90.00 | 15.75 | 100535 |
| 20/4/2007 | 7502 | Telephone | 89.50 | 15.66 | 100536 |
| 30/4/2007 | 7000 | Wages | 7,842.30 | no VAT | BACS |
| | | Totals | 8,188.80 | 60.64 | |

These payments are entered into the computerised accounting system on the PAYMENTS screen reached from BANK (see next page).

Note that the Bank Current Account and the appropriate nominal code (N/C) are used each time. The reference in each case is the relevant cheque number.

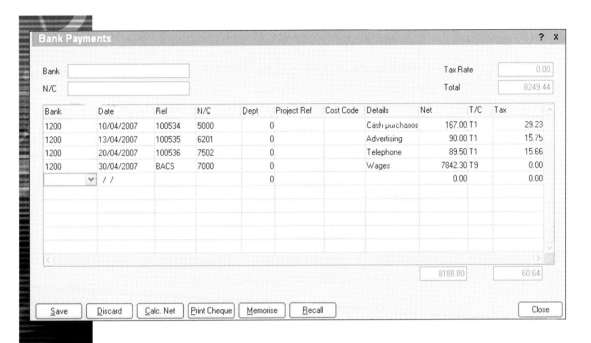

Jo then checks her listing totals against the on-screen totals for accuracy and clicks SAVE.

She prints out a report Day Books: Bank Payments (Detailed) from BANK as a record of the transactions she has processed. This is shown below. She compares the totals on the report against the totals on her original listing as a final check of input accuracy.

## Rowan Limited

### Day Books: Bank Payments (Detailed)

| Date From: | 01/04/2007 | | | Bank From: | |
| Date To: | 30/04/2007 | | | Bank To: | 99999999 |
| Transaction From: | 1 | | | N/C From: | |
| Transaction To: | 99999999 | | | N/C To: | 99999999 |
| Dept From: | 0 | | | | |
| Dept To: | 999 | | | | |

Bank: 1200  Currency: Pound Sterling

| No | Type | N/C | Date | Ref | Details | Dept | Net £ | Tax £ | T/C | Gross £ | V | B |
|----|------|------|------------|--------|---------------|------|----------|-------|-----|----------|---|---|
| 20 | BP | 5000 | 10/04/2007 | 100534 | Cash purchases | 0 | 167.00 | 29.23 | T1 | 196.23 | N | N |
| 21 | BP | 6201 | 13/04/2007 | 100535 | Advertising | 0 | 90.00 | 15.75 | T1 | 105.75 | N | N |
| 22 | BP | 7502 | 20/04/2007 | 100536 | Telephone | 0 | 89.50 | 15.66 | T1 | 105.16 | N | N |
| 23 | BP | 7000 | 30/04/2007 | BACS | Wages | 0 | 7,842.30 | 0.00 | T9 | 7,842.30 | - | N |
| | | | | | | Totals £ | 8,188.80 | 60.64 | | 8,249.44 | | |

## USING A 'CASH' ACCOUNT

A business which holds substantial amounts of cash – eg shop 'takings' – may wish to operate a separate Cash Account on the computer, just as it may set up separate 'cash' columns in the manual Cash Book. If this is the case, it will open a separate account in BANK for this purpose. Any transfers to and from the actual bank Current Account will be made using the bank transfer screen. This transfer screen will also be used when making transfers to Petty Cash Account (see below).

## PETTY CASH

### petty cash and the accounting system

As you will know from your studies, **petty cash** is a fund of money kept in the business in the same way as the bank current account is a fund of money kept in the bank. A 'bank' account will be set up for petty cash on the computer which will handle all the transactions:

■ payments of cash into petty cash from the bank current account

■ payments out of petty cash to pay for small expense items

### payments into petty cash

The Sage computer system has a default Petty Cash Account which it classes as a bank account, although, of course, the money is not in the bank. The computer sees it as a 'money fund'.

When cash is needed to top up the petty cash, the business will often cash a cheque at the bank and then put the money in the cash tin. The computer program requires the business to input the transaction as a TRANSFER from the BANK menu bar. In the screen below, a business has cashed a £100 cheque at the bank (using cheque 100533) to provide the cash.

## payments out of petty cash

Payments out of Petty Cash Account are handled in exactly the same way on the computer as payments out of Bank Current Account.

The PAYMENTS screen is reached through BANK. The details are then input from the petty cash vouchers or the petty cash book in which they are recorded.

The screen below shows a petty cash voucher and the input of the details into the Sage BANK PAYMENTS screen.

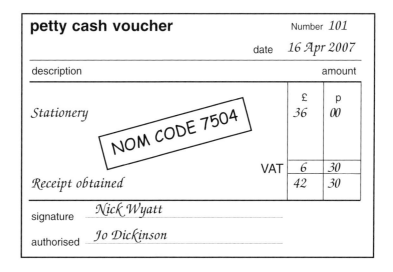

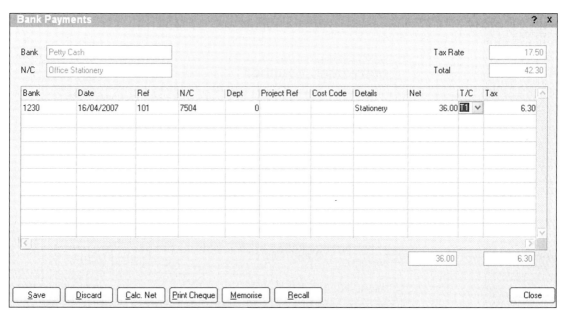

Points to remember are:

- the bank account number used is the Petty Cash Account number
- the reference is the petty cash voucher number
- petty cash vouchers and their receipts will not always show the VAT amount – the VAT and net amount can be calculated on the computer by inputting the full amount under 'Net' and then clicking on 'Calc.Net' at the bottom of the screen (using T1 code to denote standard rate VAT)
- when the details have been checked you should SAVE
- the details can also be checked against a Cash Payments Day Book printout if required (accessed through Reports in BANK)

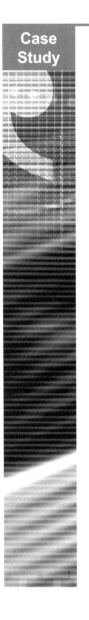

**Case Study**

# ROWAN LIMITED:
# SETTING UP THE PETTY CASH SYSTEM

At the beginning of April:

- Jo cashed cheque no 100533 for £100 at the bank on 2 April.

- The £100 cash was transferred to the petty cash tin on 2 April.

- The tin contains three vouchers for payments made during the month – these are shown below and on the next page. They are ready for entry in the petty cash book as part of the month-end routine. Note that the Sage nominal codes have been marked on the vouchers.

  Voucher 101 shows the VAT included in the total (standard rate: T1)

  Voucher 102 does not have any VAT in it (postage stamps are exempt:T2)

  Voucher 103 does not show the VAT included in the total (standard rate: T1) because it was not shown separately on the original receipt.

| petty cash voucher | | Number *101* |
| --- | --- | --- |
| | | date  *16 Apr 2007* |

| description | | amount | |
| --- | --- | --- | --- |
| | | £ | p |
| *Stationery*  NOM CODE 7504 | | *36* | *00* |
| | VAT | *6* | *30* |
| *Receipt obtained* | | *42* | *30* |

signature  *Nick Wyatt*

authorised  *Jo Dickinson*

petty cash voucher                    Number *102*

                              date    *23 Apr 2007*

| description | | amount | |
|---|---|---|---|
| | | £ | p |
| *Postage stamps* NOM CODE 7501 | | 25 | 00 |
| | VAT | | |
| *Receipt obtained* | | 25 | 00 |

signature ....... *R Patel* ......

authorised ....... *Jo Dickinson* ......

petty cash voucher                    Number *103*

                              date    *25 Apr 2007*

| description | | amount | |
|---|---|---|---|
| | | £ | p |
| *Cleaning materials* NOM CODE 7801 | | | |
| | VAT | | |
| *Receipt obtained* | | 18 | 80 |

signature ....... *P Adams* ......

authorised ....... *Jo Dickinson* ......

## the transfer to petty cash

Jo first inputs the £100 transfer from the Bank Current Account to the Petty Cash Account. The screen is illustrated below. Note the use of the cheque number as the reference.

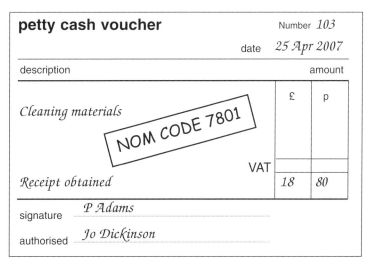

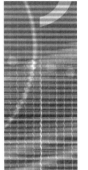

## inputting the vouchers

The petty cash payments are entered into the computerised accounting system on the PAYMENTS screen reached from the BANK menu bar.

Note that the bank Petty Cash Account number and the appropriate nominal code (N/C) are used each time.

The nominal codes are taken from the default nominal list.

The reference in each case is the relevant petty cash voucher number.

Postage stamps are VAT exempt. The VAT on the third petty cash voucher was not on the receipt but has been calculated on-screen by inputting the total amount of £18.80 in the 'Net' column and clicking on 'Calc.Net' at the bottom of the screen:

### Rowan Limited
### Day Books: Cash Payments (Detailed)

| Date From: | 01/04/2007 | | | | | | | | Bank From: | |
| Date To: | 30/04/2007 | | | | | | | | Bank To: | 99999999 |
| | | | | | | | | | | |
| Transaction From: | 1 | | | | | | | | N/C From: | |
| Transaction To: | 99999999 | | | | | | | | N/C To: | 99999999 |
| | | | | | | | | | | |
| Dept From: | 0 | | | | | | | | | |
| Dept To: | 999 | | | | | | | | | |

Bank: 1230     Currency: Pound Sterling

| No | Type | N/C | Date | Ref | Details | Dept | Net £ | Tax | £ T/C | Gross £ | V | B |
|----|------|-----|------|-----|---------|------|-------|-----|-------|---------|---|---|
| 26 | CP | 7504 | 16/04/2007 | 101 | Stationery | 0 | 36.00 | | 6.30 T1 | 42.30 | N | N |
| 27 | CP | 7501 | 23/04/2007 | 102 | Postage stamps | 0 | 25.00 | | 0.00 T2 | 25.00 | N | N |
| 28 | CP | 7801 | 25/04/2007 | 103 | Cleaning materials | 0 | 16.00 | | 2.80 T1 | 18.80 | N | N |
| | | | | | | Totals £ | 77.00 | | 9.10 | 86.10 | | |

Jo then checks the screen Total with the total of the vouchers and when she is happy that all the details are correct she will SAVE. The Day Book report will now show the petty cash payments. Note that the transaction code is 'CP' (second column from the left). This stands for 'Cash Payment'. This distinguishes the petty cash payments from payments from the bank current account (input through the same screen). These payments have the code 'BP' which stands for 'Bank Payment'.

### Rowan Limited
### Day Books: Cash Payments (Detailed)

| Date From: | 01/04/2007 | | | | | | | | Bank From: | |
| Date To: | 30/04/2007 | | | | | | | | Bank To: | 99999999 |
| | | | | | | | | | | |
| Transaction From: | 1 | | | | | | | | N/C From: | |
| Transaction To: | 99999999 | | | | | | | | N/C To: | 99999999 |
| | | | | | | | | | | |
| Dept From: | 0 | | | | | | | | | |
| Dept To: | 999 | | | | | | | | | |

Bank: 1230     Currency: Pound Sterling

| No | Type | N/C | Date | Ref | Details | Dept | Net £ | Tax | £ T/C | Gross £ | V | B |
|----|------|-----|------|-----|---------|------|-------|-----|-------|---------|---|---|
| 26 | CP | 7504 | 16/04/2007 | 101 | Stationery | 0 | 36.00 | | 6.30 T1 | 42.30 | N | N |
| 27 | CP | 7501 | 23/04/2007 | 102 | Postage stamps | 0 | 25.00 | | 0.00 T2 | 25.00 | N | N |
| 28 | CP | 7801 | 25/04/2007 | 103 | Cleaning materials | 0 | 16.00 | | 2.80 T1 | 18.80 | N | N |
| | | | | | | Totals £ | 77.00 | | 9.10 | 86.10 | | |

## JOURNAL ENTRIES

**Journal** entries enable you to make transfers from one nominal (Main Ledger) account to another. The Journal is useful if an error needs to be corrected when an entry has been input to the wrong account.

Suppose you are inputting a batch of Bank Payments which include a number of bills that have to be paid. You have written out a cheque for £105.75 for printing brochures, but when inputting it you think it is for advertising and so post it to 'Advertising' (nominal account 6201) instead of 'P.R. Literature & Brochures' (nominal account 6203).

You can correct your mistake using a journal entry. You bring up the screen by clicking on the JOURNALS icon on the NOMINAL menu bar:

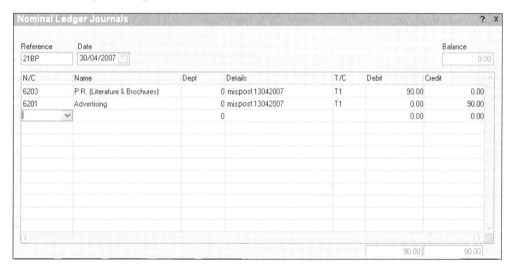

The procedure is:

- enter the reference (this could be the transaction number you can find by opening up the FINANCIALS screen and locating the transaction)
- enter the date
- enter the nominal code of the account to which you are going to post the debit; here it is PR (Literature & Brochures) because you are recording an expense
- enter the reason for the transaction – here you are adjusting a mispost
- enter the VAT tax code input on the original (wrong) entry
- enter the net amount in the debit column (ie the amount before VAT has been added on) – here the net amount is £90 and VAT (here at standard rate) is £15.75 and the total is £105.75; note that neither the VAT nor the total appear on the screen because you are not adjusting the VAT; *only the net amount* has gone to the wrong account

- enter the nominal code of the account to which you are going to post the credit; here it is Advertising account because you are effectively refunding the amount to the account – it is an income item and so a credit

- enter the remaining data as you did for the debit, but enter the net amount in the right-hand credit column

- make sure the Balance box reads zero – meaning that the debit equals the credit – and SAVE

## BAD DEBT WRITE OFF

If a customer's debt is not paid and there is no likelihood of payment, perhaps because the customer has gone out of business, then the debt must be written off in the books.

In manual accounting this is normally done by processing a journal to transfer the amount from the debtors control account (and the subsidiary sales ledger account) to the bad debt account, but in Sage you cannot process a journal to write off a debt. You must either process a sales credit note coded with the Bad Debt Write Off code (N/C 8100) or use the special procedure provided. This is shown below.

First click on Tools on the menu bar and choose 'Write Off, Refund and Returns Wizard'. Finally click Next between each of the following as you move through the wizard:

- select the Sales Ledger option

- select Write off Customer Accounts (or Write Off Customer Transactions if only part of the account is being written off)

- select the customer

- select the transaction(s) to be written off

- input a date and a summary (eg 'Customer bankrupt')

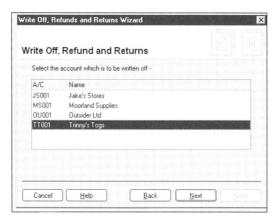

# BANK RECONCILIATION ON THE COMPUTER

A bank reconciliation statement forms a link between the balances shown in the bank statement and the Bank Account in the cash book (or its computer equivalent).

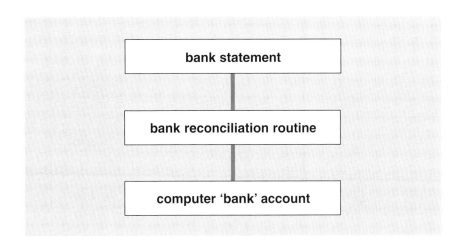

The Sage system allows you to carry out a bank reconciliation. The Bank Reconciliation screen, accessed through RECONCILE in BANK, is shown on the next page. The procedure is as follows:

1   Enter the bank statement date and closing bank statement balance at the top of the screen and check that the opening balance is the same on the computer screen and on the bank statement.

2   Compare the items on the screen with the bank statement – selecting them item by item – and update the computer with any items such as bank charges which appear on the bank statement and not on the computer screen (ie by inputting them, using the Adjustment button).

3   When you have highlighted all the items on screen which are on the bank statement and updated the computer (see **2**), check that the Sage 'Reconcile Balance' matches the bank statement closing balance and the Difference box shows zero. Reconciliation is then complete.

4   Click SAVE and then confirm 'Mark selected transactions as reconciled'. Any unselected items (ie items on the computer but not in the bank) will appear again when you next carry out this bank reconciliation process.

Now study (on the next page) the Rowan Limited bank statement produced on 30 April and compare it with the bank reconciliation screen.

**ALBION BANK PLC**

**Statement of account as at:** 30 04 2007

**Account** 90 47 19 11719881 Rowan Limited

| Date | Details | Paid out | Paid in | Balance |
|---|---|---|---|---|
| 2007 | | | | |
| 1 Apr | Balance b/f | | | nil |
| 2 Apr | Cheque no 100533 | 100.00 | | -100.00 |
| 13 Apr | Cheque no 100534 | 196.23 | | -296.23 |
| 16 Apr | Cheque no 100535 | 105.75 | | -401.98 |
| 16 Apr | Paid in ref 20636 | | 1233.75 | 831.77 |
| 23 Apr | Cheque no 100536 | 105.16 | | 726.61 |
| 23 Apr | Paid in ref 20637 | | 11958.75 | 12685.36 |
| 23 Apr | BACS receipt | | 2073.87 | 14759.23 |
| 30 Apr | BACS autopay | 7842.30 | | 6916.93 |
| 30 Apr | Bank charges | 26.00 | | 6890.93 |
| 30 Apr | Paid in ref 20638 | | 752.00 | 7642.93 |

*bank statement for Rowan Limited, dated 30 April*

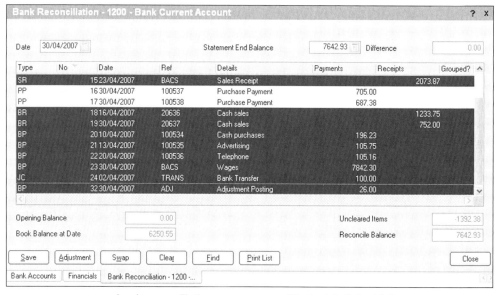

*a bank reconciliation screen – see Student Activity 15.9*

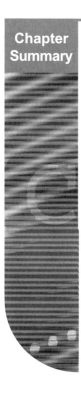

## Chapter Summary

■ A business can set up not only the bank current account in the computerised accounting system, but also a number of other 'money' accounts. These, which include petty cash account, enable the business to keep track of the processing of money in a variety of forms.

■ Payments received from customers who have bought on credit and payments to suppliers from whom the business has bought on credit can be processed through the computerised accounting system.

■ It is essential to check the input of payments from customers and to suppliers by obtaining a printout – such as a Day Book – from the computer.

■ Petty cash transactions are processed on the computer through Petty Cash Account. Cash payments and receipts are either processed on the computer through the Bank Account, or through a special 'Cash' account which is the same as Cash Account in a manual accounting system.

■ The computerised accounting system also provides the facility for making adjustments with journal entries (eg for correcting errors), writing off bad debts and reconciling the bank statement balances with the computer bank account.

## Key Terms

| | |
|---|---|
| **cash payments** | payments made straightaway |
| **credit payments** | payments made at a later date following the issue of an invoice to a customer or by a supplier |
| **remittance advice** | a document that tells a business that a payment is being made |
| **petty cash** | a float of cash kept in the office for making small purchases |
| **journal** | the part of the accounting system which enables you to make transfers from one nominal (main ledger) account to another |
| **bad debt write off** | the transfer of a customer's debt from the Sales Ledger to the Bad Debt write off account |
| **bank reconciliation** | the matching of transactions shown on the bank statement with those in the bank account in the accounting system and the identification of differences |

# Student Activities

**15.1** Set the program date to 23 April 2007. Enter the customer payments shown on page 230 into BANK (CUSTOMER). Use the reference 'cheque' or 'BACS' as appropriate.

Print out a Day Books: Customer Receipts (Summary) Report from REPORTS in BANK (see page 231). Agree the day book total with the batch total to confirm the accuracy of your input.

**15.2** Set the program date to 30 April 2007. Enter the cheques shown on page 232 that Jo is paying to suppliers into the computer (SUPPLIER in BANK).

Print out a Day Books: Supplier Payments (Summary) Report from REPORTS in BANK (see page 233). Agree the day book total with the batch total to confirm the accuracy of your input.

**15.3** Ensure the program date is set to 30 April 2007. Enter the following banked cash receipts into the computer. Check your totals before saving and print out a Day Books: Bank Receipts (Detailed) Report (see page 238) to confirm the accuracy of your input.

| Date | Details | Net amount (£) | VAT (£) | ref. |
|---|---|---|---|---|
| 16 April 2007 | Cash sales | 1,050.00 | 183.75 | 20636 |
| 30 April 2007 | Cash sales | 640.00 | 112.00 | 20638 |
| | | 1,690.00 | 295.75 | |

**15.4** Keep the program date as 30 April 2007.

Enter the following cash payments into the computer. Use the nominal accounts indicated on the listing. Take care over the VAT Tax codes used. T1 is the standard rate code, T2 is for exempt items and T9 is the code for transactions which do not involve VAT.

Check your totals before saving and print out a Day Books: Bank Payments (Detailed) Report (see page 239).

| Date | Code | Details | Net amount (£) | VAT (£) | chq no |
|---|---|---|---|---|---|
| 10/4/2007 | 5000 | Cash purchases | 167.00 | 29.23 | 100534 |
| 13/4/2007 | 6201 | Advertising | 90.00 | 15.75 | 100535 |
| 20/4/2007 | 7502 | Telephone | 89.50 | 15.66 | 100536 |
| 30/4/2007 | 7000 | Wages | 7,842.30 | no VAT | BACS |
| | | Totals | 8,188.80 | 60.64 | |

**15.5**  Keep the program date as 30 April 2007.

On 2 April Jo cashed cheque 100533 for £100 at her bank for the petty cash account.

Carry out a bank transfer dated 2 April from Bank Current Account to Petty Cash Account for this amount.

**15.6**  Keep the program date as 30 April 2007. Input the three petty cash vouchers on pages 242 to 243 into Bank Payments, taking care with the VAT element on each one (postage is VAT exempt, stationery and cleaning materials are standard-rated). Note that the coding is on the vouchers.

Note: select the Petty Cash Bank account on the screen before data input and running any reports.

Print out a Day Books: Cash Payments (Detailed) Report to confirm the accuracy of your input (see page 244).

**15.7**  Keep the program date as 30 April 2007.

Jo finds that a payment of £90 plus VAT, made on 13 April, which appears under Advertising (nominal account 6201) was actually for P.R. Literature & Brochures - account 6203.

Jo needs to make a journal entry to adjust the position, debiting account 6203 and crediting account 6201.

Make an appropriate journal entry, using the same VAT code (T1) as on the original transaction. The reference is 21 and the current date 30 April 2007. The details are 'mispost 13/04/07'. The JOURNALS screen is accessed through NOMINAL.

Print out a Day Books: Nominal Ledger report (date range 1 April to 30 April 2007) from REPORTS in NOMINAL and check the details to confirm the accuracy of your input. Check your output with the screen below.

**Rowan Limited**
**Day Books: Nominal Ledger**

| | | | | | | | | | | | |
|---|---|---|---|---|---|---|---|---|---|---|---|
| Date From: | 01/04/2007 | | | | | | | N/C From: | | | |
| Date To: | 30/04/2007 | | | | | | | N/C To: | 99999999 | | |
| Transaction From: | 1 | | | | | | | Dept From: | 0 | | |
| Transaction To: | 99999999 | | | | | | | Dept To: | 999 | | |

| No | Type | N/C | Date | Ref | Details | Dept | T/C | Debit | Credit | V | B |
|---|---|---|---|---|---|---|---|---|---|---|---|
| 24 | JC | 1200 | 02.04.2007 | TRANS | Bank Transfer | 0 | T9 | | 100.00 | - | R |
| 25 | JD | 1230 | 02.04.2007 | TRANS | Bank Transfer | 0 | T9 | 100.00 | | - | N |
| 29 | JD | 6203 | 30.04.2007 | 21 | Wrong post 13 04 07 | 0 | T1 | 90.00 | | N | - |
| 30 | JC | 6201 | 30.04.2007 | 21 | Wrong post 13 04 07 | 0 | T1 | | 90.00 | N | - |
| | | | | | | | Totals: | 190.00 | 190.00 | | |

**15.8**  Trinny's Togs have disputed the unpaid balance on their account (£143.75). Write this off as a bad debt using the Sage wizard. The date is 30 April 2007.

Then print out a Customer Activity (Detailed) report for Trinny's Togs with a date range of 1 April to 30 April 2007.

Check your output with the screen shown at the top of the next page.

### Rowan Limited
### Customer Activity (Detailed)

| Date From: | 01/04/2007 | | | | | Customer From: | TT001 |
|---|---|---|---|---|---|---|---|
| Date To: | 30/04/2007 | | | | | Customer To: | ZZZZ |
| Transaction From: | 1 | | | | | N/C From: | |
| Transaction To: | 99999999 | | | | | N/C To: | 999 |

| A/C: | TT001 | Name: | Tracey's Togs | | Contact: | | | Tel: | |

| No | Type | Date | Ref | N/C | Details | Dept | T/C | Value | O.S | Debit | Credit |
|---|---|---|---|---|---|---|---|---|---|---|---|
| 1 | SI | 09.04.2007 | 07/542 | 4000 | Karakul | 0 | T1 | 2,643.75 | | 2,643.75 | |
| 14 | SR | 23.04.2007 | Cheque | 1200 | Sales Receipt | 0 | T9 | 2,500.00 | | | 2,500.00 |
| 31 | SC | 30.04.2007 | BADDBT | 8100 | Bad Debt Write Off | 0 | T9 | 143.75 | | | 143.75 |
| | | | | | | | Totals: | 0.00 | 0.00 | 2,643.75 | 2,643.75 |

**15.9** Keep the program date of 30 April 2007. Jo has an online facility with her bank and has just printed out her bank statement as at 30 April 2007. This is shown below.

Jo decides to carry out a bank reconciliation on the computer, using the RECONCILE function through BANK.

She will have to make an adjustment for the bank charges. The VAT code is T2 for exempt items such as bank charges, and the nominal code to be used is 7901.

When you have completed the reconciliation process, SAVE and print out a 'Bank Statement - Reconciled and Un-reconciled' to show the items that have been reconciled and any that have not.

Check your output with the screen at the top of the next page.

**ALBION BANK PLC**

**Statement of account as at:** 30 04 2007

**Account** 90 47 19 11719881 Rowan Limited

| Date | Details | Paid out | Paid in | Balance |
|---|---|---|---|---|
| 2007 | | | | |
| 1 Apr | Balance b/f | | | nil |
| 2 Apr | Cheque no 100533 | 100.00 | | -100.00 |
| 13 Apr | Cheque no 100534 | 196.23 | | -296.23 |
| 16 Apr | Cheque no 100535 | 105.75 | | -401.98 |
| 16 Apr | Paid in ref 20636 | | 1233.75 | 831.77 |
| 23 Apr | Cheque no 100536 | 105.16 | | 726.61 |
| 23 Apr | Paid in ref 20637 | | 11958.75 | 12685.36 |
| 23 Apr | BACS receipt | | 2073.87 | 14759.23 |
| 30 Apr | BACS autopay | 7842.30 | | 6916.93 |
| 30 Apr | Bank charges | 26.00 | | 6890.93 |
| 30 Apr | Paid in ref 20638 | | 752.00 | 7642.93 |

**Rowan Limited**
**Bank Statement - Reconciled and Un-reconciled**

Date From : 01/04/2007

Date To :   30/04/2007

Reconciled Transactions

| No | Type | Date | Ref | Details | Debit | Credit | Balance | Running Bal. |
|----|------|------|-----|---------|-------|--------|---------|--------------|
| 24 | JC | 02/04/2007 | TRANS | Bank Transfer | | 100.00 | -100.00 | -100.00 |
| 20 | BP | 10/04/2007 | 100534 | Cash purchases | | 196.23 | -296.23 | -296.23 |
| 21 | BP | 13/04/2007 | 100535 | Advertising | | 105.75 | -401.98 | -401.98 |
| 18 | BR | 16/04/2007 | 20636 | Cash sales | 1,233.75 | | 831.77 | 831.77 |
| 22 | BP | 20/04/2007 | 100536 | Telephone | | 105.16 | 726.61 | 726.61 |
| 12 | SR | 23/04/2007 | Cheque | Sales Receipt | 6,580.00 | | 7,306.61 | 7,306.61 |
| 13 | SR | 23/04/2007 | Cheque | Sales Receipt | 2,878.75 | | 10,185.36 | 10,185.36 |
| 14 | SR | 23/04/2007 | Cheque | Sales Receipt | 2,500.00 | | 12,685.36 | 12,685.36 |
| 15 | SR | 23/04/2007 | BACS | Sales Receipt | 2,073.87 | | 14,759.23 | 14,759.23 |
| 19 | BR | 30/04/2007 | 20637 | Cash sales | 752.00 | | 15,511.23 | 15,511.23 |
| 23 | BP | 30/04/2007 | BACS | Wages | | 7,842.30 | 7,668.93 | 7,668.93 |
| 32 | BP | 30/04/2007 | ADJ | Adjustment Posting | | 26.00 | 7,642.93 | 7,642.93 |
| | | | | Reconciled Total : | 16,018.37 | 8,375.44 | 7,642.93 | |

Non-Reconciled Transactions

| No | Type | Date | Ref | Details | Debit | Credit | Balance | Running Bal. |
|----|------|------|-----|---------|-------|--------|---------|--------------|
| 16 | PP | 30/04/2007 | 100537 | Purchase Payment | | 705.00 | -705.00 | 6,937.93 |
| 17 | PP | 30/04/2007 | 100538 | Purchase Payment | | 687.38 | -1,392.38 | 6,250.55 |
| | | | | Non-Reconciled Total : | 0.00 | 1,392.38 | -1,392.38 | |
| | | | | Bank Balance : | 16,018.37 | 9,767.82 | 6,250.55 | |

## 15.10

Finally, print out a new Trial Balance as at 30 April 2007 and check it against the one below. If necessary, look at an audit trail for the same period to identify any differences or errors.

**Rowan Limited**
**Period Trial Balance**

To Period :    Month 1, April 2007

| N/C | Name | Debit | Credit |
|-----|------|-------|--------|
| 0020 | Plant and Machinery | 585.00 | |
| 1200 | Bank Current Account | 6,250.55 | |
| 1230 | Petty Cash | 13.90 | |
| 2100 | Creditors Control Account | | 4,993.75 |
| 2200 | Sales Tax Control Account | | 2,407.12 |
| 2201 | Purchase Tax Control Account | 1,020.87 | |
| 4000 | Sales Type A | | 13,755.00 |
| 5000 | Materials Purchased | 5,017.00 | |
| 6203 | P.R. (Literature & Brochures) | 90.00 | |
| 7000 | Gross Wages | 7,842.30 | |
| 7501 | Postage and Carriage | 25.00 | |
| 7502 | Telephone | 89.50 | |
| 7504 | Office Stationery | 36.00 | |
| 7801 | Cleaning | 16.00 | |
| 7901 | Bank Charges | 26.00 | |
| 8100 | Bad Debt Write Off | 143.75 | |
| | Totals: | 21,155.87 | 21,155.87 |

Reminder! Have you made a backup?

# 16 Planning and organising your work

In this chapter we explain the need for an employee to plan and organise his or her work, following the procedures of the organisation, so that the work can be carried out efficiently and effectively. This involves a number of processes:

- identifying the various tasks that have to be carried out in the workplace

- organising them in order of priority so that the requirements of the organisation and its other employees can be met

- using planning aids such as diaries and schedules to organise tasks

- identifying when priorities change and knowing how to modify schedules

- asking for help and advice when priorities do change

- letting the right person know when problems are encountered in getting the work done

## PERFORMANCE CRITERIA COVERED

### unit 31: ACCOUNTING WORK SKILLS

### element 13.3

### perform effectively in the workplace

A    Identify and prioritise work tasks taking account of organisational procedures and prepare a work plan.

B    Monitor and report progress against work plans and deadlines, adapting as necessary.

## WORKING IN AN ORGANISATION

### why work?

Employees normally come to work, not just to earn money (although many claim this as their sole motive!) but because the workplace, like a family, is a social grouping of people who work, argue and have a laugh together. By going to work, employees gain a unique sense of identity which the organisation and social grouping provides. The idea of the workplace as an extended 'family' or 'team' was vigorously promoted by the Japanese and adopted by Western business culture. Its origin, of course, has deeper roots. The chocolate manufacturer, Cadburys, which promoted the ethic of hard work and benefits for all, built a whole 'village' to house its employees – its 'extended family' – over fifty years ago.

The reason for making this point is that employees learn to treat the workplace as an environment in which they have a sense of 'social' responsibility for what they do. This responsibility extends to:

- the everyday tasks that they have to carry out

- their attitude to their colleagues when they carry out tasks

- the idea that they are working together to achieve common **objectives** adopted by the organisation

### employees and objectives

What are these 'objectives' of an organisation? They may well include:

- **customer satisfaction** – making the customer the main focus of the organisation

- **profitability** – which should benefit employees, owners and customers

- **sustainability** – reducing wastage of natural resources, eg energy and paper

In order to achieve these objectives, organisations promote:

- customer care schemes

- profit-sharing schemes

- 'green' schemes to cut down on wastage, eg of energy and paper

The example on the next page shows how a Customer Care scheme can set very specific targets for the performance of workplace tasks. Therefore, when an assistant sorts out a customer query, it is not just a case of 'that's another one out of the way' but 'I got a buzz of satisfaction in showing that our organisation cares about its customers.' In short, tasks are often seen to fulfil objectives.

## day-to-day tasks in a Customer Care scheme

### efficiency

- aim to be 100% error free
- answer all letters within 2 days of receipt
- advise customers of delivery timescales

### problem solving

- take ownership – don't blame others
- resolve complaints within 2 to 10 working days
- follow up afterwards to ensure that the customer is satisfied

### courtesy

- greet customers and smile
- use customer's name
- give customer 100% of your attention

### dealing with customers who are waiting

- serve all customers within 4 minutes
- apologise if a customer is kept waiting
- make visible efforts to reduce waiting times

### using the telephone

- answer before the third ring, if possible
- speak clearly to customers, use their name and check their understanding of what you say

### organisational procedures

The way in which employees tackle tasks is often set down in written sets of **procedures**. Larger organisations are likely to have manuals which give guidance; smaller organisations may have written 'checklists' compiled by experienced staff. Examples of jobs in an accounting context which will have set procedures for the tasks carried out include:

- supermarket checkout operators dealing with cash, debit and credit cards
- employees processing payroll
- accounts assistants paying supplier invoices

### 'what next?'

The focus of this Element is on planning and organisation. The day-to-day work will involve a wide variety of tasks competing for the employee's time. The question 'what next?' involves identifying and prioritising the tasks that need to be done. We will now examine the techniques and aids available to the employee.

## WHAT ARE MY TASKS?

### keeping to the job description

An employee needs to know:

- what tasks need to be done in the office
- what tasks the employee is able to do in the office

These are not necessarily the same. Employees should be given a **job description** which sets out exactly what the employee is expected to be able to do. It may be that a line manager puts pressure onto an employee to carry out tasks which the employee is not qualified or able to do. The employee may think 'promotion here we come!' but also may get in a mess and make mistakes for which he or she should not really be held responsible.

One golden rule is therefore to look at your job description and know what you should have to do and what limits there are to your range of activities.

### identifying types of tasks

The next golden rule is to be able to identify exactly what tasks have to be done and to identify what type of tasks they are, because this will affect the order in which you will carry them out.

There are a number of different types of task, for example, in an accounts office . . .

- **routine tasks**

  These are everyday tasks such as reading the post and emails, checking invoices, inputting runs of data, sending standard letters, answering telephone queries, photocopying and filing. They do not hold any great surprises, but their efficient completion is important to the smooth running of the office.

- **non-routine tasks**

  These are the unexpected tasks such as helping with one-off projects, working out of the office on a special assignment, or helping to clear up after the washroom has flooded. These may hold up your normal routine work.

**Routine tasks** are easy to plan for because they are predictable.

**Non-routine tasks** cannot be planned for, and they can sometimes cause problems, as we will see later in the chapter. They call for flexibility and logical thinking, skills which to some extent can be developed.

As you will know some people thrive on routine and do not like it to be upset; others get bored by it and enjoy the challenges of the unexpected.

In addition, tasks may be **urgent** and they may be **important**. These are not always the same thing . . .

- **urgent tasks**

  These are tasks which have to be done by a specific pressing deadline: a director may need a spreadsheet immediately for a meeting currently taking place; customer statements may have to go out in tonight's post.

- **important tasks**

  These are tasks for which you have been given personal responsibility. They may be part of your normal routine and other people depend on their successful completion, or they may have been delegated to you because your manager thinks you capable of them.

## working out the priorities

**Prioritising** tasks means deciding on which order the tasks should be carried out. Which one first? Which one last? Which tasks matter? Which tasks do not matter so much?

The guide to the basic order of priority is shown below. You may, of course, think of exceptions to this rule, particularly with items 2 and 3.

*an order of priority . . .*

*1*
Tasks that are **urgent and important** – they have got to be done soon and if you do not do them you are going to let a lot of people down – eg producing the spreadsheet for the MD's meeting.

*2*
Tasks that are **urgent but less important**, eg watering office plants which have dried out – if you fail to water them straightaway the job still needs doing, but the office is not going to grind to a halt if they remain dry.

*3*
Tasks that are **important but not urgent**, eg producing some sales figures for your manager for a meeting at the end of the week – the task has to be done, but it could be done tomorrow.

*4*
Tasks that are **neither important nor urgent**, eg archiving material from some old files. This task is a useful 'filler' when the office becomes less busy; it would not matter, however, if it were put off for a week or two.

## Case Study

# FLICK'S DAY – WORKING OUT THE PRIORITIES

Flick works as an accounts assistant at the Liverpool head office of Estro PLC, a company that makes vacuum cleaners. Her main job is to process the incoming sales orders. She is supervised by her line manager Josie Khan.

She is not having a good week and seems stressed by the workload she has been given. It is Thursday 6 February and things are getting no better.

She has written down her tasks on various bits of paper and has stuck post-it notes on the side of her computer screen, marking them 'Remember!' Her colleague, Kirsty, has written notes to her. She also has her daily routine sheet which came with her job description.

These are all shown below.

---

### SALES ORDER PROCESSING: DAILY ROUTINE

1   Collect mail, open, sort and refer where necessary
2   Open email and deal with queries - refer where necessary
3   Check incoming sales orders and debit notes
4   Check sales orders with credit control lists
5   Batch and process sales orders on computer
6   Print sales invoices and credit notes
7   Check printed documents
8   Agree batch total with computer day book summary
9   Pass invoices and credit notes for checking against order documentation
10  File copy invoices, credit notes and order documentation
11  Answer customer queries  - refer where necessary

---

These are the notes received from Kirsty, a colleague:

> Flick - Accounts
> Manager wants
> January sales
> figures asap!
>
> Kirsty 6 Feb
> 9.30

> Flick - we are
> moving the
> computers at
> 2.00 Thursday
> afternoon - can
> you help? Kirsty

These are the 'Remember!' post-it notes Flick has stuck on the side of her computer screen:

**REMEMBER!**
Get instant coffee for staff kitchen. Ordinary <u>and</u> decaff! Both jars now empty.

**REMEMBER!**
**4 FEB**
Josie wants printouts of top 10 customer activity reports by end of Friday.

**REMEMBER!**
Old customer sales files need moving to separate filing drawer some time.

How is Flick going to work out her priorities?

### solution

Flick takes a short morning break to discuss her various tasks with her line manager, Josie. At Josie's suggestion she thinks about the priorities involved and classifies the tasks according to how urgent they are and how important they are. She starts by prioritising the non-routine/unexpected tasks:

**urgent and important tasks**

• The Accounts Manager wants the January sales figures straightaway.

• The computers have to be moved at 2.00 pm that day.

**urgent and less important tasks**

• The staff kitchen needs more coffee.

**important and non-urgent tasks**

• The top 10 customer activity reports are required for Friday.

**less important and non-urgent tasks**

• The old customer sales files need moving to a separate filing drawer.

The non-routine tasks are fairly easily prioritised, as seen above, although there was some uncertainty over whether the staff coffee or the customer printouts had greater priority! But Flick's problem was how to combine the non-routine tasks with the big pile of routine paperwork she had to get through that day. Then there was the filing to do and customers on the telephone with 'stupid' queries.

Josie, her line manager, suggests that she should deal with her tasks in the following order:

1  urgent and important tasks – the January sales figures, shifting the computers

2  important routine tasks – these include processing and checking documentation, answering customer queries

3  urgent and less important tasks – it will not take long to get some more coffee

4  important and non-urgent tasks – the printouts for the next day (Friday)

5  less important and non-urgent tasks – filing (daily filing and shifting old files)

Josie also suggests that Flick compiles a prioritised 'To Do' list of all her non-routine tasks. She can then tick off the items as she does them. This will replace all the notes and Post-it stickers she has all over her desk. It can also be updated as she is asked to carry out new non-routine tasks.

FLICK'S 'TO DO' LIST

1  January sales figures for the Accounts Manager.

2  Thursday 2.00 pm move computers.

3  Coffee - get jars of ordinary <u>and</u> decaff at lunch time.

4  Print out top 10 customer activity reports for Josie, Friday.

5  Move old customer sales files to new drawer, as and when.

## USING PLANNING AIDS

The Case Study on the last few pages has shown how an employee has become more effective by becoming more organised and prioritising tasks. The Post-it notes are important in the process, but they are only a start. There are a number of planning aids available to help with organisation, time planning and prioritisation. These include:

- a 'To Do' list – as seen above
- a diary
- a planning schedule
- an action plan

### 'To Do' lists

Making lists of things 'to do' are very common both at work and at home, ranging from the type of list shown above to the very basic family shopping list. It is the organised person, however, who writes these lists on an ongoing basis, possibly daily, incorporating actions which have not been ticked off on the previous day in a new list. In other words, tasks that have not been done are carried forward onto a new list. Lists may be written on paper or they may be compiled on the computer as a form of electronic 'Post-it' note.

'To do' lists may be subdivided to show the priorities of the tasks to be done. Look at the example below.

---

**'TO DO' LIST**                                                    1 April

**urgent stuff**

1   Aged debtors schedules for the Accounts Manager for today.

2   Sales summaries for Costings section for today.

3   Get March statements in the post today.

**non-urgent**

1   Print out activity reports for overseas customers.

2   Set up spreadsheet for regional sales analysis.

3   Look into venues for staff evening out.

---

## diaries

The diary organises tasks in terms of time. They are very useful planning aids and ensure – if they are efficiently kept – that tasks and events do not clash. Diaries can be paper-based or electronic. They can be individual diaries or office or 'section' diaries used for a group of employees.

The traditional paper-based diary with a week to view can be used alongside 'To do' lists as an efficient way of time planning and prioritising. Some people keep the 'To do' lists in their diary. The diary shown below is kept by a line manager.

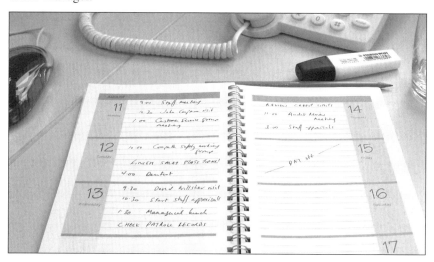

### planning schedules

Planning schedules are rather more complex planning devices which deal with situations such as projects where:

- some tasks *have to* follow on from each other – to give a simple example, you have to boil the water before making a cup of coffee – these are known as **critical** activities; you cannot achieve what you want without doing them in sequence

- some tasks are **non-critical** – they are important, but the timing is not so crucial – you will have to put coffee in the cup, but you can do it while the kettle is boiling or even the day before if you want!

So whether you are making coffee or planning a space launch, the principles remain the same. Sometimes there will be a non-routine activity in the workplace, which is complicated and involves a number of inter-dependent tasks. Organisations often use a visual representation of the tasks in the form of horizontal bars set against a time scale to help with the planning. These are known as Gannt charts and can be drawn up manually, or, more often these days, on the computer screen using dedicated software.

It is unlikely that you will have to plan a project in this way, but you may well have to interpret a chart to see *how* you or your section will be involved, and *when*. The Case Study below shows what happens when an office relocates.

**Case Study**

## HERMES BUREAU: A PLANNING SCHEDULE

### situation

You work for a computer bureau – Hermes Bureau – which provides accounting, payroll and other computer services to a wide range of commercial customers.

The business plans to invest in new premises shortly, and has purchased the lease of an office in the town, and will be able to move in six months' time.

The management of Hermes is taking the opportunity when moving to update its computer hardware and software systems.

There are a number of important tasks to carry out before the business moves, and the management has drawn up the list set out on the next page. The software needs updating and customising by programmers, and this will be the task which will take the most time. You see that all the tasks will have to be completed before the new office can become operational, and the obvious fact that the ordering of software and hardware can only take place after full assessment. The management allows itself a clear two week planning period before starting the process.

Hermes is very busy at the moment. When should the planning start?

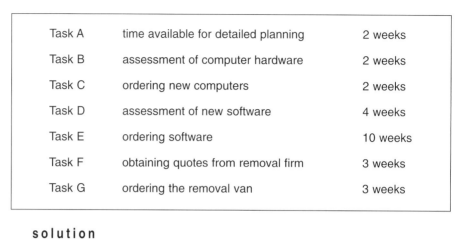

| | | |
|---|---|---|
| Task A | time available for detailed planning | 2 weeks |
| Task B | assessment of computer hardware | 2 weeks |
| Task C | ordering new computers | 2 weeks |
| Task D | assessment of new software | 4 weeks |
| Task E | ordering software | 10 weeks |
| Task F | obtaining quotes from removal firm | 3 weeks |
| Task G | ordering the removal van | 3 weeks |

## solution

The Gannt planning chart drawn up by Hermes Bureau shows:

- the activities on a weekly schedule (the weeks are numbered across the top)
- the critical activities as black bars
- the activities which are not critical as grey bars
- float times for non-critical activities – ie times during which a delay can occur which will not hold up the project – as white bars

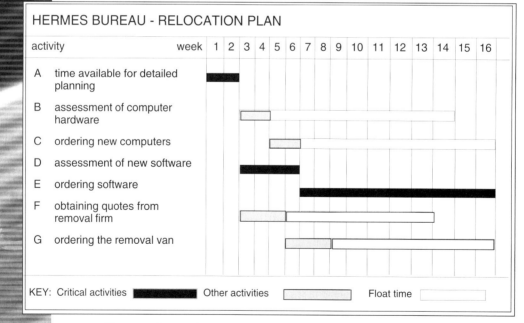

You can also see from this chart that the black bars represent the *priority* activities: planning, software assessment and software ordering. The grey bars are the non-priority activities which can be slotted in when convenient. What you effectively have in this chart is the type of prioritised list seen earlier in this chapter, but a prioritised list set on a time schedule. The visual aspect of the chart makes it easier to understand.

## action plans

After a series of activities has been scheduled over time, as in the last Case Study, the organisation can then carry out more detailed planning in the form of an **action plan** which will:

* define each activity in detail
* establish start dates for individual activities
* establish target finish dates
* state who is responsible for carrying out each activity
* in some cases state the cost of each activity

This form of plan is a form of checklist which can be regularly monitored and amended as required. Plans rarely go according 'to plan'. Computer spreadsheets are often used for setting out action plans because they can be easily amended and printed out in revised form.

The example below shows an action plan used in a marketing department which is launching a new product. As the months pass, the plan will be monitored, updated and actual costs checked to see if they are within budget.

# Enigma Limited

# marketing action plan

Product 247G - launch date April

| Month | Activity | Person in charge | completed | budget £ | actual £ |
|---|---|---|---|---|---|
| Feb | Book press adverts - trade magazines | RP | 6 Feb | 5,600 | 5,750 |
| Feb | Leaflet design | HG | 12 Feb | 1,200 | 1,200 |
| Feb | Catalogue design | HG | 12 Feb | 2,400 | 2,750 |
| March | Leaflet printing | GF | | 12,000 | |
| March | Catalogue printing | GF | | 34,500 | |
| March | Press releases | DD | | 100 | |
| April | Public launch on 1 April | DD | | 50,000 | |
| April | Leaflet mailings | DD | | 5,600 | |
| April | Catalogue mailings | DD | | 7,500 | |
| April | Mailing of samples | VF | | 3,500 | |
| May | Telesales to follow mailings | DD | | 2,400 | |

## MONITORING AND CHANGING PRIORITIES

So far in this chapter we have dealt with the techniques for planning and prioritising tasks. We have also looked at the planning aids that can be used, ranging from simple 'To Do' checklists to complex schedules and action plans for projects.

### the importance of monitoring

But things never go quite according to plan. The unexpected can occur and what seems like a quiet productive day can turn into a stressful time, full of awkward decisions. An important aspect of working is therefore **monitoring** what is going on. Is everything going to plan? If it is, tasks can be carried out in the decided order of priority. If it is not, changes will have to be made: tasks may change in order of priority, tasks may have to be delegated or delayed, or you may have to go to a higher authority and ask for help.

This planning and monitoring process can be seen in the diagram shown below.

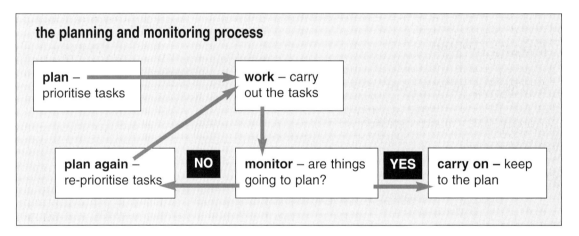

### dealing with changed priorities

At the beginning of a working day you are likely to have a set list of tasks and priorities. You may have a 'To Do' list to work from and a diary for specific timed events. But all sorts of things can happen, but hopefully not at the same time:

- your colleague, who shares your work, is off sick, so you have twice as much paperwork to deal with as usual

- the post – which brings the bulk of the documents you have to process – does not arrive because of a postal strike

- your email system breaks down because there is a virus in the server

These situations call for tasks to be re-prioritised, for resources to be assessed, and for assistance to be called for. Your work plans will have to be changed, as we will see in the Case Study which follows.

**Case Study**

# FLICK'S DAY – CHANGING THE PRIORITIES

Flick works as an accounts assistant at the Liverpool head office of Estro PLC, a company that makes vacuum cleaners.

The Case Study which starts on page 259 showed how Flick prioritised her tasks on one working day – Thursday 6 February.

In this Case Study we will see how she copes with unexpected events on that day by changing the priorities of her tasks and asking for help from managerial staff where appropriate.

To recap on what Flick had planned for Thursday:

1   The urgent tasks were to provide the January sales figures for the Accounts Manager and to help with moving the computers in the afternoon.

2   Flick had planned to get some jars of office coffee at lunchtime.

3   There was the normal daily sales order processing work and filing to be done.

4   Flick also had to provide some customer activity printouts for the following day and had been asked to move some filing records.

**Flick's problems**

Flick was faced with a number of problems as soon as she got to work on the Thursday. These meant that her carefully thought out work plan was in trouble and would have to be revised. The problems were:

1   **09.30**. Her colleague, Kirsty, who helped her with her sales order processing work had to go home sick. She had eaten a dodgy curry the night before and was in no fit state to work. There was a trainee working on the invoicing as well, but Flick doubted if this trainee could cope with the extra work involved.

2   **10.00**. Flick saw from Kirsty's note that she had to give the Accounts Manager the January sales figures 'as soon as possible'. This seemed a bit vague. Did it mean during the morning, or would later in the day be OK?

3   **11.30**. Flick's printer jammed and a long run of invoices was ruined. She could not seem to get it to work again.

4   **12.00**. The Human Resources Manager phoned through to ask if she could 'pop in' to see her at 1.45. Was she free then? Flick knew that she had to move the computers at 2.00.

5   **12.30**. Flick realised that she was going to have to work for most of her lunch break. What about the coffee she was supposed to be getting?

Flick was faced with a number of situations which clearly meant that her work plan was going to be disrupted and would have to be revised. But how was she to do this? She obviously needed to make suggestions to the management about what should be done. Some of the decisions would have to be made by the management.

**09.30 Kirsty away off sick**

Kirsty's absence would mean that Kirsty's routine processing work would have to be done by someone else – either Flick (who was busy anyway) or the trainee – unless it could be left until the next day. Flick would need to assess how much work there was and then speak to the line manager, Josie. The line manager said to Flick 'Do what you can, concentrating on orders from the important customers. The rest will have to wait. I don't think the trainee can be left on her own yet.' Flick was not too happy about this because she was very busy herself. She would have to put some of her other tasks back in order of priority.

**10.00 the figures for the Accounts Manager**

Flick realised that this was a priority job. To clarify what 'as soon as possible' really meant, she emailed the Accounts Manager who replied that the figures would be needed by lunchtime that day for a meeting in the afternoon. This job remained top priority.

**11.30 printer jam**

The printer jam had to be referred to the line manager who called in the maintenance engineer. Flick knew that the invoices would have to be printed that day, so she arranged to print them on another printer through the network. She lost valuable time in sorting out this problem and only got back to work at 11.50, by which time she was getting really stressed.

**12.00 Human Resources Manager**

Flick realised that the 1.45 appointment with the Human Resources Manager would clash with having to move the computers. The request, however, came from a senior manager and took priority over most other tasks. Flick referred the problem to her line manager who said it would be OK for Flick to go to the appointment. Flick was secretly quite pleased to miss lugging the computers about.

**12.30 coffee?**

Flick realised that she would have to work through some of her lunch hour, which meant that she would not be able to get the coffee. She explained this to Jack, another colleague, who agreed to get the coffee for her.

**17.00 end of the day review . . .**

Flick is in good spirits because she has had a productive afternoon. Her work targets for the day have largely been completed, despite the changes of plan. The sales figures have been given to the Accounts Manager and much of the sales processing work has been completed. Flick has had an interview with the Human Resources Manager and even arranged for the coffee to be bought. How has this all been achieved? Flick has successfully reworked her priorities and made the most of her resources – delegating tasks and consulting higher authorities where appropriate.

## WORKING IN ACCORDANCE WITH THE LAW AND REGULATIONS

When you work, you should always ensure that you are complying with the law and regulations, both UK legislation and European directives.

### observing equal opportunities

Employers must take great care these days with **equal opportunities** legislation in order not to discriminate in terms of sex, race, religion or age. These are covered in more detail in the next chapter.

### Data Protection Act

Employees always have to take care with confidentiality of information held both in paper records and also on computers. Unauthorised access to this information should not be given to people outside the organisation – or to employees.

The **Data Protection Act (1998)** protects the confidentiality of information about individuals. It follows the guidelines of an EC Directive and brings the UK in line with European legal principles. The Act applies to:

- a filing system of records held on **computer** – eg a computer database of customer names, addresses, telephone numbers, sales details

- a **manual** set of accessible records – eg a card index file system of customer details

All organisations which process personal data should register with the Data Protection Commission.

The Data Protection Act requires that an organisation should not reveal, without permission:

- information about one customer to another customer

- information about its employees

Data should be kept securely and must be accurate.

### retention of records

Business records are normally stored for at least **six years** (and a minimum of three years for payroll data). There are a number of legal reasons why financial data should be kept for this period of time:

- accounting records should be kept so that they can be inspected by the Inland Revenue (part of HM Revenue & Customs) if required in the case of a tax inspection

- accounting records should be kept so that they can be inspected by HM Revenue & Customs if there is a VAT inspection

**Chapter Summary**

■ Employees in an organisation are encouraged to work together to achieve the objectives of the organisation.

■ Employees are also required to work according to the established procedures of the organisation and also in line with their job descriptions.

■ Tasks can be classified in a number of different ways – routine and non-routine, urgent and non-urgent, important and less important.

■ Employees should acquire the skill of prioritising tasks according to these classifications and be able to plan their activities accordingly.

■ A 'rule of thumb' order of priority for tasks is:

1 urgent and important tasks

2 urgent and less important tasks

3 important and not urgent tasks

4 tasks that are neither urgent nor important

The second and third of these may be interchangeable, according to the context of the task.

■ Employees should be familiar with different types of planning aids. They should be able to write their own 'To Do' lists and diaries. They should be able to understand complex planning aids such as project planning schedules and action plans, but it is unlikely they will have to draw them up.

■ Employees should understand the need to monitor the progress of a work plan over time and have the flexibility to be able to re-prioritise if unexpected events happen.

■ If priorities have to change, employees should be able to consult the appropriate higher authority if help is needed; they should also be able to delegate tasks if the need arises and the resources are available.

■ Employees need to be aware of the legal restrictions on work practices. These are wide ranging and cover areas such as:

– observing equal opportunities in the workplace

– the need for confidentiality and observance of the Data Protection Act

– regulations for the retention of records

| **Key Terms** | | |
|---|---|---|
| | **objective** | a goal towards which employees work, eg customer care, profitability |
| | **procedures** | sets of instructions which dictate the way tasks should be carried out in an organisation |
| | **job description** | a formal document issued by the employer setting out the extent of the tasks that an employee should carry out |
| | **routine task** | a task which is part of the everyday work of an employee |
| | **non-routine task** | an unexpected task which is not part of the everyday work of an employee |
| | **urgent task** | a task which has a pressing deadline |
| | **important task** | a task for which the employee is given specific responsibility and the completion of which significantly affects other employees |
| | **prioritising** | deciding the specific order in which tasks should be carried out |
| | **'To Do' list** | a checklist of tasks which can be ticked off when they are completed |
| | **planning schedule** | a chart used for planning projects which organises tasks in terms of time and priority; it normally identifies the 'critical' tasks and allocates time for their completion |
| | **action plan** | a checklist for a series of activities (normally for a project) which lists the main tasks consecutively by time period (eg monthly) and allocates responsibility and sets target dates for completion – it is very useful for monitoring progress |
| | **monitoring** | the process of examining the progress of the work plan and re-prioritising tasks where appropriate |
| | **equal opportunities** | the legal protection for employees which helps to prevent workplace discrimination on the grounds of age, sex, race and religion |
| | **confidentiality** | preventing personal records of employees and outsiders (on paper and computer file) falling into the hands of unauthorised people |

# Student Activities

**16.1**   What is the difference between a routine task and a non-routine task? Give examples of both from your own experience of the workplace.  (If you have not been at work, ask family and friends).

**16.2**   Explain what is meant by the term 'prioritisation of tasks' and state why the process is necessary.

**16.3**   (a)   Define the difference between an urgent task and an important task.

          (b)   Normally an urgent task should be done before an important task. Give an example of a situation where the opposite may be true.

**16.4**   Give two examples of planning aids which are (or should be) commonly used by most employees in the workplace.

**16.5**   The eleven tasks below are examples of activities which a payroll assistant may have to carry out in an Accounts Department of a medium-sized company. It is Monday in the last week of the month and the office has just opened. Employees in the organisation are paid monthly, on the last day of the month, which is at the end of this week. The payroll has to be run through the computer on Monday and BACS instructions sent to the bank on Tuesday so that employees can be paid on Friday.

You are to reorganise the list, placing the tasks in order of priority.

■   Look at the section diary and compare with your 'To Do' list.

■   Send email to Marketing Department asking for monthly overtime figures to be sent through – they should have been received last Friday.

■   Check that details of hours worked (including overtime) have been received from all departments.

■   Distribute the departmental post.

■   Draw up a notice advertising a staff trip out for next month.

■   Process the hours of all the employees on the computer. Print out pay details and a payroll summary, including the schedule setting out the amount which will have to be paid to the Inland Revenue for income tax and National Insurance Contributions by 19th of the next month.

■   Pass the payroll printouts to your line manager for checking, and when approved, print out the payslips for distribution.

■   Put a note in the diary for the Inland Revenue cheque to be prepared on 5th of next month.

■   Print out payroll statistics from the computer for your line manager – they are required for next week.

■   Prepare the BACS payroll schedule for the bank to process on Tuesday.

■   Pass the BACS payroll schedule to your line manager for checking.

**16.6** *Note: this Activity can only be carried out after you have completed Activity 16.5.*

When you have prioritised your tasks in the payroll section, a number of events happen during the day which mean you might not be able to do all the work you had planned.

How would you react to the following situations? In each case explain what you would do and what the implications would be for your work plan for the day.

Remember that you can ask for help from colleagues or refer difficulties to a higher authority.

(a)     You get a call from Reception at 9.30, saying that your car in the car park has still got its lights on.

(b)     At 10.30 the Human Resources Manager calls to ask if you would like to sit in on a Quality Circle meeting at 14.00 to discuss Customer Service.

(c)     You get a call from reception at 11.30 saying that a friend has called and wants to talk on a personal matter.

(d)     When you are processing the email from Admin Department giving overtime hours, you notice that two employees are recorded as having worked 50 hours overtime. The normal maximum is 5 hours.

(e)     The computer system crashes, just as you are finishing processing the payroll.


**16.7** Your work routine as an employee will be affected by various legal constraints. What area of legislation is involved in each of the following situations, and how would you deal with each request?

(a)     You are asked to set up a photo shoot of members of your workforce, who vary in sex, race and age. The picture will appear in a catalogue of your products.

(b)     A customer telephones and asks for the address and telephone number of another of your customers.

(c)     A colleague has been asked to sort out the firm's old filing. She asks if she can shred the payroll records which are more than two years old. She says 'I get queries on last month's payroll, but, apart from the annual payroll return to HM Revenue & Customs, nobody seems interested in them.'

## this chapter covers . . .

In this chapter we examine the importance of maintaining good working relationships with colleagues and the part played by effective communication and mutual respect and understanding between people in the workplace.

We explain the way in which a team should work together in order to achieve the objectives of the organisation, with team members helping and supporting each other to meet deadlines.

We also discuss how team work can go wrong, with conflicts breaking out and team members becoming dissatisfied with each other and the tasks in hand. Situations such as these can either be sorted out within the team, or they may need to be referred to a higher authority to provide a solution.

The chapter concludes with an introduction to the need for equal opportunities in the workplace, specifically in the areas of discrimination (gender, race, age, disability, harassment and flexible working).

## PERFORMANCE CRITERIA COVERED

**unit 31: ACCOUNTING WORK SKILLS**

**element 13.3**

**perform effectively in the workplace**

C    *Communicate courteously with, and support, colleagues in work tasks to build effective working relationships.*

D    *Follow organisational procedures to find workable solutions to conflicts or difficulties in working relationships.*

## TEAMWORK

### what is a team?

Working with others implies the need for teamwork. It is easy to start to define a team by giving examples – a football team, a workplace team – and explaining that they work together – sometimes well and sometimes not quite so well. But what exactly is a team?

**A team is a group of people working together to achieve defined objectives.**

In the workplace a team can be a 'section group' working in one part of an office – eg a payroll section – or it can be a group working on a project, eg a group set up to improve customer service.

### benefits of teamwork

People working in a team often achieve better results than if they work on their own. The benefits include:

- **pooling of skills and abilities:** some people are better at some tasks and some are better at others, and so a team will take advantage of individual strengths and overcome individual weaknesses

- **creative thinking:** working with other people means that individuals can be stimulated to create and share ideas on a scale that would probably not be possible if they were working on their own

- **motivation:** people get a 'buzz' out of working in a team – it gets people going and brings its rewards when the team is successful

- **help and support:** team members usually support each other when support is needed – this can take the form of advice, moral support and assisting with or taking over tasks which may be causing a problem

### working at teamwork

Teamwork requires that team members are dedicated to achieving the team objective. This means that team members should:

- be committed to the work of the team

- understand their role in the team and the tasks they are allotted

- take full responsibility for what they do

- assume joint responsibility for the work of the whole team

- take note of and work to the schedules imposed by the team

Teamwork can, however, go wrong. Conflicts and their resolution are dealt with on pages 281 to 283.

## COMMUNICATION AND TEAMWORK

The vital link between team members is **communication**. Although employees will communicate with outsiders – customers and suppliers, for example – it is the effectiveness of the internal communication channels which will make a significant difference to the success of teamwork. Communication channels include:

- oral communication – talking to people face-to-face
- oral communication – talking to people on the telephone
- written notes and memoranda
- fax
- email
- word-processed documents

We will describe the effective use of these communication methods in turn.

### face-to-face oral communication

*the importance of face-to-face communication*

The time-honoured traditional method of communication is speech. This involves not just the words, but the body language and the tone of voice used. In the workplace this can take a number of forms:

- talking to and discussing work matters with colleagues informally
- passing on messages
- giving instructions
- taking part in informal and formal meetings
- interviews

Whole books have been written on the subject of communication skills and body language, but the basic guidelines for effective oral communication are:

- think about what you are going to say before you say it
- say it clearly and in an appropriate tone of voice
- look at the person (or people) you are speaking to and try to look positive and as if you mean what you are saying
- think 'body language' – do not yawn and look out of the window!
- try to make sure that what you have said has been understood by asking the person (people) involved
- listen to what is said in reply – and make notes if necessary

## oral communication – the telephone

no need to worry about facial expressions on the telephone!

The same principles apply as for face-to-face communication, but remember that when speaking on the telephone you cannot rely on body language and facial expressions to convey your meaning, unless, of course, you have a video telephone. It is important when speaking on the telephone to:

- identify yourself and make sure that you know to whom you are speaking

- if you are taking an external call you will need to comply with your 'house style' for replying – the type of ringing tone in most organisations will tell you if this is the case

- speak extra clearly – remembering that the tone of your voice will compensate for the body language that will be missing

## written notes and memoranda

Flick – Accounts Manager wants January sales figures by lunchtime today!

Kirsty 6 Feb 9.30

You can also communicate with team members using written **notes** and memoranda. Post-it notes or formal in-house notes are very useful in passing messages on – telephone messages received and reminders, for example. The important elements on a note are:

- the name of the person the note is for
- the name of the person the note is from
- the date and time
- the message, setting out clearly and concisely what is required

The **memorandum** ('memo') is a formal note used within an organisation. It can be addressed to one individual, or copied to members of a team. The use of the memorandum nowadays is on the decline as internal email becomes more popular.

---

## MEMORANDUM

**To**      John Stone, Finance Manager

**From**      Tim Blake, Sales Manager      **Ref**   TB/AC/1098

**Copies to**   n/a      **Date** 23 June 2007

**Subject**      Bad payers

---

Please can you let me have an updated list of our customers who exceed their credit period and pay late. By Friday 27th please. Thanks.

### electronic communication – fax

The fax (short for 'facsimile') enables you to transmit electronically an exact copy of the details on a sheet of paper. This can either be done on a computer or on a fax machine. If you use a fax machine you feed the sheet into the machine, dial up the recipient on the inbuilt telephone pad and transmit the document down the line. The machine at the other end will print out an exact copy of the original document.

If you are sending a fax externally – a copy invoice to a customer, for example, you normally send a 'fax header' first sheet and then feed in any further pages/documents as required. If the fax is internal you can just send an A4 sheet with a note written on it, or whatever you need to communicate – it could be a map of how to get to a client's premises.

### electronic communication – email

Email is the sending and receiving of electronic messages by means of computer. Emails can be:

- external – communications with customers through the internet, or
- internal – through a network of computers in the business – an intranet

Emails can be sent quickly and cheaply within the UK and overseas.

When someone wants to check an email account, it is necessary to log in. A list of messages is displayed. The user can read them or delete them. When a message is read, it is easy to reply to it. The original message re-appears and comments can be added to the original. If a message is of interest to someone else, it can be forwarded. Computer files – eg spreadsheets – can also be sent by email as 'attachments'.

When composing an email, a screen such as the one illustrated below is used.

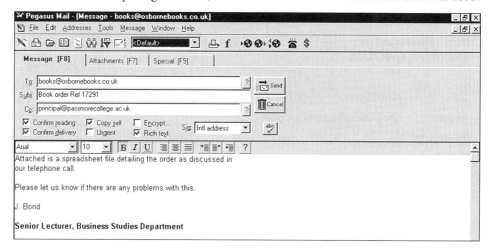

## word-processed documents

Word-processing programs are now common in the workplace. They are used for producing a wide variety of written documents, often in a set 'house style'. Standard letters and memos can easily be produced from template files set up on the computer.

Mail-merge facilities enable a word-processed letter file to import names and addresses from a computer database file and print out a batch for sending out. Word-processing programs can produce documents with sophisticated page layouts and tables; they can also import graphics and embody colour elements for illustrative purposes.

If you are working in a team – in an everyday work situation or a project team – you may well use a word-processing package for:

- letters and memos (see illustration of a memo below)
- internal forms and stationery
- order forms for customers
- meeting agendas
- meeting minutes
- notices to team members
- formal reports

You will no doubt be able to think of other ways in which word-processing is used in the workplace.

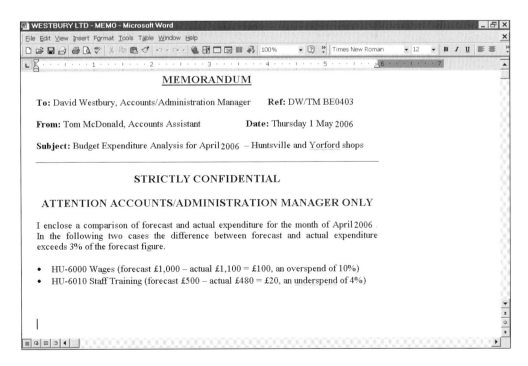

# CREATING GOOD WORKING RELATIONSHIPS

## what does a team need?

Remember that a team at work can be a group – a section – which works together on a daily basis, or it can be a special project team set up for a specific and limited purpose. A team needs to establish for itself:

- **objectives** – eg a level of quality in the case of a 'section' team, a specific result in the case of a project team

- levels of **resources** – people, equipment, time, money

- a definition of **working methods** – deciding how the work is to be carried out, and by whom

- **schedules** – time targets for specific tasks

In the case of a work 'section' team these factors will be based on current practice, and will be refined over time, improved perhaps by regular team meetings to discuss the way the team works.

In the case of a 'project' team, the team members will sit down and plan out all these factors at the start of the project.

## types of team member

If you have worked in any form of team, you will know that there are many different types of character that can make up that team:

- the leader – who may be a natural leader, appointed by the group, or who may be an employee appointed to a position of responsibility

- an ideas person who provides inspiration to the group

- the steady worker who gets things done

- the slacker and complainer who does not get things done and causes problems

- the person who provides moral and practical support to others when problems arise

## ideal qualities of a team member

In order to create good working relationships, as a team member you should ideally:

- be pleasant and polite to other team members

- be prepared to co-operate, even if you do not agree with everything that is decided

- respect the opinions of others and be prepared to listen to what others have to say

- ask others if you need help and be prepared to help others if they need it
- avoid backbiting and criticising the leader behind his/her back
- keep confidences – if information is not to be released, you should keep quiet about it (this is also a requirement of the Data Protection Act)

This probably sounds all very theoretical and ideal. In the Case Study on page 283 we examine how this works in practice. First, however, we must also explain what can go wrong in working relationships, and how those problems can be resolved.

## DEALING WITH PROBLEMATIC WORKING RELATIONSHIPS

### what can go wrong?

Problems are often caused by disagreements. These disagreements can either be resolved within the team, or exceptionally they may have to be referred to a higher authority. There are two main causes of disagreement:

- **the nature of the work** itself and the way it is carried out – for example a new line manager joining the team with very different ideas about how the work should be tackled
- **personal conflicts** within the group – clashes of personality types, even extending to bullying and other forms of harassment

Very often the two areas combine to produce a problem which can be very difficult to sort out. Look at the illustration below which shows what can irritate other people at work and cause problems in working relationships.

## causes of breakdowns in working relationships

**I do not like people who are . . .**

- inefficient
- inflexible
- rude
- over-critical
- over-sensitive
- sexist

**I do not like people who have . . .**

- an inflated opinion of themselves
- personal hygiene problems

## sorting out disagreements within a team

It is important for team members to resolve problems in working relationships themselves, within the dynamics of the team, if that is possible.

If the problem is simply one which relates to **the work itself** – for example procedures for the processing of sales orders – it could be sorted out by informal discussion between team members (ie work colleagues) and then referral to a higher authority.

If the problem is one which relates to a **personal conflict between team members** – for example 'she's too slow at her work, and always on the phone to her boyfriend' or 'he's a real pain to work with because he's always making insulting remarks' – the problem should be sorted by other means, for example:

• observing other people dealing with that person – do they have the same problems?

• talking it over with other members of the team – do they think the same way, or is it just you getting things out of proportion?

• talking to the person involved – do they actually realise how they affect other people?

If there really is a problem – and it's not just you being negative or over-sensitive – then the matter should be raised with a higher authority.

## taking the matter further – grievance procedures

If the working relationship problem is actually one of harassment – for example bullying or someone making passes at you – the matter should definitely be raised with a higher authority. If it is the line manager who is the cause of the problem, the matter should be referred to a more senior authority.

If the matter is very serious, the **grievance procedure** can be adopted. A **grievance** is a complaint against the employer. Grievances can include:

• unfair treatment by managers – for example, being passed over for promotion because of gender or race; unfair dismissal (an extreme case!)

• unfair pay – men paid more than women for the same work

All employers must have a written grievance procedure. This will be set down in writing and made available to all employees. It will state:

• the person to whom the employee must go to with their complaint – often a chat with the employee's line manager (as we saw above) will be enough to sort matters out.

• if the employee is still not happy with the way they are being treated they will be allowed to make a formal complaint to a senior manager, or even to a director

- if the employee is still not happy with the result, they may then have to go outside the organisation and take the matter to an Employment Tribunal (an independent informal court)

If the employee is a Trade Union member, the Union will be able to give advice and support in every stage of the process. The Union will also give support in the case of a disciplinary procedure.

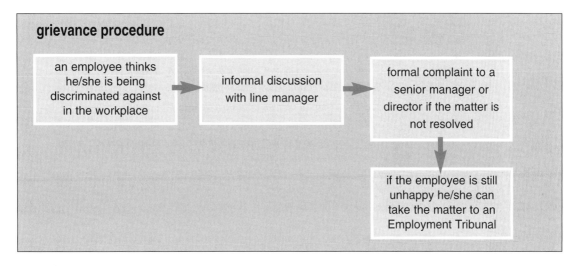

### grievance procedure

an employee thinks he/she is being discriminated against in the workplace → informal discussion with line manager → formal complaint to a senior manager or director if the matter is not resolved → if the employee is still unhappy he/she can take the matter to an Employment Tribunal

We will now look at a Case Study which shows how working relationships are developed within a work team, and the way in which problems can be resolved.

## Case Study

# WORKING ON RELATIONSHIPS

### situation

The accounts staff of Hermes Limited, which sells motor accessories, have been asked to provide sales information for the Marketing Department. The team from the Accounts Department is headed up by Jen, a line manager. She will be helped by two accounts assistants, Tom and Jacqui.

*Jen is a line manager, an organiser, experienced at her work and respected by staff.*

*She can sometimes be intolerant of people who do not seem to know what they are doing.*

*She is also old-fashioned and sexist, preferring to have female assistants, claiming privately that they are quicker and more accurate at their work than male assistants.*

**Tom** *is a mature and experienced accounts assistant, a hard worker, accurate and with an eye for detail.*

*He is not as fast as some assistants, but he can be relied upon to keep to deadlines.*

*He is also ready to help others when they need assistance. He has a quiet personality, but is popular in the office.*

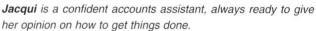

**Jacqui** *is a confident accounts assistant, always ready to give her opinion on how to get things done.*

*She is sometimes inaccurate because she tends to work too quickly.*

*She is capable of achieving her targets, however, when given help and encouragement.*

## the project

The Accounts Department has been asked by the Marketing Department to provide regular monthly statistics relating to customer sales. The requirements are:

1   sales by product and unit

2   sales by product and sales value (£)

3   the percentage of sales (in £) analysed into:
  - customers who buy on credit
  - cash sales
  - e-commerce (credit card/debit card sales from the company's website)

4   total sales (£) for each of the top 20 credit customers

This will require

- the analysis of sales figures extracted from the company's computer accounting system
- the setting up of spreadsheets to analyse the data
- the setting up of a monthly report template on a word-processing program – this will include charts imported from the spreadsheet program

## the meeting

Jen calls a meeting of her team to discuss how they are going to set up this system and maintain it to produce the monthly statistics.

They decide the following:

**objective**          the objective is to provide regular monthly sales statistics for the Marketing Department

**resources**
- two assistants (Tom and Jacqui)
- computers and computer time
- data held on the computer and in manual records
- assistance and monitoring from line manager (Jen)

**work scheduling**
- Tom, who has good IT skills, is to work on the spreadsheets and the report format. He will then help Jacqui input the data into the spreadsheets and extract the report
- Jacqui is to extract the data held on the computer accounting system and some manual records
- Jen will monitor and supervise the whole process with regular meetings

**deadlines**
- 2 weeks for Tom to complete spreadsheets and Jacqui to extract the data
- 2 further weeks for transferring data to the spreadsheets and producing the first report
- total time allowed 4 weeks

## what actually happened

### Week 1

At the end of the first week Jen calls a meeting to monitor progress on the project. Tom has worked to schedule and has prepared the spreadsheets set up to process the statistics. Jacqui has fallen behind in extracting the data, which means that Tom has insufficient test data to input. Jen says, laughing 'Don't worry, Jacqui will soon catch up, she is a good quick worker, like all the girls in this office.' Tom keeps silent about this sexist remark.

### Week 2

During week 2 Tom finds out that Jacqui's data is incomplete and inaccurate. He offers to put it right for her, so that he can ensure that the data for the spreadsheets will be accurate. Jacqui is happy to accept Tom's assistance. Tom also completes the word-processed report template. Tom knows that the deadline is important, because if the project falls behind, the Marketing Department will not get their figures on time.

At the end of the second week Jen calls a meeting to monitor progress. She is pleased with progress and jokingly remarks to Jacqui that things are going well and that Jacqui 'must have given Tom a helping hand.' Tom is very angry about this but says nothing.

**Weeks 3 and 4**

During the final two weeks, Tom and Jacqui are scheduled to work together to complete the project, and it is during these two weeks that problems occur.

Tom resents the fact that he has to help Jacqui to meet the deadlines, but what really annoys him is that Jen does not recognise his effort, but in fact makes sexist remarks at his expense.

Tom has two problematic working relationships – and neither of them are really his fault: he has to work extra hard to make up for Jacqui's shortcomings and he has to deal with discrimination from his superior.

So what are Tom's practical alternatives?

1   Tom can refuse to help Jacqui.

2   Tom can complain to Jen about Jacqui's inaccuracy.

3   Tom can complain to a more senior manager about Jen's sexist remarks.

    or . . .

4   Tom can carry on as he always has done and do more than his fair share of the work and try to ignore the sexism of his line manager, Jen.


## the solution

Tom decides to chat to his mate Dave about these problems.

**the Jacqui problem**

Dave suggests that Tom talks to other colleagues to see how they deal with Jacqui, but in the end he thinks Tom will have to accept the Jacqui situation as there will always be people at work who work less hard than their colleagues. Tom will certainly get no backing from Jen. If Tom refuses to help Jacqui, he is being unco-operative and is not helping the development of good working relations. The Jacqui problem is clearly one Tom will have to sort out himself.

**the Jen problem**

Dave points out that the sexist remarks made by Jen will be very annoying and hurtful, but unless Tom can produce any firm evidence of sexual discrimination in the workplace, he cannot bring any formal complaint against his line manager and start the grievance procedure.

Dave suggests that if Tom considers that his chances of promotion are being affected by reports given by Jen, he should talk to his departmental manager or to a Human Resources manager.

Dave also suggests that Tom takes the initiative and talks to Jen herself about the situation. This may not be the most obvious solution, but it may be that Jen does not realise that by making sexist remarks she is damaging a valuable working relationship. It may be that she thinks she is being funny. A frank and reasoned discussion with Jen may help to change Jen's attitude.

The 'right' solution to the Jen problem is far from clear. But as with the Jacqui problem, the solution is one that Tom will have to work out for himself. In the meantime he has his deadlines to meet and the project to complete . . .

## WORKING WITH OTHERS – EQUAL OPPORTUNITIES

### what are equal opportunities?

When you are working with other people it is important that you are aware of the legal implications of **equal opportunities** (often known as 'equal ops').In other words you must realise when discrimination is taking place in the workplace against certain groups of people, and when for some reason or other an employee is taken advantage of and is treated less well than a colleague. The principle here is that all employees should have equal opportunity: they should have the same rights and be treated on an equal basis.

Discrimination can occur in a number of situations, which we will deal with individually over the next few pages. For the purposes of your studies you do not have to remember the name or date of the relevant law, but you do have to recognise the legal principle involved, and perhaps more importantly, know what should be done about the situation.

The main areas of equal opportunity relate to:

- discrimination on the basis of gender
- racial discrimination
- 'ageism'
- dealing with disability
- harassment
- flexible working

### how 'equal ops' affect the employee

Employees have a number of responsibilities in the workplace. Most of them are dictated by normal social decency – in other words, they represent the behaviour of a socially responsible and normal humane person:

- being aware of any equal opportunities policy the employer may have and keeping to it
- treating everyone equally and fairly
- being able to recognise a situation where someone is being discriminated against
- having the courage to report any cases of discrimination of which he/she is aware

We will now describe the main areas where discrimination can occur and the legal protections that exist.

## discrimination by gender

This is a well-known form of discrimination, often known by the term 'sex discrimination'. The relevant Act of Parliament is the **Sex Discrimination Act 1975**. This law states that employers may not discriminate on grounds of gender. It makes it illegal to discriminate against a particular sex when:

- advertising to fill jobs available
- appointing employees for those jobs
- promoting staff into better jobs
- negotiating the terms and conditions of the job
- offering employees opportunities for training and development

If, for example, well-qualified female employees were consistently passed over for promotion in an accounts office in favour of male employees with inferior qualifications, there may well be a case to answer.

## racial discrimination

The **Race Relations Act 1976** makes it an offence to discriminate on the grounds of

- nationality
- colour
- ethnic, racial or national group

This relates to the same areas affected by discrimination by gender, ie when advertising jobs, appointing staff, promoting staff and providing staff benefits.

There are a few exceptions to the Act including ethnic restaurants wanting people of a particular race to work as waiters/waitresses to make the restaurant look more authentic and social work departments wanting to appoint staff of a particular race where they have to deal with social problems of people of the same race.

## age discrimination – 'ageism'

The **Employment Equality (Age) Regulations 2006** make it an offence to discriminate against a person on the grounds of age, for example when an organisation is recruiting for a job, and appointing and promoting staff in the workplace. Age discrimination can cover a wide range of age groups, eg:

- people seen as too 'young' for the job
- people seen as too 'old' for the job
- parents returning to work after bringing up children

Research has shown that age discrimination shows itself in the tendency for employers to prefer employees in the 25 to 35 age group.

## disability discrimination

The **Disability Discrimination Act 1995** provides protection for disabled persons. The Act requires that employers must not discriminate against disabled people when:

• advertising jobs and inviting applications

• offering jobs after interviews have taken place

• deciding the terms and conditions of the job

Once appointed, a disabled person must be treated the same as everyone else when training, promotion or any other benefits are on offer.

The employer must take reasonable steps to ensure that a disabled person can work on the premises. This includes making arrangements such as:

• modifying the buildings (entrances, ramps, lifts etc)

• allowing extra training so the disabled person can carry out the job

• putting a disabled person in a different, more convenient workplace (eg on the ground floor rather than three floors up)

## harassment

Harassment is unwanted behaviour that violates the dignity of a person or creates an intimidating, humiliating or offensive environment.

Harassment can take the form of sexual harassment or just plain bullying. It is covered in an amendment to the **Sex Discrimination Act**. Harassment can take many forms, and be related to

• age

• sex

• race

• disability

• religion

• sexual orientation

## flexible working

Under the **Flexible Working (Procedural Requirements) Regulations 2002** parents of children aged under six or disabled children aged under 18 have the right to apply to work flexibly and their employers will have a duty to consider these requests seriously. **Flexible working** includes arrangements such as flexitime, job-sharing and term-time working.

Eligible employees will be able to request a change to the hours they work or to possibility of working from home.

## Chapter Summary

- The benefits of teamwork include: the pooling of skills and abilities, the opportunity for creative thinking, motivation within the team, help and support from team members.

- Communication is important for the effective functioning of a team. Communication methods include: oral (face-to-face and telephone), notes and memoranda, faxes, email, word-processed documents.

- Teams can be normal day-to-day working groups, or they can be special project teams set up for specific purposes.

- When working in a team it is important that each member should be polite, co-operative, respectful of others, helpful, loyal and discreet.

- Working relationships within a team can go wrong, either because of the work itself, or because of a breakdown in the relationship – or both. When working relationships within a team do go wrong, they should ideally be resolved within the group. If that is not possible, they may have to be resolved by a higher authority using the grievance procedure.

- Employees need to appreciate the requirements of equal opportunity legislation, particularly in the areas of gender, race, age, disability, harassment and flexible working

## Key Terms

| | |
|---|---|
| **team** | a group of people working together to achieve defined objectives |
| **oral communication** | communication involving the spoken word – either face-to-face or telephone |
| **written communication** | communication involving writing – including notes and memoranda |
| **electronic communication** | communication involving electronic transmission of data – including faxes and emails |
| **grievance procedure** | the formal procedure to follow when you have a complaint against your employer |
| **Employment Tribunal** | an independent informal court which decides cases relating to employment problems |
| **equal opportunities** | the concept that all employees should be treated the same way, whatever their differences |
| **harassment** | violation of a person's dignity and feelings |
| **flexible working** | the ability to work hours that suits the parent of a child under six or of a disabled child |

# Student Activities

**17.1** Explain the meaning of the term 'team' and outline the benefits of working in a team.

**17.2** State the objectives of the team in which you work (or a team in which a friend or family member works).

**17.3** List the methods you (or friend or family member) use to communicate with colleagues during a working day. In each case state what type of message is involved.

**17.4** Write down the six qualities a team member should ideally possess to enable the team to function effectively.

*Optional task*: give yourself a score out of ten for each quality, add up the total score and convert to a percentage. How do you think you have done? How do you compare with your colleagues? How could you improve your teamwork skills?

**17.5** A new colleague, Jake, has just joined your team, and you find him to be an absolute pain – he thinks he knows everything, and doesn't. He also talks about colleagues and the line manager behind their backs.

What action could you take to deal with a character like Jake?

**17.6** Jasmina, a friend of yours, has worked in a payroll section for a number of years. She has a poor working relationship with her line manager, Tim, and as a result has been passed over for promotion a number of times. The line manager has been heard to say 'There's no point in promoting her and giving her all the extra training, she wants to have a baby, and may well leave the firm when it suits her.'

What practical advice can you give Jasmina about dealing with her working relationship with the line manager?

# 18 Performance, training and development

this chapter covers . . .

*In this chapter we examine the need for you to formulate and put into action a plan of self-improvement. This can involve the type of work you are already carrying out in the workplace, it can also involve career planning, ie investigating the type of work you would like to do in the future. Self-improvement involves a number of stages:*

- *taking stock of your current work activities and performance*

- *thinking about how you could develop your work activities and further your career*

- *investigating the ways in which you could acquire new skills and knowledge – by going on work training courses, taking qualifications, reading, surfing the internet*

- *reviewing your performance and progress from time-to-time to see how you are getting on*

*If you are not in employment, the same principles apply to your acquiring skills and knowledge which may help you get a job.*

## PERFORMANCE CRITERION COVERED

**unit 31: ACCOUNTING WORK SKILLS**

**element 13.3**

**perform effectively in the workplace**

E  *Review and evaluate performance and identify and agree training and development needs and objectives taking account of current work tasks and career goals.*

## WHY THIS CHAPTER IS DIFFERENT

This chapter is rather different from the other chapters in this book in that it is more loosely structured. It is intended as a series of guidance notes and hints rather than a formal 'lecture'. It is hoped that it will prove useful in helping you both with your career and with your accounting studies.

The diagram below shows you where you should be heading.

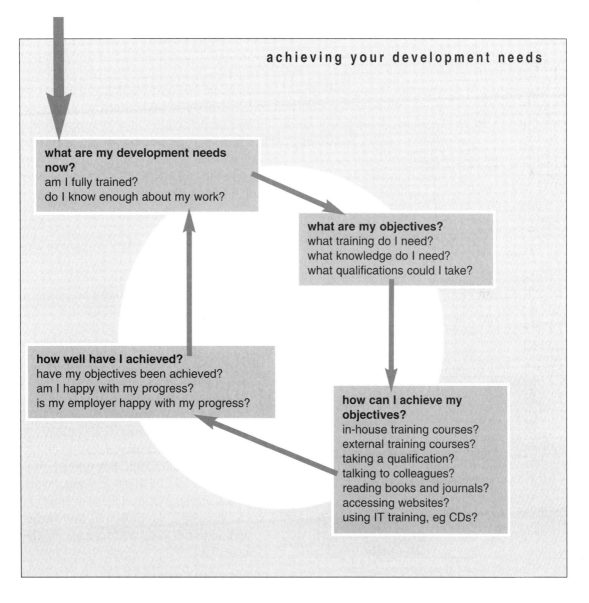

**achieving your development needs**

**what are my development needs now?**
am I fully trained?
do I know enough about my work?

**what are my objectives?**
what training do I need?
what knowledge do I need?
what qualifications could I take?

**how well have I achieved?**
have my objectives been achieved?
am I happy with my progress?
is my employer happy with my progress?

**how can I achieve my objectives?**
in-house training courses?
external training courses?
taking a qualification?
talking to colleagues?
reading books and journals?
accessing websites?
using IT training, eg CDs?

In order to improve your **performance** and career prospects – your **development needs** – you need to take stock of your current position and identify exactly where it is you want to go. The diagram on the bottom of the previous page shows a process which involves four stages:

1  what are my development needs now?

2  what are my objectives?

3  how can I achieve my objectives?

4  how well have I achieved?

The process, of course, is continuous and subject to continual review.

We will look at each of the four stages in turn.

## WHAT ARE MY DEVELOPMENT NEEDS NOW?

You may be in employment at present, or it is possible that you are not in work. Whatever the situation, you will need to take a look at what your personal development needs are. You need to carry out a form of personal 'audit' of your **knowledge** (what you know) and **skills** (how you put it into practice). How do you do this? You need to ask yourself a number of questions and also talk them over with colleagues. You will see that a number of the following questions can apply to people who are not in work:

1  Am I content with what I am doing at present?

2  Am I confident that I have the background knowledge for what I am doing at work?

3  Do I need further training for what I am doing at work?

4  Do my skills need developing? For example, do I need to go on a spreadsheet course? Do I need to improve my selling skills?

5  Where do I see myself working in a year's time?

6  Where do I see myself working in five year's time?

*talk it over at your appraisal interview*

If you are at work you may well discuss these issues on a regular basis with your management as part of the **appraisal** process. At the interview, objectives should be set, training needs identified and promotion prospects explored. You should always be given the opportunity of discussing with management how you can develop your **skills** and **knowledge** and improve your performance in the workplace.

## WHAT ARE MY OBJECTIVES?

When you have thought about your development and career needs, and discussed them with others, you will be in a position to set specific objectives – targets – for achievement. These will not be vague and woolly like 'I want to be a manager' or 'I want to be better at my work' but will be very specific. For example you might say that within the next twelve months . . . .

*'I need to learn more about spreadsheets because they are used a lot in the Accounts Department.'*

*'I need to learn more about the Sage computer accounting system. I can do the basics, but haven't a clue about doing journal entries. I don't really know my debits from my credits!'*

*'I'd like to do an accounting qualification – there seems to be a lot of opportunity in that area.'*

*'I need to know more about the theoretical background to the accounting work I am doing at the moment.'*

## HOW DO I ACHIEVE MY OBJECTIVES?

The objectives need to be made very specific. One reason for this is that your employer may have to book and arrange things for you. For example:

*'I need to go on an advanced Excel spreadsheet course at the local Training Centre so that I can process the Sales data and produce charts for management.'*

*'I need to work alongside Kulvinder for a week so that I can learn more about operating our Sage computer accounting system.'*

*'I want to enrol on a course in accounting at the local college because I want to be promoted within the department.'*

*'I need to read that Osborne Books accounting textbook recommended by my colleague because it will give me the background knowledge I need.'*

You may well already have identified the fact that what this person really needs to do is to enrol on an AAT (or equivalent) course at the local college. This will provide the theoretical and practical background to a career in an accounts office and also help with promotion prospects, as will be seen in the Case Study on the next page.

## HOW WELL HAVE I ACHIEVED?

The process of personal planning never stands still. As in any planning process, achievement will have to be monitored on a regular basis, eg every twelve months at the annual appraisal interview when both the employer and the employee will need to re-assess the situation. The planning process can then start all over again – new objectives, new targets, a new action plan.

In the Case Study which follows we look at the personal planning carried out by a typical accounting employee/student.

**Case Study**

# MAKING THE MOST OF YOUR RESOURCES

Kelly works in the Accounts Department of CompLink Limited, a computer supplies wholesaler. She moves to some extent between the sections, but spends most of her time in Sales Ledger, where she processes orders on the computer accounting system, checks documentation and has started basic work in Credit Control, sending out statements.

Kelly wants to get on in her job and career. At her appraisal interview in the Summer, she agreed with her Manager that she should achieve certain targets within the next twelve months.

These objectives included:

- in-house training in the Accounts Department, achieved by work-shadowing (working alongside a colleague in Credit Control)
- an intensive two day training course in computer accounting at a local external training provider
- enrolment at the local college to take an AAT Certificate Accounting course, which runs from September to the following June when she will have to sit an Exam

What resources can Kelly call upon to help her in her training and studies?

**colleagues**

Kelly can talk to her colleagues and make the most of their experience and knowledge, picking up tips about dealing with procedures and situations. This is particularly useful in Credit Control where Kelly can learn how to deal with slow payers - interpreting all their lame excuses about not paying (eg 'the cheque has been signed, but we haven't sent it yet' or 'we don't seem to have received the invoice'). She will also learn how to interpret debtor reports produced by the computer and to send out the appropriate letters without offending the 'important' customers who invariably pay late.

### college

Studying accounting is never an easy option, but Kelly finds that having a good teacher and a lively class helps her understand the more difficult areas of the course. She is able to ask questions about the areas she finds difficult and is given help when her trial balance doesn't balance.

### textbooks

Kelly uses the Osborne Books range of accounting texts and finds that they help her understand difficult concepts and prepare well for her Exam and Skills Test. She is online at home and finds the Student resources on the publisher's website a help (www.osbornebooks.co.uk)

### other websites

The AAT website (www.aat.org.uk) is full of useful information and links. Its Student Forums provide bulletin boards where students can post queries about study topics, and then receive replies. The website of the AAT's magazine (www.accountingtechnician.co.uk) also contains useful resources, including revision articles, reviews and job adverts.

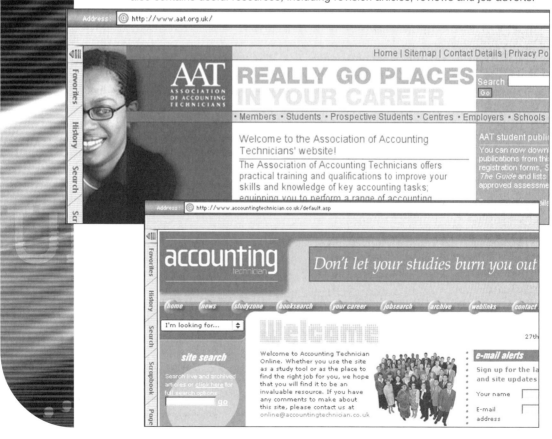

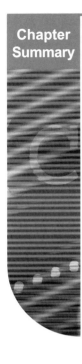

**Chapter Summary**

■ Improving your own performance involves a number of stages, starting with you assessing what you do at work (if you are in work) and thinking about where you want your career to take you.

■ You should then set defined objectives (targets). If you are at work this is best done with your employer – possibly in an appraisal interview.

■ You should then work out how you are going to achieve these objectives, assessing the resources you are going to need. The extent of these will depend whether or not you are at work: you may consider tapping into the expertise of your colleagues, training in-house and externally, taking a qualification, obtaining study material in various media.

■ The final stage in the personal development process is to review and evaluate your progress and to establish new targets and action plans. If you are at work, this may be carried out with your employer as part of the appraisal process.

**Key Terms**

**development needs**   the opportunities for improvement in your personal knowledge and skills which will help further your career (or start it, if you are not in work)

**objectives**   specific targets for development needs

**knowledge**   what you need to know to enable you to do a job at work

**skills**   the ability to put knowledge into practice

**appraisal**   the process whereby an employer interviews an employee on a regular basis, assessing past performance and identifying development needs

**performance**   your success rate in achieving your development needs

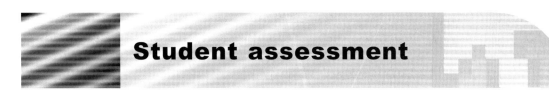

## Student assessment

**Note**

The assessment for Element 31.3 of Unit 31 is the third part of the Simulation. You will be given a project which you will be able to work on at home within a given timescale. At the time of writing this timescale was one month. You should check this with your tutor to make sure you are completely up-to-date.

# Responsibility for health and safety

*It is easy to state the obvious fact that an employee needs a healthy, safe and secure workplace. It is less easy to decide who is responsible for that level of health, safety and security – the employer or the employee?*

*This chapter examines:*

- *the hazards and risks encountered in the workplace*

- *what the law says about the responsibility of the employer and the employee*

- *some of the paperwork that the law requires the employer to complete*

## PERFORMANCE CRITERION COVERED

**unit 31: ACCOUNTING WORK SKILLS**

**element 13.3**

**perform effectively in the workplace**

F   *Monitor work methods and activities against legislation, regulations and organisational procedures ensuring that emergency procedures are adequate for potential hazards.*

## HEALTH, SAFETY AND SECURITY

Unit 31 requires you to understand the need for health, safety and security in the workplace. Both the employee and the employer have responsibilities for maintaining a reasonable level of health, safety and security.

### health

All employees need to be healthy to work efficiently. If you are suffering from malaria or have three broken ribs, your performance is likely to suffer.

Sometimes ill health can be your own fault. If you eat a dodgy curry, drink twelve pints of lager at lunchtime or go bungee jumping you may well be asking for trouble.

On the other hand, if you are required to sit in front of a VDU for six hours at a stretch, or the heating is turned down so low in the depths of winter that your fingers turn blue and you catch a cold, your employer is likely to be at fault.

### safety

Employees and employers also need to be aware of safety in the workplace. Of course, some places of employment are more obviously dangerous than others.

If you work on a building site or on a production line, you need to take great care of your personal safety, and so does your employer.

If you work in an office, you will need to take care when operating equipment such as a guillotine (which has a very sharp blade) and your employer will also need to make sure that the metal guard for the guillotine is always in place to prevent loss of fingers.

### security

Security means keeping the workplace and employees free from intrusion from outsiders and also from unauthorised employees. Threats include:

• theft of business equipment such as computers and vehicles

• theft of money and valuables owned by employees

• theft of business information held on computer and paper files

• damage to equipment

• harassment of individuals

Remember that both employees and employers are responsible for security and that breaches of security can come from employees as well.

# WHOSE FAULT IS IT?

Sophie has recently started work as an accounts assistant at the Liverpool head office of Estro PLC, a company that makes vacuum cleaners. She works with another assistant, Flick.

During the course of a working day Sophie encounters a number of issues which relate to health, safety and security.

See if you can identify the problems, decide who is responsible and realise what could happen as a result of the situation. Then read the suggested solution on the next page.

### situation 1 – Sophie trips up

Sophie was walking around Flick's desk when she tripped up over an electric lead. After she had picked herself up Flick apologised: 'Sorry. I was just charging up my laptop and the only free socket I could find for the charger was just across the room!'

### situation 2 – Sophie finds the petty cash tin

Sophie had to go to the supervisor's desk and noticed that the petty cash tin was sitting on the top of the desk. It was unlocked and Nora the supervisor was not there. The petty cash tin is officially under the supervisor's control.

### situation 3 – Sophie gets eyestrain

Sophie complained to Flick that she was getting eyestrain and headaches: 'I have to do invoicing on this computer hour after hour, inputting details from purchase orders. It is really boring. They never give a break because we are so busy.'

### situation 4 – Flick forgets her password

Flick had a bad memory and could never remember the password which she needed to get into the accounts program on the company's networked computers. She decided to write it down on a 'Post-it' note and stick it on the side of her VDU screen. 'Is that a good idea?' asked Sophie. 'No problem,' replied Flick.

### situation 5 – Flick drops her soup

Flick was having a bad day. She dropped her cuppa soup on the lino kitchen floor. 'I'll clear it up in a minute,' she said and went off to make a telephone call.

### situation 6 – Sophie goes for a smoke

Sophie was trying to give up smoking, but was not doing too well, even though the office was a no smoking zone. She was outside having a smoke with a colleague when she noticed that the despatch department had put a pallet of packages just outside the office fire escape door. 'Hope we don't have a fire today,' she muttered to her friend.

## solutions

There is not always a set solution to every problem, but an experienced colleague might have explained the situations to Sophie and Flick as follows:

### situation 1 – Sophie trips up

Flick is at fault here because she has trailed the wire across the room and tripped up Sophie. She admits the fault by apologising. Her workplace supervisor should have stopped her doing this if she had realised what was going on. The result of the accident could be an injury to Sophie which could keep her off work.

### situation 2 – Sophie finds the petty cash tin

Petty cash should always be kept under lock and key. The supervisor is responsible for the cash, even if she is away from her desk. Either she has left the cash out unlocked, or someone else has helped themselves. Security has been breached and the supervisor is responsible for what has happened.

### situation 3 – Sophie gets eyestrain

Sophie has been made to sit in front of the computer and input invoices. Eyestrain and headaches are common symptoms in people who do not take regular breaks from inputting. The employer is at fault here. The end result could be a deterioration in Sophie's health and even a case of RSI (Repetitive Strain Injury).

### situation 4 – Flick forgets her password

Passwords are used as security devices on computers to prevent outsiders and unauthorised employees gaining access to information. If Flick displays her password for the whole office to see she is breaching security and risking the company's accounting data.

### situation 5 – Flick drops her soup

Flick was certainly having a bad day. Her cuppa soup on the lino kitchen floor is a safety hazard because anyone coming into the kitchen could slip on the soup, fall over and injure themselves. The fact that Flick has gone off to make a telephone call shows that she does not think a lot about her colleagues' safety.

### situation 6 – Sophie goes for a smoke

Sophie is not helping her health by smoking, but at least she is observing the No Smoking restrictions in the workplace. She is right to point out the hazard of the pallet of packages just outside the fire escape door.

If there had been a fire, the exit would have been blocked and the result could have been loss of life. The responsibility here lies with the despatch department. As the department is under the control of the company, in the event of a fire the company would have been held responsible. In this case it would also have been Sophie's duty to alert the despatch department to the hazard.

## HAZARDS AND RISKS

The Case Study on the last two pages has used the terms **hazards** and **risks**. What is the difference between 'hazards' and 'risks'? In any study of health and safety it is important to distinguish between the two.

*A **hazard** is something that could cause you harm.*

*A **risk** measures how likely it is that the hazard will harm you.*

For example, if you are working on a building site, the hazards you face when walking along a high steel beam are:

* you could lose concentration and fall off

* someone could drop a hammer which could hit you and knock you off

* you could be struck by lightning

These are all hazards, but the risks attached to them vary. The risk of being struck by lightning, for example, is likely to be lower than that of falling off the beam through lack of concentration.

When you are examining health and safety in the workplace it is important that you:

hazards are things that can harm you

* **identify** hazards

* **assess** risks

Taking the building site example, the employer is likely to supply the employee with a safety harness, but is less likely to provide him with a lightning conductor, because the risk of being struck by lightning will be less. We will look at the need for an employer to undertake a **risk assessment** later in this book (page 319).

## hazards and risks: some facts . . .

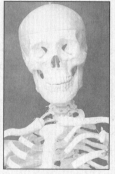

* one in every 100,000 workers is likely to be killed at work every year

* 650 in every 100,000 workers is likely to be injured at work every year

* the most common forms of accident at work are: falling from a height, being struck by a moving vehicle, being struck by moving or falling objects

* rates of fatal and non-fatal injury are higher in men than in women

* rates of fatal injury are highest for older male workers

* the rate of less serious injury is higher in young men compared with older men

*Source: Health & Safety Statistics from www.hse.gov.uk*

## HEALTH AND SAFETY LAW

We have already seen in the Case Study earlier in the chapter that responsibility for health, safety and security in the workplace rests both with the employee and the employer. This is common sense. But when there is an incident and a dispute over the incident – for example, someone injured by equipment when they should have been wearing protective gloves – common sense is sometimes forgotten. This is where the law becomes important because it lays down a structure of regulations in the workplace:

- to ensure that health and safety measures are introduced and observed both by employers and employees
- to specify the rights and responsibilities of employers and employees
- to enable employees to obtain compensation in the case of injury or ill health caused by conditions in the workplace

## HEALTH AND SAFETY AT WORK ACT 1974

The main Act of Parliament which governs health and safety is the **Health and Safety at Work Act 1974**. This not only sets out specific requirements for the employer and employee (see below), but also allows further rules to be established in the form of Regulations, Codes of Practice and Guidance.

### to whom does the Act apply?

The Health and Safety at Work Act covers:

- all work premises of any type and size
- employees and employers
- business visitors
- people and businesses brought onto the premises and employed to carry out specific tasks, eg photocopier servicing, sandwich deliveries
- members of the public who happen to call

### duties of employers

The Health and Safety at Work Act requires that employers must 'as far as is reasonably practicable':

1 Ensure the health, safety and welfare at work of employees, including:
   - the maintenance of safe entry and exit routes
   - providing a safe working environment
   - providing well-maintained and safe equipment

- • storing articles and substances safely
- • providing protective clothing where appropriate
- • providing information about safety in the workplace
- • providing appropriate training and supervision

**2** Prepare and continually update a written statement of the health and safety policy of the organisation – the **Health and Safety Policy Statement**. This requirement applies to organisations of five or more employees. The employer must make sure that the policy statement is circulated to all employees.

**3** Allow for the appointment of union members as **safety representatives** who must be allowed to:
- • investigate accidents
- • investigate potential hazards
- • follow up employee complaints
- • have paid time off to carry out their duties

### duties of employees

The Health and Safety at Work Act requires that all employees must:
- • take reasonable care of their own health and safety
- • take reasonable care of the health and safety of others who might be affected by their actions
- • cooperate with the employer and anyone acting on his or her behalf to meet health and safety requirements

## OTHER HEALTH AND SAFETY LEGISLATION

You will be relieved to hear that you are not required in your studies to memorise the names of all the laws, Directives, Regulations and Codes of Practice that supplement the Health and Safety at Work Act and protect employees in the workplace. You must, however, be aware of their existence and the impact they have on the way in which the workplace is regulated. These include:

### Workplace (Health, Safety and Welfare) Regulations 1992

These complement the Health and Safety at Work Act and regulate safety, cleanliness and the workplace environment.

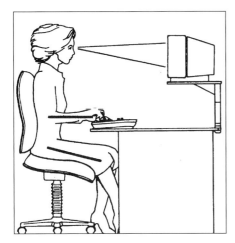

## Display Screen Equipment Regulations 1992

These Regulations set down rules for the use of computer workstations and VDU screens. A 'workstation' includes the computer equipment, furniture, space, light and atmosphere in which an employee works. Measures include:

• employees must have regular breaks

• employees must be offered eye tests

• equipment and furniture must conform to strict standards of safety and comfort

## Control of Substances Hazardous to Health 1999

Hazardous substances must be identified and stored in a safe manner. Employees dealing with a hazardous substance – whether it is radioactive waste or bleach – must be supplied with and wear suitable protective clothing. The 'Control of Substances Hazardous to Health' is often abbreviated to 'COSHH'.

## Reporting of Injuries, Diseases and Dangerous Occurrences Regulations 1995 (RIDDOR)

These regulations require that the Health and Safety Executive (a Government agency) must be notified on official RIDDOR forms of fatal or serious injuries, dangerous occurrences or serious diseases in the workplace. See page 327 for further details of the requirements of these regulations.

## other regulations

There are other regulations, the purposes of which are self-explanatory:

• Fire Precautions Regulations

• Electricity at Work Regulations

• Noise at Work Regulations

• Health and Safety (First Aid) Regulations

• Health and Safety (Safety Signs and Signals) Regulations

• Employer's Liability (Compulsory Insurance) Regulations

So that you can appreciate the extent of all these laws and regulations, you should read the Health and Safety 'checklist for office workers' our authors have compiled and which is shown on the next page. This sets out the most important office-based health and safety obligations of employers.

# EMPLOYER HEALTH AND SAFETY CHECKLIST

## an employer's duties to office employees

1   The workplace should allow at least 3.715m$^2$ of floor space and at least 11 cubic metres of space to each employee.

2   The temperature of the office should be not less than 16°C after the first hour of work.

3   The office should be effectively ventilated by fresh or purified air.

4   There must be adequate natural or artificial light.

5   The office must be cleaned regularly and frequently, and rubbish cleared away.

6   There should be sufficient toilet and washing facilities.

7   Drinking water (tap or fountain) must be made available.

8   Rest areas with adequate seating must be provided.

9   Employees must have the facilities so that they can eat on the premises.

10   Employees must be able to hang up outdoor clothing in the office.

11   There must be first aid facilities for employees – normally in the shape of a trained first aider and a first aid box.

12   There must be fire fighting equipment available and adequately signed escape routes.

13   Office equipment and machinery must be adequately maintained, and employees protected from any device which could be dangerous.

14   Doors and floors and windows must be safe.

15   Employees must be able to move around the workplace freely and without obstruction.

16   Safety rails and other safeguards must be installed in places where there is a risk of employees falling from a height.

17   Employees must be asked to read the organisation's Health and Safety Policy Statement (organisations with five or more employees).

18   Employees must be told where the accident book is.

19   Employees must be told where the Health and Safety 'poster' is situated.

20   Employees must be told about emergency and evacuation procedures.

## POLICING HEALTH AND SAFETY

There are two public sector regulatory bodies that oversee Health and Safety law and regulations:

- **Health and Safety Commission** – which has overall responsibility for research, training, health and safety information provision and the drafting of Regulations and Codes of Practice
- **Health and Safety Executive (HSE)** – which puts Health and Safety controls into practice, employing lawyers, specialists and inspectors and Local Authorities to oversee and 'police' the implementation of the various regulations

Visit www.hse.gov.uk for further details:

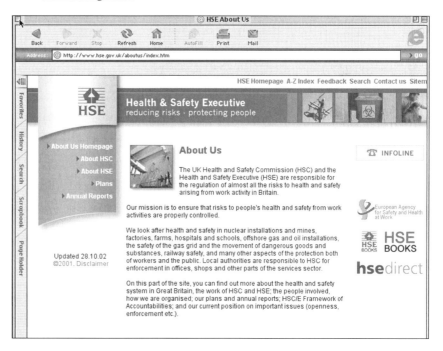

### the law in action

The **Health and Safety Executive** employs its own inspectors to visit premises, and Local Authorities employ environmental health officers to inspect shops and offices. If unsatisfactory working conditions are found an **improvement notice** may be issued. If conditions are irretrievably bad a **prohibition notice** may be issued, the faulty equipment will have to be shut down and the owner may face prosecution. (Fawlty Towers fans may remember the episode of the rat!) Do not forget that an **employee** also has obligations under Health and Safety regulations and may be prosecuted and fined in extreme circumstances for breaches of the regulations.

## HEALTH AND SAFETY REQUIREMENTS IN THE WORKPLACE

The performance criterion F of Unit 31 Element 31.3 is that you should:

*'Monitor work methods and activities against . . . organisational procedures ensuring that emergency procedures are adequate for potential hazards.'*

We will now explain where you should be able to find this information.

### Health and Safety Policy Statement

The law requires that every employer who employs five or more employees must draw up a written **Health and Safety Policy Statement**. This

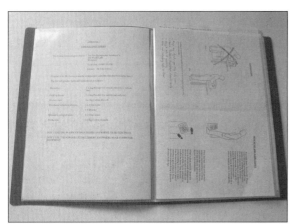

document must be shown to every employee who then has a duty to study it. Most employers will obtain each employee's signature on a form saying that they have read the Statement. The document includes:

- the names of the people responsible for health and safety

- arrangements for: risk assessment, employee consultation, safety when operating machinery, handling of unsafe substances, information, training, accident reporting, illness reporting

- emergency procedures

- forms for reporting accidents and hazards

### the Health and Safety 'poster'

Employers are also required to display a poster produced by the Health and Safety Executive, or provide an approved leaflet which summarises the employer's obligations (see below). These are very useful documents for summarising much of what has been said in this chapter.

## emergency procedures

Employees should be familiar with the emergency procedures for events such as fires and bomb threats, when they will have to evacuate the building. These situations are covered in Chapter 21 'Accidents and emergencies'.

## the accident book

Employees should also be familiar with the 'accident book'. This is a record of accidents which occur in the workplace and should be completed each time there is some form of mishap. Employers often have a trained 'first aider' on the staff who will be able to treat accidents and injuries. Serious accidents involving death, amputation, loss of sight, explosions and building collapse should be reported immediately to the appropriate Local Authority, or direct to the Health and Safety Executive.

These 'A & E' situations are also covered in more detail in Chapter 21 'Accidents and emergencies'.

## the Health and Safety Officer

Most employers will have a Health and Safety Officer on the payroll. This may be a union member, or if there is no union representation in the workplace, an employee appointed to look after health and safety matters. The name of this representative will normally be written on the 'Health and Safety Poster'. Employees should make it their business to find out who this person is. If there is a health and safety problem, the representative will need to be consulted.

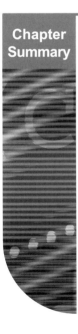

**Chapter Summary**

■ Both employer and employees have responsibility for health, safety and security in the workplace.

■ The employer is responsible for identifying hazards in the workplace and assessing the risk elements involved in those hazards. The employer should take appropriate action to protect employees against the hazards.

■ The responsibilities of employer and employee are set out in the Health and Safety at Work Act and other legislation, Directives, Regulations and Codes of Practice. These cover a wide variety of hazards, including exposure to VDUs, dangerous substances, disease, fire, electricity and noise.

■ The Government bodies responsible for health and safety in the workplace are the Health and Safety Commission (which establishes health and safety control principles) and the Health and Safety Executive (which puts the principles into practice with the help of the Local Authority).

■ Health and Safety information in the workplace may be found in the Health and Safety Policy Statement, on the Health and Safety poster, in the various emergency procedures and from a Health and Safety Representative.

| **Key Terms** | | |
|---|---|---|
| | hazard | something that could cause you harm |
| | risk | measurement of how likely it is that you will be harmed by a hazard |
| | risk assessment | formal assessment by an employer of the hazards and risks in the workplace |
| | safety officer | a person (who may be a union member) appointed to investigate health and safety problems and accidents in the workplace |
| | Health and Safety Commission | Government body which has overall responsibility for drafting of health and safety regulations for the workplace |
| | Health and Safety Executive (HSE) | Government body which puts health and safety controls into operation with the help of the Local Authorities |
| | improvement notice | a notice issued by an HSE inspector or local environmental health officer requiring the improvement of unsatisfactory workplace conditions |
| | prohibition notice | a notice issued by an HSE inspector or local environmental health officer requiring the closure of unsatisfactory workplace conditions |
| | Health and Safety Policy Statement | a document required by law stating how an employer deals with health and safety issues in the workplace |
| | accident book | a record of workplace accidents |

# Student Activities

**19.1**   Who is responsible for the maintenance of a healthy, safe and secure working environment?

**19.2**   What is the difference between a hazard and a risk?

**19.3**   (a)   What is the main Act which regulates health and safety in the workplace?

   (b)   Give <u>three</u> examples of the duties of an employer under this Act

   (c)   Give <u>three</u> examples of the duties of an employee under this Act

**19.4**  What do the following abbreviations stand for? Explain what they are.

   (a)   COSHH

   (b)   RIDDOR

   (c)   HSE

**19.5**  What is the main document drawn up by an employer which tells employees about health and safety in the workplace? Choose one from the following:

   (a)   Health and Safety Executive Statement

   (b)   Health and Safety Policy Statement

   (c)   Accident book

   (d)   Incident book

**19.6**  Study the pictures shown below. What hazards can you identify? State in each case whether the hazard is the responsibility of the employer or the employee.

   (a)

   (b)

   (c)

   (d)

## this chapter covers . . .

*In the last chapter we examined the responsibilities of the employer and employee for health and safety in the workplace. We also outlined some of the legislation that regulates health and safety. In this chapter we examine some of the health and safety hazards – and how they are dealt with – in more detail. This chapter explains:*

- *the common types of health, safety and security hazards*

- *hazards you can put right yourself and hazards that you need to report*

- *the ways in which an employer will assess risks in the workplace*

## PERFORMANCE CRITERION COVERED

**unit 31: ACCOUNTING WORK SKILLS**

**element 13.3**

**perform effectively in the workplace**

F    *Monitor work methods and activities against legislation, regulations and organisational procedures ensuring that emergency procedures are adequate for potential hazards.*

# TYPES OF HAZARD

The type of hazard you will encounter depends on your working environment. The last chapter looked briefly at the types of hazard encountered on a  building site to emphasise the fact that not everybody works in an office.  Being an office worker is clearly safer than being a lumberjack or a fire fighter, and in view of the fact that most readers of this book will work in an office, we will focus on office hazards in this chapter.

Hazards are generally:

* health and safety hazards, or
* security hazards

## health and safety hazards

Most accidents and hazards to health result from the following:

* poor flooring – slippery floors, uneven floors, frayed carpets
* electrical problems – trailing leads and cables, frayed and bare wires
* blockages and obstacles to progress – filing drawers left open, waste bins in the way, boxes stacked up in corridors
* fire doors wedged open (ie safety doors that normally swing shut)
* employees taking gymnastic risks – standing on chairs and desks, lifting items that are too heavy or not bending properly when lifting
* employees getting too excited – running around the office, playing practical jokes, tripping people up
* using harmful substances without wearing protective clothing – for example pouring bleach down a blocked toilet and not wearing gloves
* using a computer workstation and not taking regular breaks or not using suitable seating

## security hazards

Security hazards can take a number of different forms:

* money left lying around
* confidential records left lying around (the photocopier is a favourite place)
* passwords on Post-it notes on computer screens
* visitors left unattended
* strangers wandering around the office pretending to be computer engineers and 'borrowing' the equipment
* exterior doors left unattended or unlocked – particularly where there is valuable equipment, money or sensitive information in the office

The problem with these hazards is knowing when you can deal with them and realising when you have to tell someone else in the organisation about them. The Case Study that follows illustrates this.

# SOPHIE'S CHOICE

As we know from the Case Study in the last chapter, Sophie's office is not the best-run in the town. During the course of a working day she encounters a number of hazards and often has to ask herself:

'Do I deal with this, or do I need to let someone else know that there is a problem?'

What do you think Sophie should do in each of the following situations?

### situation 1 – the filing cabinet drawer

Sophie walked into the section where the customer files were kept and tripped up over an open filing cabinet drawer. She hurt her leg a bit, but there was no injury.

### situation 2 – problems with the photocopier

The photocopier in the office has a paper jam. Sophie knows that opening up the copier is relatively simple – as she has done it before – but it can be messy. She is wearing a new white shirt and is worried about getting the toner on her clothes.

### situation 3 – more problems with the photocopier

Sophie notices that the power supply cable to the photocopier is wrapped around the wheel on the base of the machine and is getting worn.

### situation 4 – problems with the ventilation

It is July and the office is getting very hot. 'Why don't you open that window, Soph?' asks Flick. 'You can easily reach it if you stand on that chair!'

'I am not too good at heights!' says Sophie.

### situation 5 – problems with the window

Sophie notices that the window has a broken lock on it.

### situation 6 – the engineer calls

A stranger walks into the office and starts fiddling with one of the new computers they have just had installed. 'Can I help you at all?' asks Sophie.

'No. I'm OK, thank you. I think I am going to have to take this one away back to the workshop to check the hard drive.'

## solutions

As with the Case Study in the last chapter, there is not always a clear cut solution to every problem, but it is likely that Sophie will react as follows:

### situation 1 – the filing cabinet drawer

Sophie has walked straight into a common office hazard and hurt herself. There is no need to involve anyone else as she is not injured and she will not need to record anything in the accident book. All she needs to do is to shut the drawer. If she finds out who has left the drawer open, she could, of course, let that person know what she thinks of them.

### situation 2 – problems with the photocopier

The photocopier with a paper jam is a common problem and is often accompanied by the potential hazard of being covered in black powder. Sophie just needs to take care when replacing the toner, or she could ask someone else nicely if they would do it for her. There is certainly no need to refer the matter to anyone else.

Sophie reports the problems

### situation 3 – more problems with the photocopier

The worn power supply cable to the photocopier is certainly a risk and needs to be referred to a supervisor or manager as soon as possible. If it is not seen to, the worn cable could start a fire or electrocute someone.

### situation 4 – problems with the ventilation

Poor ventilation in summer is a common problem. The employer has a duty to provide adequate ventilation and Sophie is quite at liberty to open the window if she wants to. She will need to take care when opening it, and it is her responsibility to make sure that she does not take undue risks, such as standing on a chair. Only if the window is beyond any employee's reach should the employer be asked to arrange for it to be opened.

### situation 5 – problems with the window

A broken lock is a serious security risk. Sophie must tell her employer about it as soon as possible so that it can be replaced.

### situation 6 – the engineer calls

It can often be easy for intruders to gain access to offices and to walk off with valuable equipment. It is Sophie's responsibility here to establish the identity of the person, and if in any doubt to contact 'Security' to deal with the intruder.

## REPORTING HAZARDS

The Case Study on the last two pages has shown that it is not good enough just to identify hazards to health, safety and security in the workplace. They have to be dealt with or reported.

It is also important to warn other people in the workplace of the dangers of hazards. The Case Study that follows shows what an employee should do when a hazard is identified.

**Case Study**

## SOPHIE'S FALL

Sophie's office has recently been extended and a new room has been added. The extension is at a slightly lower level than the old office and so going into the new area involves going down a low step where the door is.

One or two people have not noticed this drop in level and have stumbled, spilt coffee and generally been annoyed because there has been no warning notice on the door. But nobody had done anything about it.

Today Sophie was carrying a pile of files which were being transfered to the new office. She went through the new door, stumbled and dropped all the files on the floor. The papers spilled out and the air went quite blue for a while. Sophie was unhurt but very annoyed.

'I am going to do something about this. I seem to be the only person around here who is capable of doing anything!'

Sophie decided to write out a temporary notice to stick on the door straightaway:

> # Mind the step!

She also wrote a memo to Guido, the Office Manager:

---

## Memorandum

**From:** Sophie Weston, Accounts Assistant

**To:** Guido Manzini, Office Manager          Date:  28 November 2007

**Subject**:  Safety Hazards

---

This is to let you know that the step between the old office and the new extension is becoming a safety hazard. A number of people have stumbled, not knowing the step is there. I am concerned that someone, either an employee or a visitor, will be injured. I have stuck up a temporary warning notice, but recommend that action is taken soon.

## RISK ASSESSMENT BY THE EMPLOYER

So far in this chapter we have examined issues of health, safety and security mostly from the employee's point of view – dealing with questions such 'what do I need to deal with . . . what do I need to report to my employer?' But it is important to appreciate that the main burden of identifying hazards and assessing risks lies with the employer. The law states that an employer should carry out a **risk assessment**.

### what is a risk assessment?

**A risk assessment is an examination by the employer of what could cause harm to people in the workplace or cause them to become ill.**

The risk assessment is a written document prepared by the employer, often incorporated into the Health and Safety Policy Statement.

The main objectives for an employer drawing up a risk assessment are to:

- decide whether a **hazard** (something that can cause harm) is significant

- ensure that if it is significant, there are adequate precautions in place to minimise the **risk** to the employee or any other person on the premises

*some risks to assess*

For example if there is machinery to operate, the operator should be kept well away from moving parts and wear protective clothing. On a more domestic level, if there is bleach in the company kitchen, any one using it should be told to wear gloves. It all really comes down to common sense.

The Health and Safety Executive publishes useful downloadable free leaflets on www.hse.gov.uk The main HSE document is 'Five steps to Risk Assessment'. The five steps are:

**Step 1: Look for the hazards.**
As an employee you may well be consulted when your employer looks for hazards. You may be asked directly, or your union rep may be asked.

**Step 2: Decide who might be harmed, and how.**
This will include employees, cleaners, visitors, contractors, and members of the public. Special attention should be paid to new employees and pregnant employees, for obvious reasons.

**Step 3: Evaluate the risks and decide whether the existing precautions are adequate or whether more should be done**.
Risks can be high, medium or low. They should be made low if at all possible. Again, common sense should prevail.

**Step 4: Record your findings.**

This is only necessary if there are five or more employees. The findings should be written down and employees should be asked to read them. New recruits are normally asked to read them when they join. The record of findings should show that a proper check was made, employees were consulted, the hazards identified and precautions put into place which makes the risk a low one.

**Step 5: Review your assessment and revise it if necessary.**

Organisations are always changing, and so will the hazards and risks. The risk assessment should therefore be reviewed on a regular basis.

Illustrated below is a typical risk assessment for bleach, a substance classed as hazardous under the COSHH (Control of Substances Hazardous to Health) Regulations and found on most premises.

---

**COSHH SHEET**

**BLEACH**

| | |
|---|---|
| **Hazard class:** | Hazardous |
| **Handling:** | Irritant to eyes and skin. Use protective gloves. |
| **If spillage occurs:** | Wash away with water. |
| **Recommendation:** | Keep stored away safely. |
| **Conclusion:** | To be handled with care. |
| **Indication of risk:** | Irritant to eyes/skin. |
| **First Aid:** | In case of contact with eyes, hold eye open, rinse with plenty of water and seek medical advice. |
| | If swallowed do not induce vomiting. Give small sips of water. |
| | Seek medical advice. |
| | If spilt on clothes, remove any contaminated clothing and wash skin with soap and water. |

---

## taking further action

If the employer seems to ignore health and safety legal requirements, employees (or their union reps) have the right to take the matter to the Local Authority and HSE. These bodies can send in inspectors and have power to enforce the law. They can also advise employers and employees on a more friendly basis if they have health and safety queries.

**Chapter Summary**

- There are always likely to be hazards to health, safety and security, whatever the working environment – building site or office.

- Health and safety hazards in an office often relate to the physical environment: floors, doors, furniture, passageways, electrical equipment. They also relate to the people in the workplace not taking care and behaving badly.

- Security hazards involve threats from outsiders and also from employees. Security hazards relate to valuables – money, machines, data – being treated negligently by employees and being stolen by outsiders.

- Employees who have to deal with hazards in the workplace should be able to decide whether to deal with the hazards themselves or whether to report them to another person. This decision will obviously depend on the hazard.

- When an employee identifies a hazard, there may be a need both to report it and to warn other employees about it.

- It is a legal requirement for an employer to carry out a risk assessment by identifying hazards, assessing the level of risk and taking the necessary precautions.

**Key Terms**

| | |
|---|---|
| **hazard** | something that could cause you harm |
| **risk** | the extent to which a hazard can harm someone |
| **health hazard** | a hazard in the workplace which can damage the health of employees – it can take the form of a substance (including air quality), noise, and radiation from VDUs |
| **safety hazard** | a physical hazard in the workplace which can cause an accident |
| **security hazard** | a hazard in the workplace which can result in intrusion, either by an employee or by an outsider |
| **risk assessment** | a formal document, required by law, identifying hazards in the workplace and establishing precautions to minimise risk |

# Student Activities

The next two activities are based around a series of situations which you might encounter in the workplace. Consider the situations in turn and:

• **identify each hazard**

• **consider what you would do about it by choosing one of the given options, giving your reasons in each case**

20.1    You hear the fire alarm going off. It is Friday and the fire drills are often held on a Friday. One of your colleagues says she has to back up her computer data as she has just done a long run of invoices. 'I don't want to lose that lot!' she says.

The employees assemble as usual outside in the car park. The names are read out and your colleague is not there. Do you say:

(a)    'I think she has just gone to the loo.'

(b)    'She is just backing up her computer data and will be out here soon.'

(c)    Nothing.

Give your reasons.

20.2    You notice that a colleague who processes the company payroll (which is password protected) is always leaving his computer on during his lunch hour. As a result, anyone passing by can access data about employees' pay and obtain other personal details.

Do you:

(a)    Ignore the situation.

(b)    Go up to your colleague just as he is leaving for lunch and politely suggest that he logs off the payroll data in case anybody sees it.

(c)    Tell your line manager about the situation.

Give your reasons.

**The third activity involves the use of a VDU (computer screen) which is sometimes thought to be a health hazard in the workplace.**

20.3    You have been given a HSE leaflet 'Working with VDUs' by your Union rep. This covers the Display Screen Equipment Regulations and can also be downloaded from www.hse.gov.uk as a free leaflet.

Here are some extracts from the leaflet:

'. . . only a small proportion of VDU users actually suffer ill health as a result of their work. Where problems do occur, they are generally caused by the way in which the VDUs are being used, rather than the VDUs themselves.'

*'Some users may get aches and pains in their hands, wrists, arms, neck, shoulders or back, especially after long periods of uninterrupted VDU work . . .  Problems of this kind may have a physical cause, but may also be more likely if a VDU user feels stressed by the work.'*

*'Extensive research has found no evidence that VDUs can cause disease or permanent damage to the eyes. But long spells of VDU work can lead to tired eyes and discomfort.'*

*'Headaches may result from several things that occur with VDU work such as:*

- *screen glare*
- *poor image quality*
- *a need for different spectacles*
- *stress from the pace of work*
- *anxiety about new technology*
- *reading the screen for long periods without a break*
- *poor posture, or*
- *a combination of these'*

The leaflet also states that employers have a legal duty to provide adjustable chairs, a footrest if required, adequate lighting (but no glare) and sufficient desk space.

The display screens should be clear, non-reflective and adjustable.

Employees should be given suitable training and regular breaks when working.

**the situation**

Trish (see picture below) uses the computer to process sales orders most of the day.

She complains that she is getting aches and pains in her neck and arms and also bad headaches.

'My eyes really hurt at the end of each day.'

'I spend so much time doing the same process over and over again.'

'My line manager tells me to hurry up all the time. It's really offputting.'

'I am sure my machine must be at least ten years old – the screen flickers and it is difficult to read.'

'I reckon I am going to get this RSI thing, the way I feel at the end of each day.'

'I think I should take it up with the union rep.'

**the problem**

Explain, with reference to what Trish has said and what you can see in the picture:

(a) to what extent her employer has failed to protect her against VDU hazards

(b) to what extent Trish is herself responsible for her symptoms

How would you advise her to deal with the problem? Write down your advice in the form of bullet points.

# 21 Accidents and emergencies

## this chapter covers . . .

In the last chapter we concentrated on the common types of health, safety and security hazards in the workplace. We examined the ways in which they were dealt with by employees and employers. In this chapter we explain the need to set up procedures for dealing with the more extreme types of hazard:

- accidents and illnesses
- fires
- evacuating the premises for incidents such as fires and bomb alerts
- breaches of security

We also study examples of some of the paperwork that needs to be completed to report incidents of this type.

## PERFORMANCE CRITERION COVERED

unit 31: ACCOUNTING WORK SKILLS

element 13.3

perform effectively in the workplace

F   Monitor work methods and activities against legislation, regulations and organisational procedures ensuring that emergency procedures are adequate for potential hazards.

## HELP!

When accidents and emergencies such as fires, bomb threats and injuries occur, whether in the workplace or outside, you should know how to react and what to do. In the workplace there will be established procedures and routines that you will have to learn about and to follow.

### what the law requires

The law requires that every employer must:

- communicate emergency and evacuation procedures to employees and other people on the premises
- report major accidents, dangerous occurrences and diseases in the workplace

As we have seen in Chapter 19 of this book, any organisation with five or more employees must have a written **Health and Safety Policy Statement**. This document will normally include details such as:

- the names of people responsible for health and safety, for example the **Safety Officer** and the **First Aider**(s)
- where to find the First Aid box
- where to find the **Accident Book**
- **emergency procedures** – for example how to evacuate the building
- which fire extinguishers to use for different types of fire
- guidance on the handling of dangerous substances
- guidance on manual handling (lifting and moving items in the workplace)

These details should be well known by all employees in a well-run organisation.

We will now examine in a series of Case Studies the way in which employers and employees deal with more serious threats to health and safety in the workplace.

## Case Study

## THE GUILLOTINE ACCIDENT

Alex has recently started working for an insurance broker and was cutting up some A4 sheets. 'I should use the guillotine if I were you,' said Maria, 'you'll get a much cleaner cut.'

Alex was talking to Maria while he was slicing the paper and unfortunately cut into the fingers of his left hand. He was bleeding profusely and crying out in pain. What should Maria do?

## solution

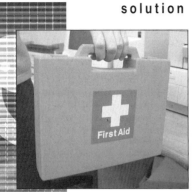

1 Maria stays calm and does not panic.

2 Maria asks around for a First Aider – fortunately her colleague Gail has recently done a British Red Cross First Aid course and is a nominated First Aider for the office. She also saw the accident.

3 Gail fetches the First Aid box.

4 Gail takes charge of the situation, runs Alex's fingers under cold water, sits him down, makes him comfortable, cleans his cuts and bandages the hand. 'He won't need to go to Casualty,' she says, 'but we will need to tell his line manager and make an entry in the Accident Book.'

5 The Accident Report Form in the Accident Book is completed by Gail as follows:

---

# Accident Report

Full name of injured person  **Alex Branfield**

Job Title  **Admin assistant**          Department  **Claims**

Date of accident  **12 December 2007**     Time  **10.40**

Location  **General office**

**Details of accident**
Cut fingers while operating guillotine. No guillotine guard apparently in place.

**Injury sustained**
Minor cuts and abrasions to four fingers of left hand.

**Witnesses**

| Name | Job title | Department |
|------|-----------|------------|
| Maria Anthony | Admin assistant | Claims |
| Gail Potter | Senior assistant | Claims |

**Action Taken**
Hand cleaned up and bandaged to staunch bleeding. No need for hospital referral.

**Further action necessary**
Wound to be monitored and redressed by Gail Potter. Guillotine guard to be checked.

Reported by **Gail Potter**          Reported to  **Asaf Patel, Line Manager**

Signature  **G M Potter**             Date  **12 December 2007**

## THE IMPORTANCE OF DOCUMENTATION

It is important to complete an Accident Report Form because the document sets out clearly what has happened and who may be responsible.

If the employer is responsible and the employee suffers in the long term as a result, the employee may sue the employer. Suppose Alex is working only part-time and his main occupation is a keyboard player in a band. If his hand is damaged in the long term and he cannot play any more, he may sue for loss of earnings. This is an extreme example, but incidents like this do occur. If a member of the public is injured on the employer's premises, similar legal action could be taken. It is for this reason that it is important that the employer takes out insurance for:

- employee liability – to cover against claims from employees
- public liability – to cover against claims from members of the public

If it is the employee who is at fault, this will be implied in the Accident Report Form and the employer will be better protected against claims from the employee. This is illustrated graphically in the Case Study which follows on the next page.

## RIDDOR REPORTING

We have already mentioned RIDDOR (Reporting of Injuries, Diseases and Dangerous Occurrences Regulations 1995) in Chapter 19 (page 307).

These regulations require that the Health and Safety Executive must be notified of fatal or serious injuries, dangerous occurrences or serious diseases in the workplace by telephone, email, online or by posting of a RIDDOR form. Specifically these regulations require reporting of:

- **death or major injury** in the workplace suffered by an employee, a self-employed person working on the premises or a member of the public; major injuries include – major fractures, amputations, dislocations, loss of sight, burns, electrocution, chemical poisoning (Form F2508)
- **'over three day' injuries** – these are less serious injuries which result in the person injured being off work for three days or more (Form F2508)
- **reportable work-related diseases** – including RSI, skin diseases (from handling dangerous substances), lung diseases (eg asbestosis) and infections such as anthrax and legionnaire's disease (Form F2508A)
- **dangerous occurrences which *could* have resulted in injury** – for example explosions at work, collapse of equipment, escape of radiation, scaffolding collapse, vehicle collisions (Form F2508)

# NICO'S ACCIDENT

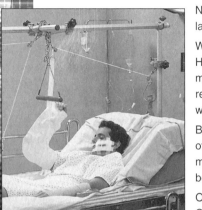

Nico Gambini is employed in the Despatch Department of a large mail order company, Mail2U.

When he was first recruited six months ago, Nico was shown the Health and Safety Policy Statement and made to read the manual handling guidance notes. These made specific reference to the ways in which boxes should be lifted and a warning that not too many boxes should be lifted at one time.

But Nico is a keep-fit and body building fanatic and likes to show off his strength, particularly if the office girls are around. His line manager has told him a number of times not to carry piles of boxes which obscure his vision.

On 19 December, just before the company was closing down for Christmas, Nico was carrying a pile of heavy boxes which were obscuring his forward vision. There was a small step down in the loading bay which was provided with warning signs 'Mind the Step!'. Nico ignored these signs, missed his footing on the step and stumbled forward, dropping the boxes and falling awkwardly on his right arm.

The First Aider was called and it was soon apparent that an ambulance would have to be called: Nico could not move his right arm and was in considerable pain.

Nico was admitted to hospital and was found to have a fracture in his right arm, bruising to his left arm and bruising to his face. The orthopaedic consultant said that it was likely that he would be spending Christmas in a hospital bed.

## the paperwork

An Accident Report Form will be completed by Nico's employer. This form is likely to state that a contributory cause of the accident was Nico's disregard for the manual handling guidance notes.

The form will also recommend that:

- the employees working in the Despatch Department are reminded of the manual handling guidance notes
- the employer ensures that the warning notice for the step is seen by despatch department employees

The employer will also have to comply with RIDDOR (Reporting of Injuries, Diseases and Dangerous Occurrences Regulations). These require that the employer must:

- telephone the local Health and Safety Authority (the local authority in this case) immediately and tell them about the business, the injured person and the accident
- within ten days of the accident complete and send to the local authority a completed Form F2508

This form is illustrated on the next two pages.

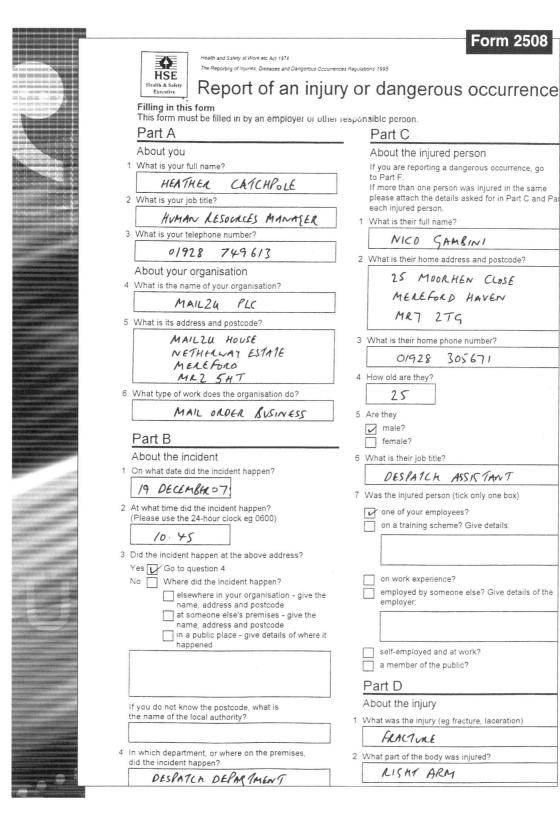

**Form 2508**

Health and Safety at Work etc Act 1974

The Reporting of Injuries, Diseases and Dangerous Occurrences Regulations 1995

**HSE**
Health & Safety
Executive

# Report of an injury or dangerous occurrence

**Filling in this form**
This form must be filled in by an employer or other responsible person.

## Part A

### About you

1 What is your full name?

> HEATHER CATCHPOLE

2 What is your job title?

> HUMAN RESOURCES MANAGER

3 What is your telephone number?

> 01928 749613

### About your organisation

4 What is the name of your organisation?

> MAIL2U PLC

5 What is its address and postcode?

> MAIL2U HOUSE
> NETHERWAY ESTATE
> MEREFORD
> MR2 5HT

6 What type of work does the organisation do?

> MAIL ORDER BUSINESS

## Part B

### About the incident

1 On what date did the incident happen?

> 19 DECEMBER 07

2 At what time did the incident happen?
(Please use the 24-hour clock eg 0600)

> 10.45

3 Did the incident happen at the above address?

Yes ☑ Go to question 4

No ☐ Where did the incident happen?

☐ elsewhere in your organisation - give the name, address and postcode
☐ at someone else's premises - give the name, address and postcode
☐ in a public place - give details of where it happened

If you do not know the postcode, what is the name of the local authority?

4 In which department, or where on the premises, did the incident happen?

> DESPATCH DEPARTMENT

## Part C

### About the injured person

If you are reporting a dangerous occurrence, go to Part F.
If more than one person was injured in the same please attach the details asked for in Part C and Par each injured person.

1 What is their full name?

> NICO GAMBINI

2 What is their home address and postcode?

> 25 MOORHEN CLOSE
> MEREFORD HAVEN
> MR7 2TG

3 What is their home phone number?

> 01928 305671

4 How old are they?

> 25

5 Are they

☑ male?
☐ female?

6 What is their job title?

> DESPATCH ASSISTANT

7 Was the injured person (tick only one box)

☑ one of your employees?
☐ on a training scheme? Give details:

☐ on work experience?
☐ employed by someone else? Give details of the employer:

☐ self-employed and at work?
☐ a member of the public?

## Part D

### About the injury

1 What was the injury (eg fracture, laceration)

> FRACTURE

2 What part of the body was injured?

> RIGHT ARM

3  Was the injury (tick the one box that applies)

- [ ] a fatality?
- [x] a major injury or condition? (see accompanying notes)
- [ ] an injury to an employee or self-employed which prevented them doing their normal work for more than 3 days?
- [ ] an injury to a member of the public which meant they had to be taken from the scene of the accident to a hospital for treatment

4  Did the injured person (tick all the boxes that apply)

- [ ] become unconscious?
- [ ] need resuscitation?
- [x] remain in hospital for more than 24 hours?
- [ ] none of the above?

## Part E

### About the kind of accident

Please tick the one box that best describes what happened, then go to Part G.

- [ ] Contact with moving machinery or material being machined
- [ ] Hit by a moving, flying or falling object
- [ ] Hit by a moving vehicle
- [ ] Hit something fixed or stationary

- [x] Injured while handling, lifting or carrying
- [ ] Slipped, tripped or fell on the same level
- [ ] Fell from a height

  How high was the fall?

  | metres |
  | --- |

- [ ] Trapped by something collapsing

- [ ] Drowned or asphyxiated
- [ ] Exposed to, or in contact with, a harmful
- [ ] Exposed to fire
- [ ] Exposed to an explosion

- [ ] Contact with electricity or an electrical discharge
- [ ] Injured by an animal
- [ ] Physically assaulted by a person

- [ ] Another kind of accident (describe it in Part G)

## Part F

### Dangerous occurrences

Enter the number of the dangerous occurrence you are reporting. (The numbers are given in the Regulations in the notes which accompany this form)

|  |
| --- |

## Part G

### Describing what happened

Give as much detail as you can. For instance

- ∟ the name of any substance involved
- ∟ the name and type of any machine involved
- ∟ the events that led to the incident
- ∟ the part played by any people

If it was a personal injury, give details of what the person was doing. Describe any action that has since been taken to prevent a similar incident. Use a separate piece of paper if you need to.

> MR GAMBINI, WHO IS AN ASSISTANT IN OUR DESPATCH DEPARTMENT SLIPPED AND FELL DOWN A SMALL STEP (10 CM). HE WAS CARRYING A LARGE PILE OF BOXES, WHICH HE DROPPED. HE FELL TO THE FLOOR AND FRACTURED HIS RIGHT ARM IN ATTEMPTING TO BREAK HIS FALL. THERE WERE WARNING SIGNS ABOUT THE STEP, BUT STAFF HAVE AGAIN BEEN ALERTED TO THE HAZARD

## Part H

### Your signature

Signature

Date

| 22 | 12 | 07 |
| --- | --- | --- |

**Where to send the form**

Please send it to the Enforcing Authority for the place where it happened. If you do not know the Enforcing Authority, send it to the nearest HSE office.

| For official use | | | | | |
| --- | --- | --- | --- | --- | --- |
| Client number | Location number | Event number | | | |
|  |  |  | [ ] INV | REP [ ] Y | [ ] N |

# REPORTING DISEASE

An employer whose employee contracts a disease as a result of the workplace environment must report the illness to the Health and Safety Authorities on Form F2508A 'Report of a case of disease.'

Employers are normally advised of serious employee illnesses by the employee's doctor. A typical disease developed by office workers is RSI (Repetitive Strain Injury) caused by overlong periods spent inputting data.

This situation is obviously bad news for the employer because it suggests that Health and Safety regulations are being ignored in the workplace, which could trigger a Health and Safety inspection. Also the employee may be demanding compensation for loss of earnings.

Form F2508A is similar to Form F2508, requiring details of the employer, the employee and the nature of the problem – in this case the circumstances that led to the disease. Extracts from the form are illustrated below.

## Part C

### The disease you are reporting

1 Please give:

- the name of the disease, and the type of work it is associated with; or
- the name and number of the disease
  *(from Schedule 3 of the Regulations – see the accompanying notes).*

> *LEGIONELLOSIS   (19)*

2 What is the date of the statement of the doctor who first diagnosed or confirmed the disease?

> *23 / 10 / 07*

3 What is the name and address of the doctor?

> *DR NICHOLAS SPOCK*
> *HALVEY HOUSE SURGERY*
> *BROCKWAY ROAD*
> *MERE FORD*
> *MR2 2LJ*

## Part D

### Describing the work that led to the disease

Please describe any work done by the affected person which might have led to them getting the disease.

If the disease is thought to have been caused by exposure to an agent at work *(eg a specific chemical)* please say what that agent is.

Give any other information which is relevant.

**Give your description here**

> *MR NEWTON WAS EMPLOYED*
> *BY ARCO LIMITED AS MAINTENANCE*
> *ENGINEER. HE IS THOUGHT TO*
> *HAVE CONTRACTED THE DISEASE*
> *WHILE CHECKING THE WATER*
> *COOLING SYSTEM WHICH WAS*
> *CONTAMINATED*

## DEALING WITH FIRES

A fire can be one of the most frightening hazards in the workplace. It can easily be started and it can easily become fatal. Fires can be started by:

- faulty electrical appliances and wiring

- people smoking illegally

- overheating of flammable substances, eg aerosols

Anyone at work – and in the home – has a duty to take care and prevent the incidence of fire.

### fire precautions and the law

The UK law relating to fire precautions in the workplace has been consolidated in the **Regulatory Reform (Fire Safety) Order 2005**, which is based on UK and European legislation.

The law requires that a person responsible for premises should:

- carry out a risk assessment and record the findings

- carry out appropriate fire safety and escape training for employees

- check that furniture and equipment comply with the safety standards

- keep proper records of compliance to reduce risk

- implement and have available the appropriate safety measures on the premises

- provide clear escape routes and exits to a place of safety

- maintain fire safety equipment

### employee familiarity with fire equipment

As noted above, it is the duty of every employer to make sure that employees become familiar with:

- fire fighting equipment in the workplace

- the procedures for evacuating the building in the event of a fire or any other emergency such as bomb scare

Fire extinguishers are the traditional and most effective means of combating fires. But it must be the right form of fire extinguisher, or the fire could be actively encouraged or sensitive equipment could be irretrievably damaged.

The illustrations on the next page show the different types of fire extinguisher. The notes explain what types of fire they should be used for.

## which fire extinguisher should I use?

**water fire extinguisher**

**yes** for paper, wood, textiles

**no** for flammable liquids and live electrical equipment

**carbon dioxide fire extinguisher**

**yes** for flammable liquids and live electrical equipment

**no** for paper, wood, textiles

**powder fire extinguisher**

**yes** for flammable liquids, gaseous fires, live electrical equipment, paper, wood and textiles

**but** it will ruin any computer equipment

## EVACUATION PROCEDURES

If there is a fire or any other emergency such as a telephoned bomb warning an organisation must have an established **evacuation procedure**. The aim of this procedure is to ensure that all people on the premises can move swiftly and safely out to a nominated place of safety. The evacuation procedure must be communicated to:

- **employees**, by means of regular evacuation drills (normally known as fire drills) and explanation in the Health and Safety Policy Statement and on notices on the premises

- any **members of the public** on the premises – for example in a shop, or in a gym – by prominent signs and notices

## FIRE ACTION!

**If you discover a fire**

1 Sound the alarm.
2 Deal with the fire as far as is safely possible using the equipment provided.
3 Telephone the Fire Services.

**If you hear the fire alarm**

1 Leave the building by the nearest exit.
2 Report to the assembly point at

*the King Street car park*

**Do not!**

1 Take unnecessary risks.
2 Return to the building until authorised to do so.

*an evacuation notice*

### help from the fire services

The Fire Services have a role to play in minimising the risk of fire in the workplace.

They can advise organisations on planning exit routes, placing signs, installing fire exits and fire doors. They can also help with training employees to become the nominated in-house Fire Officers. Note that organisations no longer require a Fire Certificate or need a Fire Service inspection of the premises. The responsibility lies with the person in charge.

### the evacuation procedure at work

Whenever evacuation takes place, either as a practice 'drill', or in response to a real emergency, there are a number of steps that have to be followed.

As you will see from the notice shown above, if you discover a fire you will need to sound the alarm. If you are unable to deal with the fire (a major electrical fire, for example) you should call the Fire Services on 999 (or whatever your emergency number is).

Most employees will first encounter the evacuation procedures when they hear the alarm sounding. The steps in this case are:

1 Leave the building as quickly and calmly as possible (not sprinting and knocking people over!)

2 Use the quickest and safest designated route – follow the Fire Exit direction signs.

3 Assemble in the designated meeting point.

4 Wait for your name to be called.

5 Return to the place where you work only after (and if) you are authorised to do so.

The person calling the 'register' of names is likely to be the organisation's appointed Safety Officer or a senior manager.

## EMPLOYEES' RESPONSIBILITIES AND FIRE RISK

Employees have two main areas of responsibility in relation to fire risk:

- helping to prevent fires starting in the first place
- in the event of a fire helping people with special needs or members of the public who are not familiar with the emergency procedures

### helping to prevent fires

There are many bad habits **employees** can get into which can help fires to start. These should be avoided. The basic rules are:

- ensure that combustible rubbish does not pile up in areas vulnerable to fire or overheating, eg behind the photocopier or any machinery that runs hot
- avoid obstructing fire escape routes, eg dumping pallets or boxes in front of fire exit doors
- ensure that all Fire Exit signs are not obstructed
- ensure that fire extinguishers are readily accessible
- do not prop open Fire Doors (ie fire-resistant doors which automatically swing shut)
- ensure that any highly flammable material is properly stored
- do not smoke

**Managers** too have additional responsibilities. They should:

- ensure that staff are properly trained in the emergency procedures
- hold regular evacuation drills
- ensure that machinery is properly maintained – particularly if it can run hot and endanger flammable substances
- arrange to have fire safety equipment regularly checked

### helping other people with evacuation procedures

If there is an evacuation drill or a real emergency, it is possible that there will be people on the premises who are not employees or who have special needs.

Members of the public and visitors should be told what is going on and guided out of the premises.

People with special needs – both employees and customers – will need to be given particular care and attention and will have to be helped out. People in this category include individuals in wheelchairs, the partially sighted and people with a hearing disability which prevents them from hearing the alarm.

## DEALING WITH BREACHES OF SECURITY

We have already seen in the last chapter that security hazards can take a number of different forms. They can involve threats from other employees:

- the theft of money left lying around
- the leaking of confidential information

They can also involve threats from outside:

- strangers being allowed in and wandering around the office on false pretences – for example, pretending to be a computer engineer
- allowing exterior doors to be left unattended or unlocked – particularly where there is valuable equipment, money or sensitive information in the office

It is an employee's duty to be alert to incidents such as these and to report them to a superior, a line manager, for example. In the extreme case of intruders on the premises, it will be up to the employee to call Security (or whoever acts as the 'heavy brigade' for the organisation) to investigate and, if necessary, to eject the intruder.

**Case Study**

# DEALING WITH DESPERATE DAN

Dan bought a computer a month ago from Compusale, a computer hardware and software company.

He has had a lot of problems with the machine he bought and has complained on a number of occasions.

You work as a customer services assistant for Compusale in a large open plan office.

You are sitting at your terminal one day and you are confronted with Dan, who has managed to get into your office.

'What are you going to do about my machine then?' he asks angrily 'It's about as much use as a biscuit tin!'

What would you do?

### solution

Dan is an intruder. He has no right to be in the office. He poses a serious security threat. You should refuse to talk to him. You should report the matter to your line manager and at the same time contact the Security Division of your company who will arrange for him to be escorted off the premises.

**Chapter Summary**

■ It is important for an employee to know what to do in the event of emergencies such as accidents, illnesses, fires and serious security breaches in the workplace.

■ The law requires that an organisation with five or more employees must prepare a Health and Safety Policy Statement which will set out details of emergency procedures to be implemented within the organisation.

■ Accidents in the workplace should be recorded in an Accident Book. This will often contain forms which record details of any workplace accidents.

■ RIDDOR (Reporting of Injuries, Diseases and Dangerous Occurrences Regulations 1995) require that the Health and Safety Executive is informed immediately in the case of fatal or serious workplace injuries, dangerous occurrences and reportable diseases.

■ An employer must by law set up procedures for the evacuation of the premises in the case of emergencies such as fire and bomb threats. These procedures must be communicated to the employees.

■ Employees must also know what action to take if there is a security breach; this normally involves reporting the matter to a superior and/or contacting the security people (the 'bouncers' ) in the organisation.

**Key Terms**

| | |
|---|---|
| **Safety Officer** | a representative chosen (by the union or by the employer) to be responsible for the implementation of safety measures |
| **First Aider** | an employee who has had First Aid training and who is responsible for the implementation of First Aid in the workplace |
| **Accident Book** | the book which records full details of accidents in the workplace |
| **emergency procedures** | procedures set down in the Health and Safety Policy Statement of an organisation which regulate, for example, the way an evacuation is carried out |
| **'over three day' injuries** | less serious injuries which result in the injured person being off work for three or more days |
| **dangerous occurrence** | an occurrence in the workplace which could have resulted in serious injury, and which will need to be investigated |

# Student Activities

**21.1** List five items which you would expect to find in a company's Health and Safety Policy Statement and which are related to workplace accidents and emergency procedures.

**21.2** Read the description of the incident below, and then answer the questions that follow.

*Percy Pratt works as an accounts assistant in the Finance Office. You are his line manager. He has just made a mug of boiling hot coffee and brought it back to his workstation. He places it on top of his computer, but unfortunately it crashes down over the keyboard, scalding his right hand and ruining the keyboard.*

*Maria Carey, the First Aider, is also an accounts assistant in the same office and she is called over to help Percy, who is in some pain. She takes him to the washroom and runs cold water over his hands to soothe the pain. She dresses his hands and sends him to the rest room to recover.*

*She reports back to you:*

*'Percy will be OK. He has a slight scalding to the back of his right hand, but I have dressed it. He will probably need to go home to recover, but I see no reason why he should not be in work tomorrow, and I have told him that. We will just need to keep an eye on the scald. I hope the computer keyboard will be alright, but I guess it is a write off!'*

(a)   Who is responsible for this accident?

(b)   You call Percy over to talk about what has happened. He says he is unhappy about the safety measures in the office. How would you reply to this?

(c)   He says that he has heard that the accident will have to be reported under RIDDOR. How would you reply to that?

(d)   What action would you recommend be taken in the office following this incident?

(e)   Complete the Accident Report Form on the opposite page in the name of Maria Carey. Use your own name for the line manager to whom she has reported the incident, and today's date.

**21.3** What are the three main circumstances in which you would complete a RIDDOR Form 2508? Write a short paragraph explaining each of the three circumstances.

**21.4** What type of fire extinguisher is best for:

(a)   a wastepaper bin fire caused by a dropped match?

(b)   a computer which has caught fire?

(c)   the engine of a delivery van which is parked just outside your loading bay?

In each case justify your choice of extinguisher.

**21.5** You have been elected Safety Officer at your place of work. One of your managers asks for a summary of what his staff should do in case the fire alarm goes off. Write down a series of numbered points summarising the emergency procedures in the case of a fire alarm. Make up any details you need, such as the meeting point. Use details taken from evacuation procedures from your own place of work, if you wish.

# Accident Report

Full name of injured person _____

Job Title _____  Department _____

Date of accident _____  Time _____

Location _____

Details of accident

Injury sustained

Witnesses
Name                    Job title              Department

Action Taken

Further action necessary

Reported by _____  Reported to _____

Signature _____  Date _____

In this chapter we explain the need for an employee to 'manage' his or her work area. This involves:

- organising your working area so that you and others can work efficiently and also comply with the organisation's rules and requirements for the workplace

- identifying and dealing with problems relating to your work area, either sorting them out yourself, or referring them to someone who can

- dealing with workplace equipment correctly, by following the manufacturer's instructions and any guidelines set down by your organisation

## PERFORMANCE CRITERION COVERED

**unit 31:  ACCOUNTING WORK SKILLS**

**element 13.3**

**perform effectively in the workplace**

G   Organise and monitor your work area so that conditions promote an effective and efficient working environment

## AN 'EFFECTIVE' AND 'EFFICIENT' WORKING ENVIRONMENT?

Unit 31 Performance Criterion 31.3 G stresses the need for an 'effective' and an 'efficient' working environment.

What exactly do these terms mean?

'Effective' means getting the result that you want. In football an effective defence prevents the opposing team scoring goals, in the dating game an effective chat-up line will win you the partner you have your eye on. An **effective working environment** will result in the achievement of the objectives of the organisation, for example – a motivated workforce, sales and profit targets achieved or exceeded.

'Efficient' is not the same as 'effective'. It means getting the job done with the minimum waste of effort and resources. This is, of course, an important objective in any organisation. But note that an **efficient working environment** will not always be 'effective'. A line manager, for example, may be ruthlessly efficient in saving time and money, but the workforce may be demotivated and levels of performance will fall off. The working environment will become less 'effective'.

The ideal working environment, therefore, is one that **balances effectiveness and efficiency**. The job is done well with the minimum wastage of effort and resources.

In this chapter we will discuss the role of the employee in making sure that the working environment – the immediate work area and the 'office' as a whole – is both effective and efficient. The two key factors in this are:

* being organised
* being aware of the needs of other employees and the organisation

## ORGANISING THE WORK AREA

### what is the 'work area'?

An employee's work area is not just the desk or workstation, it is the area which surrounds it, involving desk, chair and any furniture and filing cabinets in the vicinity.

The state of the work area is the responsibility of the employee – the user. The way in which it is (or is not) organised says a great deal about the user. A tidy desk normally means a tidy mind, just as an untidy work area often indicates a person who finds organisation rather a struggle.

An organised work area has a number of characteristics:

- it is tidy
- it is clean
- the user knows where everything is and can find it quickly
- everything is within easy reach
- the computer is correctly set up
- the chair is correctly adjusted for the user

The test of a well-organised work area is whether the user's colleagues can also find what they want. Suppose the user is an accounts assistant who deals with sales orders. She is out at lunch and an important customer telephones and asks if a recently issued sales order can be checked as an incorrect catalogue code may have been quoted on the document. Can the sales order be found? Is it in an organised filing system or pending tray, or is it buried under a pile of unsorted papers? Worse still, is it there at all?

*it helps to be organised*

It is not difficult to see from this that if a work area is organised properly, it will be:

- **effective** because tasks can be completed and the job done
- **efficient** because time (and therefore money) will not be wasted

### the importance of efficiency

Examples of **efficiency** in the working environment are:

- having resources that you need within easy reach and not in a filing cabinet at the other end of the office

- carrying out tasks in the time allotted – other people may be waiting for you to finish checking documents so that they can carry out a task
- not wasting resources such as photocopy paper
- taking care of resources so that they will last, eg storing computer disks correctly

Efficiency is important not only because cutting down on wastage means greater profit for the organisation, but also because it has a direct influence on the **effectiveness** of other members of a workplace team.

## THE ORGANISATION'S RULES FOR THE WORK AREA

Just as a teenager covers his or her room walls with 'statement' posters, employees like to personalise their working environment in order to establish their identity in the workplace and provide a psychological sense of security.

*personalising the work area*

Examples of this include:

- photographs of friends and family
- postcards received at work
- small posters saying things like 'you don't have to be mad to work here, but it helps'
- 'toys' – eg executive puzzles and fluffy animals
- plants
- bowls of fruit

An employee's work area will tell you a lot about that employee.

The organisation will, however, have **guidelines** which will regulate the extent to which an employee can put up posters, postcards and other items. It is unlikely that these guidelines will be written down, but they will normally be based on a test of what is 'reasonable' and be enforced either by a line manager or by the comments of colleagues objecting to what they think is unreasonable!

*a customer services desk
- subject to strict guidelines*

What *is* 'reasonable'? This depends on the nature of the workplace. If it is a closed office which is rarely visited by outsiders, each employee is likely to have the freedom to personalise his or her work area, as long as what is displayed is not offensive to colleagues or to management.

If the office is open plan and open to the public gaze, the organisation is likely to require that personal items should be unobtrusive. A bank customer services desk, for example will be kept very tidy and have welcoming features, such as flowers, as in the illustration on the left. The posters on the wall here are not the employees' personal choice but advertise the products of the organisation.

The working environment in this illustration gives a very positive image to the public of the financial services team that operates in the office.

## DEALING WITH WORKING CONDITIONS

We have seen earlier in this book that health and safety laws and regulations set down guidelines for the physical working environment. For example:

---

1   The workplace should allow at least 3.715m² of floor space and at least 11 cubic metres of space to each employee.

2   The temperature of the office should be not less than 16°C after the first hour of work.

3   The office should be effectively ventilated by fresh or purified air.

4   There must be adequate natural or artificial light.

5   The office must be cleaned regularly and frequently, and rubbish cleared away.

6   There should be sufficient toilet and washing facilities.

---

It is the responsibility of the employee to identify conditions in the working environment that interfere with effective working, for example a workplace that is:

• too cramped or poorly laid out

• too hot or too cold

- too stuffy or too draughty
- too bright or too dim
- too noisy

Problems like this can reduce both the **effectiveness** (getting things done) and the **efficiency** (getting things done with the minimum of wastage) of the workplace. For example:

- an office with poor heating will reduce the ability of the employees to work: some tasks may not get done and other tasks will take much longer, costing the organisation more
- poor air quality may result in staff illness: again some tasks may not get done and the organisation is likely to have the extra cost of sick pay

Sometimes the employee can do something about problems like these, and should take action. Sometimes the employee will have to refer the problem to someone else. This is illustrated in the Case Study which follows.

**Case Study**

# GETTING IT SORTED

Noor is an accounts assistant at Spira PLC, an insurance company, based in Staines.

When she started work in the office she got on well with her colleagues, but she noticed that the working environment was not as ideal as her previous office at Sanitas Limited where she trained in accounts work.

## situation

Noor has noted a number of problems and wonders how she should deal with them. Should she take action herself or should she refer them to Rashid Singh, the Line Manager? The problems are as follows:

1  Noor's desk is awkwardly situated by the photocopier. She is disturbed by people using the machine, and doesn't like the fumes it gives off. She notices that there is a space for a desk nearer to the workstations which deal with the sales and purchases processing.

2  The office is very warm to work in, particularly in the afternoon when the computers have been running for a while. The heating comes from an air conditioning system which has a thermostatic switch on the office wall. Noor often feels very sleepy after lunch and sometimes goes home with a headache. She talks to her colleagues about this and they agree with her – the office needs to be cooler and fresher, and then they will all work better.

3  The office has a big window through which the sun shines for much of the day. There are blinds, but they are stuck in the open position, and Noor, along with many of the staff, finds the light so dazzling that she cannot see her computer screen properly.

## solutions:

### problem 1 – the desk

Noor's desk is awkwardly situated by the photocopier. She works inefficiently because she is some distance from the accounts workstations. Her position also affects her effectiveness because of the fumes from the machine. She obviously cannot drag the desk across the office, and office layout is not a matter about which she can make decisions. So she will have to refer the problem to Rashid, her line manager. If there is space in the part of the office she has identified, Rashid can arrange to have the desk moved, but not before careful measurements have been made and the matter referred to the office staff.

### problem 2 – feeling the heat

Temperature and air quality in an office are critical factors for effective working. If the working environment is too hot, as could be the case here, people become drowsy and headachy; if the office is too cold, people are uncomfortable and distracted from their work. A further aspect of the problem is that some people like higher temperatures than others. The situation in this office, as in many other offices, is that the temperature rises in the afternoon. The solution is for Noor to discuss the matter with her colleagues, in one of their regular team meetings, for example. If there is a majority in favour of turning the heating down – which can easily be done using the thermostatic control on the wall – Noor could do this at the appropriate time of day. She would, of course, have to consult first with Rashid, her line manager.

### problem 3 – the stuck blinds

Dazzling sunshine can be very pleasant on a beach, but can reduce effectiveness and efficiency in a workplace. Noor and her colleagues find that not being able to see a VDU properly results in eyestrain. The solution here is simple. Noor shows some initiative and one lunchtime spends half-an-hour untangling the cords which operate the blinds. They can now be opened and closed normally, to the benefit of everyone. This is not a problem which Noor needs to refer to a line manager or even to all her colleagues – she just takes a decision and gets on with it.

## USING AND MAINTAINING EQUIPMENT

The working environment – particularly the office – normally has a wide variety of complex and delicate equipment which is in daily use. For example, an accounts assistant may have to use:

- computer hardware – processing units, backup devices, printers
- fax machine
- photocopier
- credit card terminal
- shredder

We have seen earlier in this book that both the employer and the employee have duties of care under Health and Safety regulations when using this type of equipment. In this chapter we look at the guidance that exists for the operation and maintenance of equipment in the workplace. This guidance can be found in:

*always read the instructions!*

- the instructions provided with the equipment – this may take the form of a manual, a sheet, or online assistance
- separate guidelines issued by the employer

The important point here is that these guidelines and instructions must be followed:

- when setting the equipment up and while operating the equipment
- when something goes wrong
- when maintenance is needed

An employee should never adopt his or her own remedy.

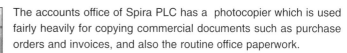

**Case Study**

# DEALING WITH THE PHOTOCOPIER

The accounts office of Spira PLC has a photocopier which is used fairly heavily for copying commercial documents such as purchase orders and invoices, and also the routine office paperwork.

The photocopier was bought outright by the business a couple of years ago, and there is a maintenance contract with Photoserve Limited, which provides toner, annual maintenance and a call out service in case of major breakdowns.

In the office there is a printed sheet of internal regulations governing the use of the photocopier by employees. This is shown below.

---

### PHOTOCOPIER USE

1. No unauthorised copying.
2. No copying of copyright material (with © symbol) without reference to line manager.
3. Switch copier off at the end of the day, but leave on at mains.
4. Renew paper in cassette tray if 'paper out' light is on.
5. Toner to be replaced by senior assistants only.
6. If you cannot clear a paper jam, please refer to senior assistant.
7. Refer major faults to line manager.
8. If the maintenance light or call light is on, refer to line manager.

The manufacturer's instructions for the photocopier are set out in a booklet, but this is rarely used because most of the common instructions are printed on the top panel of the photocopier. Some of these are illustrated below and to the right.

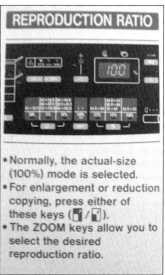

REPRODUCTION RATIO

- Normally, the actual-size (100%) mode is selected.
- For enlargement or reduction copying, press either of these keys (▤ / ▤).
- The ZOOM keys allow you to select the desired reproduction ratio.

*this tells you how to reduce or to enlarge copies*

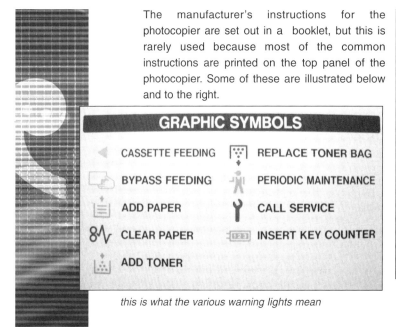

**GRAPHIC SYMBOLS**

CASSETTE FEEDING    REPLACE TONER BAG

BYPASS FEEDING    PERIODIC MAINTENANCE

ADD PAPER    CALL SERVICE

CLEAR PAPER    INSERT KEY COUNTER

ADD TONER

*this is what the various warning lights mean*

The staff of Spira PLC therefore have to know about the company procedures for dealing with the photocopier and also the operating instructions on the machine itself. Some of these relate to each other, as you will see if you carry out Student Activity 22.5 on page 350.

## Chapter Summary

- ▪ It is important that an employee organises his or her work area so that work can be carried out efficiently and effectively by all employees who use that work area.

- ▪ Employees naturally like to bring personal items into the workplace. When doing so, they should take notice of the organisation's guidelines and also their colleagues' views on what is acceptable. The aim should be to give a positive image both to colleagues and to outsiders who are visiting.

- ▪ Employees should be able to identify problems with the working environment – such as noise, heat and lighting conditions – which might interfere with effective and efficient working. They should be able to decide whether to deal with the problems themselves, in consultation with colleagues, or whether to refer them to an appropriate person.

- ▪ Equipment in the work area will normally be provided with the manufacturer's instructions for the use and maintenance of that equipment. The organisation may also provide written guidelines for the use of the equipment. It is the responsibility of every employee to be aware of the instructions and guidelines and to take notice of them when using the equipment and encountering problems.

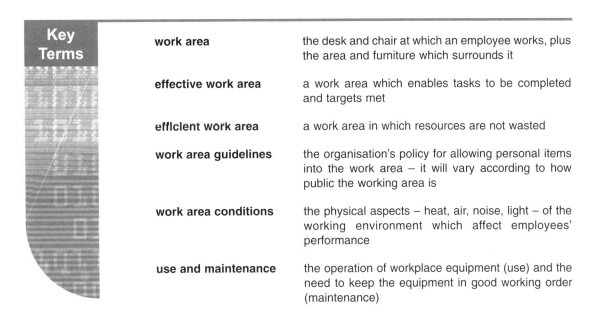

| **Key Terms** | | |
| --- | --- | --- |
| | **work area** | the desk and chair at which an employee works, plus the area and furniture which surrounds it |
| | **effective work area** | a work area which enables tasks to be completed and targets met |
| | **efficient work area** | a work area in which resources are not wasted |
| | **work area guidelines** | the organisation's policy for allowing personal items into the work area – it will vary according to how public the working area is |
| | **work area conditions** | the physical aspects – heat, air, noise, light – of the working environment which affect employees' performance |
| | **use and maintenance** | the operation of workplace equipment (use) and the need to keep the equipment in good working order (maintenance) |

# Student Activities

**Note**
*It is appreciated that not all students will be in employment. The questions that follow ask you to comment on workplace situations. If you are not in employment you should try to put yourself in the place of someone who is. If you are unsure about this, you could ask friends who have jobs, or you could even watch TV programmes which feature office life.*

**22.1**   Explain the difference between an 'effective' working environment and an 'efficient' working environment.

**22.2**   (a)   Write down three characteristics of a well-organised work area.

(b)   Describe three annoying incidents (real or imaginary) which would result from a poorly-organised work area.

How would the incidents in (b) affect the effectiveness and efficiency of the working environment?

**22.3**   Make a list of personal items which you would <u>like</u> to have in your own work space (real or imaginary).  Do you think you are likely to be allowed these items:

(a)   in an office which is normally closed to the public and has few visitors?

(b)   in an open-plan office which has a reception desk for the public (eg bank, insurance office, estate agent)?

Explain – with reasons – why some of your chosen items may be objected to, and who would object to them in (a) and in (b).

**22.4**    How would you deal with the following situations which relate to conditions in the working environment which are affecting your rate of work? Would you take the decision yourself? Consult with your colleagues? Refer the matter to your line manager?

(a)    The office is too hot, and you have an electric fan at home. You want to bring it in to put on your desk.

(b)    The office is too cold in the mornings – the office thermometer reads 15°C. You have an oil heater at home which you would like to bring in to put under your desk to warm you up.

(c)    The office is too stuffy in summer, but if you open the window everybody hears the noise from the building site on the other side of the road.

(d)    The fluorescent light above your desk is flickering and really annoying you.

**22.5**    Read the photocopier Case Study on pages 347 and 348 and explain what action you would take in the circumstances listed below. Refer in each case to the internal notice 'Photocopier Use' and to the illustrations of the manufacturer's instructions on the top of the photocopier.

(a)    The photocopier runs out of paper.

(b)    The photocopier paper jams and the jam light    8⌄    comes on.

(c)    The toner out light    [ ⠿ ]    comes on.

(d)    A colleague asks you to photocopy a funny cartoon from today's newspaper.

(e)    Your line manager asks you to photocopy some of the stock market share prices from today's newspaper.

(f)    A colleague asks you to photocopy a couple of chapters from a training manual which the office has bought. You notice that  '© Enigma Training 2003' is printed on the front cover.

(g)    Your line manager asks you to photocopy a couple of internally-produced reports. They contain some charts which are 150% larger than the normal page size you are copying.

(h)    You are photocopying some invoices and the display panel suddenly starts flashing a light, which shows a symbol which looks like a maintenance engineer.

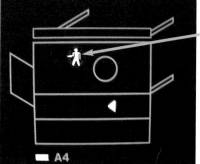

# Answers to student activities

**CHAPTER 1: MANAGEMENT ACCOUNTING – COSTS AND CODING**

1.1
- *decision-making* – deciding what action to take, eg production, new products
- *planning* – for the future of the business or organisation
- *control* – comparing actual results with forecasts and seeking reasons for discrepancies

1.2
- *costs* – materials, labour and expenses
- *income* – mainly from the sale of products or services

1.3 *Financial accounting*
- records transactions that have happened already
- looks backwards to show what has happened in the past
- is accurate to the nearest penny, with no estimated amounts
- is often a legal requirement to keep accounts (eg for HMRC purposes)
- maintains confidentiality of information (eg payroll details, VAT returns, sales figures)

*Management accounting*
- uses accounting information to summarise transactions that have happened already and to make estimates for the future
- looks in detail at costs – materials, labour and expenses – and income
- looks forward to show what is likely to happen in the future
- may use estimates where these are the most useful or suitable form of information
- provides management with reports that are of use in running the business or organisation
- provides management information as frequently as circumstances demand – speed is often vital as information may go out-of-date very quickly
- is not sent to people outside the organisation – it is for internal use
- maintains confidentiality of information (eg payroll details)

1.4
- (a) financial accounting
- (b) financial accounting
- (c) management accounting
- (d) financial accounting
- (e) management accounting (using financial accounting information)
- (f) management accounting

1.5 (a)
- cost centres – section of a business to which costs can be charged
- profit centre – section of a business to which costs can be charged, income can be identified, and profit can be calculated
- investment centre – section of a business where profit can be compared with the amount of money invested in the centre

(b)
- school or college – teaching departments, eg languages, science; also administrative departments, eg human resources, library, educational technology
- manufacturing business – by product, eg product line A, product line B, or by factory, eg Birmingham, Coventry

(c) A discussion topic which draws on the student's own experience

**1.6**

---

**MEMORANDUM**

**To:** Finance Director                                  **Ref:**  AS
**From:** A Student, Accounts Assistant         **Date:** today
**Subject:** Costs and income for last year


I refer to your request for details of the costs and income for last year of each section of the business. Details are as follows:

|                          | Newspapers and magazines £000s | Books £000s | Stationery £000s |
|--------------------------|-------------------------------:|------------:|-----------------:|
| *Cost Centre*            |                                |             |                  |
| •  materials             | 155                            | 246         | 122              |
| •  labour                | 65                             | 93          | 58               |
| •  expenses              | 27                             | 35          | 25               |
| •  total                 | 247                            | 374         | 205              |
|                          |                                |             |                  |
| *Profit Centre*          |                                |             |                  |
| Income from sales        | 352                            | 544         | 230              |
| less Costs (see above)   | 247                            | 374         | 205              |
| Profit                   | 105                            | 170         | 25               |
|                          |                                |             |                  |
| *Investment Centre*      |                                |             |                  |
| Profit (see above)       | 105                            | 170         | 25               |
| Investment               | 420                            | 850         | 250              |
| Expressed as a percentage| 25%                            | 20%         | 10%              |

If I can be of further assistance, please do not hesitate to contact me.

---

**1.7**   (a)     204250

(b)     501050

(c)     402150

(d)     503700

(e)     £240 to each centre: 203200, 303200, 403200, 503200, 603200

(f)     403050

(g)     304050

---

**MEMORANDUM**

**To:** Supervisor                    **Ref:**  AS

**From:** A Student                   **Date:**  today

**Subject:** Today's costs and income

As requested, I give details of today's costs and income that I have coded:

                                                              £

- materials (code numbers 1000–1999)          22,740
- labour (code numbers 2000–2999)                840
- expenses (code numbers 3000–3999)          90,985
- income (code numbers 4000–4999)            16,640

Please let me know if I can be of further assistance.

---

## CHAPTER 2:  FINANCIAL ACCOUNTING – FINANCIAL STATEMENTS

**2.1**  Profit & Loss Account, Balance Sheet.

**2.2**  A profit and loss account is a financial statement which summarises the revenue and expenses of a business for an accounting period and shows the overall profit or loss.

A balance sheet is a financial statement which shows the assets, liabilities and capital of a business at a particular date.

Differences: P&L covers a specific period of time, BS represents situation at a single moment. P&L deals with aspects of profitability, BS shows state of business, including value of assets and extent of liabilities and capital position.

**2.3**  (a)  Net profit = gross profit minus overheads.

(b)  Stakeholders, ie

Shareholders , ie owners, to see how their investment is faring.

Lenders, to ensure borrowing will be repaid.

Suppliers, to be reassured that they will be paid.

The public, either as investors or for ethical reasons.

Tax authorities, because they will receive tax revenue from profits.

**2.4**  (a)  Capital = assets minus liabilities.

(b)  Capital invested plus accumulated profit.

**2.5**  (a)  Gross profit = Sales (£400,000) minus Cost of Sales (£125,000) = £275,000

(b)  Gross profit (£275,000) minus overheads/expenses (£175,000) = £100,000

(c)  Net assets = total assets (£120,000 + £85,000) minus total liabilities (£55,000) = £ 150,000

(d)  Capital = net assets = £150,000

**CHAPTER 3: MEASURING PERFORMANCE**

**3.1**  (a)   61%        ([716 ÷ 1182]  x  100)

(b)   39%        ([76 ÷ 196]  x  100)

(c)   17%        ([120 ÷ 716]  x  100)

(d)   £341,000   (£310,000  x  [100 + 10]  ÷ 100)   or   £310,000  x  1.1

(e)   £102,000   (£120,000  x  [100 - 15]  ÷ 100) or £120,000  x  0.85

(f)   GB£0.72    ([10 ÷ 9]  x  GB£0.65)
     Profits are likely to be reduced, as income for the business is likely to be in GB£

**3.2**

|            | (a) units | (b) % |
|------------|-----------|-------|
| January    | 120       | 96    |
| February   | 109       | 87    |
| March      | 131       | 105   |
| April      | 136       | 109   |
| May        | 110       | 88    |
| June       | 123       | 98    |
| July       | 178       | 142   |
| August     | 135       | 108   |
| September  | 93        | 74    |
| October    | 150       | 120   |
| November   | 134       | 107   |
| December   | 112       | 90    |
| Total      | 1,531     |       |

(c)   128 and 102% respectively.

Comments:

- There are seasonal fluctuations, eg more policies than average in July, ready for the summer registrations.
- Average productivity is 128 units (target 125), reflected in efficiency of 102%.

**3.3**  (a)

|            | cost (£) |
|------------|----------|
| January    | 200      |
| February   | 192      |
| March      | 200      |
| April      | 183      |
| May        | 175      |
| June       | 186      |
| July       | 200      |
| August     | 200      |
| September  | 188      |

| | |
|---|---:|
| October | 179 |
| November | 187 |
| December | 192 |
| TOTAL: | 58,200 |

(b)  Average annual cost per unit = £58,200/308 units  = £189

Comments:

- Seasonal fluctuations (more installed just before holiday period and just before Christmas).
- Costs are lower when larger numbers of units are sold – economies of scale.

**3.4**  (a)

| | | daily utilisation % |
|---|---|---:|
| Monday | 56/56 | 100 |
| Tuesday | 50/56 | 89 |
| Wednesday | 28/56 | 50 |
| Thursday | 56/56 | 100 |
| Friday | 48/56 | 86 |

(b)

| | |
|---|---:|
| Weekly hours available  = 8 x 7 x  5  = | 280 |
| Hours worked during the week = | 238 |
| Labour utilisation for week  238/280  x  100  = | 85% |

Because the business is highly dependent on computers, idle time is likely to be the result of computer breakdown, or power cut, or even poor time recording (less likely). Idle time is high on Wednesday, which suggests that the management has not utilised the staff time efficiently – the staff could have used the time for administrative tasks, or contacting existing or prospective customers.  Friday, is of course, Friday – there may have been an extended lunchtime for some form of celebration.

**3.5**

| | | Week 1 | Week 2 | Week 3 | Week 4 |
|---|---|---:|---:|---:|---:|
| (a) | labour productivity | £60 | £64 | £68 | £70 |
| (b) | capital productivity | 16p | 20p | 22p | 24p |
| (c) | efficiency % | 103% | 105% | 110% | 114% |
| (d) | cost per unit | £7.50 | £7.50 | £8.64 | £8.75 |

Comments:

- the level of production is rising over the period to meet demand
- productivity is rising over the period
- capital productivity and efficiency are also increasing, reflecting the same trend
- cost per unit is rising sharply – reflecting the overtime worked and rising material costs
- this rise in costs is not a cause for immediate concern as the extra sales more than compensate; in the long term the company will need to look at its working practices and supplier situation

**3.6**

|  | Jan-March | April-June | July-Sept | Oct-Dec | Total |
|---|---|---|---|---|---|
| Sales (£) | 280,000 | 350,000 | 375,000 | 210,000 | 1,215,000 |
| Cost of sales (£) | 168,000 | 217,000 | 221,250 | 128,100 | 734,350 |
| Gross profit  (£) | 112,000 | 133,000 | 153,750 | 81,900 | 480,650 |
| Gross profit % | 40% | 38% | 41% | 39% | 40% |
| Overheads (£) | 70,000 | 77,000 | 80,000 | 65,000 | 292,000 |
| Net profit (£) | 42,000 | 56,000 | 73,750 | 16,900 | 188,650 |
| Net profit % | 15% | 16% | 20% | 8% | 16% |
| ROCE % | - | - | - | - | 15% |

Comments:
- sales are very seasonal – as one would expect in the agricultural industry
- gross profit remains steady, reflecting a stable gross profit margin – a healthy sign
- net profit varies with the seasonal fluctuation in sales – the main reason being overheads staying at more or less the same level, but sales being variable

## CHAPTER 4: CHARTS, AVERAGES AND INDICES

**4.1**   Errors:
- no heading to table
- there are two years 3 – year 4 in extreme right-hand column
- £ labels missing
- gross profit Year 3 should be £650
- Year 1 total £150, year 2 £250, Year 3 £270

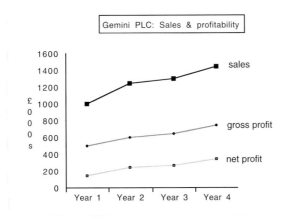

**4.2**

(a)

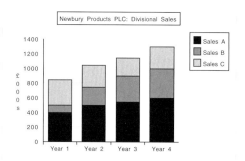

This chart shows clearly the upward trend in sales, but is less helpful in showing the *comparative* sales trends. A compound bar chart or line graph will do this more clearly (see [b]).

(b)

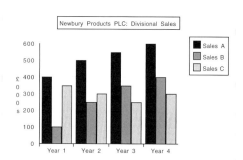

This chart makes it easy to see the divisional sales trends, but less easy to see any group sales trend (for which the component bar chart is more suitable)

(c)

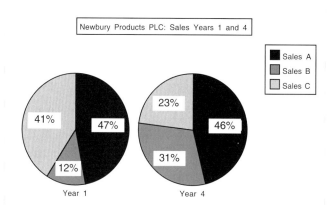

Pie charts are excellent for showing proportions of a whole – and they are widely used for this – but they do not show relative quantities. They are therefore not very helpful in this context as they are clumsy in illustrating year-to-year trends: the eye cannot easily trace changes in sectors.

**4.3**   • mean        £10.20
         • median      £5.90
         • mode        £10.00

The mean is the most arithmetically reliable as it takes all values into consideration.

**4.4**   (a) Moving average calculation:

| Week | unit sales<br>units (M) | moving average<br>units (M) |
|------|-------------------------|------------------------------|
| 1 | 3 | - |
| 2 | 5 | 6 |
| 3 | 10 | 6.7 |
| 4 | 5 | 7.3 |
| 5 | 7 | 8 |
| 6 | 12 | 8.7 |
| 7 | 7 | 9.3 |
| 8 | 9 | 11 |
| 9 | 17 | 11.3 |
| 10 | 8 | 11.7 |
| 11 | 10 | 12 |
| 12 | 18 | |

(b)   Average weekly increment 0.7M, ie (12-6) ÷ (10-1)

(c)   Forecast trend line: from week 12:  12.7, 13.4, 14.1, 14.8

Graph:

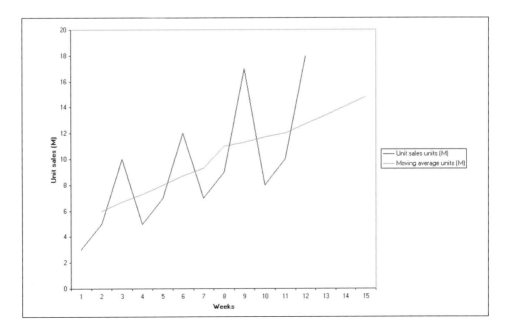

**4.5**    (a)  Calculation of moving averages.

| Year | Quarter | Historical Sales Data | 4-point Moving Average |
|------|---------|-----------------------|------------------------|
| 2001 | 1       | 2,000                 |                        |
|      | 2       | 4,500                 |                        |
|      |         |                       | 3,625                  |
|      | 3       | 6,000                 |                        |
|      |         |                       | 3,875                  |
|      | 4       | 2,000                 |                        |
|      |         |                       | 4,000                  |
| 2002 | 1       | 3,000                 |                        |
|      |         |                       | 4,375                  |
|      | 2       | 5,000                 |                        |
|      |         |                       | 4,625                  |
|      | 3       | 7,500                 |                        |
|      |         |                       | 4,875                  |
|      | 4       | 3,000                 |                        |
|      |         |                       | 5,250                  |
| 2003 | 1       | 4,000                 |                        |
|      |         |                       | 5,500                  |
|      | 2       | 6,500                 |                        |
|      |         |                       | 5,750                  |
|      | 3       | 8,500                 |                        |
|      |         |                       | 6,000                  |
|      | 4       | 4,000                 |                        |
|      |         |                       | 6,375                  |
| 2004 | 1       | 5,000                 |                        |
|      |         |                       | 6,750                  |
|      | 2       | 8,000                 |                        |
|      |         |                       | 7,000                  |
|      | 3       | 10,000                |                        |
|      | 4       | 5,000                 |                        |

(b)    Average quarterly increment $\dfrac{(7,000 - 3,625)}{(13 - 1)}$ = 3375 ÷ 12 = 281 units (nearest unit).

**4.6**

|                    | Last year (£) | Current year (£) | difference | (%)       |
|--------------------|---------------|------------------|------------|-----------|
| Sales              | 441,000       | 430,000          | − £11,000  | − 2.5%    |
| Cost of goods sold | 192,400       | 200,000          | + £7,600   | + 4.0%    |
| Wages and salaries | 89,250        | 95,000           | + £5,750   | + 6.4%    |
| Other overheads    | 58,240        | 65,000           | + £6,760   | + 11.6%   |

Although the unadjusted figures show a rise in sales, they have declined in real terms by 2.5%.

All the costs listed have increased during the year, but not by as much as the unadjusted figures would suggest.

**4.7** (a)

|  | Year 1 | Year 2 | Year 3 | Year 4 | Year 5 |
|---|---|---|---|---|---|
| Sales | 100 | 101 | 104 | 109 | 111 |
| Net profit | 100 | 102 | 107 | 108 | 109 |

Both sales and profits are increasing each year in line with each other, steadily rather than rapidly.

(b)

|  | Year 1 | Year 2 | Year 3 | Year 4 | Year 5 |
|---|---|---|---|---|---|
| Sales (£) | 350,000 | 337,577 | 334,763 | 334,659 | 319,841 |
| Net profit (£) | 45,000 | 43,742 | 44,024 | 42,713 | 40,185 |

When adjusted for the RPI, both sales and profits are declining significantly in real terms.

## CHAPTER 5: REPORT WRITING

*Tutors may wish to adopt the short formal report with headings, or the more simple report without headings. We would recommend the former, as it brings the concept of structure more forcibly to mind.*

**5.1** See chapter for headings and answer to 3.5 for points to be raised.

**5.2**

|  | performance indicator | Kidderport | Stourminster | Persham | Total |
|---|---|---|---|---|---|
| (a) | labour productivity: |  |  |  |  |
|  | units/employees | 480 | 475 | 367 | 433 |
|  | sales/hours | £27 | £26 | £22 | £25 |
| (b) | sales/£1 capital employed | 80p | 79p | 81p | 80p |
| (c) | cost per unit | 43.75 | 44.21 | 49.09 | 45.69 |
| (d) | sales per m$^2$ | £240.00 | £211.11 | £176.00 | £206.35 |
| (e) | gross profit % | 46% | 42% | 35% | 41% |
| (f) | net profit % | 13% | 12% | 2% | 9% |
| (g) | return on capital employed | 10% | 9% | 1% | 7% |

The report should *assess* the performance indicators (not just say figure A is bigger than figure B etc). In particular the poor performance of Persham and its effect on the group performance should be highlighted. Students should note:

*productivity*

Labour productivity is about 20% - 25% lower at Persham than at the other shops; this is not too serious; in fact capital productivity is highest at Persham at 82p. These indicators result from the fact that sales are buoyant at Persham – 2,200 units sold (more than Stourminster). The problems seem to lie elsewhere.

*cost per unit*

Persham has the highest cost per unit (£49.09). This again points to the root problem.

*resource utilisation*

Persham has the lowest sales per square metre of floorspace. Better use could perhaps be made of merchandising.

*profitability*

Gross profit percentage is lowest at Persham. One possible reason is that they are not getting the best terms from suppliers; alternatively they could be giving greater discounts to stimulate sales.

Net profit percentage and ROCE are poor at Persham (only 1%). Overhead costs are clearly too high here and should be investigated.

## CHAPTER 6: CONSOLIDATING AND REPORTING INFORMATION

**6.1** Figures that have been calculated and adjusted are shown in bold type.

| FITMAN WHOLESALE LIMITED | | | |
| --- | --- | --- | --- |
| Profit and Loss Account (extract) for week ended 31 March 2006 | | | |
| | Hornchurch | Basildon | Total |
| | £ | £ | £ |
| Sales | 71,000 | 55,000 | **126,000** |
| Opening Stock | 32,000 | 24,000 | **56,000** |
| Purchases | 35,000 | 25,000 | **60,000** |
| Closing stock | **32,000** | 23,000 | **55,000** |
| Cost of goods sold | **35,000** | **26,000** | **61,000** |
| Gross Profit | **36,000** | **29,000** | **65,000** |

**6.2** Figures that have been calculated and adjusted are shown in bold type.

| XYZ Retail Limited | | | | |
| --- | --- | --- | --- | --- |
| Profit and Loss Account (extract) for week ended 31 March 2006 | | | | |
| | Branch X | Branch Y | Branch Z | Total |
| | £ | £ | £ | £ |
| Sales | 80,000 | 75,000 | 80,000 | **235,000** |
| Opening Stock | 30,000 | 22,000 | 25,000 | **77,000** |
| Purchases | 40,000 | 37,000 | 38,000 | **115,000** |
| Closing stock | **28,500** | 21,000 | 24,000 | **73,500** |
| Cost of goods sold | **41,500** | **38,000** | **39,000** | **118,500** |
| Gross Profit | **38,500** | **37,000** | **41,000** | **116,500** |
| Transfers from X | **1,500** | | | **nil** |
| Transfers to Y and Z | | 1,000 | 500 | |

**6.3**

(a)   **Anne Field Enterprises: Profit and Loss Account data for 3 months ended 30 June 2006**

|  | £ | £ |
|---|---|---|
| Sales |  | 220,500 |
| Opening stock | 102,000 |  |
| Purchases | 114,000 |  |
|  | 216,000 |  |
| Less closing stock | 101,200* |  |
| Cost of goods sold |  | 114,800 |
| Gross Profit |  | 105,700 |
| Overheads |  | 87,400 |
| Net Profit |  | 18,300 |

*Includes £200 added back to the Liverpool closing stock in respect of stock in transit.

(b)   **Anne Field Enterprises: Comparison of data for 3 months ended 30 June 2006**

|  | £ | £ |
|---|---|---|
|  | **2005** | **2006** |
| Sales | 185,000 | 220,500 |
| Cost of goods sold | 112,000 | 114,800 |
| Gross Profit | 73,000 | 105,700 |
| Gross Profit percentage | 39.46% | 47.94% |
| Overheads | 62,000 | 87,400 |
| Net Profit | 11,000 | 18,300 |
| Net Profit percentage | 5.95% | 8.30% |

(c)   **compound bar chart**

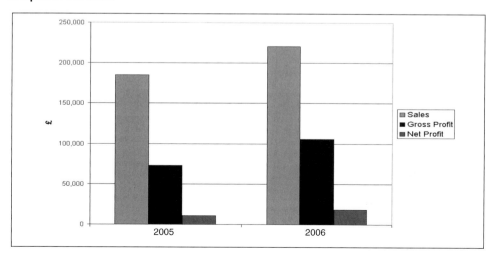

(d)    **Comments** are generally very positive:

- Sales have increased by 19.19%

- Gross profit percentage has increased by 8.48%

- Net profit percentage has increased by 2.35%

The management has clearly improved the overall sales and profitability of the business. The substantial increase in gross profit would suggest that merchandise is being successfully marked up, and this with the increase in sales has helped to improve net profitability by 39%. The only penalty has been a sharp rise in overheads by 41%. This may need investigating and the goal for 2007 should be to trim this increase.

**6.4**

| | A | B | C | D | E | F |
|---|---|---|---|---|---|---|
| 1 | Chronos Manufacturing Limited: Consolidated statement of cost and revenues | | | | | |
| 2 | Year ended 30 June 2006 | | | | | |
| 3 | | | | | | |
| 4 | | | Electronics Division | Casings Division | Admin Division | Consolidated |
| 5 | | | £ | £ | £ | £ |
| 6 | | | | | | |
| 7 | | Sales | | | 1,876,000 | 1,876,000 |
| 8 | | | | | | |
| 9 | | Cost of goods sold | | | | |
| 10 | | Opening stock of finished goods | | | 75,600 | 75,600 |
| 11 | plus | Total usage of raw materials | 226,500 | 111,200 | | 337,700 |
| 12 | plus | Total factory labour | 176,400 | 181,000 | | 357,400 |
| 13 | plus | Total factory overheads | 131,600 | 174,300 | | 305,900 |
| 14 | | | 534,500 | 466,500 | 75,600 | 1,076,600 |
| 15 | less | Closing stock of finished goods | | | 71,900 | 71,900 |
| 16 | | Total cost of goods sold | 534,500 | 466,500 | 3,700 | 1,004,700 |
| 17 | | | | | | |
| 18 | | Gross profit | | | | 871,300 |
| 19 | | | | | | |
| 20 | less | Administration salaries | | | | 310,000 |
| 21 | less | Administration costs | | | | 356,000 |
| 22 | | | | | | 666,000 |
| 23 | | Net profit | | | | 205,300 |

**6.5**

| | A | B | C | D | E | F |
|---|---|---|---|---|---|---|
| 1 | Helios Limited: Consolidated statement of cost and revenues | | | | | |
| 2 | Year ended 30 June 2006 | | | | | |
| 3 | | | | | | |
| 4 | | | Manufacturing | Assembly | Administration | Consolidated |
| 5 | | | £ | £ | £ | £ |
| 6 | | | | | | |
| 7 | | Sales | | | 2,814,000 | 2,814,000 |
| 8 | | | | | | |
| 9 | | Cost of goods sold | | | | |
| 10 | | Opening stock of finished goods | | | 96,000 | 96,000 |
| 11 | plus | Total usage of raw materials | 339,750 | 166,800 | | 506,550 |
| 12 | plus | Total factory labour | 264,600 | 271,500 | | 536,100 |
| 13 | plus | Total factory overheads | 196,500 | 261,450 | | 457,950 |
| 14 | | | 800,850 | 699,750 | 96,000 | 1,596,600 |
| 15 | less | Closing stock of finished goods | | | 93,100 | 93,100 |
| 16 | | Total cost of goods sold | 800,850 | 699,750 | 2,900 | 1,503,500 |
| 17 | | | | | | |
| 18 | | Gross profit | | | | 1,310,500 |
| 19 | | | | | | |
| 20 | less | Administration salaries | | | | 450,000 |
| 21 | less | Administration costs | | | | 525,000 |
| 22 | | | | | | 975,000 |
| 23 | | Net profit | | | | 335,500 |

**6.6 (a)** 1   gross profit margin                                             47%

2   net profit margin                                               12%

3   return on capital employed                          7%

4   manufacturing cost (£) of each radio produced          £15

5   sales revenue (£) per employee                      £14,070

**(b)**

| | A | B | C | D | E | F |
|---|---|---|---|---|---|---|
| 1 | Helios Ltd: Consolidated Statement of Revenues and Costs | | | | | |
| 2 | Year ended 30 June 2005 | | | | | |
| 3 | | | | | | |
| 4 | | | Adjusted | | Unadjusted | |
| 5 | | | £ | £ | £ | £ |
| 6 | | | | | | |
| 7 | | Sales | | 2,652,000 | | 2,550,000 |
| 8 | | | | | | |
| 9 | | Cost of goods sold | | | | |
| 10 | | | | | | |
| 11 | | Opening stock of finished goods | 95,000 | | 95,000 | |
| 12 | add | Total usage of raw materials | 484,500 | | 475,000 | |
| 13 | add | Total factory labour | 502,640 | | 488,000 | |
| 14 | add | Total factory overheads | 442,000 | | 425,000 | |
| 15 | | | 1,524,140 | | 1,483,000 | |
| 16 | less | Closing stock of finished goods | 96,000 | | 96,000 | |
| 17 | | Total cost of goods sold | | 1,428,140 | | 1,387,000 |
| 18 | | | | | | |
| 19 | | Gross profit | | 1,223,860 | | 1,163,000 |
| 20 | | | | | | |
| 21 | less | Administration salaries | 406,850 | | 395,000 | |
| 22 | | | | | | |
| 23 | less: | Administration costs | 517,920 | | 498,000 | |
| 24 | | | | 924,770 | | 893,000 |
| 25 | | Net profit before taxation | | 299,090 | | 270,000 |

**(c)**

| | A | B | C | D | E |
|---|---|---|---|---|---|
| 1 | Helios Ltd: Comparison of actual 2006 results with adjusted 2005 results | | | | |
| 2 | | | | | |
| 3 | | | | | |
| 4 | | Actual 2006 | Adjusted 2005 | Variance | Variance |
| 5 | | £ | £ | £ | % |
| 6 | | | | | |
| 7 | Sales | 2,814,000 | 2,652,000 | 162,000 | 6.1 |
| 8 | | | | | |
| 9 | Gross profit | 1,310,500 | 1,223,860 | 86,640 | 7.1 |
| 10 | | | | | |
| 11 | Net profit | 335,500 | 299,090 | 36,410 | 12.2 |
| 12 | | | | | |
| 13 | Factory labour costs | 536,100 | 502,640 | 33,460 | 6.7 |
| 14 | | | | | |
| 15 | Administration salaries | 450,000 | 406,850 | 43,150 | 10.6 |
| 16 | | | | | |

Comments could include the fact that sales, gross profit and net profit have all seen a healthy increase. The cost of administration salaries may need to be investigated. The more able students may note that the greater increase in net profit points to the fact that overhead costs on the whole have been contained.

## CHAPTER 7: PREPARING EXTERNAL REPORTS

7.1

| CUTE IDEAS | | Trading Report | | Quarter ended ......../......../....... | |
|---|---|---|---|---|---|
| | £ | | £ | £ variance | % variance |
| Sales A (actual) | 13,500 | Sales Target A | 15,000 | 1,500 | 10 |
| Sales B (actual) | 18,000 | Sales Target B | 21,000 | 3,000 | 14 |
| Total Sales (actual) | 31,500 | Total Sales Target | 36,000 | 4,500 | 13 |

10% Commission on sales £3,150      (cheque enclosed)

**Comments**
Points to include: acknowledgment of fall in sales (mentioning variance) and attributing the factors mentioned in the question; future performance could be estimated in general terms.

**signature**    *R Smith*

**date** (in first week of April + year)

**7.2**

| | |
|---|---|
| | **Great Western Bank Plc** |
| | **Quarterly Management Accounts** |
| **Customer:** | Electro Supplies |
| **Quarter ended:** | 31 March 2007 |

**Please complete details below in the column on the right:**

| | |
|---|---|
| **Sales (£)** | £340,000 |
| **Gross profit (£)** | £85,000 |
| **Gross profit %** | 25% |
| **Overhead costs (£)** | £68,000 |
| **Net profit (£)** | £17,000 |
| **Net profit %** | 5% |
| **Return on capital employed %**<br><br>**Note: Formula required   =   net profit x 100**<br>                              **owner's capital** | 4% |

**Authorised signature of customer** ........................................................

**Date** ........................................................

## CHAPTER 8: BASIC PRINCIPLES OF VAT

**8.1**   Sales of chargeable supplies and imports – sales of business goods and services by VAT registered persons and organisations.

**8.2**   Input tax is a tax on purchases and expenses and may normally be reclaimed by the supplier; output tax is tax charged on chargeable supplies and is due to HM Revenue & Customs. The arithmetic difference between the two is payable to/claimable from HM Revenue & Customs on the VAT Return.

**8.3**   A supplier may reclaim VAT if the amount of input tax in any VAT period exceeds the amount of output VAT.  VAT is also reclaimable in the case of bad debt relief (covered in Chapter 9).

**8.4**   The VAT is paid to the supplier, who is accountable, together with other businesses involved in the production process, to HM Revenue & Customs for the VAT (see diagram on page 139).

**8.5**   Standard 17.5%, reduced 5%, zero 0%. (at time of writing)

**8.6**   Zero-rated VAT is VAT at 0% charged on taxable supplies. Exempt supplies are supplies which are not taxable. See page 140 or the 'VAT Guide' for examples.

**8.7**   Unit price missing, invoice number missing, issue date missing, VAT amount has been rounded up (should be £36.67). Wrong cast in total: £36.68 taken as £63.68.

**8.8**   (a)   the invoices are valid VAT invoices as they are all under £250 and fall into the 'less detailed' category which can quote VAT-inclusive totals

(b)   using the VAT fraction of $^7/_{47}$ (or the percentage calculation) the net and VAT amounts are:

£74.47 +  £13.03 VAT  =  £87.50

£35.00  +  £6.12 VAT  =  £41.12

£40.00  +  £7.00 VAT  =  £47.00

£47.45  +  £8.30 VAT  =  £55.75

£84.30  +  £14.75 VAT  =  £99.05

## CHAPTER 9:  VAT ACCOUNTING AND THE VAT RETURN

9.1

| | Business: Uno Ltd £ | Business: Duo Brothers £ | Business: Tray PLC £ | Business: Quattro PLC £ |
|---|---|---|---|---|
| **Box 1** VAT on sales and other outputs (UK) | 21,000 | 32,375 | 17,150 | 484,000 (483,000 + 1,000) |
| **Box 2** VAT on acquisitions from EU (non UK) | NONE | NONE | NONE | NONE |
| **Box 3** Box 1 plus Box 2 | 21,000 | 32,375 | 17,150 | 484,000 |
| **Box 4** VAT reclaimed on purchases/expenses (UK & EU) | 11,375 | 15,400 (14,000 + 1,400) | 7,875 | 261,975 |
| **Box 5** VAT to be paid or reclaimed (difference between Box 3 and Box 4) | 9,625 | 16,975 | 9,275 | 222,025 |
| **Box 6** Total value of sales (UK & EU) | 120,000 | 207,511 | 103,100 | 3,350,800 |
| **Box 7** Total of purchases/expenses (UK & EU) | 65,000 | 80,000 | 45,000 | 1,497,000 |
| **Box 8** Total value of sales (EU excluding UK) | NONE | 22,511 | 5,100 | 590,800 |
| **Box 9** Total value of purchases/expenses (EU excluding UK) | NONE | NONE | NONE | NONE |

**9.2**

Before you fill in this form please read the notes on the back and the VAT leaflet *"Filling in your VAT return"*. Fill in all boxes clearly in ink, and write 'none' where necessary. Don't put a dash or leave any box blank. If there are no pence write "00" in the pence column. **Do not** enter more than one amount in any box.

| For official use | | £ | p |
|---|---|---|---|
| | VAT due in this period on **sales** and other outputs **1** | 273,000 | 00 |
| | VAT due in this period on **acquisitions** from other **EC Member States** **2** | NONE | |
| | Total VAT due **(the sum of boxes 1 and 2)** **3** | 273,000 | 00 |
| | VAT reclaimed in this period on **purchases** and other inputs (including acquisitions from the EC) **4** | 152,460 | 00 |
| | Net VAT to be paid to Customs or reclaimed by you **(Difference between boxes 3 and 4)** **5** | 120,540 | 00 |
| | Total value of **sales** and all other outputs excluding any VAT. **Include your box 8 figure** **6** | 1,684,800 | 00 |
| | Total value of **purchases** and all other inputs excluding any VAT. **Include your box 9 figure** **7** | 870,000 | 00 |
| | Total value of all **supplies** of goods and related services, excluding any VAT, to other **EC Member States** **8** | 124,800 | 00 |
| | Total value of all **acquisitions** of goods and related services, excluding any VAT, from other **EC Member States** **9** | NONE | 00 |

If you are enclosing a payment please tick this box.

☑

DECLARATION: You, or someone on your behalf, must sign below.

I, RALPH POSTGATE ..................................................... declare that the
(Full name of signatory in BLOCK LETTERS)

information given above is true and complete.

Signature ............................................... Date ...............................
**A false declaration can result in prosecution.**

L

0041633

**VAT 100** (half)

## CHAPTER 10: COMPUTER SYSTEMS AND ACCOUNTING SOFTWARE

**10.1** The visual checklist should be in numbered form and include checking of hardware components (central processing unit and peripherals), power plugs, peripheral connections, safety of cabling.

**10.2** (a) A system password enables you to gain access to the computer itself – to 'log on'. A software password enables you to gain access to individual programs on the computer.

(b) Passwords are necessary for security reasons. The system password prevents access to the system from intruders and other unauthorised people. A software password restricts access to individual programs from individual unauthorised employees, eg access to personnel records.

**10.3** A variety of back-up policies could be quoted – for example the use of a 'one disk per working day' system or a rotation of any practical number of disks. Mention should be made of where the disks are to be stored, eg there could be two sets, one stored securely on the premises, another off-site. Mention could also be made of sending data by email to a remote location as a method of backing up smaller files.

**10.4**   Paper out – normally fixed by the operator.

Paper jam – can be fixed by the operator, although assistance may be needed in more serious cases.

Toner out – assistance would normally be needed.

Software problem – the printer refuses to print or prints out nonsense – assistance would definitely be needed.

Mechanical breakdown – assistance would definitely be needed from an engineer.

## CHAPTER 11: DATA SECURITY

**11.1**   The passwords should be:

- six characters long

- easily memorised

- accompanied by explanations of the source of the password elements and the reasons why nobody could guess them

**11.2**   Rules such as the following could be adopted:

- Staff should not write down a password where other people can read it.

- Staff should make sure that noone can see them when inputting a password.

- Passwords should be changed on a regular basis.

- Any suspicion that a password has been 'leaked' should be reported to management immediately.

**11.3**   (a) It is possible that the colleague is trying to work out your password in order to gain unauthorised access to the data. You should report the fact that the password may be insecure to your line manager, who is then likely to arrange for it to be replaced.

(b) The attachment could contain a virus and should not be opened. The matter should be reported to your line manager.

(c) The colleague should be advised to move the disks as overheating could damage them and lead to file corruption and loss of data. This could be serious if the disks are the only current back-up.

**11.4**   (a) Illegal copying of software is a breach of copyright and unacceptable. You should point this out to the employee, refuse permission and ask who else has been borrowing the software so that further action can be taken.

(b) This is a question of confidentiality, and the employer is regulated by the Data Protection Act. It would be a breach of this Act if the employee gave information about one customer to another customer without authorisation, particularly if the answer might give a bad impression of the customer's credit rating. The request to give the information should be politely declined.

(c) This is a matter of health and safety and is covered by the Display Screen Equipment Regulations. It sounds as if the employee is spending too long at the keyboard and may have a problem with posture and eyesight. The employer has responsibilities to the employee, including the giving of work breaks, a free eyesight test and suitable seating. You should discuss these matters with the employee.

NOTE: The 'answers' to the computerised accounting exercises (Chapters 12 to 15) are within the text. The only exception is Activity 14.5 where the answer to the last part is that the transaction for the sewing machine purchase is posted to account 0020 and will not appear on the account 5000 Activity Report.

## CHAPTER 16: PLANNING AND ORGANISING YOUR WORK

**16.1**   A routine task is a task which is part of the everyday activity of the workplace. A non-routine task is an unexpected task. Examples should be given as appropriate.

**16.2**   Prioritisation of tasks is deciding on the order in which the tasks should be completed.

**16.3**   (a)   An urgent task is a task which is required to be done by a specific deadline; an important task is a task for the completion of which an employee is given personal responsibility.

    (b)   The situation where the urgent task is relatively unimportant.

**16.4**   'To Do' list, diary.

**16.5**   A suggested order for the list:
1   Distribute the departmental post.
2   Look at the section diary and compare with your 'To Do' list.
3   Check that details of hours worked (including overtime) have been received from all departments.
4   Send email to Marketing Department asking for monthly overtime figures to be sent through – they should have been received last Friday.
5   Process the hours of all the employees on the computer. Print out pay details and a payroll summary, including the schedule setting out the amount which will have to be paid to the Inland Revenue for income tax and National Insurance Contributions by 19th of the next month.
6   Pass the payroll printouts to your line manager for checking, and when approved, print out the payslips for distribution.
7   Prepare the BACS payroll schedule for the bank to process on Tuesday.
8   Pass the BACS payroll schedule to your line manager for checking.
9   Put a note in the diary for the Inland Revenue cheque to be prepared on 5th of next month.
10   Print out payroll statistics from the computer for your line manager – they are required for next week.
11   Draw up a notice advertising a staff trip out for next month.

**16.6**   (a)   You should go and turn the lights off as soon as an opportunity arises. It will not take long and will prevent the battery going flat.

    (b)   This should be referred to your line manager. You are very busy, but the line manager should decide whether you should go – it may be possible for the line manager to delegate your work to someone else.

    (c)   The friend should be told politely that you cannot speak during working hours. You could suggest a  lunch-time meeting.

    (d)   This looks like an obvious error, or even a fraud! You cannot take action yourself, but should refer the matter to your line manager to take action.

    (e)   The work will have to be redone as a matter of urgency. The computer will have to be rebooted and the data re-input (to the extent that it has not been saved). If there are further problems, the line manager will have to be alerted and technical assistance requested.

**16.7** (a) Equal opportunities. The workforce seen in publicity material should be representative of the employees in terms of race, sex and age.

   (b) Data Protection. This would be a breach of confidentiality and should be refused.

   (c) Retention of records. HM Revenue & Customs can ask for payroll records dating from up to three years ago. The colleague's request should be refused and the colleague recommended to refer to the retention of records policy of the organisation. Most organisations keep records for six years.

## CHAPTER 17: WORKING WITH OTHERS

**17.1** A team is a group of people working together to achieve defined objectives. The benefits of working in a team include: the pooling of skills and abilities of different team members, creative thinking stimulated by group discussion, motivation from working with others, the help and support provided by other team members.

**17.2** The answer will depend on the circumstances involved.

**17.3** See the communication methods described on pages 276 to 279. It is important that each method listed should be accompanied by some form of analysis – ie is the method formal or informal? How does it suit the type of message being conveyed?

**17.4** A suggested six (note that these are not prescriptive):

   1 being pleasant and polite
   2 being cooperative
   3 listening to and respecting the opinions of others
   4 asking for and providing help
   5 do not backbite
   6 keep confidences

**17.5** The important point here is to make sure that your objection to Jake is based on issues which relate to the work itself rather than your personal (and possibly subjective) reaction to him. You should:

   • Observe the ways in which the other members of the team deal with him – do they also have problems? If they do not, the problem may lie with you.

   • Talk the problem over with the other team members – do they think the same way?

   • Talk the matter over with Jake, if you feel you are able to.

   If it emerges that the problems with Jake extend to the whole team and the standard of work and workplace efficiency is being affected, there may be a case for taking the matter to a higher authority.

**17.6** Jasmina's problem is one of possible sexual discrimination, although the evidence is circumstantial rather than actual. (It may be, of course, that she is hopeless at her work.) She should in the first instance talk the matter over with the line manager, stressing her wish for promotion and motivation, making it clear that she intends to carry on working if she starts a family. If the line manager cannot come up with a satisfactory explanation for keeping her where she is, she should take the matter to a Human Resources Manager (or equivalent). If she has firm evidence of sexual discrimination, she may have grounds for starting the grievance procedure.

## CHAPTER 19: RESPONSIBILITY FOR HEALTH & SAFETY

**19.1**   Both employer and employee.

**19.2**   A hazard is something that could harm you. A risk is a measurement of how likely it is that you will be harmed by a hazard.

**19.3**   (a)   Health and Safety at Work Act 1974.

      (b)   -   ensure health, safety and welfare of employees

           -   provide a Health and Safety Policy Statement (where there are five or more employees)

           -   allow the appointment of a safety representative

      (c)   -   take reasonable care of own health and safety

           -   take reasonable care of the health and safety of others

           -   cooperate with the employer or anyone acting on his or her behalf to meet health and safety requirements

**19.4**   (a)   Control of Substances Hazardous to Health (regulations affecting the identification and storage of hazardous substances).

      (b)   Reporting of Injuries, Diseases and Dangerous Occurrences (regulations requiring the official reporting of these events).

      (c)   Health and Safety Executive (the body responsible for the regulation, control and inspection of health and safety in the workplace).

**19.5**   (b)

**19.6**   (a)   Emptying of bins is the employer's responsibility. If bins are not emptied the rubbish could become a hazard for two reasons: it could trip somebody up if it spills onto the floor; it could be a health hazard if there is rotting food in it.

      (b)   A drink on top of a computer is the responsibility of the employee and should be avoided at all costs; the hazard is a spill which could damage the electronic components of the computer beyond repair.

      (c)   It is the employer's responsibility to provide adequate seating; in the case of a computer workstation this means an adjustable seat. This avoids the hazard of bad backs and other muscular disorders.

      (d)   It is the employee's responsibility to use the furniture and equipment provided in an appropriate way. The hazard here is that the employee may fall off the chair or strain a muscle or damage the spine.

## CHAPTER 20: DEALING WITH HEALTH & SAFETY HAZARDS

**20.1**   The hazard here is a safety one. The danger is that the fire alarm could be going off because there actually is a fire, and the priority would then be to get everyone out alive, invoices or no invoices. As far as the options are concerned:

      (a)   This is just untrue and should be avoided at all costs.

      (b)   This is true, and while possibly getting your colleague into trouble, you would be alerting the employer to the fact that fire safety regulations are not being observed. If there was a fire you would possibly be saving her life. This is the correct option.

(c)     This is avoiding the issue entirely and shirking the employee's responsibilities for health and safety. The result would be that the employer would be unaware of breaches of fire safety regulations. This could prove fatal in the event of an actual fire.

**20.2**     The hazard here concerns security. The danger is that employees or even outsiders could obtain confidential information from the computer. Bank details may be on the computer and obtained for fraud. Addresses could also be obtained for purposes of harassment. Details of pay could be obtained and be a cause of unrest at work ('he's earning £2,000 more than me and he's useless' etc). The answer here is less clear cut and could lead to some interesting discussion:

(a)     This is avoiding the issue and shirking the employee's responsibilities for security in the workplace. The result would be that the employer would be unaware of breaches of security.

(b)     This is arguably the correct option in this situation if your colleague is at the same level of seniority as yourself. If he fails to log off next time or on subsequent occasions, option (c) would then become the course of action.

(c)     See (b). If your colleague is junior to yourself it would be more appropriate to advise the line manager who can then check out the position and take action.

**20.3**     It is possible that Trish is a serial whinger and inefficient at her work, but ...

(a)     Her employer is potentially liable for:

- a possibly substandard monitor - it flickers and is difficult to read

- not varying Trish's work sufficiently

- possibly requiring her to work for long periods of time without a break

- stressing her by telling her to hurry up

(b)     Trish is responsible for her condition to the extent that:

- her posture is poor, despite the chair being appropriate for the job

- her work area is poorly organised and a mess

- it is possible that she does not take breaks when she has the opportunity

- she may need to get her eyes tested, or may have neglected to do so when offered a test

Your advice to Trish could be to talk to her employer about her symptoms, having regular breaks, arranging eye tests, the need to improve the quality of the screen, and the lack of variation of the work (could she be trained to do something else as well?).

She could also talk to her union rep who may give her a copy of the HSE leaflet 'Working with VDUs' - or she could download it from www.hse.gov.uk

You could also tactfully mention the importance of good posture and organisation of her work area.

## CHAPTER 21: ACCIDENTS AND EMERGENCIES

**21.1**   Five from:

- name of Safety Officer
- name of First Aider(s)
- location of First aid box
- location of Accident Book
- emergency procedures
- types of fire extinguisher

**21.2**   (a)   Percy. Placing a mug of coffee on top of a computer is negligent on his part.

   (b)   Explain to Percy his own responsibilities for Health & Safety in the office – including where not to put mugs of hot coffee. Also mention the likely need to replace the keyboard.

   (c)   A light scald is not a reportable injury under RIDDOR. As Percy is likely to come back to work the next day, the 'over three day' situation will not arise.

   (d)   Circulation of a note about employee responsibility for Health & Safety in the office, mentioning specific instances such as mugs of hot coffee on computers.

   (e)   The form should give full details of the circumstances of the accident, the injury, the action taken by the First Aider and the further action of communicating employee responsibility for Health & Safety to the office staff.

**21.3**   • death or major injury in the workplace – giving examples of major injuries

   • 'over three day' injuries where the employee is away from work for more than three days for less serious injuries

   • dangerous occurrences which could have resulted in injury, but did not, giving examples of dangerous occurrences

**21.4**   (a)   Water. Most effective for paper. Powder would work, but much messier.

   (b)   Carbon Dioxide. Powder would work but would ruin computer irretrievably.

   (c)   Powder. The only choice as it deals with all substances.

**21.5**   See text in the bottom half of page 334, together with selected points from the bottom section of page 335. The meeting point should be mentioned by name.

## CHAPTER 22: MANAGING THE WORK AREA

**22.1**   An <u>effective</u> working environment is one which will result in the achievement of the objectives of the organisation. An <u>efficient</u> working environment is one in which the organisation achieves the required results with the minimum wastage of resources.

**22.2**   (a)   Three from: tidy, clean, everything in its place, everything accessible, VDU correct, chair correct

   (b)   Examples such as not being able to find a document when user is absent, user not being able to find document when present, user not passing on data needed by someone else, user not passing on message because message lost, data disk corrupted because of dirt etc. The implications on effectiveness (task not being done) and efficiency (time/money wasted) should be discussed in each case.

**22.3** The list is a very personal choice and could include pictures, posters, postcards, photos, 'toys', fruit, holiday souvenirs etc etc.

(a) Most items would normally be allowed, subject to the sensitivities of colleagues and management. Colleagues are likely to object to items that make a noise or smell. Female colleagues might object to men bringing in girlie calendars or pictures. Management would object to items that get in the way of the work processes, eg very large plants, personal stereos etc.

(b) The appearance of an office that is open to public view would be strictly controlled by the employer. Any personal items would have to be unobtrusive, eg small photos, and wallspace is likely to be used for advertising or promoting corporate identity. Any public areas would have items welcoming to the public, eg flowers, appropriate magazines.

**22.4** (a) You would have to consult your colleagues first, and then your employer. Remember that it will be noisy (affecting colleagues) and will use power (which will increase the electricity bill).

(b) An oil heater under a desk would be a fire hazard and totally unacceptable. You would need to bring to the employer's attention the fact that the 15 degree temperature is below the legal minimum of 16 degrees for an office. It would then be up to the employer to adjust and increase the level of the heating.

(c) This is a common problem and would need to be decided among the employees, particularly bearing in mind the feelings of the people nearest to the window (and the noise).

(d) A flickering fluorescent light would need to be referred to a line manager, who should arrange for it to be replaced.

**22.5** (a) You should fill up the paper tray.

(b) You should try to clear the jam, following the manufacturer's instructions. If you are unsuccessful, consult a senior assistant.

(c) Refer to a senior assistant. This is a skilled and potentially messy job.

(d) This is unauthorised copying. The answer should be 'no'.

(e) This is not for you to question, and you should do it. You may think it is unauthorised, but the line manager may be doing some research connected with work.

(f) This is copyright material and should not be copied. Sometimes you are allowed to copy short extracts from copyright material, but two chapters is not a short extract.

(g) You will need to use the reducing function on the machine. The instructions are on the top panel (see illustration on page 348).

(h) This flashing symbol is the Periodic Maintenance light. It should be referred to the line manager.

# Index